SUHA BOLUKBASI is Professor of Internatio
East Technical University, Ankara. He holds a
Virginia and has held visiting appointments a
College and Woodrow Wilson International C

Suha
Bolukbasi

AZERBAIJAN
A POLITICAL HISTORY

New paperback edition published in 2014 by I.B.Tauris & Co Ltd
6 Salem Road, London W2 4BU
175 Fifth Avenue, New York NY 10010
www.ibtauris.com

Distributed in the United States and Canada Exclusively by Palgrave Macmillan
175 Fifth Avenue, New York NY 10010

First published in hardback in 2011 by I.B.Tauris & Co Ltd

ISBN: 978 178076 759 8

A full CIP record for this book is available from the British Library
A full CIP record is available from the Library of Congress

Library of Congress Catalog Card Number: available

Typeset in Garamond by Artform, Oxfordshire

Printed and bound in Great Britain by Page Bros, Norwich
from camera-ready copy edited and supplied by the author

To my daughter Defne

Contents

List of Plates

13 Azeri woman refugee after having been expelled from Nagorno-Karabagh. She is located in the Sabirabad camp. Source: *Azerbaijan International Magazine*, paper edition, Spring 1997.

14 Fleeing on foot from Kelbejar, Azerbaijan, after the Armenians attacked this region. April, 1993. Source: http://azer.com/aiweb/categories/magazine/51_folder_/51_articles/51_editorial.html

Every attempt has been made to gain permission for the use of the images in this book. Any omissions will be rectified in future editions.

List of Abbreviations and Terms

ACP	Armenian Communist Party
AzCP	Azerbaijan Communist Party
Azrevkom	Azerbaijan Revolutionary Committee
BBC/SWB	BBC Summaries of World Broadcasts
Dashnaktsutiun Party	Socialist/Nationalist Armenian Party
Duma	Assembly, Parliament
FBIS	Foreign Broadcasts Information Service
Gorilspolkom	City Soviet Executive Committee
Gubernia (plural Gubernii)	Province(s)
Himmat Party	Toil (or Endeavor) Party
Hunchak Party	Armenian Social Democratic Party
Krunk	Organization of Secessionist Karabagh Armenians
Korenisatsiia	Nativization
Miatsum	Campaign to Unify Armenia with Mountainous Karabagh
Musavat Party	Party of Equality
Oblispolkom	Oblast Soviet Executive Committee
Orgburo	Organizational Bureau of the AzCP
Party Obkom	Oblast Party Committee
Ramgavar	Armenian Liberal Party
Rastsvet	Flourishing of national cultures under Khrushchev
Raykom	Raion Party Committee
Sblizhenie	Merger of nations into one Soviet nation

Sovnarkom	Soviet of People's Commissars (Council of Ministers)
Uezd(y)	District(s)
Zakavkom	Transcaucasian Commissariat
Zavkraikom	Transcaucasian Regional Committee

Note on Transliteration

The problems of spelling and transliteration were compounded due to a number of reasons. A major problem was that many sources referred to in this book used varying methods. To do justice to the original language I had to either pick one style of transliteration or come up with my own, combining insights from different approaches.

For Russian words, I used the most common form adopted by the standard Library of Congress system, while omitting diacritical marks. A tougher problem encountered concerned uniquely Azeri letters. Azerbaijani Cyrillic, used until Azerbaijan shifted to the use of Latin in the early independence years, included non-standard letters such as ə (pronounced like a in "hat"), y (same as ü in German), and ө (same as ö in German). While ü and ö are widely known, the letter ə is generally transliterated as ä, which in German is used as both a short and long vowel. Instead, I believe that the sound a as in "many" approximates the sound ə more adequately. Hence, to simplify reading of the text I chose a or e for ə, o for ө, and u for y. Therefore, Aliev instead of Äliev, and Efendiev instead of Äfändiev.

There were other transliteration problems. A case in point is the transliteration of the names of Azeris if the latter had immigrated to Turkey and had become also known by their Turkified names. Resulzada's Turkish name of Mehmet Emin Resulzade illustrates this phenomenon. I used his Azeri name of Mammad Emin Resulzada, although he is considered a Turkish hero and had spent a significant portion of his life in Turkey.

All in all, I have tried to use a minimal amount of foreign words in the text, transliterating only those terms for which there are no accurate English equivalent.

Nevertheless, there are many names of places and people for whom transliteration is not that simple. I spelled the name of Azerbaijan's first president as Resulzada instead of Resulzadeh or Rasulzade, although these other forms seem adequate as well. Finally, I chose to write the name of one of independent Azerbaijan's foreign ministers as Tofik Kasumov and not Towfik Qasumov.

Preface

This book would never have materialized without useful criticism of the manuscript by many of my friends in Azerbaijan and elsewhere. I also owe a considerable debt to my PhD students Burcu Değirmen and Yavuz Şir who generously agreed to review the manuscript. Obviously the failings of the book are my own.

This project is more about the past than the future. Yet, by describing issues, patterns and constants it aims at identifying current and potential challenges. As suggested throughout the book, many of the problems and dilemmas Azerbaijan is facing are not unique to this former Soviet republic. More specific to Azerbaijan are the diversity and types of challenges which have arisen since the start of the secessionist drive in mountainous Karabagh in 1988.

The book attempts to identify historical and geopolitical determinants that could re-emerge in a new guise and under very different circumstances. Having arisen from the ruins of the Soviet Union, Azeris are contemplating their history and statehood, as well as the definitions of the boundaries of their nation. A victim of partition between Iran and Czarist Russia, independent Azerbaijan has experienced a complex evolution as a divided entity which recently suffered another setback with the loss of mountainous Karabagh.

This work also focuses on the construction of modern Azerbaijani identity and statehood. It examines Soviet and post-Soviet cultural and socio-political transformations that have contributed to the contemporary sense of nationality. I suggest that the making of the Azeri nation has involved transformations imposed by the Soviet state as well as constructions created by the nation-building elite.

I hope the book will lead to a better understanding of this very colorful country and richly endowed people of Azerbaijan. I seek not to be critical, but to explain. If the history and political culture can be better understood through this work, I will be gratified.

Many of my findings are the outcome of my informal discussions with colleagues and students. Any endeavor with a decade-long history, after all, also entails a multitude of debts to Azeri friends whose personal experiences have helped me to gain more insight. This project is also heavily dependent on monographs whose wisdom and judgments have contributed to my synthesis. Their names can be found in the bibliography at the end of the book, which shows the extent of my debt.

Introduction

Ernest Gellner once said that nationalism was "natural and probably irresistible."[1] Writing years later, an observer of the Soviet scene, Alexander J. Motyl, seconded this opinion by saying that "nationalism makes sense in a world of nation states." It is rational, he said, because "it suggests an excellent solution, statehood, to a variety of contemporary problems."[2] Although it is debatable whether nationalist pledges are realistic or apocryphal, they do promise modernization such as development, industrialization, and mass education, and at the same time guarantee and promote life, liberty and the pursuit of happiness.[3] In short, nationalism is promoted as a broad symbol that entails values and goals which make it worthy of notice and acceptance.[4]

In the Soviet Republic of Azerbaijan, during the tumultuous three years from 1988 to 1991 – when nationalist, that is anti-Armenian feelings, snowballed – the self-styled nationalists challenged the local leadership, as well as Moscow, to attain the "national goal": preventing the loss of Karabagh, and achieving independence. Azeri nationalists were able to challenge Moscow's constraints partly because by the end of 1988 Gorbachev's policies of glasnost and perestroika had created conditions for opposition groups to organize and articulate political demands. Yet it was the demonstrations in Yerevan (Armenia) and in Nagorno-Karabagh in February 1988, demanding the unification of the mostly Armenian enclave of Karabagh with Armenia, which bolstered the appeal of nationalist slogans. In short, although the long-suppressed cultural, linguistic and other grievances might have, to an extent, influenced Azeri masses, they were mostly motivated by the nascent nationalist leadership's uncompromising stance on the Karabagh issue.

Although the Gorbachev reforms and the Nagorno-Karabagh dispute account for the nationalist fervor, it was the 70-year long Soviet rule that created favorable conditions for a peculiarly Soviet nation-building process. Unlike the assumptions of many Sovietologists, who argued that Moscow tried to stamp out all the remnants of nationalism, the various policies implemented throughout the USSR inadvertently made nations out of "ethnies" or proto-nations that existed prior to 1917.[5] As will be elaborated later, Soviet policies included: 1) nativization, or the employment of the native cadre in the 1920s and early 1930s, and later in the post-Stalin era; 2) economic and social transformations of the 1930s, which nevertheless preserved "national education" and "national cadres"; 3) territorialization, or the consolidation of exclusive, historically validated, national territories based on ethno-linguistic traits; 4) imperial center-periphery relations, or the natives' lack of a real capability to make important political decisions without acquiring Moscow's acquiescence; 5) traditionalism, or the survival of traditional practices and traditional social structures; 6) localism, or the establishment of ties between republican leaders and native peoples based on favoritism, patronage, limited national pride, and economic permissiveness; 7) promotion of "selective local nationalisms" side by side with patriotism, or loyalty to the USSR led to the emergence of secular, conscious, and politically mobile nations.[6] By the 1980s the republics became increasingly homogeneous, and national elites ruled by persuasion, giving concessions to the native populace, "delivering the goods" to the constituents, allowing greater permissiveness of nationalist expression, and using mafia-like networks of clans to link political power with the "second economy".

Some scholars object to the argument that Moscow helped the nation-building process because Moscow 1) weakened the historical identity; 2) confined identity to folk-dancing and handicrafts; 3) manipulated and applied artificial nomenclature to languages and vilified national literature; 4) falsified history; and 5) banned oral histories (*dastans*).[7] Although these observations do have a point, they do not preclude the possibility that a national, or proto-national consciousness – though different from the pre-Soviet characteristics of a given community – could eventually emerge. The Azerbaijani experience attests to this latter possibility.

However, for some Sovietologists, the nationalist fervor in Azerbaijan came as no surprise. For a long time they had predicted that sooner or later nations within the Soviet state would rebel and that they would be unmanageable in the long run. Yet had Gorbachev not set out to establish economic and democratic accountability throughout the USSR, it would have been much more difficult for nationalists to challenge the incumbent pro-Moscow leaders in various republics by adopting populist and nationalist programs. In the Azerbaijani case, the nationalist rhetoric emanating from the "enemy" – from Yerevan and Stepanakert (the capital of Karabagh) and the state of undeclared war since 1989 between Yerevan and Baku made the adoption of nationalist slogans by the elite and the masses all the more inevitable.

While Moscow used coercion to transform Turkic communities through official campaigns against Islam and nationalism (*millatchilik*), and promoted a uniform socialist culture, utilizing – among others – linguistic engineering (Russification of the Turkic languages and styles of expression), these policies, nevertheless, could not prevent the emergence of republican intelligentsias who increasingly managed to expand their room to maneuver. The latter served as repositories of national culture, values and history, which were transmitted more easily to the public after Stalin's years of terror ended. Despite their apparent support for Moscow's assimilation attempts, republican ruling elites tolerated such behavior for, among others, self-serving reasons.

The social compact between the republican ruling elite and the people led over time to the titular nation's acquisition of a prominent status in the republican apparatus, regardless of its decision-making capacity or incapacity. The establishment of national operas and national academies of sciences also took place during this period, and although some dismissed them as symbolic and controlled institutions, they were nevertheless perceived as an embodiment of validated exclusive national territories based on ethno-linguistic cultures.[8] Moreover, despite the Soviet transformations in economic and social life, traditional cultural practices and social structures – though not in their original form – remained either intact or were reinvented. By the 1940s traditional patterns of leadership were destroyed, religion was suppressed, and the social environment was fundamentally changed, and yet old unities based on kinship, customs, and beliefs largely survived. The second economy flourished mainly due to traditional networks protected by favors, family loyalties and codes of silence.

During the 1970s, while "official nationalism" provided "patriotism" or allegiance to the USSR, a selective local nationalism was promoted which included "ethnic pride" and respect for "historic achievements". In such an atmosphere dissidents and even human rights activists based their demands on ethnic or linguistic issues, which had become tolerable and fashionable.

Even within the Helsinki Committees, ethnic and linguistic issues were popular.[9] By the 1980s, partly due to policies pursued by republican leaderships: 1) the republics had become demographically more homogeneous; 2) articulate national, political, and intellectual elites had emerged and developed a shared national consciousness; and 3) the ruling elite ruled mostly by persuasion, concessions, and "delivering the goods" to their constituents. It was perhaps inevitable that the ruling elites consisted mostly of mafia-like networks of clans linking political power with second economy, while allowing limited nationalist expression, which Moscow tolerated or was unable to detect and/or curb.

Although republican parties promoted patronage, favoritism and economic permissiveness toward titular nationality, and enabled the latter to have national pride, the perception of a colonial or quasi-colonial situation, that is, that Russians dominated and exploited other nations, persisted in most – including Turkic – republics. This also contributed to feelings of solidarity between natives. Hence, in the late 1980s, when Gorbachev gave more leeway to expressions of dissent, indigenous activists usually referred to Moscow's discriminatory policies to explain their republics' various dire straits. As Michael Hechter said: "Where economic disadvantages are superimposed upon objective cultural differences – where a pattern of 'internal colonialism' exists – political demands are most likely to be made on a status-group basis."[10]

Ernest Gellner and Eric Hobsbawm stressed that social and cultural processes cannot be conceived simply as objective forces existing outside the given nationality. The active work of individuals, parties, newspapers and intellectuals or the state is the key to the manufacture or articulation of national consciousness. Nationalists or the nation-building elite create common (homogeneous) culture by ignoring or modifying pre-existing cultures, which are usually diverse, to invent a new "high" culture.[11] This process could be an evolving one. As Miroslav Hroch emphasized, the three-stage evolution of nationalism includes an incremental process involving: 1) scholars stressing culture, language and history of the "oppressed" nationality; 2) activists diffusing nationalist ideas; and 3) broad masses joining in the nationalist movement.[12]

Colonial states – blamed for many ills and wrongdoings – did contribute to the notion of the nation. They drew artificial boundaries, thus delimiting the "nation", held censuses to determine members of the "nation", and excavated ruins of former civilizations, thereby reconstructing the missing link in the historiography of the "nation". As in 1991, when the "nations" of the Soviet Union acquired independence almost overnight, Asian and African colonies – no matter whether there was an armed struggle or not – became independent, often too quickly. Independence for many was mostly a simple transaction of transfer of government on paper. For France, for instance, 1960 was the year of wholesale decolonization in Africa.

Characteristics of post-colonial states and those of Azerbaijan seem similar. In both cases state offices have uncertain authority, pre- and post-independence governments are highly ineffective and plagued with corruption, and the political community is highly segmented ethnically or religiously into several "publics" (including tribes, regions, and religious communities). Most elites of the newly independent states belong to two publics at the same time: the civic public and the primordial public. The elite considers itself first and foremost part of the primordial public. As Peter P. Ekeh argued, "the unwritten law is that it is legitimate to rob the civic public in order to strengthen the primordial public."[13] Government is less an agency to provide political goods such as law, order, security, justice, and welfare, and more a foundation of privilege, wealth, and power for the elite who control it. Those who occupy state offices, civilian and military, high and low, are inclined to treat them as possessions rather than positions: to live off their rents and use those to reward persons and cliques who help maintain their power.[14]

In Azerbaijan, during both the Soviet era and after independence, regional and clan influences account for patronage and frequently institutionalized corruption. Two prominent clan groups, the *Nakhichevanis* and the *Yerazi* have had the most influence, and promoted nepotism. In the Soviet era, Azerbaijan Communist Party (AzCP) leaders belonged to one of these patronage networks. In the post-Soviet period, many high government officials also are affiliated with these clans. In independent Azerbaijan, payments in return for services rendered have also become common in that bribing senior officials or buying official positions have been considered as a means to get the required export/import licenses or to land a job which would be financially very rewarding. Key bureaucratic positions can enable office holders to secure bribes, aptly defined as "transaction fees".[15] Many ministers also would either buy their positions or be related to the incumbent president. The late President Heidar Aliev's brother Jalal, for instance, is widely believed to have acquired riches as a result of his being positioned very close to the center of power. As a corollary to the system, the 125-member parliament is largely a rubber stamp, but most of its members are well positioned to reap benefits through their belonging to the ruling New Azerbaijan Party.

The first chapter of this book examines the conflicting versions of Azerbaijan's history as argued or promoted by the Soviet regime, Azeri academics, and the latter's Armenian counterparts. Their diverging and often contentious approaches have often been used for political purposes. While Soviet ideologues omitted references to Azerbaijan's Turkic roots, Azerbaijani academics – especially in the post-Stalin period – increasingly focused on the Turkic past, though they continued to embrace the Soviet theory that Azeris were indigenous to the region and hence the real inheritors of the pre-historical civilizations. This argument strengthened their claims to such disputed portions of the Caucasus as Nagorno-Karabagh (mountainous Karabagh), Nakhichevan and Zangezur. Armenian intellectuals, as well as the ruling elite, clung to the argument that Azeris were recent newcomers or invaders who destroyed ancient civilizations and cannot have any historical claim to the disputed territories.

During the fourth century BCE, two states ruled the region: while Caucasian Albania existed on roughly the territory of today's Republic of Azerbaijan, a second political entity, called "Aturpatkan", "Atropaten", or "Atropatenes" ruled southern, or Iranian Azerbaijan.[16] Azerbaijani scholars have considered both Atropaten and Albania as predecessors of contemporary Azerbaijan, and argued that the name of Azerbaijan has been in use for more than two millennia.[17] They have argued that Albanians were one of the three ethno-linguistic communities who served as progenitors of the modern Azerbaijani nation.

Arab invasions in the seventh century introduced Islam to Caucasia, and Islamic politics were established under local rulers called *shahanshah*. Some authors claimed that despite its socio-cultural impact, Islam could not change the region's Iranian traditions, because even the conquering Arabs came under the impact of the well-established Sassanian culture.[18] The fact that non-Muslims had to pay higher taxes led to the Islamization of most of the Albanian population, who consequently were more easily Turkified by the recently Islamized Seljuk Turks in the eleventh century.[19] Those who chose to remain Christian eventually melted into the Armenian community, who also inhabited the region together with other Transcaucasian peoples.

Successive Karakoyunlu, Akkoyunlu, and Safavid states strengthened the Turkic characteristic of the region, although their rule, as a result of reliance on khans (local rulers), was decentralized. Most khanates consisted of individual *mahals*, (regions), inhabited by homogeneous tribes, illustrating that tribalism was still strong.[20] Land ownership was arranged according to the *iqta* system, distributing state lands as non-hereditary grants to beys and aghas (local notables) for services rendered to the ruler, the khan.[21] The khanates regime contributed to the lack of unity and failure to establish an independent state until the twentieth century. Another legacy of the khanates regime was *yerbazlik* (regionalism), which meant that local allegiance had priority over national or supra-national loyalties.[22] As we shall see later, this legacy proved to be an important facet of Azerbaijani life to be reckoned with.

The unrelenting struggle for control of the Caucasus would lead to two Russo-Iranian (Qajar dynasty) wars from 1804 to 1812, and from 1826 to 1828. After the first war, Fath 'Ali Shah of Iran agreed to the Treaty of Gulistan, and to the Russian predominance in the northern portion of today's Republic of Azerbaijan. At the end of the second war Iran signed the Treaty of Turkmenchai, which transferred sovereignty over the khanates of Yerevan, Nakhichevan and Ordubad.[23] Although initially khans enjoyed Russia's less intrusive rule than that of the Qajars, soon Russian rule began to be detested for its discriminatory policies toward Muslims and its preferential treatment of Armenians. By the late nineteenth century the Azeri intellectual elite identified with Turkey and Iran, although "localism" remained the main tenet of cultural identity among Azeri intellectuals. It comprised the spoken vernacular, local history and problems. The "Armeno-Tatar" War of 1905–1906, while accelerating the nationalist construction of the "ethnic enemy", was to replace the previous proto-nationalism or localism with a more modern nationalism accentuating "Turkish" identity and Islam.[24]

The 1917 Bolshevik Revolution enabled Azerbaijan to have independence from May 28, 1918 to the Bolshevik invasion on April 27, 1920. After the invasion, the Azrevkom (Azerbaijan Revolutionary Committee) was established by the Baku Bureau of the Kavkraikom (Caucasian Regional Committee) of the Russian Communist Party (RCP), and the Bolshevization of the country started. The previously non-existing territorial delineation in 1921 as a "shining example" of Lenin's nationalities policy allocated Nakhichevan and mountainous Karabagh to Azerbaijan, while Zangezur was made Armenian territory. These acts ensured not only that Azerbaijan's main body was to be cut off from Turkey but also the preservation of territorial conflicts between Armenia and Azerbaijan over all these three regions.

The second chapter examines the various stages through which Azerbaijan and its people passed from the difficult 1920s to the relaxed late 1980s. Despite initially favoring Baku on the Karabagh issue, Moscow relied heavily on an ethnic Armenian and Russian cadre as well as quite a few Azeri yes-men to run the country through the mid-1950s. The post-Stalin years were similar to those in other republics in that Moscow became increasingly more tolerant of ethno-cultural revival, as heralded by Khrushchev's *rastsvet* (flowering) policy. The post-Stalin era also witnessed the rehabilitations of once denounced and liquidated literary and political figures, though the publication of their works was usually postponed or came after some editing. Nevertheless, until the 1970s, when Brezhnev increasingly granted more autonomy to the republics, nationalism had remained a serious offense to discredit and dismiss incumbent native leaders.

This chapter also focuses on the underground economy, corruption, and nepotism linked to clans and bureaucratic networks, and the failure of successive first secretaries to eradicate them. As Dmitriy Furman suggested, "[t]heft from the state ... is considerably less of a sin than, for example turning away a poor young fellow from one's own village asking to be fixed up in a graduate course, or the militia, or failing to help a fellow countryman or kinsman in trouble".[25] Patronage and institutionalized corruption influenced by regional and clan interests were major attributes of Soviet era Azerbaijan's political and economic system. In essence these traits have continued to influence the lives of the powerful and the weak in the post-independence era as well.

Soviet tolerance of diversity enabled the Azeri intellectual elite to engage in a quiet and gradual effort to reclaim the past. Historiography, arts and literature became areas where this endeavor took place. Yet the Azeri intellectual elite was initially timid. It embraced Moscow's argument that Azeris' Albanian and Iranian ethno-cultural characteristics were predominant in order to downplay Azerbaijan's Turkic past and stress ancestral links to the ancient indigenous civilizations. Yet, by the late 1970s, Azerbaijan had become more homogeneous demographically, administratively and culturally which enabled the Azeri intelligentsia to act more assertively to stress Azeris' Turkic roots. Gorbachev's policies of perestroika (*yenidengurma*) and glasnost (*ashkarlik*) were initially shunned by the Azerbaijan Communist Party (AzCP), which continued to stress the old rhetoric including the primacy of the central party leadership. Aliev's forced resignation from the Politburo in 1987, and the almost simultaneous claim by Armenian nationalists that the NKAO should unite with Armenia would radically change the attitude of the AzCP, which would begin to tolerate, if not encourage, discussion of once taboo subjects such as the NKAO's patrimony as historic Azeri territory. Soon the Azerbaijan Popular Front (APF) would come into being to challenge the constraints of the old order.

Chapter three focuses on the re-emergence of the Karabagh problem when, taking advantage of the post-Stalin relaxation, the Armenian intellectual elite began to lobby and petition Moscow during the Khrushchev years to sanction the unification of the NKAO with Armenia. Yet the contemporary dispute dates back to a more recent period, which started with another petition drive in both Armenia and the NKAO in 1987. Since Gorbachev seemed more attuned to popular demands, Armenian campaigners hoped to get better results for their efforts this time. The chapter discusses Azerbaijani reaction, first in the form of "unofficial scholarly articles" printed in the republic's various journals, outlining why the NKAO should belong to Azerbaijan. Later, the AzCP leadership itself made use of legalistic arguments, suggesting that the NKAO's secession from Azerbaijan would violate USSR's and Azerbaijan's constitutions. The AzCP also utilized statistics to show that alleged discrimination against the NKAO residents was incorrect and that the residents never wished to have the oblast transferred to Armenia.

Starting in 1989 Azerbaijan's official and unofficial media began focusing on the 1918 to 1920 period and presented the then ruling Musavat Party more favorably than before. They assailed several alphabet changes, linguistic and cultural Russification, depletion of Azerbaijan's oil, destruction of the Caspian Sea's ecology, unemployment, Moscow's implementation of unfavorable terms of trade with the republic, and shortcomings in health and education sectors. Anti-Armenian articles were more easily printed because they were less objectionable than articles critical of Moscow's policies.

The AzCP's concessions to the opposition did not reflect a genuine change of heart. The ruling elite felt that embracing popular demands would not only curry favor with the masses but also force Moscow to act favorably. The AzCP leadership, nevertheless, chose to downplay the dimensions of ethnic cleansing conducted in Armenia against ethnic Azeris. The former's attempt to conceal the magnitude of the Azeris' suffering was due to its belief that the only realistic option was to curry favor with Moscow and this required convincing the Azeris that all was well. The AzCP's assumption that acting as the good guys – as opposed to the

Armenian Communist Party's (ACP) increasingly nationalist stance – would ingratiate the former with Moscow.

Soon, however, having failed to impress Gorbachev, the AzCP's attempt to manipulate Moscow took a different turn. In late February 1989, an Azeri mob attacked and killed scores of ethnic Armenians in the Azeri city of Sumgait while Azeri authorities and security forces chose to stand by. The way the violence was handled by the AzCP suggested that the whole event was planned not only to intimidate the NKAO Armenians, but also compel Moscow to think that, unless it acted fast, popular uproar in Azerbaijan could seriously harm peace and stability in the Transcaucasus. Initially, AzCP's plan seemed to have worked. Moscow intervened and asked the parties to cease denunciations and finger pointing. All three, the AzCP, ACP and the NKAO *obkom* (Oblast Party Committee) followed suit, and banned public demonstrations. The AzCP promised improvements in almost all areas of the lives of the NKAO residents, which Moscow was eager to finance. Reflecting the still limited expectations of the parties, a group of Azeri intellectuals issued a samizdat critical of the AzCP while still treating Gorbachev and perestroika favorably.

Nevertheless, before long, strikes, ethnic cleansing and mutual recriminations would resume and Moscow would decide to take over the reins in conflict management in the NKAO. Chapter four examines the appointment of a close Gorbachev associate, Arkadiy N. Volskiy as Head of the "Special Commission" to administer the NKAO, and subsequent developments. His appointment accelerated the implementation of projects to improve the standard of living in the oblast and provide stronger ties between the NKAO and Armenia, with the latter investing in various socio-economic projects in the oblast. Yet, while these measures fell short of satisfying the Armenians' unification goal, they antagonized Azeris who felt that the NKAO was gradually being torn away from them.

AzCP's half-hearted objections to Armenia's Moscow-sanctioned involvement in construction and other projects in the NKAO made the messages of the nascent Azerbaijan Popular Front (APF) very pertinent to the life of the ordinary Azeri. On November 22, 1988 half a million people, and the following day 800,000 people gathered on Baku's Lenin Square (later renamed Azadlyg or Freedom Square) to denounce Armenia as well as the AzCP, which remained passive. The demonstrators carried the flag of independent Azerbaijan (1918–1920) and previously obscure orators rose to prominence. Soon the APF, which was established in mid-1988 by seven academics to promote perestroika, would claim that it represented the demonstrating masses and adopt a comprehensive program favoring socio-economic and cultural reforms, and political sovereignty. The front was an umbrella organization including pan-Turkists, Islamic radicals, disgruntled AzCP members and others whose major priority became to keep the NKAO within Azerbaijan and not the country's democratization to which the founding intellectuals initially aspired.

By mid-1989 it appeared that Volskiy's rule in the NKAO was not a halfway house on the road to the NKAO's secession from Azerbaijan. This realization led Armenians in the oblast and in Armenia to resume strikes and resort to the use of arms. The Azeris responded by imposing a rail blockade against Armenia and by cutting off Armenia's road link to the NKAO. The armed confrontations were relatively bloodless, mainly because the arms used consisted of pistols and hunting rifles. Soon, however, the inter-communal and inter-state conflict would become much more violent and the weapons used much more deadly.

As suggested above, the AzCP's use of the APF card, that is, reaching a modus vivendi with the latter to manipulate Moscow and to mollify the Azeris led to the legalization of the APF and the adoption of many of the APF's demands including free elections and applicability of the USSR legislation in the republic only when it didn't violate Azerbaijani sovereignty. Still, however, the Azerbaijani opposition – and certainly the ruling elite – believed that the problems of Azerbaijan, including the NKAO problem would be solved within the confines of the USSR's political system. Etibar Mamedov, one of the prominent leaders of the opposition, hailed the *rapprochement* with the government by stating that Gorbachev's perestroika had made it possible by "opening the door of democracy to people."[26]

Chapter five focuses on Moscow's attempts to retain control of the increasingly spiraling ethnic conflict. First, it abolished the Volskiy Committee to establish a new one in which Azeris and Karabagh Armenians would be equally represented. Baku rejected this apparent reduction of its sovereignty while Armenia and the NKAO Armenians declared the oblast's unification with Armenia, although this remained mainly rhetorical. Consequently, inter-communal fighting escalated, leading by late December to the AzCP's further losing ground and to the start by the militants associated with the APF to take over the government in provincial towns. In early January 1990, the AzCP's Russian Second Secretary offered seats to the opposition in the to-be-established National Defense Council to cope more effectively with the situation. Nevertheless, in mid-January lawlessness took a turn for the worse when extremists began attacking Armenian residents of Baku. The former included many deportees from Armenia who struggled to cope with their dire economic circumstances.

Worried about the increasing lawlessness in the republic and complete loss of control, Moscow decided to invade Baku. Soviet Interior Ministry (MVD) troops arrived in Baku during the night of January 19 and in the ensuing clashes many opposition activists as well as many civilian passers-by died, mostly as a result of the MVD troops' propensity to shoot at whatever moved. High casualties also occurred when troops tried to disperse the 30,000-strong crowd camped outside the AzCP headquarters. Moscow's move was all the more unfortunate in that it failed to address Armenia's growing military involvement in the NKAO, and the ongoing general strike in the former. Moscow also did not suspend the air corridor between Armenia and the NKAO through which many civilian and military supplies reached the oblast. The important roadblocks on the Aghdam–Stepanakert (Hankendi) and Stepanakert–Lachin roads remained in the hands of rival Azeri and Armenian irregulars.

Chapter six focuses on the immense contribution of Baku's invasion to the public feeling of victimization and to anti-Soviet sentiments. The fact that Azerbaijan was occupied, whilst Armenia was not, revived the centuries-old notion that Russia favored fellow Christians. For a growing segment of the Azeri population, the APF and its offshoots seemed better poised to act more assertively toward Moscow and to turn the tide of events which the AzCP was unable to cope with. Nevertheless, the AzCP dragged its feet on the establishment of a national army, which the opposition vehemently demanded. Armenia, for its part, not only elected the opposition candidate Levon Ter-Petrosyan as President in July 1990 but also established a national army immediately after.

Azerbaijan's lagging behind Armenia in uniting the various armed bands into a unified army by about one and a half years would cost the republic dearly in the coming months. Also, unlike the ACP, which tolerated the opposition Armenian National Movement (ANM) to win the July 1990 general elections, the AzCP did not permit the opposition to win more than token seats at the September 1990 Supreme Soviet elections. Moreover, unlike the ANM, the AzCP decided to participate in the referendum for Gorbachev's New Union Treaty, which resulted in Soviet-style overwhelming electoral support.

The anti-Gorbachev coup of the Soviet hardliners in August 1991 was to drastically change not only how the post-coup Soviet Union – or what remained of it – looked like, but also the nature of the warfare in the

NKAO and the participants in it. The unraveling of the coup on its third day meant the fizzling out of the AzCP First Secretary Mutalibov's adamantly argued strategy of loyally following Moscow's directives on the NKAO. Afterwards he was forced to pay lip service to such opposition demands as a national unity government and the establishment of a national army, which he had steadfastly refused for two years. In late November he even agreed to the establishment of a new legislative, the National Council, where the opposition was allocated half the seats. Chapter seven examines the creation of the Council and what happened until the cease-fire between Azerbaijan and Armenia in May 1994.

Despite his half-hearted power sharing deal with the opposition, Mutalibov, still banking on Moscow's support, signed the Commonwealth of Independent States (CIS) Treaty in Almaty on December 21, 1991. The gesture wasn't going to save his presidency, however. In late February 1992 Armenian forces attacked Khojaly, the main aerial supply location for the NKAO Azeris. On February 26, 1992 Azeri positions were overrun and the few remaining defenders of the town began fleeing the combat zone accompanied by some 3,000 civilians. What happened during the night of February 26 was nothing short of the cold-blooded massacre of about 500 people, including women and children shot at point blank range and later mutilated.

The Khojaly massacre had wide-ranging consequences. Armenian extremist factions felt redeemed in their insistence of the feasibility of a military solution, thereby undermining President Ter-Petrosyan who seemed interested in a negotiated settlement. Mutalibov's initial denial that a massacre had happened took its toll as well. The opposition charged him with *satkinlig* (sell-out), linking the tragic loss of Khojaly to Mutalibov's "deliberate delay" in creating a national army. Unable to say anything that might have extenuated his negligence, Mutalibov argued for a closer alliance with Russia, which sounded as tactless as it was heartless, coming in the wake of the Khojaly massacre in which Russian troops had allegedly participated. With crowds demonstrating outside Parliament he resigned in disgrace.

Until the June 1992 election victory of Abulfaz Elchibey, a coalition between former communists and the APF governed the country. The coalition decided to establish a national army, but as later battlefield performances would show, the decision was too little too late. The parties did make use of mercenaries, who were recruited from former Soviet bases in Azerbaijan, Armenia, and the NKAO. Often Russian commanders sold or hired heavy arms and tanks to the warring parties. Yet, having set out to establish a national army earlier, Armenian units were better trained and disciplined and had more experience.

The end of 1991 symbolized not only the break-up of the Soviet Union but also the expiration of the mandate of the Soviet Fourth Army's 366th Regiment stationed there. Almost overnight Azeri villages there found themselves exposed to ethnic cleansing by Armenian paramilitaries who by then were – albeit inadequately – restrained by Soviet troops. Armenian rebels also inherited most of the 366th Regiments' – and Armenia-based Seventh Army's – weaponry, while Azeris obtained arms from the 23rd Division in Ganja. The acquisition of heavy arms raised the level of violence and destruction, paving the way for full-scale warfare between Azeri forces and Armenian rebels as well as "volunteers" from Armenia.

Although Azerbaijan acquired significantly more weaponry from the Soviet forces, its troops' inexperience continued to take its toll on the battlefield. In May 1992, in a major offensive, Armenian forces captured Shusha, the only remaining Azeri stronghold in the NKAO, where the rearguard was holed up for a last stand. The loss of Lachin, on the strategically-located corridor linking Armenia to the NKAO, came a week later. Elchibey's election to the presidency in June 1992 seemed to have upped the morale of Azeri forces when they recaptured strategically-located Shaumyan and Agdere (Martakert) regions, which had been lost earlier. Yet Elchibey's presidency had far-reaching consequences. His refusal to join the CIS coupled with Armenian CIS membership did not bode well for Azerbaijan. By the fall of 1992, Russian military supplies to Armenia increased dramatically, as did Armenian battle victories.

While trying to weather gloomy reports from the front, Elchibey and the APF tried to govern the country with little or no experience. Some in Elchibey's entourage quickly became corrupt, while some tried to valiantly navigate in the larger administrative apparatus staffed largely by Soviet era *apparatchiks*. Socio-economic disruptions, mushrooming of petty crime, general chaos and lawlessness coupled with battlefield defeats generally chipped away at Elchibey's and APF's popularity by the spring of 1993. The public increasingly perceived that the command staff was incompetent and corrupt and this caused recruitment figures to dwindle. Soon, the government introduced compulsory conscription, which led to high numbers of the youth leaving the country to dodge the draft.

On the positive side, the Elchibey era witnessed the mushrooming of political parties and their lively and no-holds-barred public debates. Nevertheless, the government – like its communist predecessors – tried to restrict media freedoms by extending or withdrawing favors. As a result, post-Soviet Azerbaijani politics was shaped by compromises or political deals between bureaucratic cliques and political party bosses. Regional power brokers and local warlords, for their part, acquired increased significance. Some regional warlords acquired nationwide fame or notoriety, as was the case with Surat Huseinov, who from his base in Ganja would eventually challenge and topple Elchibey in June 1993. Similarly, government strongmen also did not hesitate to use, or threaten with the use of, force to subdue opponents. Such was the case with Minister of the Interior Iskender Hamidov who, among other misdeeds, beat up journalists for writing unfavorable news stories.

Increasingly, government ministers extended their writs beyond their purviews. Hamidov would give battle orders to his Internal Security (OPON) units to conduct operations in and around the NKAO without bothering to consult with the Defense Ministry. Defense Minister Rahim Gaziev, for his part, made use of the army to meddle in domestic politics. In one case he ordered Etibar Mamedov's National Independence Party to hand over the party's headquarters to him. It took Elchibey's involvement for Gaziev to back down. Although Elchibey chose to arbitrate disputes between his ministers, he wasn't always successful. His attempts to muddle through the political maze also symbolized his inability to dictate his will on the government. Eventually, he would fire both Gaziev and Hamidov, the men with guns, but their departure would leave him unprotected when Huseinov revolted to overthrow him in June 1993. In short, the Elchibey era was negatively influenced by Soviet era patterns of behavior and lack of democratic culture, as well as new forms of regional and bureaucratic rivalries and external manipulation attempts. This included Russia's not-so-covert aid to the local warlord, Surat Huseinov, to topple the most anti-Russian government in former Muslim republics.

Elchibey's brand of nationalism gave reason to various non-Turkic minorities to feel uncomfortable about their prospects in a more Turkified state. By June 1993, while several secessionist drives were in full swing, a former Deputy Minister of Defense, Alekram Hummatov, an ethnic Talish, declared his intention to form an independent Talish republic or to join Iran. In the north, secessionist Lezgin groups, including *Sadval*, were also planning to challenge Azerbaijani rule and establish a Lezgin state in order to unite it with Russia's Daghestan. For a while even the Yerevan-based tiny "Kurdish Liberation Movement" dreamed of a Lachin-centered Kurdish autonomous region affiliated with the Armenian-controlled NKAO.

The Elchibey era coincided with the start of the CSCE's (later OSCE) mediation effort in the NKAO dispute when it created the Minsk Group of eleven states to mediate between the parties. Although the Minsk Group aimed at declaring a truce, it was Russia's unilateral mediation that untied the knot in May 1994. The seventh chapter will also examine the OSCE's and Russia's continuing efforts to engineer a peace settlement and why various proposals have proved inadequate to satisfy the parties' demands. Although technically part of the Minsk Group, Russia chose to leave its imprint on a peace settlement and thus has often acted alone. The West and the US in particular have also been actively involved in unilateral mediation for fear that a "pax Russiana" could turn the strategic southern Caucasus once again into Russia's backyard.

In the Conclusion I will discuss how in the post-independence period many Soviet era habits have influenced the lack of tolerance of the ruling elite toward the opposition. All presidential and parliamentary elections since independence have been tainted by government-orchestrated practices. International observers often found "major nation-wide fraud, including ballot stuffing and improper counting and tabulation".[27] More importantly, pre-election restrictions on opposition candidates' access to media and the electorate in general seriously hampered fairness of elections. Often state resources are used to support the ruling New Azerbaijan Party candidates, and state employees are pressured to vote for particular candidates and avoid attending opposition rallies.[28] In a country where many voters depend on the state for employment and services such efforts of influence carry great weight. As suggested elsewhere, oil and gas wealth can be used "to keep entrenched elites in power, to postpone reforms, to underwrite the lavish lifestyles of the privileged … and to placate powerful special interests."[29]

Azerbaijan's Soviet past has accounted for the population's mostly quiet acquiescence in strong leadership. Elchibey's inability to reestablish law and order, and the chaotic years of early independence, including the immediate post-Soviet period's socio-economic hardships and the war in and around the NKAO, contributed to popular longing for a powerful leader. Hence Heidar Aliev, with his Soviet-era "tough" image seemed to be the most suitable candidate for the job. It might even be argued that the legacy of the Soviet era's lack of the rule of the law and an effective institutional framework necessitated government with a substantial dose of authoritarianism. Under the elder Aliev, policy-making remained largely a presidential prerogative. He relied on advisors and several power ministers who are considered well-informed, shrewd, wise, and most importantly, loyal. It is debatable, however, whether his son, Ilham Aliev, could continue to rule after popular yearning for authoritarian rule had already subsided and while deeply embedded patronage networks that promote nepotism are widely detested.

1

Pre-Soviet Era and Sovietization

Atropatanes, Medes, Albanians and Turks

Contemporary Azerbaijan has been invaded, ruled by, and exposed to the various influences of numerous civilizations since earliest times. Cyrus the Great, the Persian king, captured the land – called Media then – in the sixth century BCE, and Alexander the Great, two centuries later. The Roman legions, under the command of Pompey, also were to seize the region during the first century BCE. During the Byzantine era Caucasia was an object of dispute between the constantly-warring Byzantine and Sassanian (Persian) forces, while various Turkic tribal groups who roamed the northern Caucasian steppes frequently sided with the Byzantine against Persia.[1]

Since ancient and medieval times speakers of eastern Iranian dialects, some nomadic Turkic tribes and the Caucasian Albanians inhabited Transcaucasia. The latter lived in what is now northern Azerbaijan and converted to Christianity in the fourth century. The Armenian-speaking community, however, gradually absorbed them culturally and linguistically.[2] Although Albania vanished as a socio-political entity it survived as a geographical term for southern Caucasus, especially when referring to Nagorno-Karabagh.[3]

During the fourth century BCE two states ruled the region: while Caucasian Albania existed on roughly the territory of today's Republic of Azerbaijan, a second political entity, called "Aturpatkan", "Atropaten" or "Atropatenes" ruled southern or Iranian Azerbaijan.[4] Atropatenes was a Persian satrap during the time of Alexander the Great, lending his name to the state. One theory of the etymology of Azerbaijan suggests that it is a derivation from Atropatenes. A more popular version traces its origin to the word "azer" or fire, from which Azerbaijan, "the land of fire" might have been drawn, in reference to the various Zoroastrian temples whose fires were fed by the abundant sources of natural gas in the area.[5]

Azerbaijani scholars consider both Atropaten and Albania precursors of contemporary Azerbaijan and suggest that the name Azerbaijan has been in use for more than two millennia.[6] Zia Buniatov, a prominent Azeri historian, suggested that Albanians were one of the three ethno-linguistic communities who served as progenitors of the modern Azerbaijani nation. He claimed that the former survived well into the modern era but Armenians suppressed their church.[7]

However, some non-Azerbaijani scholars argue that Azerbaijan is a recent and fictional term, which emerged with the arrival of the Turks in the region in the last millennium. This latter group has inadvertently supported Armenian nationalists' arguments, which have claimed that Azeris are recent newcomers to the region and whose claim to the disputed territories is indefensible.[8] Azeri scholars, however, respond by contending that contemporary Azerbaijan dates back to the Albanian and Atropaten states. No matter how the name of Azerbaijan as a concept of a unique country emerged in the sixth century BCE, it seems that north and south Azerbaijan came to be known by the name of Azerbaijan by the eighth century.[9]

The region was also influenced by the reign of the Arsacids in Iran (249 BCE – 226 AD), members of whose royal family married Caucasian nobles. During the first century BCE Iranian political and military influence competed with that of Rome with current Armenia becoming a battleground between the Roman and Iranian Arsacid empires. The spread of Christianity was haphazard and Christian converts looked to Rome rather than to Iran for guidance and cultural influence.[10] In the face of Roman expansion and conflicts with Christian neighbors, for Muslims, reliance on various Muslim khanates seemed necessary and unavoidable.

The successors of the Genghisid order, the Ilkhanid and the Timurid empires, expanded their rule to the region between the thirteenth and fifteenth centuries, which further contributed to the population acquiring Turkic traits. During the Ilkhanid era, Azerbaijan became the center of the empire extending from Amu Darya to Syria with the khans residing in Tabriz. Throughout the thirteenth to fifteenth centuries, Azerbaijan was a lively center of trade and cultural activity.[11] The Turkic Karakoyunlu and the Akkoyunlu states, based in Iranian Azerbaijan, ruled the area of contemporary Azerbaijan in the fifteenth century.

The Seljuk invasions in the eleventh century changed the composition of the local population and produced the linguistic dominance of the Oghuz Turkic dialects. And yet, unlike the Ottoman Turks who ruled to the west of the Caucasus, the Caucasian Muslims in the early sixteenth century began to adopt in large numbers the Shi'a faith that set them apart from Sunni Ottomans. It was Safavid Iran's zealous proselytizing that made Azerbaijanis' conversion to the Shi'a sect a prudent and necessary choice. Joining the ranks of the Shi'a made the Azeris more receptive to Persian social and cultural influence. Yet a significant portion of the Azeris chose to remain Sunni.[12]

The Safavid rule (1502–1722) over contemporary Azerbaijan was interrupted for short durations by Ottoman rule (1578–1603) and by Russia under Peter I during the early eighteenth century. The Safavids divided Azerbaijan into four *beklerbekliks* or large administrative zones. These *beklerbekliks* included Tabriz (center: Tabriz), Shukur Saada (center: Nakhichevan), Shirvan (center: Shemakhi), and Karabagh (center: Ganja).[13]

With the assassination of Nadir Shah, who had resuscitated the Safavid rule beyond its formal collapse in 1722 until 1747, Iran's central authority ended and khans and tribal leaders asserted themselves.[14] Muslim khans continued to rule, among others, Karabagh, Sheki, Baku, Ganje Derbent, Kuba, Nakhichevan, Talysh, and Yerevan in the north, and Tabriz, Urmi, Ardabil, Khoi, Maku, Maragin and Karadagh in the south; often engaging in intra-khanate warfare, destabilizing each other. The population was multi-ethnic and multi-confessional.

Yet most khanates consisted of individual *mahals* or regions, inhabited by homogeneous tribes, illustrating that tribalism was still strong.[15] Land ownership was arranged according to the *iqta* system, distributing state lands as non-hereditary grants to *beys* and *aghas* (local notables) for services rendered to the ruler, the khan.[16] The khanates contributed to a lack of unity and the failure to establish an independent state until the twentieth century. Another legacy of the khanates was *yerbazlik* or regionalism, which meant that local allegiances preceded national or multi-regional loyalties.[17] As we shall see later, this legacy proved to be an important facet of Azerbaijani life to be reckoned with. The largest component of the population was the Turcoman tribes, some nomadic, some sedentary. In the 1830s the numbers of Sunnis in northern (former Soviet, now independent) Azerbaijan were almost equal to the Shi'a, with the Shi'a being only slightly in the majority. The Sunnis lived in the northernmost part of the country near Daghestan, a major region of concentration of the Sunnis.

The Sunnis began to emigrate to Turkey after the Russian suppression of the rebellion of the Daghestanis led by the charismatic Imam Shamil from 1834 to 1859.[18] Afterwards, the Sunni–Shi'a ratio became 1:2. The Sunni–Shi'a conflict had always been there, yet Turco–Armenian antagonism muted it toward the end of the nineteenth century.[19] Armenian and Georgian populations often appealed to Russia to capture the southern Caucasus and put an end to the Turco-Muslim khanates which many of them apparently frowned on.[20]

For Russia, Azerbaijan was important as a source of raw materials such as silk, cotton, and copper and also as a place to settle Russian colonists. It was, however, its perceived strategic significance that tempted the Czarist Empire. The Russian involvement dates back to the ill-fated Persia expedition of Peter the Great in 1722, which was aimed at expanding Russia's power toward the Indian Ocean. By 1735 the expedition had failed and Nadir Shah drove out the remaining Russian troops.[21]

Under Catherine the Great (1763–1796) Russia resumed the expansion toward the south but clashed in 1796 with the new Qajar dynasty of Iran, which by then had extended its rule to most of the former Safavid lands south of the Araz River.[22] In 1801, Czar Alexander I made Georgia a Russian province and during the first quarter of the nineteenth century Czarist Russia expanded further either by treaty or by force. At the end of the 1804–1812 Russo-Persian War Fath 'Ali Shah of Iran agreed to the Treaty of Gulistan and to the Russian predominance in the northern portion of today's Republic of Azerbaijan. At the end of the second Russo-Persian War (1826–1828) Iran signed the Treaty of Turkmenchai, which transferred sovereignty over the khanates of Yerevan, Nakhichevan and Ordubad to Russia.[23]

As a result of these treaties one-third of Azerbaijani lands came under Russian rule while the rest remained within Iran up to the present time. The khans accepted Russia's prerogative in foreign policy and defense and agreed to the deployment of Czarist troops. Another consequence of the Turkmenchai Treaty was Czar Nicholas I's decree providing for the formation of an Armenian *oblast* (district) comprising the territories of the khanates of Yerevan and Nakhichevan.[24]

At first, Russian rule in the Caucasus was military and the former khanates were reorganized into *provintsii* (provinces) and administered by army officers who ruled by a combination of local and Russian imperial law. In 1841, civil imperial administration replaced military rule and Transcaucasia was divided into a Georgian-Imeritian *gubernia* (province) with its center in

Tblisi and a Caspian oblast (region) centered in Shemakhi. Ganja (Elizavetpol) and Nakhichevan were incorporated into the Georgian *gubernia*.

In 1846 Viceroy M. S. Vorontsov (1844–1854) introduced the empire's administrative and legal institutions and drew new administrative boundaries by abolishing the former borders and creating instead four *gubernii*: Tblisi, Kutais, Shemakhi, and Derbent. Ganja remained under Tblisi's jurisdiction while Nakhichevan was transferred to the Yerevan *gubernia* created in 1849. Whereas Azeris and Georgians were the most compact populations, Armenians were the most urbanized yet scattered community. Nevertheless, the new borders paid no attention to the ethnic structure of the population or to the already existing loyalties.[25]

These reforms placed southern Caucasus more fully under Russian control but they also facilitated the region's economic integration by removing divisions, which spawned local peculiarities.[26] Soon most of the *waqf* (Muslim pious foundations) lands and properties were confiscated and the jurisdiction of the Muslim courts was curtailed. Many mosques and *madrassahs* (religious schools) were closed and the clerical establishment was required to show loyalty to Russia.[27]

A major outcome of the Treaty of Turkmenchai was that Armenians living in Iran were granted permission to resettle in the Russian Empire. As a result, 8,249 Armenian families (approximately 50,000 people) moved into the *gubernia* of Yerevan, the province of Karabagh and the Shemakhi district, the latter two being part of modern Nagorno-Karabagh.[28] A second wave of Armenian immigrants followed during and after the Crimean War and a third wave came in the wake of the relocation of Ottoman Armenians in Turkey in 1915.[29]

Armenian immigration created Armenian majorities also in some rural areas. The earliest data on the population of Transcaucasia came from the imperial census of 1897. Accordingly, in the 1860s the Baku *gubernia* (province) had grown from 486,000 to 826,716, of which nearly 60 percent were Azeris, 11 percent Tats (Persian speakers), nearly 10 percent Russians and a little over 6 percent Armenians. The latter two communities lived mostly in Baku city.[30]

Azeris comprised a large majority in four of the six *uezdy* (districts) in the Baku *gubernia* and a smaller majority in the other two districts. Azeris also constituted the most numerous communities in the Elizavetpol *gubernia* (the western portion of the contemporary Republic of Azerbaijan). In seven out of the eight *uezdy* of the Elizavetpol *gubernia*, they made up 52–74 percent of the population. In the Yerevan *gubernia*, however, the Azeris comprised 37 percent of the population whereas the Armenian community amounted to 63 percent.[31]

The Azeri community also suffered unequal treatment in other ways. Except for the vice-royalty of Prince Grigorii Golitsyn (1896–1904), which addressed some of the grievances of the Azerbaijani community, the viceroys as a rule adopted pro-Armenian and anti-Muslim postures. Muslim mullahs were brought under direct state control and were subject to state regulations, which designated their rank, qualifications, privileges, and responsibilities and proscribed their adherence to Sufi orders.[32]

The legal and administrative reforms of the Alexander II era (1855–1881) are considered major steps in the modernization of Russia but they were applied to the Muslims of Caucasia with various restrictions. One celebrated example is the restricted implementation of the Urban Reform Act of 1870 according to which suffrage was based on property ownership. Although the Azeris of Baku constituted 80 percent of people with property, the Muslims (Azeris) were prohibited from having more than half of the seats in the city council.[33] Consequently the Baku city Duma remained in the hands of the propertied Armenians and Russians.[34] The only exception to the "Muslims should hold no more than one-half of the seats" rule came with the 1908 elections. The Viceroy tacitly accepted Azeris' electing more than half of the members of the City Council in 1908 and thus violating the law.[35]

Although oil production preceded even the Russian rule in 1813, in the 1870s – simultaneous with the growth in industry, trade, banking, construction and communications network – the oil yields of the Baku wells increased dramatically, leading Baku to become the empire's oil production center and one of the world's major oil production hubs. Between 1821 and 1872, the Czarist state maintained some form of monopoly over oil extraction, refining and trade.[36] Until 1872 individual state farms held state concessions, after which the state monopoly system was replaced with the auction of oil fields, benefiting mostly Russian and Armenian entrepreneurs. In 1888 54 major companies extracted oil in Baku, of which only two were Azerbaijani-owned.[37]

Czarist preferential treatment of the Armenian community could be accredited for the latter's enthusiastic embrace of the incremental Russian annexation of the Caucasus since the late eighteenth century. Until almost the end of the nineteenth century Russia favored Armenians and the Azeri community considered them as surrogates of Russia. Armenians occupied many posts in the regional administration, imperial academic institutions, and the military and the Armenian Church kept its autonomous existence.[38]

The Armenians were among the wealthiest merchants and oilmen. They were second to Russians in terms of their size in the regional judiciary.[39] Armenian political organizations, especially the nationalist Dashnaktsutiun (Dashnakt) Party, focused on the plight of the Armenian community in the Ottoman Empire and regarded the Turks – Ottoman and Azerbaijani – as their main foe.[40] Yet, by 1907, the Dashnakts had begun to anger the Czarist state for advocating an autonomous Armenia not only in eastern Anatolia but also in Transcaucasia.[41]

Unlike Central Asian Muslims, who were accorded only inorodtsy (alien) status, Azeris were given citizenship, yet they suffered discrimination. They were legally classified as "Muslims" thus proscribed from practicing various professions. They couldn't benefit from some of the legal reforms adopted in the late nineteenth century. As suggested above, the Azeri community was barred from occupying more than 50 percent of the Baku City Council seats although it constituted 80 percent of the Baku city's electorate.[42]

The increasingly violent antagonism between Armenians and Azeris defused the hostility felt toward Russian rule. Consequently, Russian rule was less resented in the Transcaucasus than in other Muslim regions of the empire and there were no major upheavals.[43] Quite a few of the Azeri cultural elite, including the well-known Abbas Kuli Bakikhanov and Fath Ali Akhunzada (Akhundov), were attracted to the Russian culture which, they trusted, would allow them to embrace European culture and values. Most of the Azeri intellectuals and political leaders, however, looked up to the Ottoman Empire, or even to Qajar Persia as models to emulate. Until the 1905 Revolution, Russia's cultural and political influence remained less significant compared to that of Turkey or Iran.[44]

Intellectual Awakening: Constitutionalism, Nationalism and Socialism

Czarist rule contributed to the rise of market forces and capitalist relations of production. Considerations of profit and security prompted many to acquiesce to Russian rule while remaining weary of Russian supremacy in all spheres. Azerbaijani cultural revival also began in the wake of the Russian conquest and was led by the secular intelligentsia who labored to transform their ethno-religious community into a more politically conscious and articulate national grouping. Azerbaijani intellectuals studied, and wrote the history of their people, codified native language and aspired to reform education and social mores that were perceived as contributing to the backwardness of their society, including such practices as religious education and arranged marriages.[45]

Between 1875 and 1877 a Baku teacher of Sunni beliefs, Hasan Bey Zardabi, published a newspaper called *Ekinchi* (farmer), which was pro-Ottoman. There were many other papers that followed. Ismail Bey Gasprinski, a Çrimean Tatar, published *Tarjuman* in Bakchisarai, Crimea, starting in 1883. Gasprinski called for Turkic unity in spiritual, linguistic and cultural spheres (*Dilde, Fikirde, İshte Birlik*). One of his priorities was to create a literary language understandable by all Turkic peoples from the Balkans to China. *Tarjuman* used Istanbul Turkish – purged from excessive Arabic and Persian words – offering it as a common medium to be employed by all Turkic communities in Russia.[46] The Azeri intelligentsia also widely read Gasprinski.

The first Azeri pan-Turkist in a political sense was Alibey Huseynzada (1864–1941) who openly advocated pan-Turkism. Huseynzada called for one single literary language for all Turkic communities and for Azerbaijan's unification with the Ottoman Empire, "the spiritual and political head of the Islamic world".[47] There were also pan-Islamists such as Ahmad Bey Agaev (Ağaoğlu), who was initially pro-Iranian and anti-Ottoman before he embraced pan-Turkism.[48]

Until the late nineteenth century Azeris perceived their community invariably as Turkish or Muslim and/or identified themselves by their tribal/regional affiliations. Toward the end of the century, however, many began to see themselves as Azerbaijani Turks, although this did not mean that they used it in the modern sense of the term. Their national identity was bound to the territory they lived in and to regional conditions, including ethnic frictions with Armenians and discriminatory policies of the Czarist administrations.

"Localism" was the main tenet of cultural identity among many – though not all – Azeri intellectuals. It comprised the spoken vernacular, local history and problems. They avoided focusing on all-Turkic (pan-Turkist) issues while at the same time striving not to closely associate with the Russian Empire. The so-called "Armeno-Tatar" War of 1905–1906, while accelerating the nationalist construction of the ethnic enemy, was to replace the previous proto-nationalism with a more modern nationalism, accentuating Turkishness and Islam.[49]

In general, the Azeri intelligentsia was more interested in the socio-economic and political growth of the Azeri community than in the well-being of the Muslims of the Russian Empire. Although they were interested in political support from Turkey and Iran against their Armenian foes, they soon discovered that neither of these countries was in a position to back them. Starting in the early twentieth century, the search for allies among other Muslim peoples of the empire, especially among Volga Tatars, acquired importance, at least partly as a result of the 1905 Armeno-Tatar War.[50]

At around the same time, Baku industrialists, including Zain ul-Abidin Tagiev and the Ashurbeyli brothers, started to financially support a compact group of intellectuals to act as spokesmen for the Azeri community's well-being. The Young Turks' movement in Turkey influenced this group, but its pan-Turkism was more pronounced than that of the Turks or their Tatar contemporaries. This group consisted of young intellectuals, who, unlike the Berlin or St Petersburg-schooled Tatars, were mostly educated in Istanbul. It included Ahmad Bey Agaev (Ağaoğlu), Ali Husein Zadeh (Huseinov), Hashim Vazirov, Uzeir and Jayhun Hajibeyli, Mardan Bey Topchubashy, Mammad Emin Resulzada, and Nariman Narimanov. This talented group provided most of the cadre of Azerbaijani political parties established subsequently.[51]

Moreover, due to their hostility to the Iranian monarchy and the Shi'a religious hierarchy, they were anti-clerical modernists. This group was also populist and receptive to socialist ideas. All, including the more conservatives among them, gave priority to social justice and equated anti-imperialism with being against the Russian rule.[52] In short, their socialist idealism did not hinder their adherence to a nationalist agenda.

Many Azeri intellectuals, like their counterparts in the *jadid* movement in Russia and Central Asia, were exposed to such concepts as constitutionalism, nationalism, and socialism while they studied or lived in Istanbul and Europe.[53] Like other *jadids*, they were reformist and secular, "anti-clerical but not irreligious."[54] They demanded greater autonomy within Russia and control over local government and education. The education program they desired was a combination of the traditional, including religion, native language and literature, and Western, including Russian language, and science courses. Azerbaijani *jadids* would assume leadership positions in independent Azerbaijan (1918–1920) and even during the early Bolshevik era.

The aforementioned compact group of Azeri intellectuals remained united until the first Russian Revolution (1905), after which the socialist

Himmat (toil or endeavor) Party was born. The establishment of the party was preceded by the formation in 1903 of a debating circle, which assumed the title "Himmat" in 1904, and published a clandestine newspaper under the same name. Himmat included socialist intellectuals such as Mammad Emin Resulzada, Abbas Kazimzada, Mammad Hasan Hajinski as well as Russian Social Democratic Workers Party (RSDWP) members, including M. G. Movsumov, Sultan Majid Efendiev, and Asadullah Akhundov.[55] Himmat emphasized development of the native language, mass education, and native customs and denounced colonialism, Czarist oppression, the Europeanized native bourgeoisie, pro-Russian bureaucrats and the religious establishment. It resisted absorption by the RSDWP, yet it was loosely affiliated with the latter. In 1906, Russian Interior – and later Prime – Minister Pyotr A. Stolypin's repressive measures dealt Himmat a severe blow. Several of its leaders were arrested and several others took refuge in Iran. By 1909 Himmat ceased to exist as a political party, but its former members continued to be called Himmatists.[56] The overthrow of the Czardom in March 1917 enabled the re-establishment of Himmat by several former leaders after the latter considered and opposed joining the ranks of the RSDWP.[57]

In 1911 or 1912 a more nationalistic but also socialist Musavat (equality) Party – or Muslim Democratic Party – came into being. Since Musavat was inactive before the First World War, some historians claimed that it did not exist before 1917. Yet it did have a program and statutes before 1914. The party desired equality of the Muslims with ethnic Russians, but at the same time called for the freedom of all Muslims.[58] Party members had in the past flirted with Islamic solidarity, a moderate version of pan-Turkism and – as in the case of many of its members who used to be Himmat members – socialism.[59]

The evolution of views of the future leader of Musavat, Mammad Emin Resulzada, is characteristic also of the experiences of many other leaders and rank and file. After having fled Baku Resulzada arrived in Tehran in 1909 and published a pro-constitution newspaper, the *Iran-i nou* (New Iran) there, indicative of how ambiguous the convictions of Azeri intellectuals then were.[60] After the Russian military intervention in Iran, Czarist pressure forced him to leave Tehran for Istanbul. In 1913 he took advantage of the amnesty granted to commemorate the 300th anniversary of the Romanov dynasty, returning home to assume the chairmanship of the Musavat. Other than Resulzada's participation not much is known about Musavat prior to 1917.[61] Following the overthrow of the monarchy in Russia in February 1917, Musavat advocated pan-Turkism.

While in Istanbul, Resulzada had become close to the pan-Turkists. Many Russian Turkic intellectuals, likewise, had taken refuge in Istanbul where they influenced and were influenced by the pan-Turkic tendencies of the post-1908 Young Turk administration. Azeri intellectuals, such as poet Muhammad Hadi, journalist Karabey Karabekov, Mammad E. Resulzada, Ali Bey Husaynzada, together with Ismail Bey Gasprinski and Yusuf Akçuraoğlu, were invited to join the supreme council of the Committee of Union and Progress (CUP), and Ahmad Agaev became one of the leading contributors to the theoretical journal of pan-Turkism, *Turk Yurdu*, established in 1911.

Ziya Gökalp, the leading Turkish theorist of the pan-Turkist movement, who called for unity of Oghuz Turks, including Ottoman Turks, Turkmens, and Azeris, also influenced Azeri intellectuals.[62] Husaynzada called for "*Turklashtirmak, Islamlashtırmak, Avrupalashtırmak*," (Turkification, Islamization, Europeanization) as a means of deliverance from the Russian yoke. He stated: "[O]ur system of thought seeks guidance from Turkic life and from the worship of Islam. It also calls for acquiring the benefits of civilization from contemporary Europe."[63] As Husaynzada's argument suggests, there was uncertainty even in the post-1905 era as to how the educated elite identified themselves. Were they Muslims, Turks or Azeris? Obviously events such as the 1905 hostilities with Armenians and the Bolshevik Revolution in 1917 would influence this process.

1905 Azeri–Armenian Inter-Communal Fighting

By the early twentieth century the remarkable increase in oil production and the attending industrialization made Baku a city of immigrants. They came from Russia, from Armenian districts and from Iran. Consequently, in the early 1900s Baku was not a city dominated by Muslims; rather it was a multi-national city with a powerful labor movement consisting mostly of Russian and Armenian laborers. Therefore Baku was dissimilar to its hinterland for being cosmopolitan, very much unlike Ganja, which had more of a traditional/static quality. Ordinary Azeris were on the fringes of Baku's socialist movement and they even seemed immune to nationalist rhetoric. Yet the threats perceived to be coming from the Armenian socialist Dashnaktsutiun and Russian Marxists (Russian Social Democrats) gradually contributed to the nationalist construction of the ethnic enemy.

Azeris increasingly felt in solidarity with the Ottoman Turks and other Muslims though they recognized themselves as a distinct community or ethnie.[64] By the early twentieth century the accumulation of antagonistic feelings between Armenians and Azeris had reached crisis proportions. The latter detested the Armenians' ability to acquire most oil-field leases through favorable treatment by Czarist officials. In addition, the mostly rural and impoverished Azeris envied the more privileged lives of the by and large urbanized Armenians while the few urban Azeri laborers felt bitter toward the more skilled Armenian workers who took away better paying oil jobs.[65]

The start in February 1905 of the Armenian–Azeri conflict played a significant role in enabling the Azeri intelligentsia to move beyond the earlier emphasis on language, literature, and education, to demand civil rights, social justice, legal equality and representative government.[66] The immediate cause of the 1905 clashes was the murder of a Muslim by Dashnaktsutiun militants in Baku. In response, thousands of Azeris, including many arriving from the countryside, attacked the Armenian sections of the city. In the ensuing period, inter-communal fighting, widespread violence and looting engulfed the whole city.

Violence expanded to other cities, including Yerevan (February 20–21), Nakhichevan (May), Shusha (June), and others. Between November 15 and 18 one of the bloodiest clashes took place in Ganja followed by clashes in Tblisi on November 21. Fighting continued at low intensity into the following year, tapering off gradually.[67] While in Baku, Shusha, and Nakhichevan the Azeris had the upper hand, in Yerevan and Etchmiadzin Armenians overpowered the Azeris. The inter-communal fighting led to the progression of ethnic cleansing, making the neighborhoods more homogeneous and the cities more divided. The fighting did not spare rural communities. According to Armenian sources 128 Armenian and 158 Azeri villages were "pillaged or destroyed" changing the population make-up of larger regions.[68]

The clashes in the Transcaucasus came in the wake of the Ottoman suppression in the 1890s of the escalating Armenian nationalist activities. After additional clashes with Azeris in 1905, the Armenian political elite perceived irreconcilable differences with both Ottoman and "Azeri Turks" who seemed bent on destroying their socio-political presence in the region. Azeris, for their part, increasingly identified with Ottoman Turkey's policy toward its own Armenians. The Armenian perception of encirclement and suffocation would intensify with the Ottoman government's decision in

1915 to deport Anatolian Armenians to Syria, in the process of which many would perish.[69]

The Azeri political elite perceived the events of 1905 much differently. They considered the Armenian-instigated clashes as evidence of a Russo-Armenian plot of ethnic cleansing. As a result, revolutionary doctrines critical of exploitation of non-Russian regions had great appeal and they were considered a means of coping with Czarist colonialism, Russification, proselytizing, and non-native bourgeoisie exploiting Azerbaijani resources. Despite their revolutionary rhetoric Azeri radicals, including those belonging to Himmat, perceived exploitation related not so much to class struggle; rather they perceived it as a consequence of the Azeri community's subjugation.

In the post-1905 period, the anti-colonial movement moved from the cultural sphere to the political field but it was, nevertheless, reformist and not yet separatist. Some regions were, however, more assertive. The Ganja intelligentsia had a clearer national identity and its rhetoric was more anti-Russian and nationalistic than those in Baku because Ganja was more exposed to Dashnaktsutiun's activities. The frictions with the latter contributed to Ganja's emergence as the center of the national movement in the following years.

After 1905 the influence of Tatar *jadidism* became more relevant to cultural and educational life in Azerbaijan.[70] So, before the October Revolution, the Azeri intelligentsia increasingly sided with the pan-Turkic and pan-Islamic movement led by the Crimean and Volga Tatars, and for their part, contributed significantly to the pre-revolutionary political life of the Muslims of Russia. Azeri delegates participated in the first all-Russian Muslim Congress in August 1905 in Nizhni Novgorod. The Congress adopted a moderate program, resolving to create *Rusya'nin Muselman Ittifaqi* (Union of Russia's Muslims) and to struggle for the creation of a constitutional monarchy and abrogation of all laws and administrative practices discriminatory to Muslims.[71]

Iranian constitutional reforms (1906/1907) and the Young Turk revolution in Turkey in 1908 also influenced Azerbaijani politics. The Iranian experiment's failure in June 1908 at the hands of Muhammad Ali Shah led to revolts in Tabriz in Iranian Azerbaijan and the pro-constitution revolt there turned into a pan-Azerbaijani revolt led by Sattar Khan. The Tabriz insurgents, encouraged by the success of the Turkish revolution, threatened that unless Tehran reinstituted the constitutional reforms they would cast their lot with Turkey. Azeris from the north, especially Himmatists, went to

Tabriz to join the revolt. When the Shah could not bring the rebellion to an end, the Russian army came to his aid and captured Tabriz in April 1909.[72] In the meantime Russia reached an understanding with Britain in 1907 to divide Iran into spheres of influence.[73]

During the First World War Azeris first supported Russia against Germany and Austria, but following Turkey's late involvement they moved their support to the Ottoman Empire, although pro-Ottoman groups, including Musavat, publicly kept a pro-Russia stance. During the war the strongman of the empire, Enver Pasha, gave priority to the capture of the Caucasus, at least partly because of his pan-Turkist proclivity. Enver expected that the Georgian Muslim Ajars, Daghestanis and Azeris would rebel in support of Istanbul's war effort. Yet Russia's defeat of the Third Ottoman Army, commanded by Enver at Sarıkamış, eastern Turkey in January 1915, put an early end to his pan-Turkist aspirations.

The Bolshevik Revolution and the Emergence of Independent Azerbaijan

Before the overthrow of the Czar in February 1917 Musavat increasingly advocated pan-Turkism because Azeri nationalism was still not as popular, desirable or feasible. Musavat was to change course after uniting with the Ganja-based "Ademi Merkeziyyet" (autonomy) group and in the aftermath of the February Revolution adopted this group's policy of favoring autonomy within a federal Russia.[74] Uniting with Ademi, Merkeziyyet enabled Musavat to expand its influence beyond the confines of Baku and acquire the backing of rural supporters who were the former's constituency. Himmat, meanwhile, found it increasingly difficult to stay away from the cleavage between Bolsheviks and Mensheviks in the RSDWP. When in June 1917 the Transcaucasian branch of the RSDWP split, Himmat also couldn't avoid a split. Baku Himmatists sided with the Bolsheviks while in the provinces Himmat members turned pro-Menshevik.[75] The Islamists were represented by the "Rusya'da Muslumanliq-Ittihad" (Russia's Muslim Union) Party, which opposed secession from Russia and continued to advocate unity of all Muslims in Russia through Muslim cultural autonomy.

During the last months of 1917 the Russian Caucasus front collapsed, with Russian troops deserting the front lines. The Transcaucasian nations were quick to form their own armies. Whereas Armenian motives included a desire to guard against anticipated Turkish and Azeri assaults, Azeris wanted to defend themselves against Armenians who were better armed and trained, not least because they served in the Czarist army and the Muslims did not. The Musavat Party led the effort to form an Azeri army mainly in Ganja while Bolsheviks in Baku opposed national armies calling instead for the formation of proletariat forces.

Following the October Revolution, fighting erupted again between Armenians and Azeris throughout the region but the most affected areas included Yerevan, Ardahan, Ganja, and Karabagh. Whereas the Musavat Party and even some members of the socialist Himmat were increasingly in favor of independence, Armenians – especially the pro-Bolshevik factions – favored Russian rule. Even the nationalist – and self-professed socialist – Dashnaktsutiun Party cooperated in Baku with the Bolsheviks and terrorized Azeris. The Bolsheviks, for their part, preferred collaboration with Armenians, whom they considered more reliable. Baku Bolsheviks were not enthusiastic about cooperation with the socialist Himmat, which they suspected had secessionist tendencies.

On November 11, 1917 the non-Bolshevik left-wing parties of the Transcaucasian nations met in Tblisi and resolved to establish an interim government for the region under the title "Transcaucasian Commissariat" or *Zakavkom*. The participants included, among others, Georgian Mensheviks, Azeri Musavatists, and Armenian Dashnakists. In the elections for the constituent assembly these three parties received most of the votes from their communities. Bolsheviks, Himmat, Ittihad and others received few votes, possibly reflecting the enthusiasm for territorial autonomy.[76] And yet the parties which controlled the constituent assembly were aware that the Transcaucasian Commissariat was a measure of convenience which could crumble at any moment due to historical animosity between nations in the Transcaucasus.

Musavat was initially favorably disposed to the October Revolution, not least because the latter promised national self-determination. Yet by March 1918 Baku Soviet's "war communism" policies and its anti-Muslim stance had so antagonized Musavat that the latter decided to act. Assisted by some anti-Bolshevik Russian officers Musavat members and other Muslim groups fought the Bolsheviks for control of the city in a losing battle.[77] In the wake of their defeat, Armenian Dashnaktsutiun engaged in massacres and lootings throughout the city. By Armenian estimates 3,000 Azeris were killed in two days of fighting. Subsequently, many Azeris abandoned the city, leaving Bolsheviks and Armenians as the only powers in control.[78] Yet outside Baku Soviet power was not effective.

In the immediate aftermath of the Bolshevik Revolution, Russia and Turkey signed an armistice in Erzincan on December 5, 1917 paving the way for the Ottoman entry to Transcaucasian politics. Istanbul welcomed the opportunity to recover its losses incurred earlier in the War by projecting its power to the east. The Turks saw only weak neighbors to the east with makeshift or no armies at all. In addition, the Russian army had evacuated northern Iran too, which presented the Ottomans and the Musavatists with an additional opportunity for expansion. The circumstances in Tabriz were no different from those in Baku, Ganja and other regions of Czarist Russia. Musavat dreamt of a greater Azerbaijan including northern Iran as well as Daghestan and possibly affiliated to Turkey in some fashion.

Before the independendent existence of individual republics a Transcaucasian Federation came into being in April 1918. This was almost solely due to Ottoman insistence that the newly established legislative Diet could not negotiate with the Ottomans unless it declared independence. By early March 1918 Ottoman forces had already captured Kars, Ardahan and Batum, awarded to Istanbul by the Brest-Litovsk Treaty. The Transcaucasian Federation experience, however, lasted about a month. From the start, Georgians and Azeris favored independence while Armenians – including the Dashnaktsutiun – were against it.[79] The Dasnaktsutiun and the National Council, made up of representatives of various Armenian organizations, rejected the idea of independence fearing that Armenia would not be viable without Russia's protection.

On May 28, 1918 Muslim representatives of the now defunct Diet constituted themselves as the Azerbaijani National Council and declared independence.[80] The republic was perceived with suspicion especially by Iran, which feared Azeri irredentism *vis-à-vis* Tehran. Iranian fears increased when the Ottoman army briefly occupied Tabriz in June 1918. The Ottomans promised military assistance to Azerbaijan to restore peace and stability. The implication was Ottoman support for the suppression of the Armenian revolt in Mountainous Karabagh and the recovery of Baku, held by the Bolsheviks.[81]

Enver Pasha's half-brother, Nuri Pasha, headed the joint Ottoman–Azerbaijani force called the "Army of Islam", which was deployed in Ganja since its arrival at the end of May 1918. The army was a puffed up version of the Ottoman Fifth Infantry division and troops from General Ali-Agha Shikhlinski's Muslim (Azeri) National Corps and bands of irregulars. This motley army comprised up to 18,000 men. The Ottomans constituted one-third of this army and they were the only battle-tested portion of it. Shikhlinski's troops and irregulars lacked sufficient training and battle experience. Istanbul was uncomfortable with the Formation of the Army of Islam, which even Germany might have construed as violation of the Brest-Litovsk Treaty's provisions.[82]

Nuri Pasha's involvement in Azeri politics was heavy-handed. He forced the firing of socialist ministers from the cabinet and was not even favorably disposed to the participation of ministers who were Azeri nationalists but not pro-Turkey. He also intervened in Tabriz, deporting to Kars such "undesirables" as Shaikh Muhammad Khiabani, the radical leader of the Democratic Party of Azerbaijan. He disbanded the Democratic Party, enabling the pro-Ottoman *Union of Islam* to be the only political party in Iranian Azerbaijan. These interventions contributed to Azeri elite's declining confidence in Istanbul.[83]

Nuri Pasha's forces started attacking Baku in June 1918, entering the city on September 16. During the Turkish attack on Baku the British had landed some troops there but they withdrew before the Ottomans captured the city. During the British presence the Bolsheviks – knowing that the British would not tolerate their rule – had transferred power to a new government consisting of Socialist-Revolutionary Party (called Mainstream or Right-Wing SR) members and Dashnakists who were willing to cooperate with the British. On September 15 the British withdrew and the next day the Ottomans arrived. During the intervening 24 hours, some of the Azeri irregulars took part in massacres, which caused thousands of Armenian deaths.[84]

By the end of the summer of 1918 Nuri Pasha's forces held not only northern but also Iranian Azerbaijan. In October Ottoman forces also captured Daghestan, thereby controlling the greater Azerbaijan, albeit for a very short period.[85] By the end of the month the Ottomans would sign the Mudros Armistice with the Allies, undertaking the evacuation of the entire Transcaucasus. The armistice entitled the Allies to occupy the area but it did not provide a blueprint for the future status of the Azerbaijani Republic.

The British quickly took over from the departing Ottoman forces, because the region was perceived important for its geopolitical importance and Baku oil fields. Until the end of the war the British goal was to resurrect the eastern front. After the war the goal of fighting Germany was replaced with defeating the Bolsheviks. In order to further these goals, the British supported Denikin until his defeat in early 1920. Afterwards they hoped to keep the Transcaucasus as a barrier between the Bolsheviks and British-controlled territories, though Churchill would soon admit that this objective was unrealistic and that Russia would soon recover the region.[86]

After the British landed in Baku on November 17, 1918 they curtailed the authority of Prime Minister Fath Ali Khan Khoiski's Musavat government. Governor General William M. Thomson conducted business with it as if he recognized its legitimacy, although a formal recognition was never issued. In keeping with the Entente policy to recognize former *gubernia* boundaries, Thomson accepted in practice Azeri sovereignty over Karabagh and Zangezur appointing a well-known anti-Armenian, Khosrow Sultanov, as administrator of both regions and asking Armenian general Andranik Ozanian to cease efforts to capture them. Thomson characterized his moves as temporary measures, suggesting that territorial questions would be settled at the upcoming Paris Peace Conference.[87]

During its brief existence the Azerbaijan Republic experienced lively political debates and intensive legislation efforts in its constituent assembly. The Assembly was formed with the enlargement of its originally Musavat-dominated National Council by including Himmat, Muslim Socialist Bloc, Ahrar (liberal), Ittihad (Islamist), and Armenian members. Even after enlargement Musavat had the largest representation with 38 out of a total of 120. The Himmat group also included several members belonging to the Bolshevik faction. Their pro-Russia stance would later acquire additional adherents from Himmat and Musavat when the time for the Bolshevik invasion of the region approached. Nevertheless, the core group, including Karayev, Husainov, and Musavi even at the outset openly advocated "power to the Soviets" in Azerbaijan.[88]

Throughout its brief existence Azerbaijan seemed a typical post-colonial country. Training programs were instituted to train candidates for all kinds of jobs including railway and telegraph operators. Bribery was common and governmental privileges were bought and sold on the local exchange. Middle and lower-ranking Russian civil servants were allowed to conduct official transactions in Russian but they were given two years to learn the Azeri language.

Teaching of Azerbaijani became obligatory at all school levels but the lack of personnel restricted native language education in secondary schools. Many Azeris were sent to Turkey and Europe to be trained as teachers and many Turks came to Azerbaijan to alleviate the teacher shortage. The first Azerbaijani university (Baku University) instructing in Azerbaijani Turkish was opened on September 1, 1919 and a project to adopt the Latin alphabet was considered. Yet Russian continued to be the language of government, especially at mid-level state bureaucracy, due to the lack of trained indigenous cadres.[89]

At the 1919 Paris Peace Conference the Azerbaijani delegation asked for a large portion of the Yerevan *gubernia*, as well as Kars and Batum on religious and economic grounds, while the Armenian delegation demanded the establishment of Greater Armenia, including eastern Turkey and a large portion of the territories Azerbaijan controlled. Both delegations claimed Karabagh, Zangezur and Nakhichevan and demanded the conference to recognize these claims. The conference, however, did not address the intra-Transcaucasian borders' issue. Britain and France were mainly interested in thwarting the Bolshevik rule, protecting India, and carving up the Ottoman Empire.[90]

The Kemalist forces in Ankara conducting the Turkish war of liberation against the allies found the presence of the British forces in Transcaucasia less desirable. The Ankara government desired the victory of the Bolshevik forces, which would eliminate the British presence in the region and enable the Kemalists to establish a direct link to Moscow. This put them at odds with the Azeri government, which perceived in Britain a guarantee for its survival. Mustafa Kemal, then chairman of the parliament in Ankara, was even supposed to have said that if the "Caucasian nations decide to act as a barrier against us, we will agree with the Bolsheviks on a coordinated offensive against them."[91]

In order to quicken the Bolshevization of Azerbaijan, Russian Bolsheviks engineered a break-up of the left-wing Himmat into two by the end of July 1919. One faction, the "Social Democratic Workers Party-Himmat", kept its independence from Moscow, while the other, the "Azerbaijani Communist Party-Himmat", came under the influence of the Bolsheviks. In February 1920, with Moscow's prodding, the latter party dropped the name "Himmat" altogether from its name and was renamed the Azerbaijani Communist Party (Bolsheviks) or AzCP(b).[92] This party engaged in intense propaganda to discredit the Musavat Government and its links to Britain. It declared that Azerbaijan – like Turkey – was suffering from the encroachment of British imperialism and that the Sovietization of Azerbaijan would free the peasantry and the workers and make the country truly and not just formally independent.[93]

After the departure of the British forces in August 1919 the Supreme Allied Council granted recognition to Azerbaijan in 1920. Even before this the British had already acted as if Azerbaijan enjoyed independence. Yet the Bolshevik advance accelerated in early 1920 and the pro-Bolshevik leaders within Musavat gained influence. Realizing the inevitability of Russian conquest, even Resulzada sided with the pro-Bolshevik faction, including such figures as the interior minister, Mammad Hasan Hajinski, in intra-Musavat debates. Hajinski favored making widespread concessions including oil concessions, in return for Russia's recognition of Azerbaijani sovereignty.

Despite their enthusiasm about adopting a socialist system even AzCP(b) leaders desired an independent state, although they felt that they still needed Soviet military help. Nariman Narimanov, who assumed the portfolio of Deputy Commissar for Nationalities Affairs in the summer of 1919, worked hard to have Moscow recognize Azerbaijan's independence. Although his wish was granted in advance of the Soviet invasion, Moscow would soon renege on its promise.[94]

Bolshevik Invasion, the Transcaucasian Federation and the Creation of the NKAO

The Turkish leadership in Ankara was happy to see the end of the British presence in the Transcaucasus, but it also desired Moscow to reverse the invasion decision. Mustafa Kemal wrote a letter to Lenin on April 28, 1920 pleading him not to invade but the letter reached Lenin in June, which was too late. While negotiations on favorable trade terms and oil concessions were continuing with the Azeri delegation in Moscow, the Red Army invaded Baku on April 27, 1920. The same day the AzCP(b) submitted an ultimatum to the parliament to surrender its powers to the AzCP(b) and announced the overthrow of the "treacherous, criminal, and counterrevolutionary" Musavat Party government. The parliament promptly accepted the AzCP's ultimatum and the Azeri independence ended in practice.[95]

After controlling Baku, the Red Army moved to occupy the rest of the country, meeting stiff resistance in various regions, including Ganja. The armed opposition would last until 1924. The start of Soviet rule also caused ethnic frictions and a refugee problem. Armenians from Julfa demanded space in Zangezur while Azeris fled Zangezur to Shusha in Karabagh.[96]

On April 27, 1920 the Azrevkom (Azerbaijan Revolutionary Committee) was established by the Baku Bureau of the Kavkraikom (Caucasian Regional Committee) of the Russian Communist Party, the RCP(b). The respected native communist Nariman Narimanov was appointed chairman of the Azrevkom. Other native Azeris, including Mirza Davud Huseinov, Ali

Heydar Sultanov, and Dadash Buniatzada, who were prominent native communists or former Himmatists, became members. By contrast, Armenian and Russian communists mostly staffed the AzCP and the Kavkraikom.[97]

Until March 1922 Moscow's power was also exercised by the Azerbaijani party organization, the AzCP(b), which was merely an oblast-level department of the RCP(b), indicating the AzCP(b)'s total lack of room to maneuver or autonomy. Utilizing the AzCP(b)'s dependence, Moscow chipped away at Azerbaijani independence. The weakening of Baku's autonomy took place against the backdrop of its rather homogeneous (Azeri-staffed) government apparatus, falsely projecting the sovereign decision-making of its native ruling elite.[98] The native communists such as Narimanov played roles assigned to them by the Kavbiuro (Caucasian Regional Bureau of the Central Committee of the Russian Communist Party or CC RCP). Narimanov himself arrived in Baku on May 16, 1920 to assume the presidency of the Azrevkom, which had supposedly invited the Red Army on April 27, 1920. As late as 1925, less than half of the members of the AzCP were Azeris, while Russians and Azerbaijanis assumed its leadership.[99]

The Commissar for Nationalities Affairs, Joseph V. Stalin, engineered the conquest of Azerbaijan. During the Civil War (1918–1920) Stalin took charge of political activities on the southern front including Caucasia. After Azerbaijan's capture he went back to Moscow leaving his protégé Orzhonikidze in command of Kavbiuro with Sergei M. Kirov as his second in command. Lenin himself authorized Orzhonikidze to single-handedly determine Azerbaijan's domestic and foreign policies.[100]

After the establishment of Soviet rule in the Transcaucasus, Lenin desired the region to be economically and politically united. This, he thought, would best serve Soviet security. He asked Orzhonikidze to create an oblast-level (regional) economic union of all Transcaucasia.[101] Since the communist parties of each republic in the region were oblast-level branches of the RCP(b) economic unity would reinforce Moscow's political control. Nariman Narimanov, as President of Azerbaijani Sovnarkom (Soviet of People's Commissars, or Council of Ministers), was reluctant for regional integration. His reluctance contrasted with the acceptance of the plan by the Georgian and Armenian leaderships. It took Orzhonikidze some arm-twisting to persuade Narimanov to agree to the unification of trade and railways with the two other regional republics, which took place in 1921.

Among policies implemented by Orzhonikidze, the establishment in March 1922 of the Federal Union of the Soviet Socialist Republics of Transcaucasia proved to be much more controversial. He failed to consult the central committees of the individual republics and ignored the vociferous opposition of the Georgians and the Azerbaijanis. The Union's Plenipotentiary Council was bestowed with wide-ranging powers to conduct domestic and external affairs of each constituent republic.[102]

In the summer of 1921 Kirov was appointed First Secretary of the AzCP(b), making Azerbaijan the only Transcaucasian state to have a non-native highest executive and therefore strengthening Moscow's hold on the republic.[103] After February 1922 the Kavbiuro became Zavkraikom (Transcaucasian Regional Committee) whilst still headed by Orzhonikidze. He exercised his influence through Zavkraikom, the military, the AzCP(b), and Kirov personally.

Following the conquest of the rest of Azerbaijan in the summer of 1920 and Armenia in late 1920, the Bolsheviks "convinced" the Azrevkom to cede Zangezur to Armenia in November 1920. Between 1918 and 1920 Armenian militias had effectively reduced Azeri presence in Zangezur by expelling tens of thousands of Azeris.[104] A treaty in December 1920 between Yerevan and Moscow confirmed the transfer of Zangezur.[105] Pro-Armenian publications state that the November resolution of Azrevkom, as published in the Baku paper of *Kommunist* on December 2, stated that not only Zangezur but also Karabagh and Nakhichevan were to be recognized as Armenian territory.[106]

The Azeris contest the validity of this claim arguing that the aforementioned issue of the *Kommunist* omits any mention of Nakhichevan but confirms Azrevkom's acknowledgement of territorial disputes while offering Zangezur to Armenia and accepting Karabagh's right to "self-determination".[107] Given the fact that the December 2, 1920 issue of the *Kommunist* is missing, corroboration of either party's arguments is difficult. Nevertheless, it is not difficult to believe that the Azeri leadership seemed to have accepted "self-determination" for Karabagh, and hence its transfer to Armenia, because the AzCP was mostly staffed by Armenian and Russian members and their votes might have led to such an outcome.

Following the Russo-Armenian Treaty of December 1920 Zangezur was given to Armenia, while Karabagh was retained by Azerbaijan. Although Nakhichevan was geographically cut off from Azerbaijan, the treaty acknowledged that it had a "close relationship" with Azerbaijan.[108] Many Sovietologists suggest that the separation of Nakhichevan from Azerbaijan by according sovereignty over Zangezur to Armenia was a shrewd move on the part of Moscow. Separated from the main body of Azerbaijan, Nakhichevan would not serve as a direct link between Turkey and Azerbaijan. Partition of the ethnically-mixed and disputed territories in the way Moscow did would also facilitate permanent discontent between Armenia and Azerbaijan.

Nevertheless, the allocation of Nakhichevan and Karabagh to Azerbaijan in 1921 might have been due to the Russian government's desire to reach a *modus vivendi* with the nationalist Ankara government.[109] Furthermore, Nakhichevan's assignment to Azerbaijan is ascribed by many to Ankara's insistence to have a common border with Azerbaijan. However, Turkey ended up not having a common border with Nakhichevan until 1932, when Ataturk convinced Reza Shah of Iran to exchange a few kilometers of Iranian territory in this region for Turkish territory elsewhere.[110]

Nakhichevan's unification with the Azerbaijan SSR was affirmed by the March 16, 1921 Treaty of Moscow between the Bolsheviks and the Ankara government and also by the Treaty of Kars between the latter, the Transcaucasian republics and the Russian Soviet Federated Socialist Republic (RSFSR). Both treaties confirmed Nakhichevan's "close ties" with Azerbaijan. Article 5 of the Kars Treaty stated:

> The Turkish Government and the Soviet Governments of Armenia and Azerbaijan are agreed that the region of Nakhichevan, within the limits specified by Annex III to the present treaty, constitutes an autonomous territory under the protection of Azerbaijan.[111]

In December 1922 the Armenian and Russian-dominated Central Committee of the AzCP began administrative work to grant autonomy to the mostly Armenian-populated areas of Karabagh and to grant a more formal 'territory of Azerbaijan' status to Nakhichevan. Eventually, in March 1924 the latter was made an Autonomous Soviet Socialist Republic within Azerbaijan. Despite the opposition of the Azerbaijan government, dominated by the Azeris, the Transcaucasian Regional Committee, headed by Orzhonikidze, asked the AzCP Central Committee in 1923 to create an autonomous region in Nagorno-Karabagh as well. To ensure the AzCP's compliance, Sergei Kirov, a close lieutenant of Orzhonikidze, was appointed First Secretary of the AzCP, thus pushing aside any pretension of native rule.

The native Azeri leadership detested the move to create an autonomous region in western (mountainous) Karabagh. Nariman Narimanov, the president of the Azerbaijan Sovnarkom, argued that the existing constitutional provisions concerning minorities were adequately protective of Armenians and that a separate administrative unit was not needed. On July 19, 1921 he stated that mountainous Karabagh was an oblast with its own executive committee, capable of meeting the distinct needs of this region, implying that its autonomy was superfluous. On October 24, 1921, however, the Orgburo (Organizational Bureau) of the AzCP(b) Central Committee, under the chairmanship of First Secretary Kirov, resolved to create a special committee for the delineation of an autonomous portion of Karabagh (NKAO).[112]

The attempt to create an autonomous Karabagh came after the transfer of Nakhichevan – which also comprised a large Armenian population – to Azerbaijani rule in early 1921. Prior to that, in the wake of the Red Army's arrival, Nakhichevan was first placed under Azerbaijani rule in July 1920. It was then transferred to Armenia following the fall of the latter to the Red Army in late 1920, only to be reassigned to Baku a few months later. The push to create the NKAO could therefore be the outcome of Moscow's desire to strike a balance between the territorial claims of both republics.[113]

Some scholars claim that during the initial months following the arrival of the Red Army in the Transcaucasus in late 1920, Moscow decided to assign Nakhichevan, Zangezur and Karabagh to Armenia. In 1921, however, the Bolshevik leadership revised its policy. On July 4, 1921, in a broadened plenum with representatives from each Transcaucasian republic, the Soviets, the unions, and the army, the Kavbiuro decided to allocate mountainous Karabagh to Armenia. Yet Stalin, who was present at the meeting, asked for reconsideration of the decision. Next day the Kavbiuro rescinded its resolution and voted to keep mountainous Karabagh as part of Azerbaijan, provided the latter granted regional (oblast) autonomy to the area. The Central Committee of the AzCP was entrusted with delineation of the boundaries of the autonomous oblast.[114]

A major reason for the award of Karabagh to Azerbaijan was the Bolshevik belief – lasting until the demise of the idea of a world revolution – that Azerbaijan could function as a "red beacon for Persia, Arabia, [and] Turkey," and it would be a disservice to the Bolshevik project if Moscow were to be seen as undermining Azerbaijani sovereignty.[115] Lenin's interest in creating economically viable but not necessarily demographically homogeneous territorial entities also played a significant role in the award of the

NKAO to Azerbaijan. Historically Karabagh enjoyed stronger economic ties with the rest of Azerbaijan than with the territories constituting Armenia.[116]

On the suggestion of Orzhonikidze's Zavkraikom, the Presidium of the AzCP(b) established in October 1921 a so-called "Central Commission" to study the feasibility of autonomy of mountainous Karabagh and to administer the area. The three-member Commission did not include any Azeris, but included a Russian and two Armenians. The pro-Narimanov opponents of the Commission issued an unsigned letter on December 10, 1921 stating that "there is no so-called Karabagh question; [there is] general weakness of the party and soviet work in Karabagh."[117]

Nevertheless, the Presidium also appointed a seven-man committee, which included five Armenians and two Azeris, to consider the technicalities of an autonomous region in mountainous Karabagh. In the spring of 1923 the Commission recommended the establishment of a separate administrative unit for mountainous Karabagh. After the Zakraikom intervened once again in support of the Commission's report, the Presidium of the AzCP had to submit.[118] As a result of the Russian-led and Russian-controlled AzCP's resolution, mountainous Karabagh was declared an autonomous oblast in November 1924 and the Armenian head of the Central Commission that recommended autonomy, Armenak Nikitich Korakozov, was appointed chairman of the Sovnarkom (Soviet of People's Commissars) of the NKAO.[119]

The NKAO was carved out of the mountainous districts of historic Karabagh (including Shusha, Jebrail, Javanshir and part of Kubatlinsk).[120] The borders of the NKAO were drawn in such a way as to make sure that Armenians constituted a majority. In fact, since the mid-nineteenth century the Armenian community constituted a majority in the mountainous segment of Karabagh, which was used to justify the formation of the NKAO. The Armenian share of the population in Karabagh increased dramatically after the big waves of Armenian migrations there from Iran as provided for in the Treaty of Turkmenchai of 1828 and the exodus of significant numbers of Azeris to the Ottoman Empire and to Iran in the second half of the nineteenth century. The arrival of some 57,000 Armenian migrants from Iran shifted the population ratio in Karabagh (as well as in Nakhichevan), which had hitherto been overwhelmingly Muslim according to Czarist population records.[121] By 1926 117,000 Armenians and 13,000 Azeris lived in the NKAO.[122]

In the NKAO Armenian was to be the language of administration and education, and the party apparatus there consisted mostly of Armenians in the following years. The Azerbaijani people henceforth considered the institution of autonomy as a loss of their sovereignty over a portion of the Azerbaijani Republic. A similar arrangement was not made for the sizeable Azeri community in Zangezur, which contributed to the feelings of alienation and discrimination among the Azeris. Armenians in Armenia as well as in the NKAO, for their part, were also not satisfied because they had hoped for the attachment of mountainous Karabagh to Armenia.[123]

Gradually, Armenian dominance in the cultural and administrative spheres in the NKAO led to Azeri migrations from the oblast to other parts of Azerbaijan, strengthening local Armenian control and perpetuating Armenia's claims over it. All types of official transactions and instruction in schools began to be conducted in Armenian. NKAO's own Sovnarkom was established and Korakozov chaired it until 1928. Party and state organs began to be staffed for the most part by Armenians, who, for their part, promoted cultural autonomy.

2

Azerbaijan during the Soviet Era

The Transcaucasian Soviet Federative Socialist Republic (TSFSR), which Lenin had called for and Kavbiuro proposed, came into being in December 1922. The AzCP, under the chairmanship of Kirov, duly implemented the directive of Lenin and Orzhonikidze, while native Azeri party members, including Narimanov, opposed the sudden imposition of the federation. The TSFSR Soviet was empowered to make decisions on military affairs, foreign relations, trade, financial matters, communications, transportation, and economic policies of each constituent republic. In short, the establishment of the TSFSR meant the elimination of even formal Azerbaijani sovereignty.

The TSFSR Congress of Soviets met only seven times between 1922 and 1935. Real executive power rested with its small Central Executive Committee (CEC) and its Presidium. There were few Azeris who held positions of significance in TSFSR organs. Narimanov served on the TSFSR Presidium until his election to the CEC of the USSR in 1923, which required his move to Moscow. In late 1923 Narimanov wrote a letter addressed to Stalin, Trotsky and Karl Radek, accusing Orzhonikidze of nominating him to the CEC in Moscow, which he stated was aimed at eliminating his influence in Azerbaijan. Narimanov also argued that the AzCP's policies were adopted and implemented by several ethnic Azeris who would do anything to please the Russians, and by Armenians, including Mirzoyan and Sarkis, who – he claimed – were renegade Dashnakists working to undermine Azerbaijan's well-being in the name of communism.[1]

As suggested earlier, in the 1920s Russians and Armenians comprised more than 50 percent of the AzCP members, while the leadership of the party also consisted mostly of people of non-Azeri origin. There were also such Azeri yes-men as Huseinov and Karayev, who thought that it would not be wise to challenge Moscow's directives, thus augmenting non-native control of the AzCP. In 1925, at the age of 54, Narimanov died in Moscow under mysterious circumstances. The official explanation of his death pointed to heart failure. Although his funeral was one accorded to revolutionary heroes, he was denounced in 1937 for being a "devisionist, traitor, and bourgeois nationalist".

In 1936 Stalin dissolved the TSFSR, suggesting that historical conditions – meaning the disappearance of old animosities between its member nations – permitted such a decision. Each republic joined the USSR under the 1936 Constitution. The 1937 Azerbaijani constitution, which was modeled on the new Union constitution, affirmed both the Nakhichevan ASSR and the NKAO remaining part of Azerbaijan. State and law enforcement organs of both territories were to be subordinate to those at republic level. Article 47 of the Azerbaijani Constitution provided that the republic's Sovnarkom (Council of People's Commissars, or Council of Ministers) was authorized to annul the decisions of the Nakhichevan Sovnarkom and those of the NKAO Soviet of Deputies.[2]

The Purges

The first stage of the liquidation of the opposition took place in the early 1920s in the wake of the Bolshevik conquest. Thousands affiliated with the ancien regime, including former Musavat Party members as well as many with no involvement in pre-Bolshevik era politics, were exiled, imprisoned or summarily executed on trumped-up charges. Only later, in the late 1920s, did the Bolsheviks begin to liquidate well-off farmers (*kulaks*), the religious establishment and the former *jadids*, who were considered unreliable or dangerous.

In 1924 the AzCEC adopted a resolution to "Latinize" the alphabet. The decision was to be implemented gradually. The adoption of the Latin alphabet was to augment the Bolsheviks' efforts to purge all undesirable ideas and concepts related to the pre-1917 era. The native leadership was enthusiastic about the shift to Latin, but such a decision could not have been made without Moscow's approval. Stalin or his local representative Orzhonikidze probably ordered it. Central Asian republics replicated the Azerbaijani endeavor in the late 1920s, which indicated that the Azerbaijani experiment was not decided by native leadership alone.

Moscow's decision was motivated by its desire to further restrict contacts between Turkey and Azerbaijan and to alienate Azerbaijan from its cultural heritage and the pre-Soviet era literature considered "reactionary" by the Bolsheviks. In 1937, however, the Latin alphabet would be renounced in favor of the Cyrillic, as a means of facilitating the learning of Russian and supposedly to further communication between nations of the Soviet Union.[3] The fact that Turkey also shifted to Latin in the late 1920s might also have influenced Moscow's decision. The latter might have ordered the shift to the Cyrillic, not only to augment its newly adopted Russification drive, but also to sever any remaining links between Turkey and the Turkic republics.

The second stage in the purges came in the latter half of the 1920s and the early 1930s when many intellectuals and native communists were purged. The liquidations were sometimes based on genuine differences with the policies imposed by Moscow. Yet they were often subject to false accusations. An oft-used charge was "Sultan Galievism", in reference to the Tatar Bolshevik leader who was executed in 1929 for his alleged attachment to pan-Turkism. Nariman Narimanov, who had died in 1925, avoided the fate that befell many socialist natives who also enjoyed grass roots support within the Azeri community.

The third stage took place in the second half of the 1930s and was the longest, the bloodiest and in terms of its consequences, the most wide-ranging. These purges coincided with the "Great Terror" of the same period throughout the Soviet Union. During this phase many native communists and pre- and post-revolutionary intellectuals were executed. Some prominent native communists were even tried at show trials in Moscow. Stalin's henchman in Azerbaijan throughout this period was Mir Jafar Abasovich Baghirov (1896–1956). Baghirov, who had served as commissar for internal affairs and had headed the republic's security forces since the 1920s, became First Secretary of the Central Committee of the Azerbaijan Communist Party (CC AzCP) and chairman of the Sovnarkom in 1933. He held both positions until his dismissal in June 1953, a few months after the death of Stalin.[4]

The Azerbaijani "Great Terror" in the second half of the 1930s liquidated many prominent native communists who had impeccable credentials as long-time Bolsheviks and Himmat Party members who had helped the Red Army to suppress nationalist resistance in the early 1920s. Most of those purged in this period were accused of being pro-Trotsky, pro-Zinoviev, pan-Islamist, pan-Turkist, or Musavatist. Sultan Majid Efendiev was one of those prominent officials who were purged. He was President of the AzCP CEC and had been Co-President of the TSFSR CEC when he was arrested in 1937.

In the fall of 1937 there were a number of show trials in which party leaders, administrators and kolhoz managers were tried. Charges leveled against them included engaging in activities aimed at Azerbaijan's secession from the Soviet Union and endeavoring to bring back capitalism. During the trials, such party officials as Ruhulla Akhundov, Sultan Majid Efendiev, Gazanfar Musabekov, Dadash Buniatzada and Ayub Khanbudakov were accused of being followers of Nariman Narimanov, who was by then denounced as nationalist. At the end of the trials some were executed, while some were sentenced to long periods of imprisonment or exile. Even First Secretary Mir Jafar Baghirov could have been subject to purge had he not been friends with Lavrenti Beria, who was in charge of the purges in the Transcaucasus.[5] Some have estimated the number of the 1937/38 purge victims in Azerbaijan to be 120,000 out of a then total population of 2.6 million.[6]

The start of the German invasion on June 22, 1941 reversed the witch-hunt that had been plaguing the Soviet Union. The German attack led Stalin to adopt a number of measures including the abandonment of the assault against "nationalists". This reversal of policy made subtle nationalist expression tolerable once again. Traditional literature, including *dastans* or heroic epics, tales having "wrong" historical connotations and popular songs became acceptable. The times called for loving one's homeland and fighting the invaders. Mosques were reopened and one of the newly founded four union-wide spiritual directorates was instituted in Azerbaijan with Hajj Mullah Aghalizade becoming Sheikh ul-Islam or head of the directorate.[7] Nevertheless, the post-War era witnessed the rapid desertion of wartime policies. *Dastans*, folk tales, suspect popular songs and other genre were denounced once again.

A major phase in the history of Soviet Azerbaijan was the arrival from Iran of the leaders of the Azerbaijan Democratic Party (Azerbaijan Democrat Firkasi, or ADF), who had governed the so-called "National Autonomous State of Azerbaijan" (NASA) from December 1945 until December 1946 while Soviet troops were occupying northern Iran. Moscow and the AzCP initially welcomed the ADF leadership headed by Sayyed Jafar Pishevari and the rank and file warmly, after the former followed the departing Soviet troops and sought refuge in northern Azerbaijan.[8]

From the outset, Pishevari and other ADF leaders were, however, rather bitter about the USSR's withdrawal of support from the NASA, causing the latter to collapse shortly after. The ADF perceived it disdainful that it was not only US pressures but also the oil concessions Iran offered in northern Iran, which led Moscow to a quick about-face and to a rather hasty retreat of its military units.[9]

The refugees strove to preserve their Iranian identity, resisting the temptation to seek Soviet citizenship. Pishevari seemed ill at ease with the Moscow-set AzCP policies, often quarreling with AzCP First Secretary Baghirov in front of others. In July 1947, one day after he exchanged barbs with Baghirov, Pishevari's car collided with a military vehicle, severely injuring him. It is not clear if the crash was orchestrated by Moscow or the AzCP leadership to get rid of him. On his deathbed, Pishevari said that his Baku comrades betrayed him, implying that he also suspected a plot against him.[10]

Although Pishevari's death was officially blamed on an unfortunate accident, he was soon discarded to the dustbin of Soviet historiography: he joined many other prominent Azeris unfairly consigned into oblivion. By the end of 1949 many of his ADF comrades ended up in jail or in Siberia. One of them, Muhammad Biriya, spent 22 out of 33 years that he was in the USSR in prison. The rank and file were dispersed throughout the republic and ordered to undergo intense ideological training.[11]

The Fall of Baghirov and De-Stalinization

The death of Stalin on March 5, 1953 led to the end of the Stalinist era in Azerbaijan. On June 19, 1953 the Azerbaijan Communist Party expelled First Secretary Mir Jafar Baghirov from all of his positions. Unlike Beria he was not immediately arrested, but was appointed to a managerial position in Kuybishev. Nevertheless, he was belatedly tried in Baku in April 1956 and admitted that he was guilty as charged while denying that he had ever been an enemy of the party or the country.[12] Despite Baghirov's self-contradictory remarks the Soviet Supreme Military Court found him guilty as charged: he was convicted of being part of a conspiracy, joining a counterrevolutionary organization, liquidating 22 major Azerbaijani officials and cooperating with Stalin's Secret Service chief Lavrenti Beria. Baghirov was executed by a firing squad.[13] His successor as First Secretary, Imam Dashdemiroglu Mustafaev, didn't shy away from denouncing

Baghirov at the 20th CPSU Congress in 1956 as a proponent of the cult of personality.

At the 20th Party Congress in 1956, Khrushchev promoted the policy of *rastsvet* (flourishing), which was an endorsement of the equality of Soviet nationalities. In Azerbaijan, as well as in other republics, *rastsvet* and the union-wide de-Stalinization campaign turned once taboo subjects into acceptable discussion topics. The most symbolic was the legacy of Nariman Narimanov. He was not only rehabilitated, but also acquired a cult-like reputation over time. Soon a giant statue of him was erected on a hill commanding a view of the city of Baku. Yet his rehabilitation was a limited one, at least initially. This can be gleaned from the inscription carved into the base of his statue in which he praises friendship with Russia. Likewise, despite the post-1956 relaxation, Azerbaijan Democratic Republic did not cease to be judged as "Musavatist", which was the code word for its "nationalist, and bourgeois/aristocratic" leadership and for its collaboration with the imperialists, that is, the British. Nevertheless, more factual information on the "Musavatist" era became available in the print media.[14]

Another example of the timidity of the Soviet authorities was the publication in 1958 of a poem by the late Bakhtyar Vahabzade in a local newspaper in Sheki, in northwestern Azerbaijan. The poem was dedicated to the "radiant memories of Sattar Khan, Khiabani and Pishevari."[15] Such issues found exposure in limited circulation publications that did not reach a large audience. High-circulation newspapers, popular magazines and Russian-language media avoided altogether covering Shah Ismail or Sattar Khan, which must have been seen to be quite a leap in the dark. Yet historians referred to the "bleeding wound of Turkmenchai [Treaty]," "liberation from the hateful yoke of Iranian oppression" and "Iranian oriental despotism."[16] The post-1956 era was full of other examples of low-level pan-Azerbaijanism.

Except for the subject of unification with Iranian Azerbaijan, which must have been cleared, if not sanctioned, by Moscow, historians usually stuck to the distant past because doing so was safer. One such relatively safe topic was the rule of Shah Ismail, the founder of the Safavid dynasty (1501). It was more precarious to debate Sattar Khan's involvement in the Iranian constitutional struggle in the early twentieth century, because he was generally considered lacking proletarian credentials. Yet the more daring historians discussed him as well.[17] Historians carefully avoided dealing with the Musavat-led independent Azerbaijan (1918–1920) or even the ideologically more appropriate Jafar Pishevari, who headed the NASA from December 1945 until its demise in December 1946.

Iran's joining of the Baghdad Pact in 1955 and its close relations with the US contributed to Moscow's toleration of pan-Azerbaijanism. Yet in 1962 Iran announced that it would not agree to the deployment of nuclear missiles on its territory, engendering the improvement of relations between Tehran and Moscow.[18] In the following years Tehran and Moscow co-operated in more than 100 joint industrial projects in Iran. Afterwards, until the fall of the Shah and beyond, the USSR allowed only low-level pan-Azerbaijanism, which did not harm rapprochement with Iran.

Imam D. Mustafaev, who succeeded Baghirov in 1953, was a plant geneticist without much party experience. His not having a long-term party background and his low public profile made him a desirable party chief in the post-Stalin era. Such characteristics were considered necessary traits of collective leadership. Despite his modest background, Mustafaev took advantage of the favorable climate of the post-Stalin period of concessions to nationalist or quasi-nationalist demands. His catering to native interests included his encouragement of the migration of ethnic Azerbaijanis to Baku, thus tipping the ethnic balance in favor of the natives.

Among accomplishments credited to him was the revision of the Azerbaijani Constitution to make Azerbaijani Turkish the official language of the republic, although the same revisions were made in all three Transcaucasian republics and could hardly have been the result of his individual initiative. Furthermore, he opposed the November 1958 resolution of the Central Committee of the CPSU and the subsequent USSR Council of Ministers' decision, which concerned the study of languages in schools of non-Russian republics. The new resolution abrogated the compulsory teaching of native languages in Russian schools in non-Russian republics.

On the face of it, the new system seemed to grant more freedom to parents in choosing where they would send their children. Yet most parents traditionally preferred Russian-language schools so that their children would be upwardly mobile. This meant that eliminating the compulsory nature of native language teaching in such schools could drastically reduce the number of native speakers.[19] Mustafaev took issue with the language reform and favored Azerbaijani Turkish remaining a compulsory part of the curricula in schools. His intransigence led to his removal from his post on July 11, 1959 after being accused of "having caused bewilderment in the completely clear language situation."[20] Khrushchev also accused him of failing to prevent corruption in kolkhozes and state enterprises for good measure.[21]

Despite the thaw in many areas in the Khrushchev era, it was not complete, as Mustafaev's dismissal for "nationalist" tendencies showed. Although many former party leaders and intellectuals were rehabilitated, such accusations as "nationalism" and "corruption" were still used to discredit and fire incumbent officials. Mustafaev was also branded as having "tolerated" Islamic traditions, a worse offense than "tolerating" nationalism. Following his dismissal, several mosques, which had even survived the Stalin era, were closed down. Only 16 mosques throughout Azerbaijan remained operational.

Veli Yusifoglu (Yusubovich) Akhundov, a medical doctor, who had been chairman of the Council of Ministers of the AzSSR for a year, succeeded Mustafaev, Like his predecessor, Akhundov kept a low profile while in office. Despite officially denouncing the Mustafaev era as corrupt, Akhundov chose not to engage in a witch-hunt *vis-à-vis* his predecessor's lackluster economic performance. This explains why, at the CPSU Central Committee Plenum in May 1966, Secretary General Leonid Brezhnev leveled charges against the new Azerbaijani leadership for its laissez-faire attitude in the administration of the economy and failures in agriculture. Brezhnev's criticism of Akhundov was probably also related to the latter's siding with the Ukranian Party boss Alexander Shlepin in the 1965 Brezhnev-Shlepin struggle for power.[22]

Akhundov responded to the charges at the AzCP Central Committee Plenum in June 1966, implicitly holding the all-Union economic leadership responsible for Azerbaijan's dismal economic performance. Some observers suggested that during Akhundov's rule, bribery, influence peddling, widespread crime and violence spread rapidly. From an economic point of view, the Azerbaijani economy was, with the exception of Tajikistan, less advanced than Central Asian republics, which were the least developed in the Soviet Union.[23] Many observers suggested that another reason for Brezhnev's denunciation of Akhundov's leadership could have been the latter's toleration of some officials who allowed subtle expressions of Azerbaijani nationalism.[24] AzCP Third Secretary Kurbanov, for instance, insisted on delivering speeches in the CPSU Central Committee meetings in Azerbaijani Turkish, a symbolic yet noticeable demonstration of national pride.[25]

The rehabilitations that started earlier continued during the Akhundov era. In the literary field writers began to express their love for Azerbaijan.

In 1966, the 60th anniversary of the first issue of the satirical journal *Molla Nasreddin* and the centennial of the latter's founder and editor, Jelil Mamadkuluzada, were commemorated. In the same year, a series on music history in the literary journal *Azerbaijan* mentioned in a low-key manner how tragic it was that for a period in the past, *dastans* (epics) were banned and many reciters of *dastans* were purged for "national deviation."[26]

Start of the Aliev Era

Eventually, Akhundov was fired from his post and appointed Vice-President of the Azerbaijan Academy of Sciences on July 14, 1969. Brezhnev's firing of Akhundov was exceptional in that he preferred keeping in power incumbent party leaders. Yet Azerbaijan's persistent failures in meeting economic targets eventually proved intolerable even for Brezhnev. The verdict reached in Moscow was that Akhundov's economic mismanagement was due to the existence of the intricate networks of relatives, friends and clients set up by the Azerbaijani nomenklatura. The selection of Heidar Aliev as First Secretary was the consequence of the search for a leader who did not belong to any of the existing networks.

Heidar Aliev was a former KGB head in Azerbaijan. He had joined the CPSU and the KGB in 1945 and had worked in the KGB's eastern division, traveling to Pakistan, Iran, Afghanistan and Turkey. He rose rapidly within the KGB and became major general. Aliev's boss, the KGB chief in Baku, Semyon Tsvigun, was Brezhnev's brother-in-law. When he was promoted to the post of Deputy Chairman of the KGB in Moscow, he helped Aliev to become KGB chief in Baku in 1967.

Aliev's background as a former KGB chief in Azerbaijan and his well-known demanding nature qualified him for Moscow as the sought after leader who could fight inefficiency, corruption and nationalistic tendencies in the republic. For the latter goal, Aliev might have been considered an ideal candidate because to be selected as head of the KGB he must have been considered to possess impeccable anti-nationalist or "internationalist" characteristics. Moreover, unlike his two predecessors, he was an ardent advocate of the ideological imperatives of Marxism–Leninism.

After being installed in power Aliev extensively purged high party and state officials. The former KGB chief placed personal associates in many posts in the AzCP Bureau, in the Secretariat of the Central Committee and at the heads of Central Committee departments. He instituted a policy of frequent cadre rotation and insisted that party members should be moral role models.[27] His political style was such that he combined his toughness and energetic prosecution of wrongdoing with calls for moral decency and discipline.[28] Nevertheless, despite his public stance against nationalistic tendencies Aliev chose not to appoint Slavs to important positions. Although he paid lip service to the Brezhnev era slogan of *sblizhenie* (merger of nations into one Soviet nation), he pursued the policy of *korenisatsiia* (nativization), as did his contemporaries in other republics. "Of his thirty-five chief clients and protégés almost all were Azeris."[29]

Another deed Aliev was keen on was his emphasis on the learning of Russian by as broad a majority of the Azeris as possible. In his speeches Aliev emphasized the intellectual character of Russian and how knowledge of Russian would contribute to easier access to scientific and technical education. The emphasis on the teaching of Russian was not unique to Azerbaijan. It was part of a union-wide mobilization, which Aliev was eager to embrace. As a result, linguistic Russification accelerated during the Aliev era despite the emigration of Russians and Armenians.

Aliev was able to increase industrial and agricultural production while stressing the primacy of ideology and the party. Between 1971 and 1980 Azerbaijani industrial production and agricultural output doubled. In the 1960s, among all Soviet republics, Azerbaijan had ranked fourteenth in industrial labor productivity; in national income growth it was the fifteenth republic.[30] The Aliev factor changed the statistics. As early as the period of 1970–1974 Azerbaijan ranked fourth among union republics in industrial labor productivity and national income growth and sixth in industrial productivity growth.[31] Still Azerbaijan lagged behind other Transcaucasian republics. This was mainly due to Moscow's cutbacks on investment capital, which was related to the depletion of Azerbaijan's oil reserves. The reduction in investments gave rise to a perception of discrimination in that Azeris believed that they contributed more to the Soviet economy but received less in exchange, in the form of either capital investment or industrialization.[32]

The underground economy and corruption also, which were instrumental in Aliev's rise to power, proved to be difficult to eradicate. They lingered because of their connection to the traditional Caucasian reliance on close ties with family and friends. Azerbaijan suffered from an undue influence of clans, bureaucratic networks and of clientelism and all the inefficient and corrupt practices that went with it. The underground economy, corrupt political practices, ethnic favoritism and local nationalism proved difficult to end, because favors done and received were the operative currencies of both the social and political relations.[33] An expert on Caucasian politics describes the importance of kinship ties as follows:

> Since among Armenians, Georgians, and Azerbaidzhanis primary loyalty is centered on kinship groups or intimate friends, the sense of personal worth stems more from the honor or shame one brings on one's circle than from a successful career or great accumulation of wealth. Favors done or received are the operative currency of both social and political relations, and the networks built up through favors and personal ties make it possible to circumvent the official state economy and legal forms of political behavior.[34]

Indeed, one's obligations to one's relatives and friends were so important, that the shame accrued by failure to meet them was perceived more salient than any legal problem one could face. Such networks made ways into administrative and political institutions so that members of such groups frequently enjoyed quasi-immunity from apprehension.

Prior to the Aliev era, failure to abide by laws was less risky than letting down members of one's personal network. Aliev's crackdown on the second-economy restricted the maneuver room of the networks and breaking the law became more perilous, especially during the first five years of Aliev's rule. Yet in the long run the networks persevered to conduct business as usual, circumventing and resisting ways and means prescribed by the Soviet state.

Cultural Revival under Aliev

Although Aliev followed Moscow's directives enthusiastically, he tolerated, if not encouraged, the discussion of historical subjects and the articulation of national pride, provided they didn't challenge Marxist ideology openly. Aliev's behavior could perhaps best be understood in the light of Azade-Ayse Rorlich's argument that in the Soviet Union the mode of national assertiveness was different. Usually, she suggested, nations under colonial rule expressed their national aspirations by being assertive, rejecting the political system and by non-cooperation with the authorities. She argued:

> For a tightly controlled and centralized society such as the Soviet Union, flexibility and success in gaining maximum accommodation within the system are perhaps not only the most appropriate criteria

> for identifying national assertiveness, but also the best measure of national resilience.[35]

Contrary to the beliefs of many Sovietologists, the Brezhnev era enabled Azerbaijan, as well as Armenia and Georgia, to re-nationalize the republic by furthering ethnic homogenization or ethnic consolidation. Instead of being only a passive object of intensive Russification and implementing all the directives coming from Moscow, the republican leadership made use of government apparatus at its disposal to expand its area of autonomy. While promoting bilingualism and openly professing commitment to the Soviet project, the republican authorities made concessions to native intelligentsia by enabling it to utilize the republic's cultural and institutional tools to influence the forms of national discourse.

Nevertheless, toleration of the expression of national pride was not without bounds. In the mid-1970s the future leader of the Azerbaijan Popular Front, Abulfaz Elchibey, was imprisoned on charges of pan-Turkism and Azerbaijani nationalism. Elchibey's brand of nationalism was more difficult to tolerate then, because he was interested in a new Soviet system that would grant more autonomy to individual republics. Many other political activists elsewhere in the USSR were also persecuted in the 1970s despite moderation of Soviet policies in the détente era. Later on, in August 1991, Heidar Aliev suggested that he was not aware of Elchibey's conviction in 1975. Aliev, the former head of the KGB and AzCP First Secretary at the time argued somewhat unconvincingly: "It was the KGB that was responsible for his arrest and imprisonment. I don't know everybody in the KGB."[36]

Regarding Azeri *jadids* who were liquidated in the 1930s, Aliev was more tolerant. In 1981, Aliev arranged the exhumation in Siberia and reburial in Azerbaijan of the remains of poet and playwright Husein Javid. This act was symbolically significant. Javid, who is considered a great epic poet, was arrested and convicted in 1937 supposedly for counterrevolutionary activities. He died in Siberia in 1944. Although he was rehabilitated in 1956, after which his 80th birthday ("jubilee") celebration took place in 1963, his works still remained largely banned. Following his reburial in 1981, his books were published, his plays were staged and monuments to him were built in Baku and in his native Nakhichevan.[37]

In the early 1980s Aliev tolerated the quasi-nationalist discourse in unofficial journals and newspapers. An examination of such literary journals as *Azerbaijan* shows that historical "heroes", such as Shah Ismail, were praised as "Peter the Great" of Azerbaijan.[38] Other journals that discussed cultural and intellectual issues included *Gobustan* and *Adabiyyat va Injasanat*. By the end of the 1980s these journals would publish articles promoting more autonomy in economic decision-making, cultural issues and politics.

Aliev also personally stressed strengthening literary links with southern Azerbaijan. In his speech at the 7th Congress of the Azerbaijani Writers' Union in 1981 he called for "developing broad contacts within all sectors of cultural and intellectual creativity in imparting to our comrades of the pen the rich aesthetic-artistic experience we have accumulated."[39] On at least one occasion Aliev was quoted for having called for unification with Iranian Azerbaijan in the future, though whether or not this meant Baku's active pursuit of irredentism remained blurred.[40]

Before and after Aliev left Baku to join the Politburo in 1982, weekly popular magazines and books referred to peoples of the two Azerbaijans belonging to the same nation and the frontier dividing them an "open wound" which would eventually disappear. The Turkmenchai Treaty of 1828 was called a document of historical injustice. What was significant about these arguments was that popular publications did not cover these subjects before Aliev's rise to power. Earlier, scholarly journals and books had included similar statements, but popular media had stood clear of them. During the Aliev era theatrical performances also began to refer to "divided Azerbaijan".[41]

Nevertheless, Azerbaijan's Russian language journals and newspapers as well as the AzCP's official *Azerbaijan Kommunisti* were more timid than the Azerbaijani language popular media, showing that the Aliev administration was mindful of the dangers of debating sensitive issues in official and Russian language media. The Union organs would have more easily spotted reports with a nationalist tint or criticism of Moscow in Russian. An alternative explanation is that articles on the future unification with Iranian Azerbaijan were actually sanctioned by Moscow, but the latter was reluctant to be identified with them in order not to openly affront Tehran.

The motives of Aliev – as of other Transcaucasian republics' leaders – were probably self-serving. He might have been more preoccupied with the creation of a cult of personality. Yet Moscow's implementation of a second – and rather informal – *korenisatsiia* since the 1960s might have, nevertheless, enabled him to achieve two objectives at once: 1) appealing to the Azerbaijani population's ethnic/communal sensitivities by presenting himself as a leader who looked after their interests and who allowed nationalist or quasi-nationalist expression; 2) satisfying Soviet demands by coping with economic failures and corruption, not only by relying on coercion, but also by making use of the willing cooperation of the Azerbaijani population.

Whatever Aliev's motives were, his administration coincided with the era of Soviet tolerance of diversity, enabling the Azerbaijani intellectual elite to engage in a quiet and tedious yet successful effort to reclaim their past. Historiography, arts and literature became areas where this cautious effort took place. It was cautious because Moscow focused its attention on the republic for its earlier lackluster performance in fighting corruption. A well-publicized cultural revival could have drawn Moscow's ire, undermining the gradual restoration of Azerbaijani self-confidence and resilience.

The most cautious were historians, because Aliev was opposed to any revisionist discussion of such issues as the absorption of the Azerbaijani Khanates into the Czarist Empire, the impact of the 1905 Revolution on the Azeris and the short-lived independent Azerbaijani state after the Bolshevik Revolution. Instead, historians focused on the distant past to avoid ideological taboos. Buniatov's 1978 book on the Atabek dynasty (1136–1225), Farzaliev's 1981 book on the fifteenth and sixteenth century Azeri history or Farandzhev's 1981 monograph focused on the last several centuries of the Azeri past, as well as the examination of the works of such Azeri/Turkish thinkers as Nizami, and Nesimi.[42]

Another example is the publication of a new edition of *Gan Ichinde*, a novel by Yusif Vezir Chemenzeminli (1887–1943). In 1940 Chemenzeminli was arrested for his alleged flirtation with the Musavat government and exiled to Nizhny Novgorod, where he died. The leading character of *Gan Ichinde* is Vagif (1717–1797), the chief vizier of Karabagh's Ibrahim Khan. Given Karabagh's significance as an issue of tension between the Azeris and the Armenians, the republication of a novel affirming Karabagh's centrality in Azerbaijani history was not by accident. Chemenzeminli's novel was first published in 1960 when he was rehabilitated for his flirtation with the Musavat regime.[43] Its republication in the 1980s drove home once again the point that communism did not necessarily mean sacrificing national interests.

Another book one should mention is A. M. Akhmedov's 1983 monograph on Azeri enlightenment. Akhmedov dealt with the diversity and complexity of the Jadidist thinking, without, however, naming it as such. Akhmedov periodized the evolution of the Azeri Jadid phenomena, including: 1) Muslim-reformist enlightenment (Akhundov, Zardabi, Agaev, et al.); 2) Liberal-democratic enlightenment (Narimanov, Agamaliogli, et al.); and 3) Radical-democratic enlightenment (Mekhmandarov, Shakhtakhtinskii, et al.).[44]

Earlier in 1977 Mammad Dadashzada wrote an article entitled "Ethnographic Information Concerning Azerbaijan Contained in the *Dada Gorgud Dastan* (*Dada Gorgud* Epic)."[45] The article was yet another attempt to reclaim Azeri historical and cultural heritage. Dadashzada raised many issues which were first raised by previous generations who were liquidated by Stalin in the 1930s or later in the 1950s. He suggested that the Turks began to inhabit the southern Caucasus much earlier than Soviet and Western historians suggested.[46]

Dadashzada selected his words and presented his argument cautiously, because in 1977 he knew he had to operate within constraints.[47] In his article, Dadashzada stated that the Dada Gorgud epic shows that the Oghuz tribes began to arrive in southern Caucasus in the sixth and the seventh centuries along with the Khazars and the Kipchaks. Hence, the epic disagrees with modern historiography that dated the arrival of the Turkic tribes to the eleventh century. Dadashzada even went as far as saying that although what the epic talks about concerns the Turks and the Turkmens as well, "its vocabulary, phraseologic expressions and grammatical structure is closer to Azerbaijan[i Turkish] than to others," which might have been an attempt on his part to avoid being branded as pan-Turkist in an era when such labels were still dangerous.[48]

For obvious reasons historical works were few, yet historical novels proliferated. I. Guseinov's 1981 novel, *Sudnyi Den'* (Day of the Verdict) examined the opposition of the Hurufis, an offshoot of the Shi'a sect, to the Timurid conquest. The book provided the reader with a discussion of a part of the Azeri religious/historical past, which was ignored by the Soviet curricula.[49] In 1981 also, A. Jafarzada's three-part novel, *Baku-1501* was published in which he discussed the Safavid role in Azeri history. In its epilogue, there is a quote from Shah Ismail, the founder of the Safavid state in 1501. His words were powerful and were apparently cited by the author to boost Azerbaijani self-esteem. Shah Ismail declared:

> I hold every grain of the motherland's soil dearer than a handful of gold; the tiniest word of our native tongue more precious than jewels. All this for a never-ending life of both; the motherland and the native tongue .... Our fathers and forefathers left us a three-fold testament: our language, our honor, our motherland. They left us our lives to be ours.[50]

The Population Factor

In Azerbaijan, the nativization process was greatly influenced by the very high birth rates characteristic of most Muslim Soviet republics, although Azerbaijan's population growth was the slowest among them.[51] The emigration of Armenians and Russians from Baku and the NKAO and the relatively low mobility of the Azeris, typical of most Soviet Muslims, contributed to the homogenization. Between 1970 and 1989 the Armenian population in Azerbaijan declined by 19.4 percent, from 484,000 to 390,000.[52] The departure of non-ethnic Azeris was mostly a consequence of Azerbaijan's relative underdevelopment which especially forced educated non-titular nationalities to migrate to other republics in search of better paying jobs. The mutual dislike between Armenians and Azeris and the real or perceived discrimination against Armenians also played roles in the Armenian exodus.[53]

Smaller ethnic minorities in Azerbaijan faced assimilation rather than discrimination. In the 1920s Kurds living in Azerbaijan were allocated an autonomous region to the west of the NKAO known as "Red Kurdistan". In 1930 this entity was abolished and most Kurds were registered as Azerbaijani. Some estimates put the Kurdish figure as high as 200,000 while official statistics show a Kurdish population of around 12,000.[54] In the NKAO the Armenian population also shrunk proportionally. Whereas in 1926 there were 117,000 Armenians and 13,000 Azeris in the oblast, by 1979 the Armenian population had increased by a mere 6,000 to 123,000 while the Azeri population almost tripled to 37,000.[55] As elsewhere in the republic, the stagnation of the Armenian population in the NKAO was due to many educated Armenians leaving the oblast to go to Yerevan or Moscow where upward mobility for them was a more realistic prospect.[56]

The fact that by the 1980s only 29 percent of Azeris felt comfortable with the Russian language, while most of the Russians and many Armenians living in the republic did not speak the Azeri Turkish, also had an impact. Heidar Aliev enthusiastically encouraged the extension of the Russian language education during the 1970s as provided by Brezhnev's policy of "Drawing Nearer of the Nationalities".[57] Nevertheless, Azeris remained one of the least linguistically Russified people in the USSR. These factors reversed the Azerbaijani demography's rather heterogeneous nature. While in 1959 Azeris made up just over 67 percent of the republic's population, the 1970 census showed that Azeris constituted nearly 74 percent of people living in the republic. In 1979 they exceeded 78 percent and by 1989 they comprised 83 percent of the republic's population.[58]

Throughout the USSR, from 1959 to 1989, the number of Azerbaijanis grew by 131 percent, Armenians by 66 percent and Georgians by 48 percent.[59] The Azerbaijani population grew from 3.7 million in 1959 to 5.1 million in 1970 and to 6 million in 1979 before it grew to 6.8 million in 1989.[60] In 1989 85 percent of all Azeris in the Soviet Union lived in Azerbaijan.[61] Moreover, although the latest censuses did not disclose the ethnic composition of the cities, the Azeri elite believed that Azeris recovered from being a minority within the capital city.

The Impact of Azerbaijani Historiography

Throughout the last century, such factors as industrialization, urbanization, the spread of mass education and greater exposure to print and other media have contributed to transforming ethno-linguistic groups into communities, which perceived themselves in terms of nation and nationality. In the Soviet Union, in addition to these factors, there were more unique features that distinguished this country's nation building.

Although the Soviet Union had embarked upon the eradication of nations and creating the "Soviet man", its practices and institutions had accomplished just the opposite: It created "a set of institutions and initiated processes that fostered the development of conscious, secular, and politically mobile nationalities".[62] This nation building was not intended; it happened despite Moscow's 70-year long effort aimed at weakening national consciousness. Yet it happened nevertheless.

During the early twentieth century none of the Turkic peoples in Czarist Russia had a clear idea about their national identity. The Azeris called themselves Turks, yet the real uniting bond was Islam. Over time Azerbaijani and other republican identities increasingly became national identities as a result of Soviet policies. This doesn't mean Azeris owe their national identity to the Soviet Union or that nation-building methods are all alike. A different historical fate might have created Azerbaijani national identity at a much earlier time, or perhaps not at all, if Azerbaijan were to have remained part of Iran.

While trying to create a Soviet state based on "socialist internationalism" Moscow also created national histories and cultures. Azerbaijan's history was drawn from the region's Iranian heritage without explicitly acknowledging it. The Iranian heritage was, however, often denigrated even when it was openly mentioned. Moscow, as well as Baku, argued that the division of Azerbaijan was a consequence of its partition between Iran and the Czarist state, ignoring the fact that Iran was forced to turn over its Transcaucasian territories to Russia with the treaties of Gulistan in 1813 and Turkmenchai in 1828.

The Azeri intellectual elite posited that Azerbaijan was culturally colonized by Iran, while in times of relative intellectual freedom it would also make remarks critical of Czarist Russia. Nevertheless, exigency dictated that the discussion of Azerbaijan's continued division should mention Iran's complicity unequivocally while Moscow's post-1920 role was ignored. In 1948, for example, the AzCP sent a telegram to Iran's Azerbaijan Democratic Party praising its efforts to liberate "the southern part of our homeland that for years ha[d] been suffering under the cursed hands of Persian chauvinists."[63] The criticism of Iran intensified when Soviet–Iran relations were tense.

During the 1940s and the 1950s, due to Stalin's fear of pan-Turkism, Azeri intellectuals were forced to associate Azeri people's roots with the *Medes*, an Iranian tribal union, which inhabited areas around Hamedan and Isfahan from the middle of the ninth century BCE and later formed a kingdom. Yet by the 1980s Azeri intellectual elite started objecting to this theory, which distanced their ethno-genesis from those of the Turks of Turkey. In 1988 when glasnost was in full swing, Suleyman Aliyarov, an Azeri historian, wrote that Azeris were not related to the Medes and that the earlier Soviet era official historiography disregarded the obvious Turkic past of the Azeris.[64]

Yet even then there were others who clung to the still official description of Azeri ethno-genesis. Igrar Aliev wrote in 1990 that Aliyarov's views were "utter nonsense", arguing that the Medes played a decisive role in the ethno-cultural make-up of the Azeris.[65] Moreover, he suggested that the Athropatenes, also of Iranian origin, came to put a final shape to the Azeri ethnos in late fourth century BCE. Likewise, he argued, the Hurrians and the Mannai, who preceded the Medes and were culturally and linguistically Iranian, had influenced the composition of Azeri identity.[66] Most Azeri books published in the 1970s adopted Aliev's interpretation. J. Guliev, for instance, argued that the name Azerbaijan stemmed from *Atropat* or *Atropatenes*, an Achaemenid satrap, who established the Atropatene state in 320 BCE in southern Azerbaijan or today's northern Iran. The dominant ethnic element of this state was supposedly the Medes too.[67]

Another building block of the Azeri ethno genesis, Azerbaijani historiography alludes, were the Caucasian Albanians who inhabited southern Caucasus. The Albanians were a union of 26 tribes, which came together as a political entity as early as 500 BCE. The Caucasian Albanian state acquired stable borders between the third century BCE and the eighth century within which the southern portion of Daghestan, the NKAO, the current Azerbaijan republic and much of eastern Armenia laid.[68]

Later, the argument went, in the fifth and sixth centuries AD Turkic tribes began to arrive in the Transcaucasus, which resulted in the linguistic and ethnic mixing of the Turkic and Albanian populations. Although Christianity took root in the region from the fourth to the eighth centuries its influence was eroded following the Arab invasions that started in 654. In the face of the conversion of a significant portion of the regional population to Islam, the Albanian church drew closer to the Armenian church contributing to the Armenianization of Christian Albanians.[69]

Further, Azeri historians explained, during the eleventh and twelfth centuries Oghuz and other Turkic tribes, taking part in the Seljuq push to the west, settled in southern Caucasus and continued to mix with the indigenous population, further Turkifying them linguistically. Nevertheless, the indigenous people preserved many of their Albanian and Iranian cultural characteristics.[70] This interpretation allowed Azeri official historiographers to downplay Azerbaijan's Turkicness and stress the ancestral links to the ancient indigenous civilizations. Moscow preferred this interpretation because it could entitle the Soviet Union to claim Iranian Azerbaijan in the future. This interpretation was also expected to put distance between Turkey and Azerbaijan.[71]

The Azeri intelligentsia went along with this interpretation partly because it was expedient to do so, but also because it supported the Azeri claim to the NKAO, as this theory strengthened the Azeri argument that the Azeris were the indigenous people of their country. The NKAO factor became more obvious when the February 1988 issue of *Azerbaijan*, the literary-artistic journal of the Writers' Union, published an open letter written by eminent poet Bakhtyar Vahabzade and historian Suleyman Aliyarov. The letter, written chiefly to refute Armenian claims to the NKAO, argued that the oblast had been part of Caucasian Albania and since the Middle Ages part of various Azerbaijani khanates, all political units the Azeri elite claimed as their own.[72]

Earlier, in 1978 M. K. Sherifli, taking advantage of the Aliev/Brezhnev era tolerance, had emphasized the roles played by local Turkic dynasties and the continuous arrival of Turkic tribes that, he claimed, started as early as the tenth century AD Turkic tribes lived side by side with other inhabitants, including the Tats, the Talish, the Albanians, the Lezgin and others, before Turkification accelerated.[73] This version of history would be fully developed during the late 1980s when the Karabagh conflict and the lessening of Moscow's control led to a less cautious discourse. Historian Suleyman Aliyarov argued in 1988 that Albanians were actually Oghuz Turks, as attested to by the *Dada Gorgud* epic, which refers to Albanians twice.[74]

Also, in the early 1960s, a prominent Azerbaijani historian, Zia Buniatov, argued that Albanians were the progenitors of most of the population in Azerbaijan, including the NKAO. His argument, which became the standard Azeri thesis, suggested that Albanians survived till the Middle Ages, but Armenians suppressed their church. He stated that not only the NKAO but also a large part of the Soviet Republic of Armenia used to be parts of Albania.[75] This argument flew in the face of the Armenian thesis by suggesting that NKAO Armenians were either nineteenth-century immigrants, descendants of Albanians or even Oghuz Turks who had inhabited the region for millennia.[76]

Armenian historian Arthur S. Mnatsakanian responded by arguing that Albania was actually located to the northeast of the NKAO bordering the Caspian Sea and that it had disappeared by the tenth century. He claimed that the medieval Albania, which was located in and around the NKAO, was the new Albania and the only Albanian trait it had was its name. For Mnatsakanian, the new Albania's population consisted entirely of Armenians and was ruled by Persia.[77]

By the 1970s younger historians took up the fight. A student of Buniatov, Farita Mamedova entitled her PhD thesis "The Political History and Historical Geography of Caucasian Albania". She located the Albanian state to the west of the NKAO, to the present day Republic of Armenia, whereas, she argued, Armenians then lived further west upstream of the Euphrates River in present day Turkey. She claimed that all churches and monasteries in present day Armenia were Albanian, but Armenians who began to arrive in the fifteenth century destroyed all the Albanian inscriptions on these buildings to make them look Armenian.[78]

Not much is known about the Caucasian Albanians. The dominant belief about them is that they were a tribal federation and during the seventh century Muslim/Arab expansion in the region their 24 tribes began to disintegrate. By the tenth century only small traces of them were left. The general understanding is that the Udins, a Christian minority who used to live in northern Azerbaijan, were the descendants of Albanians. The few writing samples in Albanian have not been deciphered, thus further making it difficult to know more about them.[79]

After the start of the NKAO conflict, Zia Buniatov, then head of the Academy of Sciences in Baku, continued his anti-Armenian treatises. In 1990 the Academy re-published a long forgotten racist book by the turn-of-the-century Russian controversialist Vasil Velichko. Velichko's 1904 book, *Caucasus*, argued that Armenians were by their very racial traits politically unreliable while he praised Azeris as obedient and respectful to Czarist monarchy. Velichko blamed the Armenians' "short skulls", which like those of the Jews, he said, made them racially suspect for disobedience.[80]

Buniatov's Armenian counterpart, Zori Balayan, who, like the former, was a party member, published the book *Ochag* (The Heart) in 1984 in which he described his impressions of the so-called Armenian lands. In the book, Balayan characterized Turks – implying Azeris – as enemies of Russia and Armenia, which instantaneously created a big uproar in neighboring Azerbaijan. The very publication of such a work even before Gorbachev's glasnost was very telling as to what extent Armenians or Azeris felt secure enough to engage in nationalist propaganda.[81]

A post-independence era monogram by Igrar Aliev and Kamil Mamedzade suggested that Armenians of the former NKAO and Azerbaijanis of Azerbaijan proper were all descendants of Albanians. Hence, they argued, Armenians had no justifiable claim to the former NKAO.[82] Aliev and Mamedzade as well as Zia Buniatov, who incidentally was killed in Baku by assassins in February 1997, did not, however, successfully link the two existing theories prior to or after independence: whether the NKAO Armenians were Armenian emigrants who were settled there by the Czar or were descendants of Albanians and thus ethnic kin of the Azeris.[83]

Gorbachev's Reforms and their Impact on Azerbaijani Nationalism

Aliev's real and perceived successes in fighting corruption and achieving economic development contributed to his promotion by Andropov to the Politburo in 1982. In Moscow, Aliev also became Deputy Chairman of the Council of Ministers, a powerful position. Shevarnadze, the first secretary of the neighboring republic of Georgia, followed him to Moscow in 1985 when he too was awarded for his policies with a Politburo seat. Kamran

Baghirov succeeded Aliev as First Secretary. He was to remain in office until May 1988 when Gorbachev removed him and Armenia's First Secretary Karen Demirchian, partly because of the start of Armeno-Azeri interethnic conflict. Suren Arutrunyan and Abdul Rahman Vezirov replaced them.

The last two years of Aliev's tenure in the Politburo coincided with Gorbachev's rule as Secretary General of the Communist Party of the USSR. Aliev "retired" in 1987, although the circumstances contributing to his retirement have not been brought to light. The Gorbachev entourage included some influential Armenians who could have swayed Gorbachev into getting rid of Aliev. They included Abel Aganbegian, who advised Gorbachev on economic matters, and Georgy Shakhnazarov, the political consultant.

When Gorbachev came to power in March 1985, the USSR had experienced years of economic stagnation and lack of stable political leadership. These conditions had "enabled local ethnic and regional mafias within the party-state apparatus to increase their power."[84] Moreover, the war in Afghanistan had internationally isolated and economically drained the USSR. To cope with economic problems and international isolation Gorbachev felt that he needed to move against the well-entrenched party and state establishments in the union republics.[85]

Gorbachev purged the republican leaders of Central Asia and Transcaucasia between 1985 and 1988, though not always without resistance. The removal of Karen Demirchian, First Secretary of the Armenian Communist Party, could only take place after the NKAO crisis erupted, which weakened the Armenian Party's resistance.[86] Yet despite personnel changes local party machineries' control over their republics remained largely intact.

When, however, the various popular fronts began to act, their impact was much more considerable in the Transcaucasus and the Baltic republics. The emergence of nationalist popular fronts eliminated the very constraints of the old order, sweeping away the very elements of the old guard Gorbachev himself was trying to liquidate. While some members of the old political elite lost political power, others became born-again nationalists in a matter of weeks or even days. This process was helped by the "general democratization of political practices, the delegitimization [sic] of Communist Party rule in the center [Moscow], and the growing reluctance and inability of Moscow to use force to impose its will...."[87]

As it happened, at the outset of his tenure, Gorbachev seemed intent on reversing the exclusive hold of the titular native elite networks on their republics and putting an end to the promotion of elites from outside Russia at various decision-making institutions in Moscow, including the Politburo. As one Sovietologist stated, the initial behavior of Gorbachev indicated that "[t]he pattern of dismissals and promotions in the years following Brezhnev's death, at the center and the regions, made it clear that the policy of according circumscribed participation at the center to minority elites, characteristic of the late 1970s and early 1980s, had ended."[88] As a result, key positions in Moscow began to be filled by Russians and by non-Russians who did not have strong links to their respective republics.

Gorbachev became more sensitive to ethnic issues after the December 1986 riots in Almaty, Kazakhstan, but he still seemed convinced that economic necessities required that Moscow employ reliable cadres anywhere within the Union, without much consideration paid to their ethnic background or to the already acquired autonomy of the republics. The "informal groups" that Gorbachev encouraged to organize, initially focused on ecological and cultural issues, leading Gorbachev to think that the December 1986 riots were an exception.

Another aspect of Gorbachev's reform program, democratization, had, however, a counter-wailing effect on Gorbachev's emphasis on efficiency and restructuring. Democratization of the political system inadvertently made republican elites more susceptible to pressures on their peoples. Even those elites who were eager to put an end to the republic-level corruption and mismanagement found it necessary to be responsive to public demands in order to strengthen their public base. Their receptivity to public demands, however, led them to either tolerate ethnic or nationalist demands or become overnight nationalists themselves. The NKAO issue, for instance, showed that Gorbachev's glasnost strengthened the hands of the nationalists in Azerbaijan and Armenia because they were more easily able to challenge Soviet and republican leaderships, and that under the conditions created by glasnost the latter found it extremely difficult to withstand nationalist demands.

Gorbachev's policies of perestroika (*yenidengurma*) and openness (*ashkarlik*) initially did not receive much publicity or the Republican Party's support in Azerbaijan. Instead, such conventional rhetoric as the "primacy of central party leadership" continued to be widely used. Yet in 1986, the party organ *Azerbaijan Kommunisti* started to publish articles on the need to love one's homeland, Azerbaijan, which sounded so nationalistic that one could have hardly anticipated such rhetoric only a few months previous.[89] Nevertheless, despite its embrace of nationalistic or quasi-nationalistic rhetoric, the AzCP continued to consider perestroika as a program of economic efficiency and socio-political restructuring, not so much as democratization.[90] Thus, until the emergence of the NKAO conflict in 1988 political activity was almost as heavily restricted in Azerbaijan as in the pre-Gorbachev era.

Between 1985 and 1987, *Azerbaijan Kommunisti*, as well as *Azerbaijan*, the literary journal of the Azerbaijan Academy of Sciences, published some articles, which were critical of some low-level government officials and policy failures in the low politics area. The latter journal increasingly emphasized the need to preserve Azerbaijan's historical and cultural heritage.[91] Yet all in all, the Azerbaijani leadership seemed mostly unaware as to what the Gorbachev reforms entailed. Aliev's forced resignation in 1987 and the almost simultaneous demand of the Armenian nationalists to annex the NKAO to the Armenian SSR were to radically change this state of affairs and make open discussion of many taboo issues tolerable.

In Azerbaijan – as in many other republics – Gorbachev encouraged "informal groups" to organize around such topics as ecological and cultural issues. In the second half of the 1980s these groups concentrated on the reassertion of Azerbaijani culture, the restoration of the original historical names of towns and places and the changing of the alphabet from Cyrillic to either Latin or Arabic. Some even favored reunification with Iranian Azerbaijan. These groups included the Kizilbash (favoring reunification), Birlik (calling for an Islamic state), Dirchelish or renaissance (demanding more nationalism) and various environmentalist groups.[92] As elsewhere, these informal groups focused increasingly on ethno-cultural issues, especially when the NKAO problem emerged in full force in 1988.

Ronald G. Suny posed the question of why anti-Moscow popular movements inevitably adopted nationalistic agendas. His answer was that

> in important ways, the Soviet empire was like other empires that "modernized" through economic development programs but facilitated the possibility of communication and interaction … making nationality more articulate and nationalism the most potent expression of denied ambitions.[93]

No matter how accurate this explanation is, it was obvious that the emerging civil society in the Soviet Union had used since the 1960s the rhetoric of nationalism, and dissidents presented themselves as spokespeople of their nations. The development of civil society and democracy did not fortify the Soviet Union as Gorbachev had imagined, but rather reinforced centrifugal tendencies. The NKAO crisis was the first calamity that could not be contained, which hastened the fading of the Soviet authority.

One could also ask why, during the Gorbachev era, ethnic nationalism and hatred took hold in some republics but not in all. The missing ingredient, according to some, was ancient hatreds.[94] For instance, although Crimea was transferred from Russia to Ukraine in 1954, the Crimean Russians did not start an armed rebellion in the late 1980s to secede from Ukraine. Yet NKAO, for both Azeris and Armenians, was a piece of land whose fate could easily evoke ethnic hatred. Already in the 1960s intellectuals on both sides had started to instigate hatred and denigrate the claims of the other side.[95] Armenian poet and political activist Silva Kaputikian, who also served in the Armenian Supreme Soviet from 1975 to 1980, stated in 2000 that Soviet authorities did not suppress nationalist expression in Armenia even in the 1960s. She said

> …when I was in America in 1964, I gave one of my books that was completely devoted to Armenia, Armenian questions, the Armenian tragedies, and so on to a Dashnak[t] woman….[S]he was astonished by how it could have been published under Soviet rule."[96]

The NKAO events accelerated the pace of Gorbachev's reforms, which were rather timid and slow between 1985 and 1988. After failing to democratize the Communist Party through multi-candidate elections, Gorbachev introduced such elections for the to-be-created Congress of People's Deputies in 1988. This meant in practice the end of the supremacy of the Communist Party. The sprouting of mass nationalist movements in Transcaucasia, the Baltic republics and later in Ukraine and Belorussia, at first seemed to conform to Gorbachev's policies of glasnost and perestroika. Intellectuals and nationalist activists referred to these policies while demanding more autonomy and later, sovereignty for their republics.

Eventually, the nationalist movements turned against the General Secretary after he tried to restrain them in order to stem the tide of dismemberment. By the end of 1990 Gorbachev attempted to revive the union with a New Union Treaty, but the nationalist movements in general were not favorably disposed to the resuscitation of the Soviet Union. By 1990 many republics had declared sovereignty while a few had even proclaimed independence. The election of Boris Yeltsin as chair of the RSFSR Supreme

Soviet and the subsequent declaration of sovereignty by the Russian Republic also contributed to centrifugal propensities throughout the union.[97]

The Emergence of Nationalist Discourse in Azerbaijani Publications

Azerbaijan was the monthly literary journal of the Azerbaijani Writers' Union or Azerbaijan Yazichilar Ittifaqi and was published in Azeri. Although principally a literary journal, it also dealt with cultural events and political developments. In the post-Stalin era the Azerbaijani Writers' Union was faced with a difficult task in that it was interested in taking advantage of the more liberal atmosphere union-wide to revive Azeri literature and language, while making sure it was not perceived by the Soviet regime as unduly nationalist. By the late 1980s the membership of the union had not changed much, but *Azerbaijan* discussed much more controversial subjects than before.

Earlier, as part of the post-Stalin effort to revive native traditions and celebrate ethnic pride and historic achievements, the journal had printed some articles that were too controversial even for the Brezhnev era tolerance. In such situations the republican leadership would intervene and these issues of the journal would simply disappear from circulation and not reach their subscribers.[98] With the increased boldness the journal adopted in the Gorbachev era, its circulation grew. In 1985 its sales were 51,516, which by December 1989 had jumped to 70,307.[99] More official tolerance shown by the authorities was as much a factor in increased sales as the growing nationalist tone of the articles due to the eruption of the NKAO conflict.

Until 1987 *Azerbaijan* remained favorably disposed to the AzCP and Moscow regarding ideological issues. In 1986, for instance, the then first secretary of the Azerbaijani Writers' Union, Ismayil Shixli, wrote that Gorbachev's policies were turning a page in history and making peace with the West meant a return to Lenin's truly Marxist policies.[100] Although Gorbachev encouraged the criticism of the past, Shixli did not attempt to criticize the Union's past policies of Moscow, the AzCP or even his own. 1986 was just too early to go out on a limb to take chances. Yusuf Samedoglu, the post-October 1987 editor in chief of *Azerbaijan*, criticized in his first editorial the CPSU's past mistakes, Stalin's personality cult (*Shahsiyete Perestish Illeri*) and the policies implemented during the period of stagnation or the Brezhnev era.[101] Although what Samedoglu wrote was not uncommon in

Russia proper in those days, it was nevertheless still unconventional for Azerbaijan, whose ruling elite continued to be publicly very cautious.

Jabir Bovruz, a poet and a former editor of *Azerbaijan*, sounded in a similar way, when in July 1987 he spoke at the Congress of the Writers' Union of Azerbaijan. He stated that after Gorbachev's rise to power, many formerly banned novels and films were freely printed and shown in Russia. Yet banned Azerbaijani literary and artistic works, he added, still awaited the green light from the Azerbaijani authorities.[102] After the 1987 Congress, a mass rehabilitation of the remaining Stalin-era intellectuals who were exiled, imprisoned and executed took place. Nevertheless, the publication of their works was postponed.

In April 1988 three members of the editorial board of *Azerbaijan* were replaced and nine new members joined the board, expanding the size of the board from 16 to 25. The enlargement of the editorial board enabled several APF members, who in general were also members of the AzCP, to join the board. Moreover, the spectrum of issues that the editorial board was interested in was enlarged to include such issues as the NKAO dispute, the unification with Iranian Azerbaijan, Moscow's long-running policy of discrimination against Azerbaijan regarding the NKAO problem, the award of Zangezur to Armenia in the early 1920s, the drawing of the Azerbaijan–Armenia border to the detriment of Azerbaijan, and various forms of Russian exploitation of the republic, including the price of Azerbaijani oil being set artificially low while manufactured goods that the republic bought from Russia cost relatively high.[103]

The post-1985 publication of formerly "perilous" literary works included various poems of Samed Vurgun (1909–1956) and "1937", the famed poem of I. Ismayilzada, a member of the editorial board of *Azerbaijan*.[104] The author had written the poem earlier, but chose not to publish it even in the Brezhnev era of stagnation (*durgunluq dövrü*), fearing that doing so was too risky. Literary works by non-Azeris, including Chingiz Aitmatov, Valentin Rasputin, Anna Ahmatova and others, which criticized certain aspects of the Soviet system, also found their way into the journal.[105] After October 1987, when Samedoglu became editor of the journal, more critical articles began to appear. Among others, one could mention banned writings of Alexander Twardkowski, Anatoly Rybakov's *Children of Arbat* and Aitmatov's more critical works.[106] Probably the most important work made public was the publication in installments of the translation of Kurban Said's novel *Ali ve Nino* (Ali and Nino). The novel deals with events in Azerbaijan during the tumultuous years of 1917–1920 and was banned in the country until it appeared on the pages of *Azerbaijan,* starting in its January 1990 issue.[107]

Still, many remained blacklisted even in 1988. A nationalist poet, Muhammad Hadi, (1879–1920), was rehabilitated in 1988 but only a handful of his apolitical poems were published. He was classified as having written some poems under the "misleading nationalistic influence of the Musavat Party."[108] Another blacklisted writer with a much more substantial political involvement was Mammad Emin Resulzada (1884–1955) who served as president of independent Azerbaijan and as the head of the then ruling Musavat Party. In 1988 Resulzada was still not rehabilitated, although some called for a more impartial treatment of his political and intellectual role during the 1918–1920 period.[109]

While in Russia, Ukraine and Estonia, the dissidents and non-conformists were more at ease with challenging the party line in the second half of the 1980s, in Azerbaijan – as Abbasali Djavadi argued – Azerbaijani intellectuals stuck to the already existing tradition of not openly challenging the boundaries set by the AzCP.[110] They acted circumspect, believing that the liberal political atmosphere created by Gorbachev could be reversed and that Moscow was traditionally less tolerant of dissent in Muslim republics. Another indication of this timidity was the paucity of articles demanding democratic reforms. A few articles that were published included the translation in 1989 of Sergey Andreyev's article, in which he advocated multiparty democracy.[111]

Starting in 1989, when Armenian activists had already started the NKAO campaign, Azerbaijan's official and unofficial press focused more easily on the 1918–1920 period and presented the period and the Musavat regime more favorably. They talked about the harmful effects of several alphabet changes, linguistic and cultural Russification, depletion of Azerbaijan's oil, destruction of the Caspian Sea's ecology, unemployment, Moscow's implementation of unfavorable terms of trade *vis-à-vis* the republic's products and the education and health sectors' shortcomings. Anti-Armenian arguments were more easily printed because the AzCP considered them less objectionable.[112]

A good example of this behavior was the treatment of Ahmad Ağaoğlu (Agaev) (1869–1939) whose rehabilitation had earlier proved problematic. Ağaoğlu was a pan-Turkist and had served as a prominent member of the independent Azerbaijan's government, after whose demise he escaped to Turkey, where he eventually died. He was rehabilitated in an article in *Adabiyyat va Injasanat* on June 10, 1988, but his works remained blacklisted.

The article praised his literary abilities but did not mention his political role during 1918–1920 and that he was once considered an enemy of the revolution. The article suggested that Ağaoğlu was actually in favor of the revolutionary changes in the socio-political life in Azerbaijan and that he was not a reactionary as once thought. Another nationalist and pan-Turkist writer, Alibey Huseynzada (1864–1941), was also rehabilitated, but his works also remained taboo.[113] Even as late as 1988 the restraint shown by the Azerbaijani regime was characteristic of how cautious the authorities were before the NKAO dispute turned into an inter-state dispute.

Another ban until the late 1980s was on the religious works of such poets as Nasimi (1369–1417), Fuzuli (1498–1556), Sarraf (?–1907), and Shahriyar (1906–1988) in which they dealt with such religious themes as tasawwuf (spiritual development) and the lives of the Prophet, Imam Ali, and Imam Husayn.[114] Even anthologies omitted their religious attributes while mentioning their secular works.[115] The Qur'an too was not published in Azerbaijan in Azerbaijani Turkish or in Arabic till the late 1980s. Elsewhere, only in Kazan, Russia, was Qur'an published in limited numbers.

As could be expected, most articles in late 1980s characterized Azerbaijan as *vatan* or homeland, and were disproportionately preoccupied with the Karabagh conflict. The writers denounced state neglect of mosques and other historical/religious sites and their use for purposes contrary to Azerbaijani mores. An article in the December 1988 edition of *Azerbaijan*, for instance, disapproved of the destruction of 31 out of 41 mosques in Shusha and the use of the remainder for non-religious purposes.[116]

Abulfaz Aliev (Elchibey), the Popular Front leader who became President of independent Azerbaijan in 1993, wrote in 1989 an introduction to a reprint of an article by Mirza Bala Memmedzada, a *jadidist*, who had left Azerbaijan in 1923. In his introduction Elchibey argued that Azeri history is part of Turkish history and not part of Iranian history.[117] He also wrote that "Al-Ban" was the name Shamanism used for the forces of the "sacred sky" and that Albanians were Shamanist when Turkic communities were all Shamanist. Although Aliev avoided openly describing the Albanians as Turkic, he nevertheless insisted that without knowing the pre-Islamic history of the Turks one could not understand Azerbaijani history.[118]

Similarly, in the December 1988 issue of *Azerbaijan*, Historian B. Memmedov claimed that the NKAO was a former center of the Azeri-Muslim culture. In the June 1988 and September 1989 issues he argued that even in Armenia proper old place names were in Turkish, which, he claimed, demonstrated that the whole area's Turkish roots predated Armenian presence.[119]

By 1990 *Azerbaijan* would publish essays which further emphasized the Turkishness of Azerbaijan. One of them was the republication of an essay by Mammad Emin Resulzada, which was first published in Istanbul in 1928. In this essay Resulzada argued that diverse Turkic tribes moved south from northern Caucasus towards Azerbaijan in the fifth century AD. The Khazars, another Turkic people, arrived in the region at the beginning of the seventh century. Yet the more significant portion of the Turks, he said, came with the Seljuq conquests in the eleventh century. He argued that until the thirteenth to fourteenth centuries Turkification continued, but a thorough Turkification was possible after the Mongol invasions of the thirteenth and fourteenth centuries. He argued that the Safavids (1501–1722) completed the process of Turkification by settling more Turkic tribes in Azerbaijan. Resulzada also referred to Albania, but for him the Albanian factor was marginal in the context of the Azerbaijanis' ethno-linguistic make-up. For him, Albania was not even an independent entity. He argued that Albania, like southern Azerbaijan, was merely a region of the Sassanian Empire.[120]

The reprint of Resulzada's article was not coincidental. The post-1988 discourse on Azerbaijani ethno-genesis increasingly focused on proving that Albanians were actually Turkic. Historian Suleyman Aliyarov contributed to the endeavor by writing a reader's letter to the September 1988 issue of *Azerbaijan*. There, he argued that Albanians were part of the Oghuz ethnos and they were hence Turkic. He also argued that in the Dada Gorgud epic, the name "Alban" was used twice and hence Albanians were truly Turkic.[121]

A similar view was presented by the reprint in 1989 of Mirza Bala's article, which was originally published in Ankara in 1951. Bala was a member of the *Turk Adem-i Merkeziyyet Partiyasi-Musavat* and a close associate of Resulzada in Istanbul and Berlin after the two escaped the Bolshevik takeover in 1920. In the article that was reprinted, Bala too argued that Albanians were of Turkic origin and that for the last two millennia they and their forefathers were in control of, among others, Zangezur, Karabagh, and Nakhichevan, three regions that were contested by Armenians and the Azeris throughout the twentieth century. Bala added that Armenians had never constituted a majority in any portion of the Transcaucasus throughout history.[122]

Iran, another neighboring country with whose cultural characteristics Azerbaijanis strongly identified, did not enjoy the positive coverage that was accorded to Turkey and Turks. During the days when almost all things non-Soviet were viewed sympathetically, Iran continued to be mentioned as the oppressor of Azeris. Both the Pahlavi dynasty and the post-1979 Islamic regime could not escape the scorn of the late 1980s' Azerbaijani assertiveness. Hostility towards Iran was also expressed by projecting the Shah regime and Moscow as major culprits of the division of Azerbaijan.[123]

Articles abounded that decried Azerbaijan's ecologically endangered state. A. Abbasov, for example, argued in an article that cotton farmers in Azerbaijan used 90 kilograms of pesticide per hectare while cotton growers in western republics of the Soviet Union used only three kilograms per hectare. In Azerbaijan, he argued, this led to high rates in child mortality, exceeding by 50 percent the Soviet average.[124] Abbasov complained that in order to achieve record production levels the kolkhozes even bought chemicals on the black market, amplifying the environmental disaster Azerbaijan already faced. In the early 1980s, the same *Azerbaijan* that published Abbasov's 1989 article had carried articles in support of efforts to increase cotton production in the raions.[125]

3

Armenia Claims Mountainous Karabagh
Start of Hostilities

During the latter half of Stalin's rule, as well as after, the NKAO leadership pursued a policy of "Armenianization" by stocking local libraries with native language books, adopting native language curricula, promoting radio broadcasts in Armenian and, in general, pursuing ever closer ties to Armenia.[1] Despite the various Stalin-era restrictions, since the mid-1940s Armenians raised the issue of the "return" of the NKAO to Armenia, in the name of rectifying a historic injustice.[2] In 1945 the head of the Armenian Communist Party, Grigory Artyomovich Arutyunov (Arutyunyan), asked Stalin to attach the province to Armenia. After Stalin's death, Karabagh Armenians continued their coaxing of Moscow. In 1965, 13 local party officials and intellectuals wrote a joint letter to the Soviet leadership complaining about Baku's discriminatory policies. This resulted in many of them being sacked from their positions by the Azerbaijan leadership.[3]

After Aliev became First Secretary in 1969 he tightened Baku's reigns even further. He moved against local party bosses, including NKAO's First Secretary Gurgen Melkumian and head of the NKAO's Executive Committee, Musheg Ohanjenian. They were replaced in 1974 with more reliable locals.[4] The new party Secretary in the NKAO was Boris Kevorkov who proved to be very loyal to Aliev. He was an Armenian from outside the NKAO and had an Azeri wife. During his 14-year tenure he never visited Armenia.[5] Azeri policies included an attempt to revise population ratios in the oblast. The percentage of ethnic Armenians in the NKAO dropped from 84 percent in 1959 to 76 percent in 1979.[6]

Since Moscow perceived Armenian nationalism as not necessarily anti-Russian, it was historically more tolerant and supportive of Armenia. This contributed to national revival in Armenia taking place earlier than in Azerbaijan. In the post-Stalin era, symbols of Armenian nationhood began to appear almost everywhere in Yerevan. Stalin's statue was replaced by one of "Mother Armenia" and memorials were erected to honor the fifth-century Armenian warrior Vartan Mamikonian, and even the pre-Soviet era guerrilla commander Andranik. Moreover, in 1965 a memorial was built in Yerevan to commemorate the 50th anniversary of what many Armenians claim was the "Armenian Genocide."[7]

While the relaxation of Moscow's restrictions imposed on freedom of expression led elsewhere to more benign forms of dissidence, in Armenia and in some other locations it augmented ancient hatreds. National revival in such locations was not restricted to dissident publications. It also involved active participation of official historians as well as communist party functionaries. In 1965 and 1966 a signature collection campaign in Yerevan, which aimed to unify Armenia with the NKAO, produced 45,000 signatures, which were submitted to Moscow, while a separate letter signed by thousands was presented to the 27th Party Congress of the CPSU. The reply in both instances was that accommodating Armenian demands would lead to a plethora of other demands for border changes throughout the union. The 1966 campaign did, however, result in the emergence of an Armenian dissident movement with a hint of nationalism.[8]

In Azerbaijan it was difficult to combine local nationalism with dedication to the Soviet ethos. Yet Aliev – in addition to his contribution to self-assertiveness discussed earlier – made the Azeri language more acceptable in public life and unveiled monuments to Vagif, Nizami and others in recognition of their contribution to Azerbaijani literature.[9] As suggested earlier, Aliev could afford such behavior not only because of the post-Stalin relaxation but also because of his impeccable credentials as a committed Marxist.

The contemporary phase of the conflict over the mountainous portion of Karabagh began in August 1987 when Armenians in the NKAO as well as in the Armenian republic started another petition drive to convince Moscow to agree to Armenia's annexation of the oblast. The petition drive was followed by a speech made in Paris by prominent Gorbachev's advisor Abel G. Aganbegian, in November 1987. In his address Aganbegian stated that Karabagh as well as Nakhichevan were historic Armenian territories and that Karabagh should revert to Armenia.[10] Armenian demonstrators in

Yerevan initially did not stress the NKAO issue in their demonstrations. Environmental problems related to Lake Sevan's shrinkage and pollution, the potential dangers of the Medzamor nuclear power station and the Nairit chemical plant were presented, and even air pollution in Yerevan were issues protestors seemed to be more preoccupied with. The demand to make the NKAO part of Armenia appeared to be put on the back burner for a while.[11]

When Armenians began to demonstrate for the NKAO, they claimed that Karabagh was part of historic Armenia and that Stalin incorporated it into Azerbaijan for reasons of expediency. Armenian nationalists had argued all along that Azeri authorities discriminated against NKAO Armenians in various ways, tried to stall the oblast's economic development and prevented socio-cultural links between residents of the NKAO and those of the Republic of Armenia. Emphasis was placed on the fact that the USSR constitution allowed for the exercise of self-determination, and since Armenians in the NKAO constituted there a significant majority, they should be allowed to decide their own future.

Initial reactions to the Armenian demands came not from the official Azerbaijani establishment but from the Azerbaijani intellectuals and ordinary Azeris. On February 19, 1988, on the seventh day of the rallies held in Armenia, a group of Azeris including academics and laymen marched from the Academy of Sciences, located on a hill in Baku, down to the republican parliament, the Supreme Soviet, carrying banners and placards that proclaimed NKAO belonged to Azerbaijan.[12] In February 1988, with the probable acquiescence of the Azerbaijani ruling elite, the journal *Azerbaijan* published an open letter by late Bakhtiyar Vahabzade and Suleyman Aliyarov positing that Karabagh had always been Azerbaijani territory.[13] No matter how passionate the authors of the "open letter" about the "national question" were, they nevertheless tried to substantiate their arguments with references to the Leninist ideology and to the Soviet constitution's restrictions on the revision of republican borders.[14]

A major reason why the NKAO dispute struck a raw nerve in Azerbaijan was that Karabagh was home to Shusha, one of the historically most prominent Azerbaijani population centers. In 1740 Panakh Khan, a renegade general of the Persian army, founded his Javanshir dynasty in Karabagh, building a series of fortresses. One of these fortresses was in Shusha, a mostly Muslim population center. Under Panakh's successor, Ibrahim Khan, the city prospered. Vagif, a major Azeri poet and politician from Karabagh, served as Ibrahim's court poet and Chief Vizier. By the end of the eighteenth century Karabagh would once again come under Iran's Qajar dynasty's influence and would become part of Czarist Russia after the Russo-Persian War (1804–1813).

In the nineteenth century Shusha was larger and more prosperous than Baku or Yerevan. It was at the crossroads of a series of caravan routes and was well known for its silk production.[15] Shusha was also famous for its carpets, as well as for the mughams, traditional Azeri vocal and musical compositions. The region is also known as the cradle of Azerbaijan's musical tradition. Composer Uzeir Hajibeyov (1885–1948) and the famous Azeri singer and actor Bulbul (1897–1961) were Karabagh natives.[16] Beside Vagif the town was also the birthplace of Azerbaijan's most famous female poet, Khurshud Banu Natavan (1830–1897), who was the daughter of Karabagh's last khan (Mahdi Kulu Khan) who fled to Iran in 1822.

Notwithstanding the diverging arguments, the ethnic or religious make up of the NKAO was not a constant. Personal observations of travelers, such as Johann Schiltberger in the early fifteenth century and Baron von Haxthausen in the mid-nineteenth century point to a mixed Christian/ Muslim population in the mountainous portion of Karabagh.[17] Moreover, there were seasonal fluctuations in the composition of the population. Muslims living in the territories of the NKAO have all along been nomadic. While they constituted a majority in mountainous Karabagh in summer, Armenians rose to majority status in winter, with Muslims relocating to the plains of Karabagh.[18]

Armenian Activists Begin Struggle for the NKAO (Mountainous Karabagh)

In the NKAO an underground secessionist movement existed since the 1940s, if not earlier. In 1945, 1965 and 1977 NKAO activists collected signatures and sent letters to Moscow calling for unification with Armenia.[19] In Armenia such underground groups as the so-called "United Armenian Party" existed since 1965, which under the leadership of Paruyr Hayrikian played a role in the *miatsum* (unification) campaign in the late 1980s.[20] Yet the Gorbachev era pro-secession activists differed from those who participated in the earlier ones. The activists of the 1980s were mostly Armenians from the NKAO who were no longer residing in the oblast. A major reason was that since the Second World War, many belonging to the intelligentsia in the oblast had moved to Moscow, Yerevan or elsewhere, where they set up more easily an informal network aimed at putting an end to

Azeri rule in the NKAO. One of the organizers of the late 1980s was Igor Muradian, who was then in his early 30s, and – despite being from the NKAO – grew up in Baku. He worked in Yerevan and was more comfortable in Russian than in Armenian. In February 1988 Muradian succeeded in acquiring signatures from eight Armenian Communist Party (ACP) members, including Abel Aganbegian, before presenting them to the Union authorities. Muradian sought and received from the ACP some help for his NKAO campaign. He also contacted the then underground Dashnaktsutiun Party's members in Yerevan and abroad. Through their help he acquired weapons whose first shipment arrived in the summer of 1986.[21] Aganbegian was also rumored to have taken part in the alleged effort of nationalist Armenians' termination of Heidar Aliev's Politburo career.[22] On November 16, 1987 Aganbegian met with French Armenians in Paris and stated that unification would be achieved in the context of perestroika and democracy in the Soviet Union.[23]

Another close Gorbachev aide who was also Armenian was Georgy Khosroevich Shakhnazarov. In his memoirs Shakhnazarov suggested that he opposed the unification of the NKAO with Armenia and believed that the raising of the NKAO's status to an autonomous republic would have solved the oblast's problems while keeping it part of Azerbaijan.[24] This self-professed internationalist Armenian was probably less involved in lobbying Gorbachev than others, including Aganbegian.

Aliev did indeed resign his post in the summer of 1987, ostensibly for health reasons. It is not clear whether the anti-Aliev campaign played a role in his resignation. Yet many Armenians, including former ACP chief Karen Demirchian, stated that Aliev's removal from the Politburo helped the Armenian cause.[25] Aliev suggested in an interview in August 1991 that Gorbachev did not grasp the complexity of the NKAO dispute and did not consult him. He added that Gorbachev had already made up his mind to turn over the NKAO to Armenia before events began to unfold.[26]

Dissidents in the Baltic states, Ukraine, Russia and elsewhere supported the Armenian stance on the NKAO dispute, partly because the NKAO Armenians were perceived as victims of Stalin's divide-and-rule policy. Personal ties were probably also important. Andrei Sakharov, the prominent dissident, whose wife's stepfather was incidentally Armenian, was also a staunch supporter of the Armenian position. In general, Azeri-committed violence received much more publicity than Armenian-committed atrocities in Western as well as in the Soviet media, which the Azeris interpreted as Christian bias against Muslim Azeris.

On February 20, 1988 110 Armenian deputies of the NKAO Soviet passed a resolution which appealed to the Supreme Soviets of the Azerbaijan and the Armenian republics, calling for the transfer of the NKAO from Azerbaijan to Armenia and for the USSR Supreme Soviet to sanction such a transfer.[27] Before the emergency session took place, the NKAO Party boss, Boris Kevorkov, a loyal ally of AzCP First Secretary Kamran Baghirov, tried in vain to forestall it. For their part, Azeri members of the NKAO Soviet refused to participate in the voting and walked out.

The organization that pushed for a more assertive stance regarding secession from Azerbaijan was Krunk, the Armenian word for the crane, which supposedly symbolized longing for the motherland, Armenia. An alternate explanation was that in Russian Krunk is the abbreviation of the Committee for the Revolution in Nagorno-Karabagh.[28] The organization came to light during the demonstrations that took place in Armenia proper and in the NKAO in February 1988. Krunk was registered a few days later by the *oblispolkom*. Krunk included 47 Communist Party members, seven members of the party *obkom* and *gorkom*, four oblast and city soviet deputies, 22 enterprise and association leaders, three secretaries of plant party committees and representatives from the media and the intelligentsia. It was headed by an 11-member council. Its chairman was A. Manucharov, who was a party member and director of the construction materials combine.[29] Robert Kocharian, who at the time served as the head of the AzCP organization at the Stepanakert Silk Factory, was responsible for Krunk's ideological work. Although Krunk was banned at the end of March 1988, it continued to function in the oblast under the name of *miatsum*. Robert Kocharian, President of Armenia since 1998, headed *miatsum* before assuming the post of prime minister in 1992, and president in 1994 of the breakaway region.

In Armenia the Karabagh Committee, chaired by an 11-member leadership council led the *miatsum* campaign. The committee, which quickly sidelined the ACP as the agenda-setter on the NKAO, consisted of 11 intellectuals. Originally, Igor Muradian and Zori Balayan, two Armenian men who belonged to the ACP and were originally from the NKAO, led the movement, but men who were mostly Yerevan intellectuals soon replaced them.[30] The Committee's agenda was larger than the initial leaders Balayan and Muradian had intended. It wasn't only concerned with the NKAO, it was also aimed at *Hai Dat* or uniting Armenians worldwide.[31]

Within a short period the Karabagh Committee would come to power under the banner of the Armenian National Movement (ANM). The Committee owed its success especially to two men: Levon Ter-Petrosyan and Vazgen Manukian. Ter-Petrosyan was a philologist and a historian, whereas Manukian was a mathematician who taught at Yerevan University. In an interview in 1990 with the official organ of the ANM, *Hayk*, Manukian stated that Armenia traditionally relied on Russia for security and well-being. Yet, he added, Russia has always been preoccupied with imperial interests, a good example of which was its award of the NKAO and Nakhichevan to Azerbaijan in the 1920s. Manukian, who would assume the post of prime minister in 1990, was referring to such activists as Zori Balayan, who preferred a moderate nationalist stance to acquire Moscow's support on the NKAO.[32]

Years later, Ter-Petrosyan stated that the first Karabagh Committee, including Silva Kaputikian, Zori Balayan, and Igor Muradian, campaigned for *miatsum*, but were not so enthusiastic to challenge the Soviet system. He said:

> For them issues like democracy or the independence of Armenia simply did not exist. And this was the ground where the split occurred. When they felt we were already becoming dangerous for the Soviet system, they left .... They thought that the Karabagh question had to be solved by using the Soviet system. And we understood that this system would never solve the Karabagh issue and that the reverse was true: you had to change the system to resolve this problem.[33]

Despite the activists' rather uncompromising tone, most Armenians were not swayed easily to their side. Their oldest Armenian political party, the Social Democratic Hunchak Party, had declared in 1923 that the "Armenian Question had been resolved satisfactorily" with the establishment of Soviet Armenia.[34] The Hunchak position was paradoxical because at the time of its founding in 1887 it had called for independence. The more nationalist, yet still socialist, Dashnakt Party and the rather liberal Ramgavar Party accepted the Sovietization of Armenia as a matter of fact. Both, as well as Hunchak, believed that Armenia had no chance to become independent any time soon, and even an independent Armenia would need Russia's support to survive on account of Turkey's perceived threat.[35]

Yet despite its initial disinclination the Dashnakt leadership would quickly change its position by the end of 1988 and would espouse not only the creation of independent Armenia but also a greater Armenia (*hoghabavak*) to include most of the supposed historical Armenian lands and gather together most Armenians (*azgahavak*). These goals meant that in the future an independent Armenian state would not only include the Soviet republic of Armenia but also eastern Turkey, the NKAO, Nakhichevan, and Akhalkelek (Georgia).[36] In 1989 the Dashnakt leadership would establish an underground armed organization called *Vrezh* (vengeance) which would engage in bombings of targets within Azerbaijan proper.[37]

The CPSU Central Committee's response to the demonstrations and violence in the NKAO and Armenia was as expected. On February 21, 1988 it issued a warning to the parties involved, declaring that their demands "contradict[ed] the interests of the working people" of Azerbaijan and Armenia. The Central Committee's warning came after weeklong demonstrations which engulfed the Armenian SSR and the NKAO.[38]

In Kremlin Gorbachev told the Politburo the same day that there were 19 potential territorial conflicts and agreeing to the NKAO's secession would set a terrible precedent for others to follow.[39] What Gorbachev could also have said was that while Article 72 of the Soviet Constitution reaffirmed the right of the Union Republics to secede from the USSR, Article 78 stipulated that "the territory of a Union Republic may not be altered without its consent".[40] This latter article ensured, at least on paper, that Azerbaijan's territorial integrity was constitutionally guaranteed. Gorbachev tried dialogue and compromise, dispatching delegations to Azerbaijan and Armenia, but to no avail.

On February 26, 1988 Gorbachev met in Kremlin with two prominent Soviet era Armenians: Zori Balayan and Silva Kaputikian. Balayan was a writer and journalist with the Soviet newspaper *Literaturnaya Gazeta.* Kaputikian was a famous poet and Raisa Gorbacheva was one of her fans. Kaputikian beseeched Gorbachev for some concessions to take back to Armenia's demonstrating crowds. Georgy Shakhnazarov, who was present at the meeting, told her that she could tell the crowds that there would be a conference to deal with "nationality questions" which would have an impact on the NKAO question.[41]

AzCP First Secretary Kamran Baghirov also tried to influence Moscow and his people. On February 23, 1988 he issued a statement denouncing the demands made in Armenia and the NKAO. Using Marxist terminology and avoiding appeals to national sentiments, he said:

> The reports that Nagorno-Karabagh will be affiliated with the Armenian SSR are unfounded. Such rumors conflict with the Constitution of the Soviet Union and … the Constitution of the Azerbaijan SSR.

> In fact, such thoughtless activities are aimed at creating an argument on the essence of the policy pursued by the CPSU and the Soviet state in accordance with Lenin's national policy.[42]

While demonstrations were continuing in the NKAO, violence erupted near Askeran village in the oblast on February 22. At the end of the day two Azeris lost their lives while two Armenians were wounded.[43] As reported later, these two Azeris were part of a group from nearby Aghdam, who, after hearing about the demonstrations in the NKAO, went to Askeran to "teach a lesson" to the unruly Armenians. Armenian irregulars also attacked and ransacked a dozen other villages in the region causing hundreds of Azeri residents to flee to Azerbaijan proper.[44] Following the hostilities, Moscow sent airborne military units to Yerevan to be used when necessary. Moscow also sent four senior emissaries to the region to help restore order.[45]

The same day, the plenary meeting of the Nagorno-Karabagh *obkom* resulted in the dismissal of Boris Kevorkov "for shortcomings" from his post as First Secretary of the Karabagh *obkom* bureau, which he held for 15 years. In his place the Nagorno-Karabagh *obkom* elected Genrikh Pogosyan, a former mayor of Stepanakert, who was at the time deputy chairman of the NKAO Soviet of People's Deputies.[46] AzCP First Secretary Kamran Baghirov was present at the NKAO meeting. Following these measures, the new office holders called for an end to demonstrations and strikes, and Gorbachev announced that the Central Committee of the USSR would examine their demands. Consequently, the demonstrations lost some of their intensity, but a complete halt was not achieved.

Armenia Starts Ethnic Cleansing

During the February protest rallies many ethnic Azeris who were Armenian citizens escaped to Azerbaijan. They came from the Kafan, Dilizhan, Idzhevan and other raions in Armenia and were temporarily settled in the Apsheron, Imishli, Zangelan and other raions in Azerbaijan. *Bakinskiy Rabochiy*, which reported on the exodus of the Azeris from Armenia, nevertheless tried to conceal why so many ethnic Azeris were leaving Armenia. Trying to tow the line expounded by Moscow, the paper stated: "Deliberately or otherwise, the new arrivals are beginning to spread various rumors and absurd conjectures which have nothing in common with reality."[47] *Bakinskiy Rabochiy*'s cautious behavior was partly due to the Azerbaijani elite's belief that their country's fate was still in the hands of the Union leadership. Azerbaijani party leaders thought that a favorable outcome of the NKAO crisis could only come if they curried favor with Moscow by public displays of loyalty.

Earlier, in November 1987 two freight trains carrying Azeris who fled from the southern Armenian town Kafan had arrived in Baku, although the Azerbaijani media did not report on their arrival. By the end of January 1988 2,000 more refugees from Kafan arrived in Baku. They reportedly carried signs of beatings or fights.[48] Azeris living in Yerevan constituted a tiny minority and the police protected them. In rural areas, however, Azeris faced widespread violence. Armenian gangs raided villages, beating and shooting Azeris, burning homes and forcing the villagers to leave on foot. By the end of 1988 there were dozens of deserted villages and 200,000 Azeris and Muslim Kurds had fled the republic, which largely completed ethnic cleansing in Armenia.[49]

In Armenia most murders took place at the end of November and the beginning of December 1988. During this period 127 Azeris were murdered. In one instance 12 Azeris from the northeastern village of Vartan were burned to death.[50] Armenian officials condoned, if not outright encouraged, the deportations. On one occasion, on November 27, 1988, police and ACP officials visited two Azeri villages in northern Armenia, Saral and Gurasly, and told the villagers to leave within two weeks. When Azeri villagers refused to comply, Armenian gangs attacked the villages. Afterwards, the police came once again and reiterated its ultimatum for the villagers' departure. This time Azeri residents were eager to comply. They were bussed to the Azerbaijani border.[51]

In the Politburo there was no consensus on how to deal with the dispute. Hence, both the Azeri and Armenian elites tried to exploit Moscow's vacillation, hoping that they could sway Moscow's opinion to their side. A Politburo assistant, the so-called nationalities specialist, Vyacheslav Mikhailov, stated years later that in May 1988 Moscow considered granting ASSR status to the NKAO, which would have provided the oblast with its own parliament, constitution and government, making mountainous Karabagh almost a Union republic. The Politburo also planned to construct a highway between Armenia and the NKAO passing through Azerbaijani Lachin to provide closer ties between the two. Mikhailov stated that the then local party boss of the NKAO, Genrikh Pogosyan, rejected the plan, which for Armenian radicals was also unacceptable on account of its being a short-term palliative.[52]

In Moscow Gorbachev sympathized with Armenians' past grievances, although he rejected out of hand the nationalist leaders' demands. While critical of the nationalist nature of the demands, he praised them for being expressed peacefully. In a Politburo session he said:

> For my part I see two causes: on the one hand, many mistakes committed in Karabagh itself plus the emotional foundation, which [engulfs the Armenian] people. Everything that has happened to this people in history remains, and so, everything that worries them provokes a reaction like this [sic].[53]

Nevertheless, Gorbachev criticized AzCP and ACP leaders for cooperating with the nationalists and for hiding crucial information from Moscow.[54]

Azerbaijani official media's attitude reflected the AzCP's statements, which contained pledges stating that there was no reason for Armenians in the NKAO to feel alienated or neglected, economically or socially. As, however, the ethnic Armenian editor of the journal *Glasnost*, Sergei Grigoriants, argued, the Azerbaijani TV, ironically a major part of the official media, and the Azerbaijani Writers' Union, which had been more interested in Gorbachev's policy of glasnost, adopted more nationalist stances. Grigoriants said that there was a series of programs on Azerbaijani TV in which the viewers were reassured that Azerbaijan would "never give up Nagorno-Karabagh." The chairman of the Azerbaijani Writers' Union, Grigoriants said, had supposedly stated that "the border [with Armenia] is open, and those who do not feel comfortable in Nagorno-Karabagh can go home."[55]

The Sumgait Massacre

Sumgait is a relatively new town of 250,000 located 11 miles north of Baku. Before the Second World War the place was an empty shoreline on the Caspian Sea. In the late 1940s it began to emerge as a town whose population consisted of political prisoners sent from Stalin's camps, Azeris who were deported from Armenia and poor Armenians from the NKAO in search of jobs in Baku. Soon Sumgait became an industrial hub consisting of various chemical plants. Azeris and others who settled there suffered high death rates due to environmental pollution. The controversy over the NKAO took a turn for the worse after a group of unruly Azeris took part in atrocities against local Armenians during February 27–28, 1988 in

Sumgait. Figures of Armenian casualties ranged between 17 and 180, depending on which source did the reporting. Whereas Azerbaijani authorities submitted the lowest figures, the Armenian side claimed that the loss of life was in the hundreds. Although the details are hazy, it seems that a group of mostly young Azeris attacked Armenian homes and establishments, believing that their action was in retaliation to Azerbaijani loss of life in the NKAO and the expulsion of ethnic Azeris from Armenia. The Soviet media characteristically put the blame on "hooligans" who, reacting to events in Armenia and the NKAO, supposedly decided to take the law into their own hands.[56]

The events began to unfold on February 26 when a small group of 50 recent refugees from Armenia demonstrated peacefully in Sumgait's Lenin Square. Next day a larger crowd of several hundred people demonstrated and the Second Secretary of the Sumgait Party Committee, Bayramova, addressed the crowd and demanded the expulsion of Armenians from Azerbaijan. In the evening, the frenzy of some of the demonstrators led them to use force while local police stood by. Still, violence was random and not as ferocious as it would be next day. Coincidentally, on the very same evening the Soviet military prosecutor, Alexander Katusev, announced the murders of two young men with obvious Azeri names in the central NKAO town Askeran. By the morning of February 28 the NKAO murders had further incited the crowds. The first secretary of the local Party Committee, Jehangir Muslimzada, addressed the demonstrators promising that the NKAO would not be given to Armenia and the local Armenian community in Sumgait would be expelled from the city. His words, apparently to calm the crowd, failed, however, to do so and gangs of various sizes began to hunt for Armenians using mostly homemade weapons.[57]

While killings continued on February 29 in some parts of Sumgait, Soviet marines from the Caspian Sea flotilla and a parachute regiment arrived and martial law was imposed. The same evening, several thousand Azeri youth held a demonstration in the square by the bus station, which the Soviet military dispersed with the use of force, causing several Azeri casualties. The official death toll of the Sumgait violence was 32, of which six were Azeri, and more than 400 alleged culprits were arrested.[58] Following the killings, 14,000 Sumgait Armenians were evacuated from the city and the republic and several thousand additional Armenians from throughout Azerbaijan joined them.

Excessive violence might not have been planned in advance, but the fact that high casualty figures were obviously linked to the Azerbaijani police forces' standing by raised suspicions about the Azerbaijani authorities' complicity in at least the initial part of the demonstrations, which were probably later hijacked by the extremists.[59] One of the Azeri authorities who was accused of involvement in the violence was Jehangir Muslimzada, First Secretary of the Sumgait party gorkom (city committee). Muslimzada argued that "in order to restrain" the demonstrators he joined them, but when an extremist group split from the main column, he couldn't stop them. The court accused Muslimzada also of not asking for reinforcements and for failing to evacuate Armenian families to safe areas.[60] The case against Muslimzada displayed how the Azerbaijani ruling elite was swept by the rising tide of nationalist euphoria of the Azerbaijani population. Muslimzada was removed from office by the Sumgait party gorkom for "political negligence, major shortcomings in organizational and political work, and conduct not befitting a party member, which led to tragic consequences in the city."[61]

In the wake of the massacre additional Soviet troops were sent to Sumgait to restore order. Several Azeris were arrested and were prosecuted for participating in the riots and massacres. Those who were considered major culprits appeared in the courts of the Russian Federation to facilitate Armenian witnesses to testify more freely, while those whose involvement was minor were tried in secret sessions of the courts in Sumgait. Since Armenia had demanded that Moscow prosecute the Sumgait rioters in courts outside Azerbaijan, Azeris' doubts regarding impartiality of Moscow seemed to have been vindicated.[62] At the end of the trials 80 people were convicted and one of them, Akhmed Akhmedov, was executed.[63]

Although Armenians accused even First Secretary Baghirov of masterminding the Sumgait violence, Moscow exempted him from prosecution. Many Armenian survivors of the violence accused AzCP officials of providing the mob names and addresses of Armenians and for supplying homemade weapons. A Sumgait paper, *Kommunist Sumgaita*, claimed that the Azerbaijan Pipe-Rolling Plant produced axes, knives and other objects used during the attacks by "hooligan elements".[64] For their part, Azeri residents of Sumgait blamed Armenian provocateurs for instigating the hostilities.[65] Azerbaijan's Prosecutor General, however, rejected both the Azeri and Armenian claims that the violence was premeditated.[66]

Although it is difficult to ascertain to what extent official complicity, if ever, was the case, the way authorities handled the violence suggests that the former probably wanted to intimidate Armenians in the NKAO by demonstrating what could befall them if they "didn't behave". If this was the case, the actual use of force must have far exceeded what the authorities had planned for. The magnitude of the Sumgait events also led some of the Azerbaijani intelligentsia to assume, publicly if not privately, positions reminiscent of the pre-1988 era when most paid lip service to friendship between Soviet peoples. "People's Poet", Bakhtiyar Vahabzade, wrote an article in early March, calling for the continuation of the friendship between the Azeris and the Armenians throughout the Azerbaijani territory.[67] A year later, when interethnic conflict began to turn into civil war, Zia Buniatov wrote an article in which he denied Azerbaijani culpability. He maintained that the Sumgait events were planned and implemented by Armenian nationalists to discredit Azerbaijan, and the murderer of the first five Armenians was an Armenian named Grigorian.[68]

In the Politburo session on February 29 Gorbachev argued that what was needed to stop violence in the region was ideological work. He said: "The main thing now is we need to send the working class, people's volunteers into the fight with the criminals. That, I can tell you, will stop any hooligans and extremists."[69] It was ironic that Gorbachev, who in general was discarding Marxist discourse, wanted to rely on it to call for socialist brotherhood of peoples. His statement showed that he failed to understand the magnitude of the rising nationalist tide that was engulfing the whole region.

Strikes Resume in the NKAO

In mid-March 1988 there were mass demonstrations in Yerevan, which were organized by a 1,000-strong committee supposedly representing a multitude of grass-roots organizations of various cities and enterprises. The committee was called "the Union for National Self-Determination", which Moscow tried to discredit as extremist.[70] Demonstrators carried placards bearing two dates, 1915 and 1988, comparing the Sumgait massacre to the 1915 massacres in Turkey. Arkady Gukasian, now president of Karabagh, characterized the Sumgait events as "an attempt to frighten [NKAO Armenians], to say 'look, the same thing will happen to you'."[71]

The local Communist Party apparatus in the NKAO, staffed mostly by ethnic Armenians, was also swept by nationalist excitement. The NKAO *obkom* called for the "restoration" of the oblast to Armenia after 70,000 people demonstrated earlier in the day in the capital city of Stepanakert. The same *obkom* had called for restraint earlier during the February 1988 demonstrations when it was prodded by Moscow to do so. The March resolution of the NKAO *obkom* was all the more significant because Boris Kevorkov, the oblast's first secretary for 15 years, was sacked on February 24 for failing to carry out his duties, by failing to stem the rising nationalist tide. Genrikh Pagosyan replaced him with the Baku leadership's approval.[72] Pagosyan was expected to bring calm to the NKAO, but during his term it would be more difficult to rein in nationalist agitation.

The strikes in Stepanakert, the major population center in the NKAO, resumed in late March 1988. They paralyzed factories and public transport. A spokesman for the town's official newspaper, *Sovietski Karabagh*, stated that only essential services were working, such as water pumping stations and bakeries, and that the strikes would continue until the NKAO was transferred to Armenia.[73] The immediate cause for the strikes seemed to be the USSR Supreme Soviet's March 24, 1988 resolution. NKAO Armenians ceased demonstrations in late February 1988 after Gorbachev had promised that the Central Committee of the CPSU would deal with their grievances. The fact that the Supreme Soviet, rather than the Central Committee, dealt with the issue and that secession of the NKAO was not considered an option was a major reason for the resumption of the demonstrations.[74] The fact that strikes in Armenia did not resume when they did in the NKAO might be indicative of the fact that the NKAO Armenians enjoyed a substantial amount of autonomy from the Yerevan activists.

One of the reasons for the rise of nationalistic feelings in the NKAO was that its population had long harbored grievances related to the perceived shortcomings of the Azerbaijani authorities. The *Moscow News*, a weekly English language journal, published in March 1988 a report by Karen Khachutarov, an ethnic Armenian, which referred to undated census figures to suggest that the Azerbaijani authorities deliberately tried to reduce the NKAO's Armenian population. He argued: "[O]ver two decades (1959–1979) the percentage of Armenians [in the NKAO] dropped from 84.4 to 75.8 percent while that of the Azerbaijanis increased from 13.8 to 22.9 percent."[75] He added that Armenians were once a majority in the Nakhichevan Autonomous Republic, but their ratio there dropped to 2 percent eventually. He added that the reason for the situation in the NKAO was "the deformation of the socio-economic and cultural conditions of life in the autonomous region [sic]." He argued:

> Statisticians have prepared for the NKAR [NKAO] a place under the sun in all indices. But there are weighty reasons for doubting these optimistic calculations. The rights to autonomy have been limited and

> are sometimes even fictitious. Even an appointment to the job of doctor or teacher is sanctioned by the republican ministry. A blind curtain has been put up between the NKAR [NKAO] and Armenia, from where [NKAO residents] could [have] at least receive[d] books in their native language. Even the curricula of the humanities faculty of the Stepanakert Pedagogical Institute, the only higher educational establishment in the autonomous region, have no course on the history and geography of Armenia. The social sphere has been particularly neglected. The metal structures of the planned sports complex have turned rusty. The promises to build a house of Young Pioneers and other childcare institutions have not been honored for years. … There is much bitterness and resentment that have been accumulating for decades in Nagorno-Karabagh, and people lay the blame on the former leadership of Azerbaijan and the Nagorno-Karabagh Autonomous Region.[76]

Reports drew links between the socio-economic shortcomings, which they blamed on the Azerbaijani authorities and the nationalist euphoria that engulfed the oblast. In March the Moscow newspaper *Trud* reported that among the NKAO residents' grievances, lack of housing, intermittent supply of tap and irrigation water and the disrepair of public highways as compared to those in Azerbaijan proper ranked highly. The paper also alleged that the Azerbaijani authorities and their NKAO subordinates deliberately misled the USSR *Gosplan* (Central Planning Organization) by trivializing the needs of the NKAO. Although *Trud* also mentioned that there were quite impressive achievements attained by the NKAO, including dramatic increases in industrial and agricultural outputs in the last 15 years, the overall emphasis was on shortcomings, which probably reflected how the inhabitants of the oblast saw the balance sheet as well.

Other reports drew attention to lack of childcare centers and the unfulfilled promise of a new sports complex in the NKAO, whose construction progressed very slowly. More importantly, however, NKAO Armenians complained that their autonomy remained just on paper. They protested that security personnel, as well as bureaucrats who assigned apartments in the oblast were mostly ethnic Azeris. They criticized that the authorities as having deliberately complicated all kinds of links between the NKAO and Armenia and that they were still unable to watch TV broadcasts originating in the Armenian Republic.[77]

In referring to NKAO Armenians' grievances, a well-informed observer, Thomas de Waal, suggested that the Azeris of the NKAO for their part complained that the local Armenian authorities discriminated against them, their towns and villages. Yet he suggested:

> The Armenian intelligentsia had a long list of cultural complaints. For example, there was no Armenian-language television in Nagorn[o] Karabagh; the history of Armenia was not taught in Armenian-language schools; 24 April, Genocide Day, was not marked in Stepanakert; the director of the local museum, Shagen Mkrtchian, was sacked on orders from Baku. One strongly felt grievance was that the dozens of Armenian medieval churches in Karabagh were not only closed for worship, but falling down for lack of upkeep. Karabagh Armenians contrasted their situation to that in Armenia, where national culture was undergoing its officially sanctioned revival. In other words, their complaint was that Azerbaijan was suppressing their demands to have Nagorn[o] Karabagh as a distinctly Armenian region. To Azerbaijanis, this was insupportable, for they had their own notions of Karabagh as a distinctly Azerbaijani region, with long cultural and historical traditions.[78]

Indeed, Azeri political and academic elite adamantly refused Armenian claims that the NKAO was more backward socio-economically than the rest of the republic and that the republican authorities were responsible for it. The republic's various media organs published data that argued that the NKAO was ahead of the rest of Azerbaijan in terms of hospital beds and doctors per capita as well as the number of child care centers and libraries. If there were a few fields in which the oblast lagged behind the rest of the Republic, the Azeris argued, these were the consequences of the Soviet command system and not of deliberate policy decisions of the AzCP or the Azerbaijani government.[79] To prove their point, Azeris argued that the NKAO received more in terms of budgetary allocation than the more populous Nakhichevan, inhabited mostly by ethnic Azeris.[80] Another observer of the Azerbaijani scene, Audrey Altstadt, argued that the NKAO's administrative and party apparatus was heavily Armenian and most of whom spoke no Azeri, which, she claimed, proved that the oblast enjoyed genuine autonomy.[81]

The above-quoted Thomas de Waal suggests that although visitors to the NKAO in the late 1980s were struck by its apparent neglect, the oblast was not worse off than the rest of Azerbaijan.[82] In 1994 Robert Kocharian, who was then president of the breakaway region, told an interviewer that neglect was not the real issue for Karabagh Armenians, saying the latter would still have revolted even if they were more affluent. For him, it was Armenian nationalism that motivated them.[83]

Moscow's Measures Falter after Initial Success

On March 9, 1988, anxious to cope with the spiraling ethnic upheaval in both republics, Gorbachev charged the Secretariat of the Central Committee to come up with solutions to the NKAO problem.[84] Later, the USSR Supreme Soviet, headed by Andrei Gromyko, stated that unification of the NKAO with Armenia through efforts of "extremist organizations" was intolerable and this unification could "lead to unpredictable consequences." To foil the attempts of the "extremists", the Supreme Soviet resolved that "the USSR Council of Ministers should work out measures for solving ripe problems of the economic, social, and cultural development of the Nagorno-Karabagh autonomous region [sic]."[85]

Next day the Central Committee of the CPSU and the USSR Council of Ministers adopted resolutions to "accelerate the social and economic development" of the NKAO "in the 1988–1995" period, which were later approved by the Politburo of the Central Committee of the CPSU. The Politburo statement asserted that

> … considerable expansion of construction of housing, general education schools, preschool establishments, hospitals, and other social and cultural facilities is envisioned. Work on ensuring reliable reception of the all-union television channel, as well as the full range of broadcasts by Azerbaijani and Armenian television will be completed. There will be an increase in the amount of literature published in Armenian, and there will be an expansion of restoration and renovation work on historical and cultural monuments.[86]

Immediately afterwards, the Communist Parties of Azerbaijan, Armenia and the NKAO *obkom* backed the Politburo statement and stopped denouncing each other. All three banned public demonstrations and passed resolutions similar to that of the all-Union Politburo. Moreover, withdrawing their earlier objections to the Armenian claims of neglect, the AzCP and the NKAO party officials announced that economic and social reforms and investments in the NKAO would eradicate existing economic problems and would provide the NKAO residents with more Armenian language books and access to Armenian TV broadcasts from Yerevan.[87]

During the same week, a group of senior officials of the USSR Gosplan, all-Union government ministers and high-level bureaucrats traveled to Stepanakert. There they outlined a program of economic and social development for the NKAO providing for: increase in the availability of adequate housing, single shift teaching in "general education schools" by 1995, a palace of culture, a 400-bed oblast hospital, a young "pioneers' house", a city library in Stepanakert, access to Armenian TV broadcasts, modernization of the NKAO airport, provision of natural gas supplies to rural areas, and elimination of tap water shortages.[88] The program made it obvious that the CPSU was trying to cope with the nationalist fervor by throwing money on tangible problems.

In October 1988 First Secretary of the Armenian CP, Suren Arutrunyan, declared that Moscow's efforts had already begun to bear fruits and that Armenia had established close economic, spiritual and cultural contacts with the NKAO. He stated: "Active assistance will be rendered [to the NKAO] in establishing production facilities for electrical engineering, electronic and light industries. Preparatory work is under way to lay on a gas supply pipeline for the oblast. [sic]" Arutrunyan added that Armenia would also invest in the agro-industrial enterprises in the oblast and would help the NKAO to solve its housing problem. He stated that quotas were set aside for the NKAO students at higher education institutions in Armenia.[89] The fact that Armenia was allowed to get involved in such a substantial way in the neighboring republic indicates that Moscow was trying as vigorously as possible to respond to the gripes of the NKAO activists. However, the fact that the Azerbaijan CP was compelled by Moscow to stand by while Armenia was actively interfering in the oblast's internal affairs further harmed the Azerbaijani ruling elite's public image, contributing to the appeal of the Azerbaijani nationalist activists.

The fact that Moscow was still able to influence Yerevan became apparent when the Armenian SSR Supreme Soviet Presidium banned on March 25, 1988 the Karabagh Committee that had organized the "unification with the NKAO" demonstrations in Armenia.[90] Yerevan's deed might have been part of an effort to curry favor with Moscow, although such action did not preclude the possibility that it was just a face-saving measure. Despite its banning of "extremist" groupings, Yerevan probably still expected unification with the NKAO and hoped that such an outcome would reduce the appeal of the non-party opposition.

Media organs of the Armenian CP, furthermore, denounced such "extremist" leaders as Paruir Airikyan and Sergei Grigoriants as anti-Soviet and as "troublemakers."[91] Yerevan's move exhibited all the hallmarks of an administration struggling to preserve its authority as "defender of national rights" by isolating obvious contenders in various ways. Yerevan believed that convincing the Armenian public to support a subtle approach toward Moscow could allow it to use moderate repression of the "extremists". Azerbaijan, for its part, banned the pro-unification Krunk committee from operating in the NKAO.[92]

A samizdat, supposedly issued by "senior and junior members of the Institute of Art and Architecture in Baku" throws some light on the emergence of popular excitement centering on "the national issue", the Karabagh problem. The samizdat is all the more important because intellectuals in Azerbaijan, as in other Muslim republics, did not have the habit of issuing samizdats. The Azerbaijani samizdat hence epitomized how significant an impact the NKAO had on the Azerbaijani intelligentsia who felt the urgency of presenting its disapproval of the Baku regime and Moscow. The date of the samizdat is unknown, but one could surmise from its content that it came out sometime during the February–May 1988 period.

The samizdat blamed the Sumgait events of February 1988 on the erroneous policies of Moscow and Baku and on social and ecological factors, including the overcrowding of the city, excessive pollution, and lack of communal housing. The writers, apparently still impressed with Gorbachev's reforms, mostly blamed the Baku leadership, who, they said, failed to defend the interests of the refugees who were expelled from Armenia and were later housed in cramped quarters in Sumgait. The samizdat also blamed the Azerbaijani intellectuals for having failed to challenge the authorities to correct the mistakes made during recent years. The writers claimed that the Karabagh events served as a watershed in the evolution of the increased "social" awareness, a code word in those days for "national interests", and that "Azerbaijani intellectuals would henceforth be more actively involved in politics."[93]

Another samizdat that appeared in late 1988 or early 1989, though it praised Gorbachev's perestroika policy, was more boldly anti-AzCP, which showed that time that passed since mid-1988 had radicalized the nationalist intelligentsia. The samizdat even complimented the USSR CP for dealing successfully with the NKAO crisis but warned that tensions could rise again. The samizdat blamed the AzCP for being ineffective and weak because the latter "avoided taking decisions on a series of ideological problems related to internationalist education in the NKAO, [and] leaving the autonomous oblast to its own devices". It also criticized the Azerbaijani leadership for failing to contain Armenian nationalists in the oblast at the right time. More importantly, the samizdat threatened that unless the NKAO problem was solved to the satisfaction of Azerbaijan, the Azeris could become more nationalist and religious, which could lead them to seek closer ties with "brothers", meaning the Turks of Turkey and the Azeris of northern Iran.[94]

In Armenia, despite Yerevan's ban, demonstrations continued. On May 29, 1988 Armenians demonstrated in the Opera Square calling for the USSR CP Central Committee to unite the NKAO with the republic. During the six days immediately preceding the May 29 rally, 1,000 students had taken part in a sit-in in the Square, which contributed to the public fervor. On May 30, 1988 thousands again took part in public rallies. In the NKAO most Armenians had been on general strike since May 22, 1988 and there were daily public rallies as well.[95] On May 31, in accordance with the trend of bowing to public pressure, the recently appointed party boss, Genrikh Pogosyan, called on Moscow to place the NKAO under direct Russian rule. Although this demand fell short of the nationalist demand of uniting the oblast with Armenia, its implementation, nevertheless, could have led to the separation of the NKAO from Azerbaijan.[96] Pogosyan's advocacy of such a solution shows that Baku's hold on the oblast was increasingly becoming untenable.

During the same week, Azerbaijani authorities of the NKAO's mainly Azeri town of Shusha began firing ethnic Armenians from their jobs, while ethnic Azeris were sacked from jobs in the mostly ethnic Armenian NKAO town of Stepanakert. This was low-intensity ethnic cleansing conducted by both sides, although it was not clear who started it.[97] Large-scale population exchanges had started in the wake of the Sumgait violence when Armenians from throughout Azerbaijan began migrating to Armenia and the NKAO, while the Azeris – after being intimidated by similar violence in Armenia – began leaving for Azerbaijan.[98] One such incident took place on May 11, 1988 when anti-Azeri intimidation forced ethnic Azeris in Armenia's Araratskiy raion to migrate to Azerbaijan in large numbers.[99]

Moscow's reaction to the Azeri and Armenian officialdoms' growing embrace of nationalistic rhetoric, and their inability to stop ethnic cleansing and escalating violence, came on May 21, 1988 when republican communist parties in both republics were forced to replace their first secretaries. With Gorbachev's prodding they sacked Kamran Baghirov and Karen Demirchian from their posts as republican first secretaries and appointed in their place Abdur Rahman Vezirov, who was serving as Soviet Ambassador to Pakistan, and Suren Arutrunyan, who was with the USSR Communist Party in Moscow.[100] Apparently Gorbachev hoped that these "outsiders" would be less vulnerable to the sentiments dominating their republics. Yet soon Gorbachev would begin to criticize Harutiunian for currying favor with the nationalists. At the July 18, 1988 session of the USSR Supreme Soviet, Gorbachev quarreled with some Armenian delegates, arguing that they proved less introspective than Azerbaijani delegates and took part in an anti-perestroika campaign.[101]

Indeed, the replacement of the first secretaries did not seem to have had an impact on the developments in the NKAO when strikes entered their third week at the time. In Stepanakert and such raion centers as Martuni, Mardakert, and Askeran, strikes brought most industrial enterprises and public transport to a standstill during the last week of May 1988. Shops selling consumer goods and foodstuffs remained closed, and economic and other links with Baku were disrupted. Armed Armenian militants were spotted setting up what they called "self-defense posts" to militarily defend the areas they began to control in the oblast. The banned Krunk Committee seemed in charge of public rallies and strikes, while the oblast CP organization seemed ill at ease or unwilling to stem the tide of nationalist euphoria.[102]

4

Inter-Communal Fighting and Ethnic Cleansing

On June 9, 1988 a group of deputies of the Armenian Supreme Soviet asked the Presidium of the same body to discuss the resolution adopted on February 20, 1988 by the extraordinary session of the NKAO Soviet of People's Deputies, petitioning the Armenian and Azeri Supreme Soviets to transfer the NKAO from the AzSSR jurisdiction to the ASSR.[1] After learning of the Armenian deputies' behavior, the Presidium of the Azerbaijani Supreme Soviet met at once and belatedly rejected the NKAO's petition, which had earlier been left unanswered by both Baku and Yerevan.[2] The same day, Vezirov told this decision to a crowd of "workers" and AzCP members.

On June 13 the Armenian first secretary, Arutrunyan, told participants at a rally that the response of the republic's Supreme Soviet would be positive and consequently the general strike in progress should be ended.[3] As heralded, the Armenian Supreme Soviet voted unanimously on June 15 to accept the NKAO's demand.[4] The resolution adopted by the Armenian Supreme Soviet was

> requesting the Supreme Soviet of the USSR to consider and settle positively the question of the transfer of the Nagorno-Karabagh Autonomous Oblast from the structure of the Azerbaijan SSR into the structure of the Armenian SSR; and [t]o address the Supreme Soviet of the Azerbaijan SSR in the hope that such a resolution will not disturb the traditional good-neighborly relations between the two

> republics, but will be received by the Azerbaijani republic with understanding.[5]

Azerbaijani and Armenian CP resolutions further demonstrated that the ruling elites were openly embracing popular demands which would have been unthinkable only months ago.

Meanwhile, ethnic cleansing went unabated. Armenians who fled Sumgait and other Azerbaijani towns and villages were settled in homes in Armenia, which had been abandoned by ethnic Azeris who were forced to leave for Azerbaijan earlier. Some of the Armenian refugees were resettled in the NKAO, especially in the mainly Armenian town of Stepanakert.[6] The fact that Baku, which had tried to reverse the Armenianization of the oblast for decades, was helpless to physically prevent Armenian refugees from settling in the oblast suggests that Armenian paramilitaries in the oblast were in control. For their part, Azeri refugees fleeing Armenia usually sought refuge in Nakhichevan, where most were resettled. Others were resettled in other raions, including Shamkhor, Kuba, Kazakh, and Zhdanov.[7]

At the 19th National Conference of the CPSU, which started on June 28, both the AzCP and the ACP first secretaries, Vezirov and Arutrunyan, spoke. The speech of Vezirov was predictable in that he promised the improvement of life in the NKAO and offered cooperation with the Armenian CP to solve the oblast's problems.[8] Arutrunyan's speech was, however, unconventional. Drastically revising the standard rhetoric of his party, he said that the demonstrations in the NKAO and Armenia were not caused by extremist elements. He stated that such a characterization would be

> [a] very simplified representation. … I cannot omit to say here, comrades, that such explanations are painfully offensive to the national feelings of the communists and the working people of our republic. … It is now urgently necessary to elaborate new political thinking on the national issue. … [N]ot a single serious problem can be solved without renouncing old-fashioned approaches and stereotypes.[9]

Arutrunyan added that one could argue that national problems were artificially created. Yet once created, he said, they became real and should not be dealt with using old-fashioned approaches. After the Conference, Arutrunyan addressed a crowd in the Theater (*Teatralnaya*) Square in Yerevan, where his pleas for calm were rejected by the "strike committee". He said that now Moscow was going to deal with the problem and that Armenians should stop demonstrations and give Moscow a chance. The strike committee, however, called for a general strike.[10] Although for a while the general strike was not widely observed, it eventually acquired widespread adherence.

On July 12 the NKAO Soviet of People's Deputies once again voted to join Armenia. Out of the Soviet's 150 members, 102 ethnic Armenian deputies voted in favor of the resolution, while ethnic Azeri members once again did not participate in the session. The Presidium of Azerbaijan's Supreme Soviet declared the resolution null and void based "on the strength of Article 87 of the Constitution of the USSR, Article 114 of the Constitution of Azerbaijan, and Article 42 of the Law of the Azerbaijani Soviet Socialist Republic on the Nagorno-Karabagh Autonomous Region."[11] The first two articles barred territorial changes without the consent of the republics concerned.

Volskiy's "Special Commission"

Within a few days the Presidium of the USSR Supreme Soviet took up the question of the NKAO. The result was a decision on July 18, 1988 to establish a "special commission" to "observe" the conditions in the NKAO to "strengthen and develop" its autonomy.[12] Arkadiy N. Volskiy, a USSR Central Committee member and close associate of Gorbachev, was appointed head of the special commission. Although by referring to the earlier decisions the Supreme Soviet affirmed the NKAO's status as part of Azerbaijan, its involvement of Armenia in the settlement of the dispute implied its recognition of the dispute as a virtual inter-republican dispute rather than an intra-Azerbaijan dispute. Volskiy imposed martial law in such areas as Stepanakert and the adjoining Aghdam to the east of the oblast. By doing so, the Volskiy Commission detached the NKAO from Baku's direct rule.

In the NKAO Volskiy functioned like a governor-general, feeling responsible, in his own words, for everything "from inseminating cows to military issues."[13] He enjoyed the respect of both parties and was initially able to dampen tensions. Economic recovery was among his priorities because strikes in the oblast had brought the economy to a standstill. Boris Nefyodov, Volskiy's chief aide, suggested that a strike at the condenser factory in Stepanakert had undermined production at 65 television and radio factories throughout the union.[14] Volskiy even had to get involved when Armenian militants of Vank prevented Azeri shepherds from bringing down half a million sheep from their summer pastures. He protested saying "sheep have no national ambitions."[15]

The above-mentioned July 18 meeting of the USSR Presidium of the Supreme Soviet was interesting also in that it witnessed the speeches of the chairman of the Azerbaijani Supreme Soviet, Suleiman Tatliev, and first secretary of the NKAO Committee of the AzCP, Genrikh Pogosyan.[16] Tatliev was unequivocal about his rejection of any change in the status of the NKAO. He complained that the Baku-appointed first secretary of the NKAO, Pogosyan, did not follow Baku's directives, implying that Moscow had imposed him on the AzCP and that Pogosyan's allegiance lay more with his ethnic kin rather than with his formal superiors.[17] In his rebuttal Genrikh Pogosyan argued that for Armenians, Karabagh was historic patrimony and the NKAO Armenians' grievances were not solely economic and social. He suggested that the oblast's population could not be mollified solely by material benefits and that its national, cultural and spiritual wants needed to be satisfied. Pogosyan ended his speech by calling for an outright secession of the oblast from Azerbaijan.[18]

On September 19, 1988 clashes took place between Armenians and Azeris in Khojaly village near Stepanakert. Later, paramilitary Armenian forces from Stepanakert joined the fight, leading to an increase in the number of casualties.[19] This was one of the earliest signs that intercommunal fighting was getting out of control. In the following days, in the mostly Azeri town of Shusha, Armenian residents fled their homes, which were subsequently burned by local Azeri paramilitary forces. By early October 1988 both sides conducted ethnic cleansing in regions where they had the upper hand. Ethnic Azeris were thrown out of Stepanakert while ethnic Armenians were forced out of Shusha and Aghdam. Those who were forced to leave their hometowns, in most cases also lost their jobs there.[20] The continuation of the inter-communal warfare led Arkadiy Volskiy to declare on September 21 a state of emergency and introduce a night curfew in Stepanakert and Aghdam, although the latter was outside the NKAO, which was outside Volskiy's jurisdiction. Later, the state of emergency and curfew was extended to the whole NKAO, where demonstrations and strikes were outlawed.[21]

The Karabagh Committee, which since February 1988 had organized the demonstrations in Armenia, issued in September 1988 a list of "short-term" demands to make Armenia more sovereign. The list included such goals as economic independence, the closure of the Medzamor nuclear power plant near Yerevan, the struggle by Armenians to reclaim territories lost to Turkey, acknowledgement by the USSR Supreme Soviet of the 1915 massacres of Armenians in Ottoman Turkey and the creation of the Armenian-only divisions within the Soviet Army.[22]

The Azerbaijani side's response to such demands in those days was still relatively timid. Many unofficial grass-roots campaign publications referred to the dispute within the limits of glasnost as delineated by Moscow. A number of samizdats and letters to editors of various publications in the Soviet Union and written by members of Azerbaijan's intellectual elite were published in the West. One of them was signed by the so-called "Initiative Group of the Institute of Oriental Studies of the Academy of Sciences of the Azerbaijan SSR". The authors praised perestroika and characterized Armenian secessionism and irredentism as "serious and well-organized counter-action[s undertaken] by anti-perestroika forces, and as challenge[s] to democracy and to the Soviet [C]onstitution."[23] The authors blamed the anti-Gorbachev bureaucracy for "fanning nationalism among the passive masses" because it failed to neutralize the "healthy forces of the party leadership through the usual 'palace revolution'." The authors also blamed the ACP leader, Demirchian, for channeling the dissatisfaction of the masses regarding economic, social and ideological shortcomings in Armenia into "nationalist ambitions".[24]

The timidity of such Azerbaijani initiatives was to disappear by late 1988. Starting in November 1988 the demonstrations in Baku – while still focusing on the NKAO problem – also put forward such demands as revival of the Azeri language, preservation of historical monuments, and protection of the environment. They also called for Moscow's more equitable economic and pricing policies, which, they argued, were hitherto contrary to the interests of the Azerbaijani population. During this period, a number of unofficial newspapers and journals also cropped up to campaign for the same demands.[25]

Violence also spread throughout Azerbaijan. On November 24 Azeri irregulars attacked Armenians in Kirovabad (Ganja) and Nakhichevan, and Soviet Interior Ministry troops had to intervene to stop the violence. Nakhichevan and Kirovabad had been, as was Baku, under emergency rule since November 20, but this didn't prevent hostilities.[26] As a result 1,700 Armenians were airlifted from Kirovabad and Nakhichevan to Armenia.[27] In Azerbaijan emergency rule meant control by Soviet military forces, which, it appeared, were not accountable to the AzCP or the Azerbaijani government.' Soviet military commanders issued orders and imposed curfews as they deemed necessary. Their decrees not only dealt with riots but also with matters such as sanitary measures, municipalities or civilian health authorities were supposed to deal with.[28]

Meanwhile, the first secretary of the NKAO, Genrikh Pogosyan, increasingly made use of nationalist rhetoric. By November 1988 he was committed to the policy of unification with Armenia. In mid-November 1988 he stated that

> the oblast [NKAO] should immediately be brought out of the structure of the Azerbaijan SSR. ... The Artsakh [NKAO] people firmly believe that traditional justice will be revived and that the Armenian people, who have been artificially [divided] will be united again.[29]

While Pogosyan was making this statement, he was virtually powerless because the Moscow-appointed administrator Volskiy and Soviet military forces were in charge in the oblast.

While Moscow was trying to keep violence from expanding, its concessions to the Armenian inhabitants of the NKAO had begun to bear fruits by November 1988. From February 1988 the Armenian Republic undertook many projects in the oblast while Azerbaijani authorities stood by. TV and radio relay stations were built to enable broadcasts from Armenia to reach the oblast. The Armenian SSR State Construction Institute began the construction of two nine-storey housing units in 1988 and projected the construction of two more such units in 1989. The Institute set up an office in the NKAO to work on plans to build up to 10,000 square meters of housing units, 1,000-seat schools, and 300-seat kindergartens annually.[30] The ACP first secretary, Suren Arutrunyan, explained that in 1988 feasibility studies for a culture center, a "pioneers' house" and a city library in Stepanakert were conducted. He also suggested that Armenia prepared to build a road linking Stepanakert to Goris, thus connecting Armenia with the NKAO.[31]

While Azerbaijani authorities seemed to half-heartedly raise objections to Armenia's construction and economic activities in the NKAO, the nascent Azeri grass-roots organizations adopted a more vocal opposition. On November 22, 1988 500,000 people demonstrated in Baku to demand that the NKAO remained a part of Azerbaijan. Next day 800,000 Azeris held a rally in the same city to call a halt to the construction activities of Armenia in the NKAO. A particular project, the rumored construction of an aluminum plant in the Topkhane area near Shusha, drew the ire of the protesters. Later, it turned out that the construction was a resort for the workers of the Kanakert aluminum plant in Armenia, but this did not dull the rage Azeris felt.[32] Azeri protesters opposed the project because: 1) it symbolized Armenia's involvement in the NKAO affairs; 2) its construction near the Topkhane natural park raised environmental concerns; and 3) it could change population ratios in the mostly Azeri Shusha.

Escalation

Like the Baku demonstrators, members of the Azeri intellectual elite also began to leave behind their enthusiasm for Gorbachev's reforms. Since the 1970s they had aired ethno-cultural grievances and taken part in the subtle celebration of Azerbaijan's pre-Soviet historical and literary achievements. Sometime during the second half of 1988, these few elite concluded that the Azerbaijani and Soviet party and state apparatuses were mishandling the current problems and moved to a more independent stance. Nevertheless, initially the intellectual elite's impact on the demonstrators would be limited. Instead, activists with little or no background in politics would rise to the challenge and control the crowds.

On November 17 mass demonstrations began to take place on a daily basis in Lenin Square, facing the House of the Soviets. Crowds, in general, carried the flag of independent Azerbaijan (1918–1920), while occasionally the national flags of Turkey or Iran would be spotted. Virtually unknown leaders emerged due to their ability to get hold of the crowds. One such leader was Neimat Panakhov, who in 1988 was a 27-year-old factory worker. By the end of 1988 the number of "informal" organizations had reached forty. The more prominent ones among them included Dirchelish (Revival), the Committee of People's Aid for Karabagh, the People's Front of the Kizilbash, Yurd (Homeland), Birlik (Unity), and Yeni Musavat (New Musavat).[33]

After the daily demonstrations many remained in the square at night seeking shelter in makeshift tents. Hundreds of thousands of demonstrators called for an end to Armenia's involvement in the NKAO, including the former's socio-economic investments. The "People's Poet", Bakhtiyar Vahabzade, for his part, spoke to demand the establishment of an autonomous oblast in Armenia for resident ethnic Azeris, the equivalent of the NKAO for the Azeris.[34] Although the immediate cause for the participation of most protesters was the anxiety they felt over the Karabagh dispute and Armenia's increased prominence in the NKAO affairs, their endeavor led to the emergence of the Azerbaijan Popular Front (APF), a mass movement that eventually adopted a more comprehensive program.[35]

Several AzCP and government officials also addressed the crowds and tried to present the AzCP's stance in the NKAO dispute as the correct one. In the meantime, the AzSSR Council of Ministers abrogated on November 30 the NKAO Gorilspolkom's November 1, 1988 decision to allocate six hectares of land to Armenia's Kanakert aluminum plant in the Topkhane region.[36] Even AzCP First Secretary Abdul Rahman Vezirov attended some of the demonstrations in Lenin Square and listened to the grievances of some of the participants.

Nevertheless, the continuation of the demonstrations made the AzCP uneasy, leading the President of Azerbaijan Supreme Soviet to adopt on November 23 "special measures" including curfews in such cities as Baku, Ganja and Nakhichevan. Yet, despite the curfew, the Lenin Square protests lasted for one more week during which armed clashes between the demonstrators and the police took place. In the end, on December 5 security forces arrested those who had remained in the square and the square was closed to public rallies.[37] People such as the aforementioned Neimat Panakhov were arrested and remained in custody for six months.[38]

While demonstrations in both Armenia and Azerbaijan were continuing, ethnic cleansing persisted. Those who fled were in most cases forced to do so. There were, however, meandering ways employed by both sides: Azerbaijani and Armenian factories began dismissing workers who had the "undesirable" ethnic credentials.[39] In Armenia, Azeris in Kalininskiy, Gorisskiy, Gugarkskiy, and Vardenisskiy raions faced armed assault by paramilitary forces if they chose to stay behind.[40] Most Azeris expelled from Armenia used to live in Kafan (in Zangezur in the south), Idzhevan (in the north, near the border), Razdan (in the north), Dilidzhan (in the north), and Masis (in the west, near Yerevan and the Turkish border).

On December 7 there was a strong earthquake whose epicenter was in Spitak, Armenia, and more than 25,000 lives were lost. The disaster did not end the struggle for the NKAO, however. An article in *Krasnaya Zvezda* noted that the officially disbanded Karabagh Committee continued under the "Karabagh Movement of Armenia" and that after the earthquake it met almost daily in the building of the republic's Writers' Union.[41] More importantly, new means began to be employed in the conflict. Azeri and Armenian militants stopped trains in either direction along the Yerevan–Nakhichevan–Baku railroad. These militants belonged mostly to the Karabagh Committee in Armenia,and to the APF in Azerbaijan.[42]

Azerbaijan Khalg Jabhasi (APF)

The Armenian National Movement (Haiots Hamazgain Sharzhum or ANM) was born with the Karabagh demonstrations in Yerevan in 1988 and its leaders were mostly intellectuals.[43] The ANM combined Armenian nationalism with ecological concerns, the struggle for economic independence and a democratic political system. In Armenia, already in the moderate atmosphere of the 1950s and the 1960s, "unorthodox" nationalism or even separatism had emerged. This nationalism was different from the Moscow-sanctioned "official nationalism" or the republics' sanctioned celebrations of traditions, ethnic pride and celebrations of the achievements of selected national heroes.

In 1988 a reporter of Komsomolskaya Pravda described how the Soviet-era subtle anti-Turkish stance evolved into irredentism focused on the NKAO:

> For nearly two years in the Nagorno-Karabagh Autonomous Oblast, there have been collections of signatures among the population, meetings in the labor collectives, and sessions of some raion soviets. In Armenia, over that same two-year period, signatures have been collected for petitions. Hundreds of letters and telegrams have been sent to Moscow requesting that the problem of Nagorno-Karabagh be [re]examined.[44]

In Azerbaijan, however, Azerbaijan Khalg Jabhasi (APF) was never as organized or as disciplined as the ANM. The APF displayed at its initial stage, an impressive assertiveness of the Azerbaijani intelligentsia, who desired to utilize the NKAO problem as a means of democratizing the political system. Yet, when broad masses began to join the ranks of the APF, democratization lost its significance as its single most important goal. After the less-educated and less-privileged began to join the organization, such popular figures as Neimat Panakhov denounced not only the AzCP but also the urban intelligentsia who had established the APF. In 1989 the APF became an umbrella organization, including many AzCP members, pan-Turkists, Islamic radicals and those who desired a greater Azerbaijan. Many refugees from Armenia and the NKAO, as well as militant groups who favored armed action, also joined. Eventually there emerged a divide between those who wanted to focus on the NKAO dispute and those who had a larger agenda, including abolishing the one-party rule in the republic.

One might even argue, as did Ronald G. Suny, that the NKAO issue led to the failure of the democratization drive because no intellectual associated with the APF dared to accept self-determination for the NKAO.[45]

Seven "research workers" or academics at the Azerbaijan Academy of Sciences, including Araz Alizade, Leyla Yunusova, Hikmat Hajizada, Tofiq Gasymov, Yaqub Salamov, Isa Gambar and Aydin Balayev, formed the APF in all but name in mid-1988. This group originally came together to promote perestroika and was probably sanctioned by Baku, and even Moscow.[46] Initially, it was perceived as pro-perestroika, or even pro-Gorbachev. Its first program was modest, aimed at Azerbaijan's socio-economic, cultural and political sovereignty within the USSR. The founders of the APF were in general born in the 1930s, and consequently had avoided Stalin's bloody purges and military service during the Second World War. Their avoidance of major Soviet era calamities enabled this generation of the intellectual elite to be more outspoken about various socio-political issues.[47]

The APF held its formal founding congress in July 1989 at which Abulfaz Elchibey, a former dissident who was imprisoned in the 1970s on charges of pan-Turkism and Azeri nationalism, was elected chairman. The escalation of the NKAO conflict accelerated the APF's acquisition of a legal status, which took place in October 1989. The APF platform included many socio-economic and political demands, which had been increasingly debated by many APF leaders in the Azerbaijani publications during 1988 and 1989. These educated and articulate elite seemed united on the need to pursue a more assertive policy on the NKAO, but felt free to disagree on other issues. As at the turn of the century, the vagueness of the distinctions between political organizations, including those between Musavat and Himmat, the APF's differences with other organizations and the peculiarities of the various groupings within the APF were not clearly identifiable.

The first program of the APF, adopted at its founding congress, reflected its pro-Gorbachev, pro-perestroika stance. The APF, indeed, was initially wary to stay within limits set by Gorbachev. Its original name, the "Popular Front of Azerbaijan in Support of Perestroika" showed that the APF wanted to take advantage of the freedoms created by Gorbachev by presenting itself as a reformist rather than a revolutionary organization. Some alleged that its program was adapted from the Estonian Popular Front program though programs of many popular fronts then looked alike.[48] It called on all "progressive forces" to strive to facilitate the implementation of perestroika. Consequently, it stated that the APF formed a united front with the AzCP so that "along with the healthy forces within the party [AzCP] we can ensure that perestroika is carried out. …"[49]

In reality, however, Azerbaijan in 1988 was one of the most conservative Soviet republics with no dissent being tolerated. By contrast, the Armenian Communist Party (ACP) had already started to collaborate with the nationalists. A major reason for this difference was the AzCP's belief that Moscow would not tolerate the NKAO's secession and tolerating dissent could only hurt the republic, while the ACP believed that tolerating the nationalist dissent was expedient because it would help the legitimacy of the ACP as well as force Moscow to deliver on the NKAO.[50]

The APF described itself as a "general social movement aiming to improve and democratize all spheres of our lives." It argued that "the goal of the APF [was] legal government, a fully developed civil society and [Azerbaijani] citizens enjoying all their rights ands freedoms."[51] Consistent with its still timid approach, the APF added that "[t]he main task of the APF is to achieve political, economic and cultural sovereignty for the republic." Although the APF did not demand outright independence, it nevertheless portrayed its demands in such a way as to imply that it desired full-blown independence. Its program stated that "[t]he Republic of Azerbaijan should be represented as a sovereign government within international organizations such as the UN and UNESCO." The APF called for "elections at all levels [to be] general, equal, direct and by secret ballot." Still clinging to the official rhetoric, the APF professed that it was supporting Lenin's dictum "all power to the Soviets" and for that reason it would fight to transform the USSR Supreme Soviet into a genuine parliament. The front argued that the slogan: "[f]actories and plants to the workers" could be implemented "if workers' collectives played significant roles in running the enterprises, and competent factory managers were elected through free and fair elections." The People's Front further affirmed that the dictum: "[l]and to the Peasants" could be implemented if peasants enjoyed "complete freedom to cultivate the land as individual farmers or as members of collectives."[52]

Regarding the economy, the APF stated that instead of Moscow-based, all-Union ministries, Azerbaijani authorities should run the republican economic enterprises. It argued that "[i]n order to ensure equality in product exchange between republics, the system of prices and tariffs should be reviewed and brought into line with the world market."[53] This demand was the consequence of a long-term grievance that the Moscow-set terms of trade was to the detriment of Azerbaijan and other non-Slavic republics and that Azerbaijan was selling its oil too cheaply and buying such finished goods as car tyres too expensively. The program also stated that the government of Azerbaijan, rather than Moscow, should make the decisions regarding Azerbaijan's economy and that Azerbaijan should be economically self-sufficient.

The APF demanded an end to all privileges of the party *nomenklatura*, corruption, excessive bureaucracy, and regionalism (*yerbazlik*).[54] It asked for respect for human rights, individual freedoms and democratization of the legal system. It called for a re-examination of the Stalin and Brezhnev eras to determine the wrongs done to Azerbaijan during the periods of the cult of personality (Stalin) and stagnation (Brezhnev), including the forced expulsion of Azeris to other Caucasian states and to Central Asia. The APF program also demanded that long-neglected and decaying religious buildings should be renovated, freedom of conscience granted, military training in middle and high schools abolished, and in universities curtailed.

The APF also objected to Azerbaijani conscripts serving in international conflict zones, an obvious reference to Afghanistan. Despite its nationalist rhetoric, the APF did not yet call for the establishment of a national army, which was probably related to Armenia not having decided to do so as well.[55] Although the APF program did not display an irredentist stance toward Iranian Azerbaijan, it nevertheless argued that "the APF supports the restoration of the ethnic unity of Azerbaijanis living on both sides of the border."[56]

The front called for broad cultural contacts with the world community, especially with Middle Eastern nations. It stated that the official policy of attacking Islam needed to be stopped and steps taken "towards the development of understanding and cooperation with Islam."[57] Although critical of the traditional practice of the Soviet regime, the APF program, nevertheless, was moderate in demanding more respect for religion. This was indicative of the overall secular nature of the APF leadership.

Like most grass-roots organizations of the Gorbachev era, the APF dwelt on ecology. It complained about the destruction of Azerbaijani forests and the degrading of Azerbaijani agricultural lands. Moreover, the APF stipulated that any industrial enterprise harming the environment could be shut down by the decision of the local Soviet or Azerbaijan's Supreme Soviet, and all-Union decision-makers should not possess the means to reverse such decisions. The program went on to demand that Baku, Sumgait, Kirovabad (Ganja) and Ali Bayramli should be declared areas of ecological disaster.[58]

The APF considered the revival of the native language, or Azeri, as one of its most salient goals, as did other similar organizations in the Soviet Union, Although unlike other Turkic states, the Azerbaijani constitution mentioned the Azerbaijani language as the state language, Russian was the official language in practice. The APF declared that Azeri should be used in official transactions, in academic activities, and as a language of interethnic communication, a status reserved for Russian up until then. The program stated that "[t]he APF is fighting for the reinstatement of the national symbols of Azerbaijan, the nation's own name (Azeri Turks), surnames and geographical names."[59]

Gradually, the APF-AzCP relations became strained and Vezirov accused the former of undermining the AzCP's authority. Vezirov, for his part, had been First Secretary since May 1988, yet the AzCP was still dominated by former clients of Heidar Aliev, who by 1988 had retired and continued to live in Moscow.[60] The APF, for its part, increasingly came under the influence of extremist factions. The extremists, including Neimat Panakhov, were to play a major role in the late December 1989 riots at the Azerbaijan–Iran border along the Araz River. They were the ones who would attack border posts in Nakhichevan and Lenkoran and demand the unification of the two Azerbaijans.[61] Yet despite their control of the streets, the extremists in the APF failed to grab control of the APF. On July 16, 1989 Elchibey was elected chairman of the APF executive board, although at the 3rd Conference of the APF on January 6–7, 1990, the supporters of Etibar Mamedov – another moderate nationalist – would capture a majority of the seats of the Executive Committee.[62]

Moscow Introduces Direct Rule over the NKAO: January 1989

When Mikhail Sergeyevich Gorbachev came to power in 1985 the Soviet Union was relatively stable, the Communist Party rule was not challenged, the economy muddled through and the population, as Motyl suggested, was "quiescent" and to a large degree "satisfied" and "open opposition" was minimal.[63] There was a plethora of problems and the totalitarian system seemed bent on long-term demise, but this imperfect totalitarian state could have survived for an indeterminate time.[64] By 1990, five years after Gorbachev had come to power, the Soviet state was trying in vain to contain the socio-political upheaval that the Gorbachev reforms had unleashed. "The party was thoroughly delegitimized, the economy was virtually in a shambles, the population was in the streets, and open opposition was the order of the day."[65] The Gorbachev-initiated reforms had created the process of change that permitted the non-Russians to contemplate rebellion. The Gorbachev reforms from above ironically enabled the revolution from below. The reforms raised popular expectations, attacked traditional values of the Soviet state, encouraged mass participation and initiative, and attempted to democratize an imperfect totalitarian state.[66] The theory that "[r]ebellions are most likely to occur when expectations greatly outstrip the capacity for attaining them" was borne out by the events during 1988–1991 throughout the USSR.[67]

By eliminating the fear, which had been perpetuated even under Brezhnev, glasnost allowed the expression of grievances, which had built up over decades, including the arbitrary measures adopted under Stalin. Gorbachev's attempt to overhaul the corrupt political machines of the Brezhnev era led to the rise of the popular fronts, especially after the 19th Party Conference in the summer of 1988. The Secretary General's belief that he could control the newly emerging political movements was mistaken. He had to use force in the Baltic republics and Georgia (April 1989), Azerbaijan (January 1990), and Tajikistan (February 1990).[68] His reforms pushed the ruling elites to embrace freer political systems, which included competitive elections, toleration of popular fronts and criticism of the existing political regimes.

On January 12, 1989 the USSR Supreme Soviet Presidium decided to elevate the status of Arkadiy Ivanovich Volskiy from that of "special representative" to that of "Chairman of the Committee for the Administration of the NKAO."[69] Although since his earlier appointment six months previous, Volskiy in practice ran things in the oblast without interacting with Genrikh Pogosyan, the pro-Armenia first secretary of the NKAO Party Bureau, this new appointment strengthened his hand. The NKAO was now under the direct jurisdiction of USSR central organs, while the oblast remained formally part of Azerbaijan. Volskiy was empowered to tackle social, economic, cultural, ethnic and other problems. The Volskiy Committee, replacing the NKAO Council of Ministers, would consist of eight people: two ethnic Armenians, one ethnic Azeri from the oblast and five Russians. Having become redundant by this development, Genrikh Pogosyan announced on January 20, 1989 that he would retire "for health reasons."[70]

Upon assuming full responsibility, Volskiy announced that traditional links with Azerbaijan would be preserved

> as far as power supply, transport and many other types of co-operation and production [were] concerned. To destroy these today is suicide for the oblast. A boycott of that sort would be a blow not to Azerbaijan but to the population of Nagorno-Karabagh ….

Volskiy also announced that if it would make sense economically, the oblast would trade directly with Armenia or Russia, a possibility that would further enhance ties with Armenia.[71] Although the establishment of Moscow's direct rule in the NKAO was rather a pro-Armenian development, not only the ACP but also the AzCP welcomed the Supreme Soviet Presidium's decision.[72] No initial reaction came from the Armenian Karabagh Committee or the NKAO Krunk Committee or from the Azerbaijani activists.

The start of Moscow's direct rule led AzCP First Secretary Vezirov to assume his pro-Moscow role once again, because he interpreted Moscow's decision to establish direct rule over the NKAO with formal Azerbaijani sovereignty as pro-Azerbaijan. He seems also to have concluded that this development would undermine the yet insufficiently organized opposition in Azerbaijan. Vezirov denounced the latter as extremists. He also condemned those AzCP members who cooperated with the opposition, characterizing them as members of the mafia and as enemies of perestroika. Although Vezirov tolerated, and at least on one occasion took part in, the Lenin Square rallies in late November and early December 1988, he condemned them after Moscow's direct rule over the oblast started.[73] Direct rule by Moscow could have been interpreted as a stepping-stone for the long-term independence of the NKAO and its eventual annexation by Armenia. The ACP first secretary, Arutrunyan, might have thought likewise, because he also considered the establishment of direct rule as an encouraging development.[74] Perhaps the ACP's enthusiasm was the reason for the arrest of all 11 members of the Karabagh Committee active in Armenia.[75]

In an interview in April 1989 Volskiy suggested that Armenian and not Azerbaijani enthusiasm for direct rule was justified. Openly embracing the cause of the NKAO Armenians, Volskiy said:

> In many cases we are dealing with the consequences of Stalinism and the anti-democratic and anti-ethnic decisions concerning the destinies of ethnic groups. … And if today we are restoring historical and political justice in the relations among individual citizens, this means that

> we certainly must restore the same justice in relations among ethnic groups as well. … The land should belong to the person of today, the one who works it, cares for it, harvests the crops from it, the one who has built his home there, and lowered the remains of his loved ones into the ground. This is my personal opinion, but I am convinced of it.[76]

The March 1989 elections to the Congress of People's Deputies, in which multiple candidates competed for each seat, allowed more freedom of speech to the nationalist factions on the NKAO dispute.[77] Zori Balayan, for instance, was elected deputy of the NKAO and he and others advocated more openly the Armenian stance.[78]

In March 1989 agreements were signed between the Volskiy Committee, the Armenian Architects Union and the Armenian SSR Council of Ministers' main administration for the protection and maintenance of historical and cultural monuments. They targeted maintenance and repair of architectural monuments in the NKAO. In addition they provided that NKAO architects would be trained in Armenia.[79] A similar occurrence was the incorporation of the NKAO's "NKAO 60th Anniversary" electrotechnical factory at Stepanakert into the "Luys" production enterprise of Armenia, an electrical equipment producer. The Volskiy Committee approved the transaction.[80] Moreover, the "Cooperatives Union" in the NKAO decided in April 1989 to join the newly-formed "Cooperatives Council" of Armenia.[81] All these cases illustrated that – hoping to stem the nationalist tide in the oblast – Moscow had adopted a more pro-Armenian stance.

Consequently, it was not too surprising that after a lull of three to four months, strikes, rallies and inter-communal clashes resumed in May 1989. What was startling, however, was that they took place in Armenia and the NKAO first and were mimicked in Azerbaijan subsequently. The demonstrators argued that unification of the NKAO with Armenia was the only desirable solution, and it appeared that the Volskiy Committee could not satisfy the long-term goals of Armenians.[82] Armenian nationalists might have calculated that the Volskiy Committee would strengthen ties between Armenia and the NKAO in the long run, but a speedy unification would require more drastic action on their part. A USSR "People's Deputy" from Armenia, Sero Khanzadyan, wrote an article for an Armenian paper, in which he suggested:

> I was duped; we were all duped. It [Volskiy Committee] exists only in name. The Committee started its work in the oblast by only introducing the so-called socio-economic improvements; it has no intention of contributing to the realization of the just national demand. There is only one way to help the NKAO and that is political solution entailing the oblast's reunification with Armenia. There is no alternative.
>
> This was the demand of the Armenian as well as NKAO deputies at the Congress of USSR People's Deputies.[83]

On August 16, a so-called "Congress of Plenipotentiary Representatives of the Population of Nagorno-Karabagh" was held in Stepanakert, and the "National Council" it elected demanded an end to Volskiy's rule and the unification of the NKAO with Armenia.[84] It is not clear how representative this Congress was of the people of the oblast. Armenia claimed that local party branches and soviets elected the Congress participants, but obviously such an organization was not legally entitled to ask for secession from Azerbaijan.

The above-mentioned NKAO Congress declared on August 22 that it would no longer abide by Azerbaijani laws and would terminate all existing links with the AzSSR. It stated that "the intervention of the [AzSSR] in the affairs of the autonomous oblast will be regarded as an act of aggression." The Congress appealed to world governments and to the Secretary General of the United Nations to assist the NKAO in achieving "self-determination and independence".[85] The Congress empowered the National Council to take decisions for the NKAO until the Oblast Soviet of People's Deputies and the Oblast Party Committee were reinstituted.

Rail Blockades and More: The APF Extends its Influence

In July 1989 Armenia accused the Azeris of halting the rail service between Baku and Yerevan, especially at various points in Nakhichevan. In early August Azerbaijan government representatives accused Armenians of sabotaging the railway by laying mines and firing at conductors. Azeris halted trains bound for Armenia; Armenians sabotaged the railway in Armenia's Zangezur region, on which trains traveling from Azerbaijan proper to Nakhichevan had to traverse. Some Azerbaijani militants threw stones and shot at passing trains, while Armenians blew up the railway line linking Azeri-controlled Shusha in the NKAO to the rest of Azerbaijan.

In addition, Azerbaijani conductors of trains refused to enter Armenian territory and Azeri militants blocked rail traffic between Nakhichevan and Armenia. From July 28 to August 2, 1989 no freight trains were allowed to go from Nakhichevan to Armenia. The Armenian side accused the Azerbaijanis of acting in bad faith, arguing that those trains were carrying relief supplies and construction materials to the victims of the massive earthquake of December 7 in Leninakan, Armenia.[86] Some 87 percent of the flow of freight intended for Armenia had to use the railroad passing through Azerbaijan and the remaining 13 percent used the railway connection through Georgia.[87] Similarly, the Azerbaijani side barricaded the Baku-Stepanakert railway at the Aghdam station, located just outside the NKAO border.[88]

An APF representative Vilayet Kuliev, told the Armenian newspaper *Kommunist* that the NKAO Armenians first began to use blockades a year and a half before, when they stopped trade and other transactions with the rest of Azerbaijan. In June 1989, he said, they blocked roads to the mountainous areas of Azerbaijan, accessible only through the NKAO. He also argued that Armenians in Zangezur often stoned trains going from Azerbaijan to Nakhichevan, a route also used by trains going to Armenia. In retaliation, he said, the Azerbaijani side introduced an economic blockade of the NKAO and Armenia in September 1989.[89]

In response to the Azerbaijani blockade, Armenian militants, allegedly belonging to the Dashnakt-affiliated *Vrezh* underground armed group, bombed a Tblisi-Baku bus on September 16, 1989, killing five people and wounding several others. Azerbaijani authorities held *Vrezh* also responsible for the bombing of another bus from Tblisi to Aghdam on August 10, 1990 that cost 17 passengers their lives. There were two more *Vrezh* bombings on April 30, 1991 and July 31, 1991, both on the Moscow-Baku trains in which several dozens were killed or wounded.[90]

On August 12, 1989 the APF held a rally in Lenin Square, with 200,000 attending. At the rally, the APF leadership announced that it demanded from the AzCP: 1) the adoption of laws on sovereignty, citizenship and economic independence; 2) the Volskiy Committee's abolishment and Azerbaijani sovereignty's reinstitution over the NKAO; 3) the immediate lifting of curfews and states of emergency in Baku and other regions; 4) the broadcasting on republican TV of the Supreme Soviet's discussion on these issues; 5) the holding of democratic elections for local soviets and the republican Supreme Soviet; 6) the freeing of all political prisoners; and 7) the official recognition of the APF.[91]

The AzCP avoided addressing these demands and instead took an initiative to recover lost ground. In late August 1989 the officially sanctioned Committee to Assist Nagorno-Karabagh (Karabaga Yardim Komitesi) was established. The 384 founders, including USSR People's Deputies, convened in the meeting hall of the Azerbaijan Academy of Sciences. Their first announcement stated that the Committee was established "in compliance with the demands put forward in a meeting held by the republic's intellectuals and representatives of the residents of Baku for solidarity with the Azerbaijanis in the [NKAO]." The AzCP thus tried to create its own APF by establishing the Karabagh Committee, which the government announced "ha[d] the right to intervene in all matters related to Nagorno-Karabagh."[92] Later, on October 1, 1989, the Committee began publishing a newspaper entitled *Azerbaijan*.[93]

To increase its popularity, the AzCP also attempted to adopt a critical stance *vis-à-vis* Moscow's economic policies. A pro-AzCP paper, the *Bakinskiy Rabochiy*, published an anonymous article on September 21, 1989, which argued that there was a significant discrepancy between national (Azerbaijani) production and its use by Azerbaijan, because between 1980 and 1988 national production amounted to 21.5 billion Rubles, but more than 2 billion Rubles remained annually unused. The article went on to argue that the republic had control over only a narrow sphere of productive activity, because "the fundamental part is planned and controlled by all-Union ministries and organizations which act in discord and ignore the interests of the republic, and thus hold back its social and economic development."[94]

The AzCP's attempt to steal away the APF's appeal by adopting some of its goals took place while both started a dialogue in late August 1989, which continued in early 1989. Throughout this phase the APF tried to force the AzCP to adopt policies through such means as strikes and demonstrations. On September 9, 1989, in a public meeting in Lenin Square, the APF stated that if by next day the government had not accepted the APF demands (cited above), the general strike, which was suspended for a few days, would continue.[95] On September 10 Abulfaz Elchibey, accompanied by other leaders of the APF including Yusuf Samedoglu and Etibar Mamedov, announced on Azerbaijani TV that the government had accepted the APF's requirements. These included the demand that for Union laws to be effective in Azerbaijan, they needed to be approved by the Azerbaijani

Supreme Soviet. For that reason, the APF called the strikes off, although it continued to block rail links to Armenia and the NKAO.[96] The rail blockade included the Aghdam–Stepanakert railway, while the government, for its part, closed to traffic the road linking Armenia to Stepanakert, which passed through the Azerbaijani border town, Lachin.

On September 11 Abdul Rahman Vezirov, who was in Moscow when the APF-AzCP deal was struck, returned to Baku and showed reluctance to sign the deal. Yet the same day another rally of 500,000 threatened that unless Vezirov accepted the deal by 9 p.m., the strikes would resume. Vezirov signed the agreement the same day, though it is not clear exactly what swayed him.[97] It may have been his realization that unless he did so, the AzCP would lose its already weakened grip on the country and that the APF would fill the gap.

On September 15 the Azerbaijani Supreme Soviet convened in an extraordinary session. The session was broadcast live on republican TV while thousands gathered in front of the Supreme Soviet building. Fifteen of the APF's prominent leaders were present at the meeting and two of them, Isa Gambar and Etibar Mamedov, addressed the assembly.[98] Vezirov put up a strong fight to lessen the impact of this extraordinary session. He said that the Supreme Soviet should only issue a statement asking from Moscow for the termination of Volskiy's Special Administration, instead of unilaterally ending the latter's operation. He also opposed the Supreme Soviet's consideration of the APF's other demands, including the lifting of the curfew, free elections, Azerbaijan's economic independence, adoption of a law on sovereignty, and the legalization of the APF.[99]

While the live broadcast continued, APF leaders addressed the assembly, stating that if the Supreme Soviet session were to be adjourned without considering their demands, then the APF would call for a general strike next day. Faced with this ultimatum broadcast live nationwide, Vezirov asked for an intermission of the session at 1 a.m. in the early hours of September 16, 1989. After presumably consulting with Moscow he returned to the Azerbaijan Supreme Soviet at 2 a.m. and accepted the vote on the APF demands. The Supreme Soviet overwhelmingly passed resolutions confirming Azerbaijan's sovereignty and abolished the NKAO Special Administration. It also amended Article 70 of the Azerbaijani Constitution, whose modified version provided that referenda should be held to secede from the USSR and to change the status of such regions as the NKAO and Nakhichevan.[100]

Etibar Mamedov, then a member of the Executive Committee of the APF, said later that the dialogue between the APF and the AzCP started because of the NKAO dispute. He said: "I believe that our participation in the work of the parliament … and in the preparation of the latter's many resolutions has become a turning point in the APF-AzCP relations." Still considering the APF's struggle within the context of perestroika and glasnost, Mamedov suggested: "We are the children of restructuring, and it would be unfair not to mention that … restructuring has opened the door of democracy to people."[101]

The USSR Presidium declared the Azerbaijani resolution of September 16 invalid on the grounds that it violated the USSR Constitution. Nevertheless, on September 23, a referendum was held in the republic and people voted in reaffirming Azerbaijan's sovereignty. The same day, Azerbaijan's Supreme Soviet amended Azerbaijan's Constitution to reaffirm Azerbaijan's status as a sovereign republic within the USSR.[102] The amendment, which some considered as the AzCP's capitulation to the APF, went into effect on September 25.[103] It required that for all-Union laws to be enforceable in the republic, approval by Azerbaijan's Supreme Soviet was necessary.[104] The law also stipulated that Azerbaijan could leave the USSR and become independent if the outcome of a referendum were to require it so.[105]

On October 5, 1989, making use of a 1932 decree, the Azerbaijan Council of Ministers officially registered the APF. The APF also compelled the AzCP to announce that the rail boycott would end in return for Armenian concessions including the provision of autonomy to ethnic Azeris comparable to that enjoyed by ethnic Armenians in the NKAO.[106] Yet the APF failed to convince the AzCP that Azerbaijan should have its own defense forces.[107]

Armenian Response to the Radicalization of the Azerbaijani Stance

Worried by the increasing influence of the APF in Azerbaijan proper, on September 7, 1989 the NKAO National Council called on the UN and the Armenian SSR to protect the oblast from Azerbaijan. It asked Armenia to send military units to the NKAO to defend it against armed Azeri groups who had besieged Armenian positions.[108] The Armenian Supreme Soviet responded diplomatically by stating that the struggle waged by the NKAO was a fight for self-determination in which Armenia was not involved. The

Azeris were also in full control of the tiny airport near Khojaly, an Azeri village not part of the NKAO, which contributed to the Azeri stranglehold.[109]

Moscow tried to cope with the Azerbaijani blockade that began on August 20, 1989 by organizing an enormous airlift of basic necessities. The supplies were flown to the airport in Stepanakert, which was under the control of Armenians. Throughout September, cargo aircraft arrived in the NKAO from Tblisi, Yerevan and other locations, but the bulk of supplies came from Armenia. Soviet fighter jets protected the airlift.[110]

One unexpected outcome of the blockade was the opening of an air corridor between Armenia and Stepanakert, the Armenian-held capital of the NKAO, which strengthened ties between them. Eventually, limited supplies began to be sent to the NKAO on Azerbaijani trains.[111] Nevertheless, inter-communal fighting between Azeri and Armenian irregulars and between the latter two and Soviet Interior Ministry troops in the NKAO accelerated.[112]

The APF eased the blockade against Armenia in mid-September 1989 by allowing trains that carried construction materials. Yerevan reacted by arguing that this gesture was meaningless because Azerbaijan still prevented fuel and food supplies from reaching Armenia and consequently construction supplies to the earthquake zone could not be delivered.[113]

In October 1989 the APF also began blockading the Azerbaijan-Georgia railway because Moscow had begun to use it to supply fuel and food to Armenia.[114] The APF admitted that it had decided to halt the train traffic to Georgia as a means of influencing the outcome of the NKAO dispute.[115] Later, on October 6, 1989, the APF resolved to lift the rail/road blockade of Armenia, and by the end of October 1989 Moscow was able to restore rail traffic between Azerbaijan and Armenia, although the blockade of the NKAO continued.[116]

Perhaps another unintended outcome of the rise in tensions was the establishment of the Armenian National Movement (ANM) on November 4, 1989 in Yerevan with the participation of 1,500 delegates. The ANM had existed informally and had undertaken various initiatives for two years before its formal founding. Although formerly banned, Karabagh Committee members made up a significant portion of the ANM, though the latter had a much larger agenda than the former. At the ANM's establishment congress on November 4 the first secretary of the ACP, Suren Arutrunyan and representatives of various diaspora parties including Ramgavar (liberal), Hunchak (social democratic) and Dashnaktsutiun (socialist) were present.

The Armenian Supreme Soviet officially registered the ANM, an important hurdle on the way to its existence as a legal entity.

In his speech at the congress Levon Ter-Petrosyan, the informal leader of the ANM, said that the ANM had already succeeded in having the Armenian Supreme Soviet adopt resolutions providing for unification with the NKAO, the closure of the Armenian nuclear station of Medzamor, the condemnation of the 1915 genocide and the calling for recognition of May 28, 1918 as the date of the establishment of Armenian statehood.[117] The ANM program called for: 1) Armenia's unification with the NKAO; 2) Moscow's acceptance of Armenia's right to secede; 3) the restructuring of Armenia's military forces so that they would all be based in Armenia and constitute the National Army of Armenia; 4) Armenia determining its own economic policies and foreign trade; 5) privatization of agriculture, industry and commerce; 6) the struggle to convince the United Nations to recognize the 1915 genocide; 7) international recognition of the injustice done to Armenia through its loss of territory to Turkey and Azerbaijan; 8) the annulment of the March 16, 1921 Russo-Turkish treaty, which recognized the territorial losses the Armenian side incurred up to then; 9) the abrogation of the July 5, 1921 decision of the Kavbiuro (Caucasus Bureau) of the Russian Communist Party determining the borders with Azerbaijan; and 10) the right to establish state-to-state diplomatic relations with other states.[118]

5

Black January and After

As suggested earlier, by mid-1989 the growing appeal of the APF had begun to worry Moscow and the AzCP. The latter tried not to lag behind the APF in adopting bold demands. Both demanded the disbandment of the Volskiy Committee and the re-establishment of Azerbaijani rule in the NKAO. Moscow responded on November 28, 1989 when the USSR Supreme Soviet, by a vote of 348 in favor, four against and 20 abstentions, adopted a resolution on the NKAO, eliminating Volskiy's direct rule and recognizing Azerbaijan's sovereignty over the oblast even while expanding the latter's autonomy. Armenian deputies present at the Supreme Soviet session walked out in protest at the closed-door Supreme Soviet session, and the Azerbaijani side seemed to have attained a major goal.[1]

Yet the resolution's pro-Azerbaijan appearance was misleading. It also provided for the creation of a so-called "Republican Organization Committee" (ROC), in which representatives from the AzSSR and the NKAO would be equally represented, and it would have the power to supervise the NKAO authorities. Whereas previously the mostly Armenian NKAO administration was subordinate to Baku, with the ROC in place, the NKAO administration was made equal to the AzSSR government in deciding the oblast's affairs.[2] Even though the USSR Supreme Soviet recognized Azerbaijani sovereignty over the oblast in practice, the NKAO Armenians were granted equal say over their affairs. The Supreme Soviet resolution also provided for the establishment of a "Union Monitoring and Observation Commission" (Soyuznaya Kontrolno Nablyudatelnaya Komisiya), which would be subordinate to the USSR Supreme Soviet. Adding insult to injury, the USSR Supreme Soviet stipulated that the Commission and not the AzSSR authorities – as they did in the pre-1989 period – would command the USSR Ministry of Internal Affairs, troops in the NKAO.[3]

Nevertheless, the ACP regarded the USSR Supreme Soviet's resolution as pro-Azerbaijan, and the Armenian Supreme Soviet and the newly formed National Council of the NKAO jointly convened on December 1, 1989 in order to determine a common response to the resolution. Next day, members of both assemblies unanimously resolved to unite the NKAO with Armenia and extend Armenian citizenship to the NKAO inhabitants. The fact that it was Levon Ter-Petrosyan, head of the ANM and also a member of the Armenian Supreme Soviet, who presented the draft unification resolution to the joint meeting, showed that the nationalists were calling the shots in Armenia.[4] Despite its unanimous adoption of a nationalist stance, the ACP continued its relations with Moscow with business as usual. On December 15, 1989 First Secretary Suren Arutrunyan, for instance, made a speech at the Congress of People's Deputies in Moscow praising Gorbachev's policies.[5] Moreover, Armenia abstained from effectively enforcing the unification decision and continued to rely on the Moscow-established air corridor with the NKAO as a means of preserving links with the oblast.

The AzSSR Supreme Soviet Presidium, for its part, accepted the USSR Supreme Soviet resolution on November 28, 1989 on the same day it was adopted. The APF, which on November 27 had started a ten-day strike to call for an end to the Volskiy rule, however, objected to the resolution, stating that the to-be-established Monitoring Commission would be the resurrection of the Volskiy Commission under a different name, further undermining Azerbaijani sovereignty over the NKAO.[6] The APF's objection forced the AzCP to back out of its acceptance of the Supreme Soviet resolution, which it had earlier considered as the better of two evils. On December 5 the AzCP Supreme Soviet Presidium – cognizant of Armenia's annexation decision – announced that Articles 3, 4, 5, 6, and 7 of the November 28 resolution were contrary to the Azerbaijani and the USSR Constitutions. Instead of the Republican Organization Committee (ROC), the Azerbaijani Supreme Soviet decided to establish the 'NKAO Organization Committee', which would supervise the NKAO's administrative and elected bodies and be subordinate to the AzSSR.[7] The Azerbaijani version of the committee would accrue more control to Baku than it enjoyed prior to the start of the hostilities.

The AzSSR Supreme Soviet also asked the USSR Supreme Soviet to define the authority of the to-be-established "Union Monitoring Commission" and to ensure that the USSR Ministry of Internal Affairs troops be subordinate to the Azeri-established "NKAO Organization Committee" and not to the "Union Monitoring Commission", in which Azerbaijani control would be expected to amount to next to nothing.[8] Nevertheless, despite the formal establishment of rival union and republican institutions to supervise NKAO authorities, Volskiy remained in the oblast and he and his committee exercised the same powers they enjoyed prior to November 1989. They would leave the oblast only after the Black January of 1990 crackdown by the Soviet forces in Baku.[9]

Radicals Flaunt Baku's Political Impotence

The weaning of the Azerbaijani Republic away from the USSR took place in ways very much reminiscent of the shapes it took elsewhere in the USSR. The Russian-language daily *Bakinskiy Rabochiy* announced on September 30, 1989 that it would sell to its readers a four-volume edition of the Qur'an, consisting of the Arabic text, the Azerbaijani translation, and two volumes of commentaries. Altogether, 50,000 sets would be printed and the deliveries would be made by the end of 1989.[10] Two weeks later, on October 10, 1989, Sheikh ul-Islam Allahshukur Pashazada, chairman of the Muslim Religious Directorate for Transcaucasia, announced on Iranian television the opening of a religious seminary (*madrassah*) in Baku, the first in 70 years.[11]

On November 11 the Azerbaijan Council of Ministers announced that Azerbaijan would improve relations with such union republics as Turkmenistan and Tajikistan, and joint protocols would be signed to broaden cultural ties and cooperation between the party apparatuses.[12] In late December 1989 the AzSSR Supreme Soviet Presidium renamed Kirovabad, a major historical, industrial and cultural city, as Ganja. Ganja was renamed Kirovabad in 1935 to honor Sergei M. Kirov, who had played a significant role in the Bolshevization of the Transcaucasus in the 1920s.[13]

Another significant move on the part of the AzCP was the resolutions of the AzCP Central Committee and the AzSSR Supreme Soviet to place more emphasis on the study of a part of Azerbaijani history long regarded as taboo. They stated that the period of 1918–1920 had long been one of the blank spots of Azerbaijani history and this problem should be addressed. They charged the Azerbaijan Academy of Sciences and other scholarly institutions to study archival material to shed light on this period.[14] A striking example of the new historiography came when Vilayet

Kuliev, an APF member, stated in an interview with Armenia's *Kommunist* in late October 1989 that Armenians always associated Azeris with the Turks of Turkey in order to also hold the former responsible for the "alleged" genocide of 1915. He added that this was a moot exercise because such event had never occurred.[15]

Events in December 1989 and January 1990 indicated that the NKAO conflict and the expansion of the purviews of the APF and the ANM at the expense of their respective Communist Parties were becoming increasingly difficult for Moscow to cope with. The Armenian Republic's decision of December 1 to annex the NKAO and the failure or reluctance of Moscow to rescind Yerevan's move were probably the main reasons why militants who were tightly or loosely linked to the APF decided to challenge local authorities wherever and whenever it seemed opportune or necessary.

Throughout December 1989 the number of demonstrators along Azerbaijan's border with Iran grew to several thousand, and by late December 1989 the tone of the speeches was becoming more uncompromising. Protestors also began to attack sections of the fence separating the border zones of the two countries and several watchtowers. In an interview, the then Prime Minister, Ayaz Mutalibov, stated that the events panicked First Secretary Vezirov who told him that "[the AzCP] should ask for help from Moscow because Azerbaijan did not have its own Interior Ministry forces."[16]A participant in the demonstrations stated:

> For decades barbed wire has cut us from our homeland – south Azerbaijan – which is situated on Iranian territory. For decades we have been unable to see our relatives. … [M]any people have sisters and brothers on the other side of the Araz [also known as Aras or Araks]. … It has been extremely difficult for us to visit our forefathers' graves and see our ancient monuments – they too … are also in the border strip.[17]

On December 29, 1989 APF militants including Neimat Panakhov seized AzCP offices in the southern town of Jalilabad, during which dozens of people were wounded.[18] Then Panakhov arrived in Nakhichevan and during three days, from December 31 to January 2, 1990, hundreds of Azeris, many of whom supposedly self-identified with the APF, attacked the so-called communications and signaling lines, watchtowers and border signs along the Nakhichevan-Iran and Nakhichevan–Turkey borders. Some of the attackers were even able to swim across to the Iranian side of the Araz River.[19]

According to the KGB, the APF had earlier asked the border guard command in Nakhichevan for more favorable conditions for Nakhichevanis to visit cemeteries and to cultivate 7,000 acres of fertile land located in the no-man's zone along the Soviet side of the border.[20] Moreover, some APF activists had sent a letter to the Presidium of the USSR Supreme Soviet comparing the partition of Azerbaijan in 1828 to the division of Vietnam and Korea, and called for the relaxation of border controls along the Iran–Azerbaijan border.[21]

Similar incidents of less severity took place at other portions of the Azerbaijani–Iran border near Zangelan and Lenkoran. The APF defended these actions as the venting of long pent-up frustrations due to a very long period of state-imposed border constraints.[22] In response to the border incidents, Soviet and Iranian Foreign Ministry officials held talks in January 1990 to facilitate easier crossings between the two countries.[23] As will be discussed later, after January 20, 1990 over 20,000 Azeris crossed into Iran while Soviet border guards refrained from the use of force to stop them.[24]

Some members of the APF were critical of border incidents. Leyla Yunusova, who belonged to the social democratic wing, said that these actions were the work of right-wing members of the front led by Neimat Panakhov.[25] The criticism of Yunusova reflected the schism within the APF that of late had taken shape. On January 7, 1990 she and another prominent member of the APF, Zardusht Alizade, resigned from the APF. Alizade, for his part, stated that the Azerbaijani Social Democrats desired a West European style of social democracy and more harmony with other Union republics, and that the capture of the APF by the extremists was leading to violence and chaos.[26] The not-so-extremist nationalists within the APF, including Etibar Mamedov, Rahim Gaziev, and Abulfaz Elchibey, though enthusiastic about the unification of the two Azerbaijans in future, were also disturbed by the events, but they failed to rein in the radicals.

By late 1989, while the APF leadership was losing its already shaky grip on the radicals, AzCP First Secretary Vezirov, for his part, did no longer have the ability to contain the latter. The perception of his political frailty and lack of resolve on the "national question" was such that during the demonstrations in Lenin Square, crowds called him Vezirian, Armenizing his name. Consequently, Victor Polyanichko, the Second Secretary, having earlier played a significant political role in occupied Afghanistan, stepped in to take over informal decision-making.[27] He attempted to manipulate the turn of events by even trying to influence the APF. Once he invited such APF leaders as Towfik Qasimov and Zardusht Alizade to his office, and told them that they should incorporate radical Islamic demands to the APF program because Islamist sentiments were much stronger outside Baku.

By December 1989 radicals were dominating the APF, and Polyanichko tried to utilize their prominence in various ways to influence Moscow. Among the means he used was to frequently give airtime on Azerbaijani TV to a select group of radicals who espoused their often radical views.[28] Ironically, giving radicals a larger public profile was Polyanichko's and the AzCP's way to pull Moscow to the Azeri side. Public perception of the AzCP's collaboration with the APF, the AzCP calculated, would also enable the former to augment its already much diminished popularity.

During the first half of January 1990, armed clashes between Armenians and Azeris accelerated in the NKAO, Azerbaijan, Armenia and Nakhichevan. Fighting was concentrated in Goriskiy raion in Armenia, in northern Nakhichevan and Zangelan in Azerbaijan between Armenian and Azeri infiltrators, in the NKAO between the two communities and volunteers or irregulars from Azerbaijan and Armenia, and in Azerbaijan's Shaumyanovskiy and Khanlarskiy raions between the two communities and irregulars from Azerbaijan and Armenia. Ammunition depots, police and militia offices were ransacked and thousands of arms were looted in both republics.

In Azerbaijan's Shaumyanovskiy (Shaumyan) and Khanlarskiy (Khanlar) raions – in Azerbaijan proper, north of the NKAO – military helicopters without identification marks fired shots at the Azerbaijani forces, indicating that Armenian irregulars had acquired sophisticated weaponry or Armenia was actively participating in the conflict.[29] The fact that the looting of ammunition depots was accomplished with few casualties indicates that the authorities in both republics were turning a blind eye to such acts.[30] In early January 1990, in Shaumyan and Khanlar raions, irregulars from each community took hostages from the other. In one instance, on January 9 Azeris kidnapped 19 Armenians in Shaumyan, including the first secretary of the raion party apparatus. In response, Armenians kidnapped 43 Azeris in the region.[31]

Armenian nationalists operating in the Getashen sub-raion of Khanlar and in Shaumyan, had in January 1990 started to demand the detachment of these regions from Azerbaijan proper and their incorporation into adjacent NKAO. Delegates supposedly representing the Armenian population of Getashen, Martunashen, Azat and Kamu villages located in Shaumyan and Khanlar convened and elected a 21-person National Council to govern and represent the people living there.[32] To the AzSSR authorities, this step amounted to virtual secession. On top of these developments came the Armenian SSR Supreme Soviet's discussion and adoption of the NKAO's budget as part of the Armenian SSR's budget on January 9.[33]

On January 10–14 anti-Armenian violence erupted in the Shaumyan raion, when about 100 irregulars wearing paramilitary uniforms attacked the Armenian village of Manashid.[34] During the assault, which lasted for five days, to strengthen the defense of Manashid, Armenian fighters, from Armenia or the NKAO, were brought in on board military helicopters whose insignia were painted over. It was reported that those who attacked Manashid belonged to the APF, which had begun to organize volunteers into 100-men military units.[35]

The toughening of the stance of the APF, or rather of the more radical groups within the APF, had already begun in late December 1989. As mentioned briefly earlier, on December 29, 1989 the local APF members in Dzhalilabadskiy raion (Jalilabad) revolted against the unpopular first secretary of the local party organization. During the mêlée that ensued one person died and about 100 were injured.[36] The Soviet media reported that by early January, militants loyal to one of the local APF hardliners, Mirali Bayramov, began to run government institutions in Jalilabad without formally replacing those in charge. Bayramov's men took the decisions and Baku-appointed directors signed the related forms. *Pravda* reported that Bayramov's men asked for payments from the directors of the state farms and industrial enterprises and defeated a militia detachment sent from Baku in early January.[37] *Pravda* suggested that poverty was the cause of these events, reporting that there were 22,000 unemployed in the *okrug* (district).[38]

On January 10, 1990 the USSR Supreme Soviet Presidium, chaired by Mikhail Gorbachev, annulled Armenia's December 1, 1989 decision to unite with the NKAO, and abrogated the January 9, 1990 incorporation of the NKAO into Armenia's state budget, stating that these acts violated the USSR Constitution. With regard to Azerbaijan SSR's decision to ignore the November 28, 1989 USSR Supreme Soviet resolution and the former's establishment of the so-called Organization Committee, the Presidium stated that this act was also in contravention of the Soviet Constitution.[39] The Presidium asked both republics to rescind their decisions.

Two days later, Armenia's Supreme Soviet not only rejected Moscow's demand out of hand, it also revised Article 75 of the Armenian Constitution. In its revised form, Article 75 stipulated that for the laws and resolutions of the USSR Supreme Soviet to be effective in Armenia, they needed to be "ratified by the Supreme Soviet of the Armenian SSR."[40]

The Azerbaijani Soviet had earlier passed a similar bill to amend its constitution. The APF, for its part, reacted to the January 10 decision by resuming the blockade of Armenia by cutting off rail links to the latter.[41]

By 1992 the Azerbaijani blockade of Armenia had led to shortages of various goods, including food staples. Power cuts and termination of train services were common. After a short thaw in 1992 Turkey closed its airspace to Armenia, augmenting the Azerbaijani embargo. Armenia, whose roads, gas pipelines and railways were often shut down, relied on Iran, whose cooperation enabled the former to survive "two miserable winters in 1991 and 1992."[42] Armenians used wells for water, cut down trees to burn in stoves and used candles for light. Armenia restored electricity in 1996 with the re-opening of the Metzamor nuclear power station.[43]

On January 11, 1990, one day after the USSR Supreme Soviet Presidium's decision, militants belonging to the APF occupied the soviet building of the city of Lenkoran, the police and public prosecutor's offices. A 15-member Provisional Defense Committee, including Alekram Hummatov, who would later become APF's deputy defense minister, seemed to be in charge. The Committee demanded the restoration of Azerbaijani sovereignty over the NKAO.[44] At the time, Hummatov was deputy director of a transport warehouse in Lenkoran and had joined the APF in 1989. *Komsomolskaya Pravda* wrote that the first secretary of the Lenkoran party gorkom had tried to pacify him by offering him a good job and an apartment in Baku. Later, he was also offered money to leave Lenkoran. Hummatov said that the coup in Lenkoran was not only due to the NKAO problem but also due to social problems such as unemployment. In Lenkoran there were 24,000 unemployed and those employed were paid very little.[45]

Isa Gambar, who later became Defense Minister of the APF government, told reporters that the republic's leadership was paralyzed and having failed to defend the Azeri people's rights, was following Moscow's orders. He said that Soviet troops that were present in Lenkoran did not oppose the APF's occupation of government offices. APF militants prevented the AzCP officials and the local police from returning to work in the following days.[46] Later, on January 14, 1990, the AzCP officials in Lenkoran stated that they were supporting the APF's demands on the NKAO and that they would not return to their positions until the APF Lenkoran Branch called upon them to do so.[47] Although this statement might have been made under duress, it also shows that the AzCP local officials felt that their party's monopoly on power was shaken and that the APF was a force to be reckoned with.

On January 12, 1990 AzCP Second Secretary Polyanichko came up with another unexpected plan at the end of talks he held with the APF. The parties agreed for the APF to establish a National Defense Council that would oversee defense efforts to protect the republic against Armenian incursions. Several APF leaders, including Etibar Mamedov, Neimat Panakhov and Rahim Gaziev became members of the Council. On the same day, Panakhov and Gaziev stated on Azerbaijani TV that Baku was full of Azeri refugees who tried to survive in squalid conditions while thousands of Armenian residents of Baku enjoyed a comfortable life.[48]

Their statement was an important factor that contributed to what started next day: the eruption of new violence against Armenian residents of Baku. It started after a Baku Armenian shot and killed one Azerbaijani and wounded another, after they told him he should leave Azerbaijan permanently. As soon as news of the killing reached 70,000 Azeris demonstrating in Lenin Square, some recent Azeri refugees from Armenia and extremists, with or without any association with the APF, accounts vary, went to Armenian neighborhoods to take revenge. In the following hours they committed atrocities against Armenians and the death toll eventually reached 56.[49]

The high number of those murdered was due to the standing on the sidelines of Azerbaijani police who were ordered by First Secretary Vezirov to do so.[50] Despite the possible involvement of at least some APF members in the massacres, many APF members rushed to shield Armenians from the unruly crowd. Some argued that those APF members who took part in the atrocities belonged to the extremist or right wing of the APF, which had split in late 1989 into moderate and extremist factions.[51] Thousands of Armenians sought refuge in police stations and in the huge Shafaq cinema protected by troops. From these mid-way stations they were taken to the harbor, put on ferries and shipped to Krasnovodsk across the Caspian Sea. From there thousands were flown to Yerevan.[52] Most would not return to Baku.

Azeri refugees from Armenia, who, as some argued, were heavily involved in the atrocities, had been objects of ethnic cleansing when they were forced to leave Armenia in 1989. After arriving in Azerbaijan, many remained unemployed and had to live in derelict refugee camps in or near Baku. They were irate not only because they had lost most of what they had worked for through most of their lives but also because the Azerbaijani government had failed to accommodate them with badly needed assistance. Many felt hateful *vis-à-vis* Baku Armenians who had good homes and good jobs. After the departure of Armenians from Baku the government assigned their apartments to some of these refugees.[53]

The AzCP's reluctance to stop the violence might have been the consequence of its attempt to appease the APF and most of the republic's population, who had come to believe that Armenia was acting ever more assertively as a result of the AzCP's passivity. The AzCP's behavior might also have been intended as a warning signal to Moscow, indicating that the republic's population was losing patience with the AzCP's relative moderation, and in order not to draw the wrath of the Azerbaijanis upon itself, Moscow needed to be more supportive of Azerbaijan's sovereignty over the NKAO.

Another reason for the AzCP's behavior could be that it could not have decided to act more assertively against extremists in Baku because it was almost paralyzed politically, and in the near absence of Moscow's prodding, it was unable to cope with challenges unprecedented throughout the Soviet era. A good example of the self-doubt and self-worthlessness felt by many of the AzCP ruling elite is AzCP Secretary Hasan Hasanov's speech as published by the APF's newspaper *Azadlik* on the very same day that massacres were committed against Armenians in Baku. In his speech Hasanov likened his party colleagues to "*mankurtlar*", who sacrificed their nation in order to save their careers. In Chingiz Aitmatov's novel *A Day Lasts Longer than an Age*, *mankurtlar* were men, who, after being captured and tortured, forgot their past, and became obedient slaves.[54]

Moscow also chose to stay passive after the pogroms started. Before January 12 Moscow had sent thousands of Soviet Interior Ministry troops to Baku and their use could have stopped a substantial portion of the attacks. Moscow's attitude brings to mind the possibility that Moscow desired the involvement of the APF in violence which would justify Moscow's crackdown and which actually came within a week. Some even suggested that the establishment of the National Defense Council, under the auspices of Second Secretary of Polyanichko, was also aimed at justifying a military crackdown.[55]

Matters seem more confusing when one takes into account the arrival in Baku on January 14 of Yevgeniy Primakov, a Politburo member and Gorbachev ally, and the Soviet Defense Minister, Dimitriy Yazov, to take charge of crisis management. Despite their presence, thousands of Soviet troops remained in their barracks on the outskirts of the city throughout the violence in Baku. More confounding is Moscow's imposition of a state of emergency in the NKAO border regions between Azerbaijan and Armenia and in the Azerbaijani city of Ganja, but not in Baku, despite the violence.[56]

Belatedly, on January 15, 1990 the Presidium of the USSR Supreme Soviet adopted a decree asking the Azerbaijani and Armenian governments to impose states of emergency in such Azerbaijani regions as Baku, the NKAO, Shaumyan, and Khanlar, and in the border areas of Azerbaijan and Nakhichevan with Iran and Turkey, and in Goris in Armenia. The Presidium banned political meetings and rallies, as well as such non-political gatherings as sports events unless a prior permit were obtained from the authorities. The Presidium decree also provided a ban on strikes, the imposition of curfews if authorities felt them to be crucial, searches for illegal weapons, restriction of entry to some sensitive regions, censorship of radio and TV broadcasts, deployment of USSR armed forces, KGB and Ministry of Interior forces in trouble spots, administrative detention up to a month for "troublemakers" and ensuring railway security by the USSR security forces.[57]

Despite the announcement of these measures, the APF openly challenged them, and the AzCP failed – or rather did not try – to implement them. What followed was a total breakdown of law and order. Demonstrations continued unabated and the demonstrators grew ever more reckless with each passing day. In protest rallies on January 18 and 19, 1990 some shouted "*azadlyg*" (freedom) and carried the three-color flags of the Azerbaijan Republic (1918–1920). Protesters belonging to or sympathizing with the APF barred entry to and exit from Salyanski Barracks housing Soviet Army units. APF units also blocked access roads to Baku, signaling to Moscow that Soviet troops that could be dispatched to Baku would not enter Baku unhindered.[58]

On January 16, 1990 Azerbaijani irregulars blew up the pipeline supplying water to Stepanakert (Hankendi), the mostly-Armenian inhabited capital of the NKAO. Earlier, in December 1989, the Armenian side had done the same to the pipeline supplying water to Shusha, the mostly-Azeri town in the NKAO.[59] The obstruction of trains by both sides resumed once again. Near Ganja, Armenian militants captured some Azeri villages and blocked the road to the Khanlar raion to prevent Azerbaijani reinforcements from reaching the region in order to end the Armenian control of the area. On January 17 Armenian irregulars also shelled from the Armenian side the Nakhichevani border village of Kerki. Meanwhile, the evacuation of most of the 200,000 Armenian inhabitants of Baku was completed after they were ferried to the Caspian port of Krasnovodsk (today Turkmenbashi).[60]

The formation of guerrilla bands by the ANM and the APF was in full force in both Armenia and Azerbaijan. Weapons continued to be stolen or voluntarily turned over to the guerrillas by government forces. Lachin and Khanlar became battlegrounds. Armenians from Goris on the other side of the border continuously shelled Lachin on the Azerbaijani side of the border. The Khanlar raion, north of the NKAO, witnessed pitched battles between the warring parties.[61]

On January 18, 1990 the military commander of the NKAO Major General Kosalapov, declared a state of emergency in the NKAO, as well as in Kubatli, Lachin, Fuzuli, Aghdam and Jebrail, all situated outside the NKAO but in close proximity. Not only did he declare a state of emergency in areas outside his area of responsibility, he did so even though the USSR Presidium's decree had only entitled the Azerbaijani authorities to impose states of emergency. It seems that the AzCP's unwillingness or inability to declare a state of emergency led Moscow to give an informal go ahead to military commanders on the grounds of taking the initiative. Kosalapov's deed came on the eve of the invasion of Baku on January 20.[62]

In Baku, radicals had set up barricades on roads leading to the military barracks and the airport, and on January 17 they started a rally in front of the Central Committee building which lasted non-stop until the Soviet military crackdown a few days later. Their demonstration served as a means of blocking the entrance of the Central Committee building. The demonstrators even erected a gallows in front of the building to demonstrate the gravity of the situation.[63] Meanwhile, the Politburo delegation, led by Primakov, met with APF leaders, including Elchibey. The former asked the APF to take down the barricades, cautioning that failure to do so could lead to a dangerous military confrontation between Soviet troops and the demonstrators. The APF's reluctance led Gorbachev and his advisors to go ahead with the invasion knowing full well that it would lead to high casualties. The invasion of the city would be undertaken during the night of January 20 after the imposition of a state of emergency at midnight.[64]

Soviet Forces Invade Baku

Hours prior to the arrival of the MVD, or the Ministry of Interior forces in Baku, Moscow asked the Second Secretary of the AzCP, Victor Polyanichko, to deliver an ultimatum to Etibar Mamedov, a member of the National Defense Council set up by the APF, that the latter should clear the APF-manned roadblocks within two hours.[65] Meanwhile, to prevent a coordinated resistance to the imminent assault, Soviet Special Forces incapacitated the power units of the state-run Azerbaijani TV, which had come under the influence of the APF. Had the broadcasts not been interrupted, innocent bystanders, who were unaware of the arrival of the MVD forces and the curfew, could have been informed and not borne the brunt of the gunfire.[66]

On January 20, at 12.20 a.m., the first MVD troops arrived in Baku, and using tanks and armed gunships they moved forcefully against the APF barricades. Other MVD convoys attacked similar APF fortifications in other cities and regions, including Ganja, Nakhichevan and Zangelan. While Moscow stated that in the ensuing battles in Baku and elsewhere 89 people – including 14 Soviet troops – had died, the APF claimed that in Baku alone the death toll approached 300, including many civilians.[67] Many independent journalists reported that the MVD troops opened fire not only on armed militants but also on unarmed demonstrators and even on bystanders. Most of the casualties took place near the Salyanski Barracks, housing Soviet troops in Baku. Demonstrators had besieged the barracks for several days. The invading MVD forces tried to lift the siege, opening fire on those who refused to disperse. Later, the troops demanded that 30,000 people who were camped outside the AzCP headquarters should disperse. When the crowd refused, the troops opened fire leading to the deaths of many.[68]

The intervention took place without the public approval of the AzCP leadership. On January 19 the USSR Supreme Soviet Presidium had adopted a decree imposing a state of emergency and a curfew in Baku as of January 20, 1990 to fully implement the January 15, 1990 Decree of the Supreme Soviet, which the AzCP had failed to implement. The January 19 Decree was used as a legal basis for the MVD clampdown on the night of January 20.[69] According to the then Soviet deputy foreign minister, Alexander Bessmertnykh, Soviet invasion prevented a virtual coup by the APF, because the APF, he argued, had mobilized its members, established barricades on Baku streets and the roads leading to the city and surrounded the Azerbaijani radio and TV offices in order to take them over.[70] Partly as a result of the barricades outside the TV and radio studios, broadcasts had become in tune with the APF program, which alarmed Moscow. The AzCP's failure to influence developments in the NKAO and thereby reduce the appeal of the APF and its nationalist rhetoric might also have influenced the change of heart of the journalists. Even on the morning after, Azerbaijani radio continued its anti-Moscow tone and denounced the invasion.

Moscow also witnessed that before January 20 the AzCP Central Committee building was encircled by APF militants to influence the deliberations and that the APF demanded the resignation of the Azerbaijani government. On the eve of the intervention, arms depots were ransacked and roadblocks were set up by the APF to engage in identity checks. Armed APF-affiliated or independent groups went to the NKAO or to Shaumyan, Lachin and Khanlar to fight the Armenian paramilitaries there.[71] On the eve of the invasion most Azerbaijanis felt that open support for the APF would not draw the ire of the AzCP because the latter was no longer in a position to react.

As it happened, the AzCP seemed as nationalist as anybody else the morning after. On January 20, 1990 the AzCP Central Committee Bureau declared a three-day mourning period for the victims of the invasion.[72] On January 21, 1990 the AzCP Supreme Soviet convened in an extraordinary session with the participation of several APF leaders who were not members. After the all-night session the Supreme Soviet criticized the Soviet invasion and the state of emergency imposed by the MVD forces as unconstitutional because Moscow did not inform, let alone receive permission from, the constitutional authorities of its actions. The Supreme Soviet demanded the immediate lifting of the state of emergency and withdrawal of troops other than those deployed in the NKAO and along the Azerbaijan–Armenia border. If its demands were not met, the AzCP Supreme Soviet threatened it would reconsider Azerbaijan's membership in the Union.[73]

Despite the curfew, on January 20 crowds returned to Baku's newly renamed *Azadlyg Meydani* (Freedom Square), defying the state of emergency's ban on demonstrations, and surrounded the AzCP Supreme Soviet once again. Yet this time about a dozen Soviet Army tanks and 100 troops were guarding the building.[74] January 20 was also the day when thousands of AzCP members began to publicly burn their membership cards in Baku and elsewhere in the republic. The sense of dismay felt by most Azeris was such that the same day, the Chairman of the AzSSR Supreme Soviet Presidium, Elmira Kafarova, a pro-Moscow apparatchick, felt the need to condemn the Soviet intervention as unnecessary, brutal, and violent. In her speech on Azerbaijani radio she stressed that Moscow declared the state of emergency and no Azerbaijani state organ had anything to do with it. She denounced the invasion as a "gross violation of the Azerbaijan SSR's sovereignty" and added: "The responsibility for the blood that has been shed lies directly with the USSR organs and their officials. ... The people of Azerbaijan will never forgive anyone for the tragic way their sons and daughters have been killed."[75]

Aftermath of Black January

The invasion of Baku also heralded the end of the reign of the First Secretary of the AzCP, Abdul Rahman Vezirov, whom Moscow considered disastrously ineffective. He had failed to prevent the rise of the APF and the Republic-wide anti-Armenian violence from getting out of control. In Moscow's eyes he had almost devolved all of his crucial decision making prerogatives to the APF. The invasion of Baku was for that reason not an endeavor on Moscow's part to save Vezirov, rather it was an effort to re-establish law and order through installment of a more capable and reliable leadership at the helm of the AzCP. On January 20, 1990 Moscow announced the sacking of Vezirov, who had gone to Moscow in the wake of the coup suffering from "nervous exhaustion", without going through the motions of the AzCP doing the dirty job.[76] Apparently there was no time to do so, and on the day of the invasion Moscow desired to work with a new administration that had not denounced Moscow's action. Ayaz Niyazioglu Mutalibov, an erstwhile manager of a machine-building factory and then chairman of the Council of Ministers, and the then Second Secretary, Victor Polyanichko, were hastily put "in charge of the AzCP Central Committee", a vague but nevertheless useful endorsement that would tide them over till their predictable election by the Supreme Soviet a few days later.[77]

The election took place on January 24, 1990, when the first secretary, Abdul Rahman Vezirov, who had already been sacked by Moscow, was "relieved" of his position, which was subsequently offered to Ayaz N. Mutalibov, who had already been functioning as such for a while. Mutalibov received 82 votes in favor, 31 against, thus beating the alternative candidate, Hasan Hasanov, then Third Secretary of the party, who had a good rapport with the APF.[78] Hasanov was later mollified by his appointment on January 26 to the post Mutalibov had held earlier, chairman of the Council of Ministers.

Heidar Aliev used Black January to his advantage. Like Etibar Mamedov, he too held a press conference at the Azerbaijan Representation in Moscow to condemn Baku's invasion. Aliev's favorite for the position of First Secretary was Hasan Hasanov, who later served as Aliev's foreign minister from 1993 to 1998, though the party chose the Moscow-installed Mutalibov. A major reason for Moscow's decision was probably Hasanov's speeches critical of Moscow, the last of which he had delivered on January 8, 12 days prior to the Soviet invasion.[79]

While Moscow was involved in restructuring the leadership of the AzCP, on January 22 a burial ceremony was held for the victims of Black January. The organization committee consisted of the APF, the Muslim Board of the Transcaucasus, and the Baku City Soviet Executive Committee. Given that the invasion was aimed at forestalling the APF's rise to power, the Soviet authorities must have felt ill at ease at their inability to prevent the APF's participation at such a ceremony, which had a big symbolic importance. The Baku Radio repeatedly broadcast the time and date of the "funeral ceremony for the martyrs", which implied that the APF was still very much a major political factor Moscow had to reckon with.[80] The victims were buried in *Shahidler Khiyabani* (Martyrs' Cemetery) in a long row along a granite wall.[81]

The same Baku Radio continued to broadcast commentaries on January 21, lamenting the biased attitude of Moscow towards Armenia. One commentary stated that Moscow ignored Armenia's military involvement in the NKAO, Shaumyan and Khanlar regions. The commentary argued that not only the Soviet Union, but also the United States and Europe favored Armenia in the conflict.[82] The same day, Heidar Aliev, the former Politburo member and the chief of the republic, stated from his retirement in Nakhichevan that the Soviet invasion was "inhuman, undemocratic, and unlawful."[83]

A day earlier, on January 20, 1990 Nakhichevan, where Aliev resided, had declared independence in reaction to the Soviet invasion. On January 20 Sakina Alieva, head of the Nakhichevan ASSR Presidium, read to the press a four-point resolution of the Presidium declaring Nakhichevan's independence. The resolution called on Turkey to help safeguard Nakhichevan's territorial integrity. It also sought help from the United Nations, Iran and other states. It insisted that the Presidium's resolution was legal according to Article 81 of the Soviet Constitution and was in response to the violation of the territorial integrity of Azerbaijan and Nakhichevan by Armenia and the Soviet Union.[84] The Nakhichevani resolution was influenced by the local APF which ignored for eight days the occupying Soviet forces' orders.[85]

The measures Moscow took after the invasion seemed timid and half-hearted. They seemed to be aimed at damage control rather than the re-establishment of the full authority of the AzCP, which seemed unrealistic given the escalation of the NKAO conflict. There was also a lack of co-ordination, and the policies of officers implementing emergency rule lacked uniformity. While in some cities and regions APF members were arrested and APF offices shut down, in others the APF continued to function as a legal organization.

The military administration in Baku arrested many APF leaders, including mathematician Rahim Gaziev, who later became defense minister in the post-independence Elchibey Government. Etibar Mamedov was arrested later in Moscow at the office of the Azerbaijan Representation after he held a press conference there denouncing the invasion. Both men were to remain in the Lefortovo Prison in Moscow for nine months.[86] Both were earlier named in the APF Defense Council, the organization set up by the APF to conduct the warfare in the NKAO. A third member of the Defense Council, the firebrand Neimat Panakhov fled across the border to Iran and then to Turkey. Despite its tough crackdown, the military administration stopped short of outlawing the APF. The commander of the military administration, Vladimir S. Dubinyak, did ban, however, the APF Defense Committee, which had been setting up military units to fight in the NKAO.[87] The APF's newspaper *Azadlik* and another pro-APF daily, *Azerbaijan*, were also proscribed after January 20.[88]

Another good example of the military rule's diffidence was its toleration of the local APF's de facto control of Nakhichevan's TV and radio broadcasts, newspapers and post and telegraph services. The APF took part in joint sessions with the oblast's *obkom* to discuss important matters. The general strike that was organized by the APF in the wake of the invasion remained in force in Nakhichevan as in Baku. The military emergency rule did not also strongly challenge the Azerbaijani railway strike that stopped the Armenian use of the Azerbaijan–Armenia railway. The general strike, however, that began after January 20 slackened by the end of the month. Close to 80 percent of strikers returned to work by January 31.[89] The Soviet military units imposing the state of emergency did not interfere in the APF's prominence, which the latter exercised prima facie from the sidelines. The Soviet units did re-establish control along the Nakhichevan–Iran, and Azerbaijan–Iran borders, which had less than a month previously been overrun by enraged crowds protesting the Soviet era's callous border regime.[90]

The Nakhichevan APF also conducted ceasefire talks with the ANM that were organized by Major-General Mikhail Surkov, head of the Political Department of the Yerevan Garrison. AzCP and ACP officials from Nakhichevan and Armenia were also present at the talks, held in the Ararat raion of Armenia, which culminated in a ceasefire agreement on January 25, 1990.[91] The parties subsequently engaged in negotiations to lift the Azerbaijani blockade of Armenia and the Armenian blockade of Nakhichevan, but to no avail.[92] At another part of Azerbaijan, transition was less smooth. In Lenkoran, Alekram Hummatov, who had forcefully seized power from the local AzCP on January 11, chose to go underground when the MVD forces began to arrive after Black January. On January 25 and 26 APF personnel who had occupied the party *raykom* and its *ispolkom* (Soviet executive committee) vacated the premises peacefully. Yet fighting could still not be avoided. There ensued clashes between Soviet military units and armed men belonging to the APF, leading to the arrest of 50 of them.[93] In other parts of Azerbaijan, reactions to the Soviet invasion were often vocal and boisterous. In the central Azerbaijani city of Barda, the city party committee (gorkom) first secretary resigned in response to the APF demands. In the nearby city of Mingechevir a mass rally took place, in which crowds called on the local AzCP officials to dissociate themselves from the party. In response the gorkom first secretary, the city soviet executive committee chairman and the local internal affairs and KGB chiefs publicly burned their AzCP membership cards. Similar burnings of party cards were repeated elsewhere, including Shusha.[94]

In the NKAO the Armenian-organized general strike also continued after Black January. Following Black January, Volskiy, whose mandate had lapsed much earlier but who had remained in the NKAO to conduct business as usual, left the oblast. Volskiy's departure from the oblast after January 20, 1990 left the NKAO without an administration. Victor Polyanichko, the second secretary of the AzCP, was speedily made head of the quickly established Republican Organizing Committee to run the oblast. Polyanichko took advantage of Moscow's desire to restore its influence in the republic in the wake of its bloody military operation. He also enjoyed a good relationship with Defense Minister Dimitriy Yazov and the

KGB boss Vladimir Kryuchkov, which he hoped to utilize to bring peace and order to the oblast.

On January 26, 1990 Polyanichko arrived in the oblast accompanied by General Vladislav Safanov, head of the State of Emergency in the Republic. From the start Armenians who refused to cooperate shunned Polyanichko and the ten-member Organizing Committee, forcing Polyanichko to remain isolated at the Regional AzCP headquarters. Nevertheless, the oblast's Armenian residents feared Polyanichko and even viewed him as an evil person for his ardent pursuit of Azerbaijani sovereignty over the oblast.[95] The new administration arrested many Armenian activists, while also trying to create rifts within the Armenian camp. His chief aid, Seiran Mirzoyev, stated later that Polyanichko spread rumors and false allegations to split the then united NKAO Armenian nationalists. Eventually, the conservative party chief Genrikh Pogosyan and the young radical Arkady Manucharov engaged in a public quarrel. So there was at least a crack.[96]

In May 1990 Mutalibov returned from Moscow, announcing that he had succeeded in the abolition of the NKAO's separate budgetary allocation in the Gosplan, Soviet Planning Agency, which had been the case during the Volskiy administration since February 1988. After May 1990 the NKAO was again formally part of Azerbaijan's economy.[97] Also, in the spring of 1990, Azerbaijan established its own special police force (OMON), which was made possible with the new Union legislation. Incidentally, most OMON recruits were Azeris recently deported from Armenia.[98] Some of these OMON units were deployed in the NKAO.

In the NKAO, AzCP and government offices remained closed, because the mostly ethnic Armenian staff refused to hoist the Azerbaijani flag as demanded by the Soviet military. The NKAO Party organization also published for a while the nationalist National Council's Armenian newspaper *Khorhrdayin Karabagh*, which was banned by the military, as a party newspaper to circumvent the ban.[99] In late February 1990 the commander of the emergency rule, Major General Safonov, decreed that *Khorhrdayin Karabagh* was inciting ethnic hatred and hence was placed under censorship.[100]

The military emergency administration placed the oblast's radio under its control and ensured the resumption of the Askeran–Stepanakert train service under heavy military supervision. Yet the NKAO civilian and Armenian-dominated administration refused to receive provisions sent by the AzSSR.[101] Despite the emergency rule's emphasis on Azerbaijani sovereignty over the oblast, it did not put an end to the air corridor between Armenia and the NKAO that had started earlier, an indication of

Moscow's desire to avoid identification with the Azerbaijani position on the NKAO dispute.

The military cleared many roadblocks within the NKAO, which created the image that things were not so bad in the oblast. Nevertheless, the blockades on the Aghdam–Stepanakert and on the Lachin–Stepanakert roads remained, while rival militias belonging to the APF and the ANM manned them.[102] Polyanichko described this rather mixed picture as the success of his mission, though the reality was more nebulous. Vadim Byrkin, the Soviet News Agency's correspondent in the NKAO, suggested that Polyanichko's authority was not real:

> [Polyanichko] had no real mechanism of administration because he had no power structures at his disposal. He had his Organizing Committee of ten people, which held meetings that the Armenians didn't attend. There were reports to Baku that everything was fine here, that the Armenians had begun to cooperate. In fact there was no cooperation. . . .[103]

The AzCP Loses Further Ground

After Black January the AzCP lost prestige in the eyes of the Azerbaijanis, not only because it could not avert the Soviet invasion, but also because it was unable to reassert control over the NKAO. The failure or reluctance of Soviet troops in the oblast to ensure full Azerbaijani sovereignty over the oblast was perceived by many Azeris as evidence of Moscow's long-suspected pro-Armenian bias. Since it was perceived as being propped up by Moscow, the Mutalibov administration lost points with the Azeri public, no matter how critical it pretended to be of Black January. The new first secretary, who was handpicked by Moscow, tried to shed this unflattering image by embracing some of the policy goals of the APF. He demanded the withdrawal of Soviet forces from Baku and the ending of the state of emergency in Baku and the NKAO. Yet he needed to walk a tightrope because he had to please both Moscow and the Azerbaijanis, which sometimes proved unfeasible.

Conscious of his credibility gap, Mutalibov, nevertheless, attempted the impossible. In his speech at the CPSU Central Committee plenum on February 5, 1990 he stated that perestroika gave momentum to the secessionist drive in the NKAO and a civil war was taking place in the oblast, which even the Soviet army failed to contain. Trying to appeal to the home front, he accused Armenia for opening up Pandora's Box:

> Someone must have been the first to start this vile provocation. So, why have the[ir] names… not been spoken aloud for all to hear? Many of them are continuing to fuel the interethnic conflict with enviable persistence worthy of better application…. Thus, the open, totally unsubstantiated territorial claims by one republic against another have been the cause of the conflict.[104]

In a surprisingly frank acknowledgement of the dilemma in which he and the AzCP found themselves, Mutalibov added that the inability of Moscow and the AzCP to sustain Azerbaijani sovereignty over the NKAO

> did serious damage to the republic party organization's authority, and formed a vacuum between it and the people. … This led to a virtual paralysis of … [the AzCP] for some time and … [the AzCP] is going to feel the effects of the 1990's difficult January for a long time to come."[105]

Mutalibov's credibility gap was all the more plausible given that Moscow reacted differently to the pre-January 19, 1990 events in Azerbaijan and Armenia. In early January 1990, while the APF in Azerbaijan was challenging the AzCP's authority, the Armenian paramilitary forces under the command of the ANM were also expanding their areas of control at the expense of the ACP. The ANM irregulars were not only openly operating in Armenia to cross the border to the NKAO but they were also infiltrating western Nakhichevan for hit and run operations. In various parts of Armenia the ANM guerrillas continued the ethnic cleansing operations against Azeri villagers who had proved reluctant to emigrate. In the Krasnosel raion, an Azerbaijani enclave or sovereign territory of Azerbaijan within Armenia, armed guerrillas laid siege around the Azeri village of Artsvashen, while unmarked helicopters flew over it.[106] Soon in Armenia and Azerbaijan deportations of the "others" to their "original homeland" would accelerate. Armenians living in enclaves within Azerbaijan and Azeris populating Azerbaijani enclaves within Armenia would not be exempt from such acts.

In many regions of Armenia, attacks were carried out on the police, militia and the Soviet army units to seize weapons and ammunition. In one case Major General I. Kondratyuk and four other officers of the Soviet

Army were taken hostage, only to be released later.[107] On January 20, 1990, the day the Baku invasion took place, another meeting of the "Operational Committee" bringing together the ACP Central Committee members, Government Ministers and the ANM representatives took place. Apprehensive of a similar fate that befell the APF across the border, the Armenian radio stated that the ANM was cooperating with the Soviet Army to preserve law and order in the republic.[108]

The same day, the ACP established the "Republican Council for the Special Situation" under the chairmanship of ACP First Secretary Suren Arutrunyan. The Council was to work to prevent the escalation of the crisis within the republic and maintain law and order. The new Council included the ACP Central Committee, Armenian SSR Supreme Soviet Presidium, and the Council of Ministers. It did not include the ANM. It was announced that the Operational Committee that did include the ANM would be affiliated with the Republican Council.[109]

This operational maze, it seems, was to serve two purposes. It would show the Soviets that unlike Azerbaijan, Armenia was trying to keep law and order by even co-opting the ANM. It would also help to convince the ANM and other nationalists that the ACP was sharing power with them while going through the motions to appease Moscow. The proliferation of councils and committees might also have been an ingenious way for the ANM to fool Moscow. Given that in Armenia, the ACP and the ANM rank and file, and increasingly those in leadership positions were the same people, enabled both organizations to execute a smooth transition of power.

The APF Adopts a More Radical Rhetoric

The APF leaders were people who were initially inspired by Gorbachev reforms, other Soviet republics' desire for more sovereignty and the struggles of the popular fronts in the Baltic Republics for independence. Yet Armenia's irredentism and secessionism of local Armenians in the NKAO forced the APF to busy itself almost solely with the NKAO problem. The APF acted in response to day-to-day developments, coming up with makeshift solutions to problems that the AzCP failed to cope with. Throughout 1989 it organized blockades of roads and railroads against Armenia and the NKAO Armenians and mobilized Azeri masses to demonstrate and apply pressure on the AzCP to act more assertively. It also formed armed militia to fight the Armenian paramilitary groups who gradually came to control

1 Contemporary Azerbaijan map, including Armenian-occupied Nagorno-Karabagh.

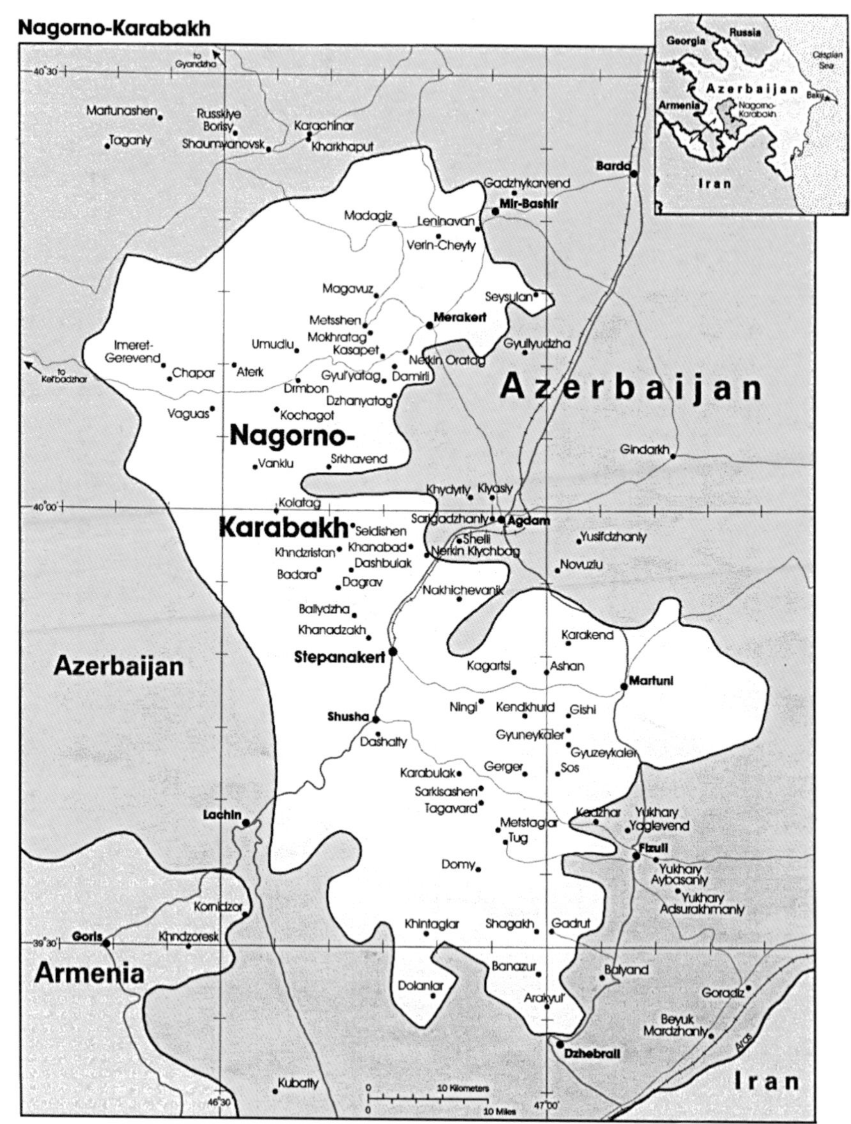

2 Nagorno-Karabagh map, currently under Armenian military forces.

3 Azerbaijan map.

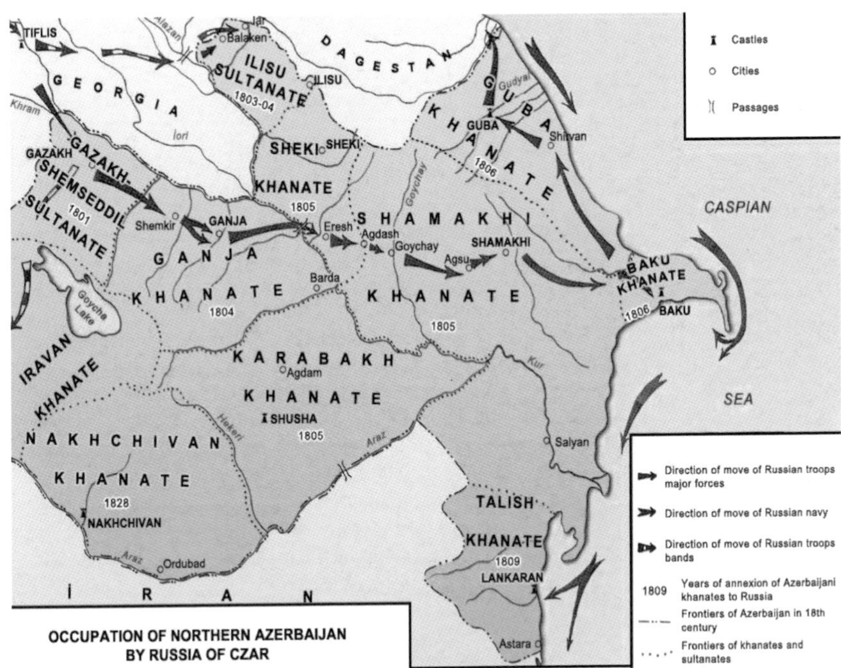

4 Nineteenth-century occupation of Azerbaijan by Russia: with dates for the occupation of different parts.

5 Abulfaz Elchibey.
First President of independent Azerbaijan.

6 Haidar Aliev. USSR era First Secretary
of Azerbaijan and post-independence second president.

7 Abulfaz Elchibey together with Turkish President Turgut Ozal and Prime Minister Suleyman Demirel at the celebration of the Turkish Republic Day in Ankara. October 29, 1992.

8 Azeri President Ilham Aliyev met with Russian President Dmitry Medvedev. April 20, 2009.

9 Ilham Aliev. Current President of Azerbaijan who succeeded his father, Haidar Aliev.

10 Post-Black January demonstrations in Baku. Demonstrations after the January 20, 1990 Soviet invasion of Baku.

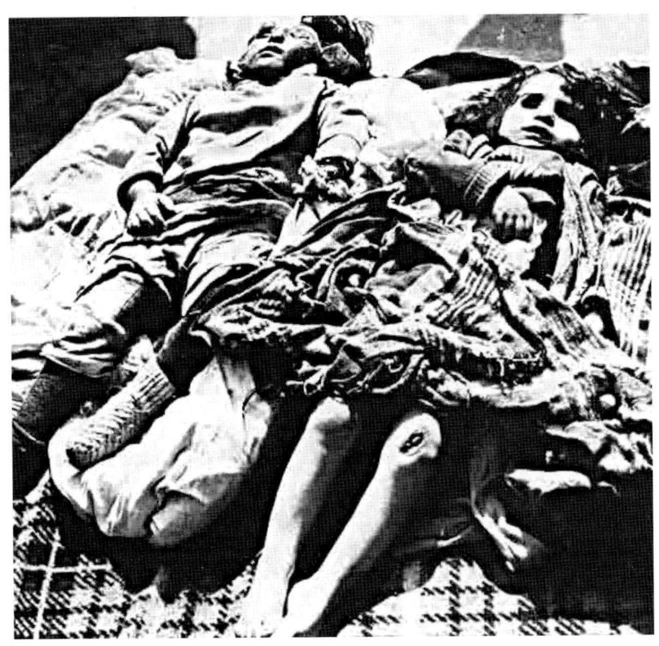

11 Khojaly massacre in 1991.

12 Azeri Martyr's Cemetery in Baku.
Burial place of Nagorno-Karabagh war victims.

13 Azeri woman refugee after having been expelled from Nagorno-Karabagh. She is located in the Sabirabad camp.

14 Fleeing on foot from Kelbejar, Azerbaijan, after the Armenians attacked this region. April, 1993.

the NKAO. By early 1990 the APF had become better organized and had even begun to serve as an informal government in many parts of the country. The invasion of Baku contributed immensely to the public feeling of victimization and to anti-Soviet sentiments. The fact that Azerbaijan was invaded, while Armenia – also in the midst of a turbulent nationalist upheaval and perceived by the Azeris as the culprit of the interethnic strife since 1988 – was spared such a misfortune, strengthened the centuries-old feeling that Russia was favoring Armenians, or fellow Christians. After Black January the average Azerbaijani began to believe that they should only expect unfair treatment at the hands of the Soviets. Consequently, most thought that more assertiveness was necessary, and the APF, with its ever-growing reputation for acting tough, seemed a suitable candidate for the public's trust.[110]

The remarks of Allahshukur Pashazada, the chairman of the Spiritual Directorate of the Muslims of the Transcaucasus, one of four throughout the USSR, shows to what extent the Azeris were alienated from Moscow. In the immediate aftermath of Black January, he said that the invasion was unnecessary and it caused fatalities among the civilians, including women and children. He stated that Moscow had a pro-Armenian bias, because earlier when Armenia expelled Azeris, Moscow did nothing to stop it. For this reason, he claimed that although the Azerbaijanis initially supported Gorbachev, they now disliked him.[111]

The increasing appeal of the APF led many to think of and articulate ideas that were not spoken aloud earlier. Etibar Mamedov, then an APF leader, stated on January 25, 1990 that the APF's long-term goal was to unite Soviet Azerbaijan with Iranian Azerbaijan. Yet, he said, the moment was not right for such a struggle.[112] Next day Mamedov was arrested in Moscow for "inciting nationalist passions" and "straining interethnic relations".[113]

Another indication of Azeri, and Armenian alienation, was that more and more conscripts from the Transcaucasian republics deserted their military units in various parts of the Soviet Union to join paramilitary units in their individual republics. In late 1989 and early January 1990 up to 770 recruits, including Georgians, deserted their units. Furthermore, in 1989 alone, 6,603 people in the Transcaucasus dodged the draft, although it is not clear what percentage they constituted of the pool of their respective republics' draft age population.[114]

The APF's self-confidence was such that despite Black January ten days previously, it engaged in quasi-official negotiations with the ANM in Riga,

Latvia, between February 1 and 4, 1990. The talks were organized by the Latvian and Estonian Popular Fronts and the Lithuanian Sajudis (Movement for Reconstruction). The parties agreed to release hostages by March 1 and establish permanent contacts. Yet on the issue of substance, namely the sovereignty over the NKAO, the parties disagreed. The ANM insisted that Azerbaijan should recognize the right to self-determination for the NKAO, while the APF argued that respect for the current borders would stabilize the "situation". The talks ended in deadlock.[115]

Struggling to pull the carpet from underneath the APF, the AzSSR Council of Ministers, as suggested earlier, announced on February 13, 1990 that it would establish "the NKAO Organization Committee". This resolution was seemingly in reaction to Moscow's December 1989 proposal to establish a Republican Organization Committee with significant ethnic Armenian participation. The NKAO Organization Committee was supposed to supervise the NKAO's administrative and elected bodies and be subordinate to the AzSSR (see above). The Azerbaijani version of the Organization Committee (OC) came into being in mid-February 1990 and was headed by the second secretary of the AzCP, Victor Polyanichko.[116] The OC was to prove just another ring in a chain of demised projects to resuscitate Azerbaijani hegemony in the NKAO.

There were other symbolic steps the AzCP took to stress its commitment to the "national cause" and redeem itself as the defender of Azerbaijan's rights. In early February 1990 the AzCP Central Committee decided that the Organization Committee should publish a newspaper by the name of *Karabagh* in Azeri Turkish. The Central Committee also decided to erect a statue of the famous Azeri/Turkish poet Nizami in Moscow in 1991 on his 850th anniversary.[117] Later, on March 13, 1990 the AzSSR Supreme Soviet adopted a resolution making March 21 of each year, which is the start of the Iranian New Year (Nevruz) a national holiday.[118] Nevruz is considered a quasi-religious date and has been celebrated by Turkic peoples in Central Asia and the Caspian basin for centuries. However, it was banned for most of the Soviet era.

Mutalibov Increasingly Moves to a quasi-Nationalistic Stance

In a speech in early April 1990 the first secretary of the AzCP, Ayaz N. Mutalibov, talked about the problems faced by the country, and more importantly about issues that negatively affected the legitimacy of the

AzCP. It had been less than three months when he was handpicked by Moscow to lead the country in the aftermath of Black January. He argued that the republic faced considerable socio-economic and ecological problems, but the main cause for the people's pain and suffering was the consequences of events that started back in February 1988 in the NKAO.[119] Although he did not say it openly, he was clearly referring to the AzCP's inability to successfully deal with the crisis and its being sidelined by a more vigorous political entity, the APF.

Mutalibov boasted, however, that under his leadership the AzCP was able to achieve rapprochement with the masses because the AzCP took measures to meet the people's demands. Referring to the ACP's partnership with the ANM and to his predecessor Vezirov' informally following the lead of the APF, he argued that the AzCP was now taking its own initiatives. He said: "What is changed is that we have taken a firm position. Whatever the motives – sovereignty, the integrity of the republic and so on – [we] must have a clear position and a clear plan of action."[120] Yet, contradicting what he said regarding the AzCP assertiveness, he criticized Moscow's "inability" to solve the NKAO problem, Mutalibov suggested: "There are problems which are the center's [Moscow's] prerogative to solve." Otherwise, he said, no matter how hard-working the AzCP were, they could not create miracles. Once again undercutting his argument, he went on to say that Moscow encouraged him to take initiatives, but that he didn't possess the means to do so. He asked rhetorically: "Given the centralization that exists [in the USSR], what do I have? Do I have an army or legions of some sort? I have nothing. My weapons are party influence, words, propaganda, and in the final analysis, appeals and requests [from the CPSU]."[121] He then promised to work harder to have more democracy within the AzCP and to make the latter more independent from Moscow.[122]

Although Mutalibov sounded critical of his predecessor's affiliation with the APF, he too sought to involve the latter in policy formulation. On May 17, 1990 AzCP officials met with the APF leadership to discuss border skirmishes with Armenians, the APF's proposal to set up a republican army, relations between the APF and government institutions, and the military emergency rule. The meeting produced the so-called Consultative Council, which was to make suggestions towards strengthening the republic's sovereignty. AzCP and APF members and several non-APF members of the intellectual elite would be represented in the Council. Following its foundation, the Council suggested: 1) the president of the republic should be elected in general polls, but because of the extraordinary situation of the republic, the Supreme Soviet could elect him; 2) Azerbaijan should consider emulating Armenia and put a stop to Azerbaijani troops serving outside the republic; and 3) the anniversary of the establishment of the Republic of Azerbaijan on May 28, 1918 should be publicly commemorated.[123]

Next day, on May 18, 1990 the Azerbaijan Supreme Soviet elected Mutalibov President by a vote of 316 in favor and three against. Following the trend elsewhere in the Soviet Union, the post of the presidency was established the same day by the AzSSR Supreme Soviet, implying, mostly symbolic, reduction of the AzCP role in politics.[124] Before his election, Mutalibov went on expanding upon the nationalist theme he had borrowed from the APF. He stated that he was in favor of Azerbaijan's economic autonomy, especially because Azerbaijani oil was sold to the Soviet state for a virtual pittance. After being processed by the Union, the same oil was exported to the world at a much higher price, while Azerbaijan continued to suffer from a trade imbalance. Mutalibov's statement was not necessarily anti-Moscow because Gorbachev himself had advocated economic autonomy and efficiency for the republics.[125] On another sensitive subject, the language issue, Mutalibov also seemed to be going out on a limb, suggesting that the use of the Azerbaijani language should be encouraged and other nationalities living in Azerbaijan should gradually learn it. Yet, to make sure not to offend Moscow, he added that "Russian has been and remains the language of interethnic communication in Azerbaijan. I would like to state that quite definitely."[126]

Despite his attempt to put distance between himself and Union authorities, it was obvious that Mutalibov was towing Moscow's line on most major issues. Yet there were more sincere efforts by the once major section of the ruling elite, members of the AzSSR Academy of Sciences. In February 1990 it was reported that a group of scholars from the academy began working on the adoption of the Latin alphabet by the end of 1990. Among other issues, they discussed whether Turkey's version of Latin or a revised version of it should be adopted.[127] It is not clear if the Mutalibov administration was involved in it, or if it was opposed to it. Such activities did indicate, however, that nationalist ideas had made significant inroads into the academic establishment.

6

Baku Courts Moscow while the ANM Comes to Power in Yerevan

The NKAO Soviet of People's Deputies resumed its sessions on March 27, 1990, after a lull of several months. Yet ethnic Azeri deputies of the Soviet did not participate in the sessions, fearing for their safety in Stepanakert.[1] The appearance of normalcy received another boost in early April 1990 with the cessation of strikes.[2] A major reason for the termination of the strikes was heavy Soviet troop presence after Black January and the Soviet army's emergency rule in the oblast. The promise of a return to normalcy was reinforced a few days later when the Azerbaijani and Armenian Prime Ministers, Hasanov and Markaryan, met in the Georgian capital, Tblisi, and agreed to adopt joint measures to normalize rail traffic between their republics and to work harder to curtail ethnic violence.[3] This summit took place amid Armenian violence directed against such Azerbaijani border regions as Kazakh, Lachin and Nakhichevan's Ilich (Ilichevskiy) raions.

Despite the Tblisi meeting and the termination of strikes in the NKAO, the nationalist commotion and euphoria emanating from Armenia and the NKAO continued to fuel Azerbaijani furor and anxiety, contributing to the APF's gradual reappearance as defender of Azeri rights. One of the earliest of such Armenian provocative acts as perceived by the Azeris was the establishment in late January in Yerevan of the so-called *Hamahaykakan Paykari Miatsyal Chakat* (United Front for Pan-Armenian Struggle), bringing together 34 Armenian organizations from Armenia and throughout the USSR. The front announced that its foremost goal was the solution of the urgent problems facing the Armenian nation.[4]

On February 17, 1990 the Armenian Supreme Soviet elected as members Levon Ter-Petrosyan, chairman of the ANM, and others, including Robert Kocharian, head of the NKAO Armenian fighters, and Khrachik Simonyan, one of the leaders of the Yerkrapah (Defender of the Country) movement, which dispatched Armenian paramilitary forces to the NKAO.[5] This was yet another indication that the ACP was trying to co-opt the ANM and other groups either to contain their criticism of the ACP's policy on the NKAO, or that it proved impossible not to do so given their popularity. Kocharian's and Simonyan's gaining seats at Armenia's Supreme Soviet also showed that Armenia had abandoned all pretension that it was not officially involved in the NKAO hostilities. The Azeris could not have overlooked the radicalization of Armenia's administration or Moscow's failure or reluctance to clamp down on the latter, which provided further validation for the argument that Moscow had a pro-Armenian bias.

In the last week of March 1990, irregulars from Armenia infiltrated Azerbaijan's Kazakh (Kazakhskiy) raion, killing several Azeris. Other guerrillas attacked the border towns of Sederek and Kerki in Nakhichevan, killing another ten people.[6] In reaction, Azerbaijan closed its borders with Armenia on March 29, 1990. Undeterred, Armenian fighters attacked the Nakhichevan Shahbuz (Shahbuzskiy) raion's town of Shada on March 31.[7] During March and April 1990, Armenian fighters continued to attack Azerbaijani trains when the latter entered the Zangezur region of Armenia on their way to Nakhichevan.[8]

On May 3, 1990 the Armenian Supreme Soviet adopted a resolution which stated that the 1921 Treaty of Moscow and the decision of the Bolshevik Party's Caucasian Bureau in 1921 led to the loss of 80 percent of Armenia's territory.[9] The resolution suggested that the 1921 Treaty recognized the loss to Turkey of "Western Armenia" whereas the Caucasian Bureau's decision involved the award of the NKAO and Nakhichevan to Azerbaijan. The resolution also made reference to Azerbaijan's decision on April 21 to redraw the boundaries of individual districts within the NKAO, arguing that Baku's intention was to reverse ethnic Armenians' demographic preponderance.[10]

On May 20, 1990, elections for the Armenian SSR Supreme Soviet took place. Armenia tried to also enable Armenian residents of the NKAO to participate in the elections. Presumably aware of the symbolic nature of its move, Yerevan sent to the NKAO ballots and ballot boxes and set aside seats in the to be elected Supreme Soviet for the NKAO Armenians. The military emergency administration in the oblast banned the participation of the NKAO Armenians in Armenia's elections, though 11 *okrugs* (districts) in the oblast supposedly held elections, choosing 11 representatives to the Armenian Supreme Soviet.[11]

The May 1990 elections to the Armenian Supreme Soviet resulted in a victory for the ANM and other nationalist parties, which came to control more than 50 percent of the seats of the Assembly and elected ANM chairman Levon Ter-Petrosyan as President of the legislative body. Ter-Petrosyan received 140 votes whereas First Secretary Vladimir Movsisyan of the ACP his main rival in the elections, received only 76 votes.[12] The ANM leader was a staunch advocate of incorporating the NKAO into Armenia, and his activities in 1988 had led to his imprisonment along with 11 other members of the Armenian Karabagh Committee (AKC). Later, Ter-Petrosyan headed the successor of the AKC, the ANM, and the increasing influence of the latter within the republic forced the ACP to invite him, along with other ANM leaders, to the Armenian Supreme Soviet in August 1989. His election as President by the newly elected Supreme Soviet symbolized the transfer of power from the ACP to the ANM. Nevertheless, Ter-Petrosyan appointed a significant number of ACP members to governmental and administrative positions to make use of their expertise, as well as to co-opt them into his regime.

One of the very first resolutions of the new Armenian Supreme Soviet came on July 31, 1990, which suspended Gorbachev's July 25 ban on illegal armed groups in Armenia and the NKAO, and demanded the surrender of their weapons by August 10. The Armenian Supreme Soviet declared that the Soviet Constitution did not entitle Gorbachev to issue such a decree, and hence announced the suspension of it in "Armenia, including the NKAO."[13] The resolution thus formally legalized the ANA and other smaller paramilitary units.[14] Nevertheless, the same day Ter-Petrosyan decreed the establishment of the core of a national army, the 2,000-strong self-defense detachments.[15]

These developments showed that while trying to curry favor with militant armed groups in the republic, Ter-Petrosyan desired to restrain and eventually eliminate them as independent centers of power. He was worried that these armed groups caused more harm than good in Armenia, and they were to be relocated to the NKAO and to mostly Armenian inhabited villages near the oblast.[16] These forces would begin to engage Soviet forces in a low intensity conflict in the NKAO in the last months of 1990. In the meantime, Ter-Petrosyan met with the Soviet Prime Minister, Nikolai Ryzhkov, on August 9 and assured him that the Armenian Government would incorporate the truly "nationalist" guerrillas into its police force, whereas the unruly gangs would be disbanded. At the meeting, he spoke of Armenia's intention to declare independence, though the full realization of it, he said, would take some time.[17]

Earlier, on May 27, 1990 there were clashes between Armenian guerrillas and Soviet Interior Ministry (MVD) troops in Armenia, in which 22 people, mostly guerrillas, died. Next day, the commander of MVD troops, Yuriy Shatalin, who was incidentally in Yerevan, accused the Armenian Republican leadership for conniving with "illegal armed formations" of the nationalist parties.[18] General Shatalin suggested that although there were thousands of illegally armed guerrilla groups serving as paramilitary forces of various Armenian political parties, the ACP leadership shied away from calling upon him to disarm them. He argued that the Armenian Supreme Soviet's resolution to set up military units to keep public order amounted to legalizing the existing paramilitary formations.[19]

While such groups as the ANA or even the relatively moderate ANM, which was practically in control of most of Armenia, flouted the writ of the Soviet state in practice, the AzCP leadership was still banking on endearing itself to the latter. The AzCP did not do so publicly, because identification with Moscow, in the aftermath of Black January, would have cost the AzCP its already diminished public support at home. The AzCP did try, however, to keep a low profile while facilitating the re-establishment of the status quo of a year ago.

Earlier, the AzCP's intermittent public outcry *vis-à-vis* Moscow's NKAO policy had helped to project the ruling party's image as a somewhat genuine defender of national rights. Yet, during the turbulent events in Armenia in early June 1990, the AzCP chief, Mutalibov, discussed with equanimity the tenets of perestroika at the 32nd Congress of the AzCP in Baku.[20] The APF, for its part, also displayed composure, and – unlike its previous hard-line stance – argued that ethnic quarrels would be easier tackled if those in charge had democratic credentials. In June 1990 Yusuf Samedoglu called on "democratic organizations" in Azerbaijan, Armenia, Georgia, and Daghestan to set aside their interethnic problems and to cooperate with each other, so that they negotiated with Moscow from a position of strength.[21] Evidently, the APF expected that it could opt for a more relaxed stance and offer dialogue to the ANM, which the latter could ill-afford at a time when it was about to adopt a more assertive policy.

As the AzCP hoped for, formal Azerbaijani rule was re-established in the NKAO by the end of June 1990. The Azerbaijani (Republican)

Organizing Committee, headed by AzCP Second Secretary Victor Polyanichko, ensured that Soviet Interior Ministry troops, who enforced the state of emergency in the oblast, restored a semblance of normalcy in the oblast. Blockades manned by Armenian paramilitaries on roads and railway tracks were removed, rail traffic between Azerbaijan proper and the NKAO resumed, and the general strike conducted by the Armenian side tapered off.[22]

The Moscow-enforced state of emergency in the NKAO also enabled the AzCP to fire several raion party committee (*raykom*) chiefs. They included the first secretary of the Gadrut (Gadrutskiy) *raykom*, Grisha Bageyan, who in the May 20, 1990 elections in the NKAO, which were banned by the AzCP, was elected to Armenia's Supreme Soviet. The AzCP accused Bageyan with the pursuit of a nationalist and separatist policy, disregard of the AzCP's decisions, and obstruction of the NKAO Organization Committee's work. Gadrut's local party administration was also suspended, and replaced with a temporary raion organization committee to implement Baku's directives.[23] Such administrative fiat, however, was not to last too long. Sooner than later Armenian paramilitaries would successfully eliminate any residue of Azerbaijani influence in the oblast.

Despite the momentary lull in fighting, the steady stream of border crossings by ANA guerrillas continued. These infiltrations originated mostly from Goris in Armenia, the region closest in distance to the NKAO. Clashes that took place in Azerbaijan's Lachin, bordering Goris, gave the impression that the ANA forces were bent on carving out for themselves a niche in Lachin, so as to build a safe corridor between Armenia and the NKAO. Other Azerbaijani regions subject to ANA infiltrations and guerrilla fighting included the Kazakh region in the northwest portion of Azerbaijan, and Nakhichevan. To reduce the permeability of the border, the Azerbaijani government offered an agreement to Armenia in early June 1990, involving the demilitarization of ten kilometers of the border on either side, and the removal of all "illegal armed units" from this area. The Armenian side refused the offer.[24] Later, Azerbaijan tried to cope with the problem by involving Soviet military forces. On June 15, 1990 Azerbaijan's Supreme Soviet asked President Mutalibov to impose martial law along the border raions with Armenia, to be enforced by Soviet KGB units and Soviet MVD forces, already deployed in the republic.[25]

Armenian Radicalization Forces the Azerbaijani Leadership to Adopt Opposition Demands

The increasing influence of irredentists in Armenia, and the fact that his was a Moscow-installed leadership led Mutalibov to increasingly use nationalist slogans and symbols to redeem his regime in the eyes of Azerbaijanis. He knew that without Moscow's support he would be unable to cope with battlefield challenges posed by the ANA guerrillas. Hence Mutalibov needed to be perceived embracing national/religious symbols to project himself as the true son of the Azeri nation. In many ways, he acted like many republican leaders elsewhere in Soviet republics, who adopted some of the policies of their popular fronts as their own.[26] On June 21, 1990 he met with a group of Muslims who were preparing to depart for the hajj in Mecca.[27] The group was small, but the event carried symbolic importance. Although the Soviet Union had sent Muslim pilgrims to hajj in recent years, the republic on its own was doing so for the first time. This event was followed by the start of publication on November 22, 1990 of the twice-monthly journal *The New Islam* by the Baku-based Transcaucasian Muslim Spiritual Board. It included articles on Islamic moral values and religious life in the region.[28] The Spiritual Board announced in late November that 30 renovated mosques had been recently reopened.

Despite Mutalibov's adoption of nationalist rhetoric, the APF went ahead with demanding more. Regarding the plan for a New Union Treaty, another Gorbachev brainchild, the APF counseled caution. It suggested that a new union would not protect Azerbaijan's territorial integrity, because in the past also, it added, the Soviet Union gave away Azerbaijani territory to others. The pro-APF newspaper articles also opposed the new union, arguing that Moscow would continue to keep decision-making powers and would make sure that the republics did not stand on their feet economically.[29]

Mutalibov, for his part, would not go as far as refusing a New Union Treaty out of hand. His record shows that he was adamant in his insistence for a new union. Nevertheless, he did not also refrain from finger pointing. On July 4, 1990 he made a speech at the CPSU Congress, in which he highlighted Moscow's culpability in the emergence of Armenian nationalism. He said that while some Politburo members, such as Yegor Ligachev, supported Azerbaijan's territorial integrity, others, such as Alexander Yakovlev, rationalized support for the NKAO's secession by referring to the people's right to self-determination. Mutalibov charged the CPSU for turning "Azerbaijan into a test bed for rehearsing ill-considered decisions." He added that the consequence of this policy was military confrontation between Azerbaijan and Armenia, and the deaths of many people. Mutalibov accused Moscow of tolerating the formation in Armenia of a, as he put it, 140,000-strong national army commanded by the republic's "informal authorities."[30]

While Mutalibov and the AzCP were embracing some of the APF's arguments, the APF itself was in the process of adopting new goals. In an interview with a Turkish newspaper in July 1990, the leader of the APF, Abulfaz Elchibey, stated that whereas the APF earlier sought sovereignty within the USSR, it had moved away from this goal in favor of "full independence". Displaying his pro-Turkey sentiments, Elchibey said that he desired a confederation between Turkey and Azerbaijan in 20 or 30 years.[31] Elchibey also criticized Mutalibov for refusing the APF's proposal that Azerbaijan should have its own national army, even after the ANA's troop strength reportedly reached 140,000.[32]

Two weeks later, on August 23, 1990, Ter-Petrosyan remained true to his promise when the Armenian Supreme Soviet declared independence and adopted "Republic of Armenia" as the name of the state. The declaration, which was passed by a vote of 183 in favor, two against and two abstentions, announced that a constitution and new laws were being prepared. The declaration proclaimed a multi-party system, freedoms of expression, assembly and the press, as well as separation of powers of the executive, legislative, and judicial branches.[33] Despite the declaration of independence, however, Armenia did not secede from the Union, with the declaration stating that it would happen when the conditions were right, an all too obvious reference to the fate of the NKAO.

The declaration granted citizenship not only to all the residents of the now defunct ASSR, but also to Armenians living in other parts of the USSR, including the NKAO, and those in the diaspora. Article 11 of the declaration affirmed that "[t]he republic of Armenia stands in support of the task of [achieving] the international recognition of the 1915 genocide in Ottoman Turkey, and Western Armenia" while another article proclaimed as an inalienable right the unification of the territories of the Republic of Armenia and the NKAO.[34] Article 11 as well as the preamble, which called for the "restoration of historic justice", became objects of discussions in parliament, with some moderates cautioning against addressing issues other than independence. Yet even the moderate Ramgavar faction joined the more radical pro-Dashnakt group in insisting on the more radical version.[35]

Throughout August 1990 Armenian paramilitaries belonging mostly to the ANA attacked border towns along the Azerbaijani–Armenian border. Most attacks took place from across Azerbaijan's northwest region of Kazakh. In response, towards the end of August, Azerbaijan stopped natural gas deliveries from Kazakh to Yerevan. The Azerbaijani government also closed the Kazakh–Idshevan (Armenia) railway. The escalation of the crisis forced President Ter-Petrosyan to ask for the endorsement by the Armenian Supreme Soviet of a state of emergency, the imposition of curfews, the disbandment of the ANA, and the latter's surrender of arms by the evening of August 29, 1990.[36]

Sharing a common desire with the nationalistically minded Ter-Petrosyan government, which is the avoidance of a Soviet invasion a la Baku, the ANA announced the disbandment of its militia and called on its members to surrender their arms to the government forces.[37] The disbandment of the ANA and its surrender of arms, an operation oozing orchestration by the Armenian government and the ANM, took place within 24 hours, almost belying the sincerity of the ANA and the government. Within days, the demobilized ANA troops were incorporated into the recently established national army of Armenia.

The democratization of the Armenian political landscape found its reflection in Azerbaijan, whose political players closely watched and often emulated what was going on in the territory of the adversary. The APF had often taken its cue from the ANM's expansion of its influence at the expense of the ACP. The AzCP, for its part, often found it hard not to grant more leeway to the APF when the ACP had already accorded significant privileges to the ANM. The election of the head of the ANM as President of the Armenian Supreme Soviet hence had a salient impact on both the government and the APF in Azerbaijan. In the September 30, 1990 Supreme Soviet elections the AzCP allowed the APF to participate, though the latter boycotted them even while allowing members to participate as independent candidates.[38]

Events in Armenia, including the declaration of independence, probably influenced the APF to adopt a new program, or platform, which would later influence the rhetoric and legislative acts of the "Democratic Azerbaijan" bloc made up of independent deputies elected in the September 30, 1990 elections. Although by May 1990 Mutalibov had adopted many of the APF goals, the new APF platform comprised more ambitious ones. Unlike the first APF platform, which singled out the AzCP in its criticism, and avoided harsh denunciations of the USSR, the second platform was blunt in its hostility towards Moscow. It declared the establishment of the Azerbaijan SSR illegal because it was the consequence of the Red Army's invasion in April 1920.[39]

Other articles of the program stipulated that relations between Azerbaijan and the Union should be modified in accordance with the Constitution and the laws of Azerbaijan. It called for Azerbaijan to conduct its own foreign policy, separate from that of the Soviet Union. The document seemed to contradict itself by also demanding independence, yet, within the then Soviet context, independence was still largely understood as wide-ranging autonomy. It asked for an end to the AzCP apparatus' domination of the republic's government, the justice branch and the media. Criticizing the Soviet legal system, it suggested that the accused should not be presumed guilty, referring to the Soviet era practice of considering trials as merely the presentation of the prosecution's case. It demanded that freedom of speech, conscience and religion be under the protection of the state. Favoring free market economy, it called for the creation of suitable conditions for foreign investment and foreign trade. The program also asked for reforms in various socio-cultural fields, including adoption of the Latin alphabet, new national, cultural and education policies, and more diligent protection of the environment. Perhaps the most popular part of the program was its demand that to ensure Azerbaijan's territorial integrity, the autonomy of the NKAO should be abolished.[40]

When the APF began calling for independence and the establishment of a national army, the AzCP was still balking at the idea of Azerbaijan having its own armed forces. On September 14, 1990 Prime Minister Hasan Hasanov, articulating the AzCP policy, stated that neither Azerbaijan nor Armenia needed armies of their own.[41] The AzCP's stand spoke of its continued advocacy of Moscow's involvement in the NKAO dispute. The AzCP reckoned that while Armenia declared independence, the AzCP's preservation of its deferential behavior towards Moscow would coax the latter into countenancing Baku's NKAO policy. This logic hence deemed the establishment of a national army counterproductive. In an interview Mutalibov acknowledged this view by saying that for him the most important weakness of the draft New Union Treaty was its failure to address national integrity of the republics, that is, the NKAO problem.[42] The Azerbaijani official stance thus differed from that of Armenia, Georgia, Moldova, and the Baltic republics, which desired independence.

On September 30 and October 14 two-stage elections were held for the Azerbaijan Supreme Soviet. The election campaign was restricted by the continuing martial law, which practically meant suppression of opposition activities while the AzCP continued to enjoy its control of republican institutions. Such prominent APF leaders as Rahim Gaziev and Etibar Mamedov remained in prison. The AzCP also prevented some APF members from registering, and closed some APF offices in the provinces. Observers reported widespread fraud in favor of the AzCP.[43]

On election day the electorate displayed obvious apathy, indicating that it perceived the vote as not essentially differing from previous Soviet elections. Official figures spoke of only around 50 percent participation in Baku, though in the provinces the participation rate was around 80 percent. The opposition did not fare well: it was able to capture only 26 seats, while the rest of the 350 seats went to the AzCP.[44] The Azerbaijani election results contrasted sharply with election results in neighboring Georgia and Armenia. In both, ruling communist parties were defeated, and nationalist movements led by Zviad Gamsakhurdia and Levon Ter-Petrosyan came to power. It would be fair to assume, however, that voters, especially in the provinces, did probably vote for the AzCP because the opposition led by urban intellectuals was calling for drastic changes in many areas of life which did not resonate well with the rural population.[45] Nevertheless, the AzCP made a gesture to the opposition by electing a moderate APF member, Tamerlan Karayev, as deputy speaker of the parliament. Some claimed that Karayev was too close to the ruling elite. Thomas Goltz, who observed the events unfolding, suggested that Karayev "was given to hand-tailored suits and flashy ties and a taste for traveling with presidential entourage."[46] Karayev, however, believed that he was doing the right thing: "The reason I chose to work with the government is that without compromise the situation in Azerbaijan would end in confrontation and bloodshed. … And with violence, we will never have our freedom."[47]

The opposition in the Supreme Soviet, which named itself the Democratic Bloc, was wrongly identified with the APF. Indeed, many of its members supported the APF, though there were quite a few who weren't involved with it. In general, however, the Democratic Bloc was a lively group, dominating the parliamentary deliberations and articulating views the rest of the AzCP-dominated parliament could not dare to address. Some of the colorful Democratic Bloc members included "the molish-looking Isa Gamberov, … tiny and sweet Towfig Gasimov (a theoretical physicist who greatly resembled Albert Einstein.), pugnacious and paranoid Rahim Gaziev (another diminutive fellow who was previously a professor of Mathematics), roly-poly Tahir Karimli…, and razor blade Arif Xadjiev (regarded as the 'brainy Bolshevik' of the Bloc.) Etibar Mamedov (an historian known locally as 'the little Napoleon') was already in the process of splitting with the Front and forming his own National Independence Party with money supplied by oil baron (and defender of the interests of the 'national bourgeoisie') Resul Guliev. There were others from the Bloc who had their moments on the floor, but the lion's share of assaulting the government was left up to Iskender Hamidov, a hick from the west of the country (and reportedly a Kurd) who had graduated from putting fear in the hearts of criminals to putting fear into the hearts of the neo-communist deputies in the Chamber whenever he approached a microphone."[48]

Among those who were elected to the Azerbaijani Supreme Soviet in elections in October 1990 was an unlikely candidate, Heidar Aliev, who ran unopposed in his native Nakhichevan, receiving 95 percent of the votes. Heidar Aliev had returned to the republic from Moscow only a few weeks before the elections. His push into his indigenous republic's political life came three years after his forced retirement from the Politburo in 1987. Aliev also ran for a seat of the Nakhichevan ASSR Soviet and won by 95 percent as well. During the election campaign, Aliev denounced AzCP leadership, including Mutalibov, for slandering him and his time as First Secretary of the AzCP. He argued that he favored multi-party democracy in Azerbaijan and criticized the current leadership in Baku for standing in the way.[49]

After his election, Aliev's speeches and votes at the Supreme Soviet were in conformity with those belonging to the opposition, although he labeled himself an independent deputy. He chastised Gorbachev, Defense Minister Yazov, Internal Affairs Minister Bakatin, and various AzCP leaders for Black January. Among the AzCP officials he held culpable were former First Secretary Vezirov, President Mutalibov, Chairman of the Supreme Soviet Elmira Kafarova, Second Secretary of the AzCP Polyanichko, and many others.[50]

Some argued that Aliev was in contact with several APF leaders. Indeed, quite a few APF leaders saw no reason not to collaborate with Aliev who also opposed the AzCP leadership and Gorbachev's policies as well. One such figure was Neimat Panakhov, who due to his firebrand oratory was considered a radical within the APF. Before Aliev's return from Moscow, Panakhov frequently met with Rafael Allahverdiev, an Aliev lieutenant. Later on, after Aliev's arrival in Nakhichevan, Panakhov was in close contact with him. Aliev would reward Panakhov's loyalty – the latter was from Nakhichevan too – by appointing him to the Presidential administration after coming to power in 1993.[51]

There were Mutalibov opponents also within the AzCP. His former rival for the seat of first secretary, Hasan Hasanov, who incidentally became Mutalibov's Prime Minister, criticized in mid-1990 the past policies of the AzCP while still relying on Moscow for remedies to Azerbaijan's problems. He stated:

> We delegated to the Center [Moscow] the responsibility for securing equal development of all the Union republics, but in return we have suffered inequality at the distribution of profits, with the result that every year we have been losing 15 to 20 percent of our national income, our standard of living has been reduced to one of the lowest in the Union, we have hundreds of thousands of unemployed and a devastated environment. We delegated to the Center our foreign trade, but our hard currency account consists only of pitiful crumbs, no use for reviving the economy.[52]

Despite its reliance on Moscow, the AzCP, which controlled more than 300 seats in the newly elected Supreme Soviet, nevertheless, partook in observing a minute's silence for the victims of Black January during the opening ceremony of the assembly on February 5, 1991. The AzCP had also commemorated the first anniversary of the invasion of Baku on January 20, 1991. Moreover, continuing its endeavor of embracing symbols of Azeri traditions, the AzCP assigned to Shaykh ul-Islam Allahshukur Pashazada, head of the Spiritual Directorate of the Muslims of the Transcaucasus, the task of reading prayers during the opening session, a first during the Soviet era.[53]

Unimpressed with the opening ceremony, the APF and others making up the Democratic Bloc, proposed the same day a number of draft resolutions. They provided that Azerbaijan's Supreme Soviet should: 1) lift the states of emergency and the curfews in many parts of the republic; 2) refuse to hold a referendum to approve the New Union Treaty in March; 3) refuse to sign the New Union Treaty; and 4) ensure a better defense of the border with Armenia. The AzCP-controlled assembly refused to discuss these demands, which prompted the Democratic Bloc deputies' walkout.[54]

In January 1991 Mutalibov submitted a written report to the USSR Central Committee. He warned Moscow that the situation in Azerbaijan was deteriorating and that well-armed Armenian militias supported by Armenia were active in the NKAO. He predicted that there could be armed clashes between Azerbaijan and Armenia and extremist elements of the APF could seize power. He cautioned that if Moscow failed to act quickly the AzSSR Supreme Soviet would create a national army, abolish the autonomy of the NKAO and refuse to approve the New Union Treaty. He also warned that Moscow's behavior was undermining AzCP's authority.[55]

The Central Committee's nationalities expert, Vyacheslav Mikhailov, examined the report and suggested that USSR Ministries of Defense, Interior and the KGB implement an operation in the region in cooperation with Azerbaijan and Armenia to disarm the militias. On January 17, 1991 the USSR Central Committee agreed to his recommendations.[56] The Mutalibov letter and the Central Committee's response show that Mutalibov's strategy worked and could have succeeded had the union not come to an end. Yet his reliance on Moscow led him to oppose the formation of a national army, which after the demise of the USSR would place Azerbaijan in a very disadvantaged position *vis-à-vis* Armenian militias militarily.

Armenian guerrillas fighting in the NKAO were superior in terms of their fighting skills. This was not so much due to their strong warrior traditions, as some observers argued, but due to much earlier formation of armed militias in Armenia while Azerbaijanis were still debating the merits of doing likewise. Initially the *fedayin* (freedom fighters) in Armenia and the NKAO were undisciplined, unorganized, and under-trained. The arrival of diaspora Armenians from Lebanon, who had been battle-tested during the Lebanese civil war, and members of the ASALA (Armenian Secret Army for the Liberation of Armenia), who had committed terror acts against Turkish diplomats in the 1970s and the 1980s, strengthened the Armenian hand. One such man was Monte Melkonian, a California-born archeologist, who had been an on-the-run ASALA member before he arrived in 1990. He was asked to command the Armenian forces in the Martuni (part of Hojavend) region. He disciplined his troops by prohibiting consumption of alcohol and looting.[57]

Although the AzCP placed its trust in Moscow, and hence was careful not to offend the latter with projects such as the establishment of a national army, it had, nevertheless, enough savvy not to look like Moscow's lackey. Therefore, the AzCP continued with its "nationalization" drive, which had started after Black January. A month after the Armenian SSR had changed its name to the Republic of Armenia, the AzCP Central Committee decided to recommend to the Azerbaijan Supreme Soviet a similar name change. By November 1990 many Soviet republics had already dropped SSR extensions from their titles. By then, preparations for a new Union agreement were also in full swing in the USSR, and the AzCP had stated publicly that it preferred sovereignty within a new federation. Azerbaijan began to use its "Republic of Azerbaijan" title in early December and its new colors in February 1991.

AzCP officials quickly took the initiative of hoisting the new republican flag at all government buildings, including the office of the military commander of the emergency rule in Baku. At first, Soviet troops took down the Azerbaijani flag, but eventually the parties agreed to hoist both the Soviet and the Azerbaijani flags.[58] Taking its cue, in late November, Azerbaijan's "Leninist Communist Youth League" changed its name to the "Communist Youth League for the Progress of Azerbaijan".[59] In early December came another name change: Kirov University was renamed Mammad Emin Resulzada University. The name Kirov was engraved in marble at the entrance of the university, but was scraped off after the name change.[60]

In early February the Azerbaijani Supreme Soviet changed the administrative status of the Shaumyan (Shaumyanovskiy) raion. Shaumyan was united with the mostly Azerbaijani Kasum Ismailov raion, and the new entity was renamed Gorenboy raion. Shaumyan's unruly Armenian rebels and the *fedayin* sent from Armenia had challenged the Azerbaijani control since early 1989. The Armenian side argued that the Shaumyan raion was part of mountainous Karabagh but was separated from it at the time of the NKAO's formation. The Azerbaijani decree revising the administrative borders stated that it was aimed at "stabilizing the sociopolitical situation" in the region.[61]

The AzCP leadership's disgruntlement in February 1991 led to the scuttling of a Gorbachev decree, which – according to Ter-Petrosyan – would have enabled the NKAO to hold elections for the NKAO Soviet, which were banned by the Volskiy Committee in January 1989. The AzCP, for its part, avoided holding elections in the oblast, fearing that a pro-secession majority could come to control the legislative body. The elections – according to the forestalled Gorbachev decree – would have been held under Moscow's Union Monitoring and Observation Commission to prevent any Azerbaijani government role in the elections. The averted decree would also have required the withdrawal of the Azerbaijani OMON (Special Purpose Militia Detachment) forces, which were sent to the NKAO in late 1990.[62]

To bolster Azeri power in the oblast, by mid-February Azerbaijan had built a railway freight-unloading center at Khojaly, an ethnically homogenous Azeri town in the NKAO. By shipping goods and supplies to the Azeri-controlled portion of the oblast Azeris would not have to go through

Armenian-controlled areas. The Azeri-staffed Republican Organization Committee was since mid-1990 already in control of the NKAO airport at Stepanakert (Hankendi), which must have dealt a blow to the logistical supplies the Armenian rebels needed.[63]

In various interviews, the leadership of the AzCP was keen on stressing loyalty to the union, or the new union that was to be voted upon. Nine days prior to the republic-wide referendum on the New Union Treaty, Mutalibov told *Izvestiya* that no republic could survive the formidable challenges of independence, no matter how rich or potentially wealthy a republic was. He said that the existing interdependence between republics was so strong that its interruption would prove disastrous, and added that for this reason the Azerbaijani population would approve the New Union Treaty.[64]

Mutalibov also reflected the zeitgeist when in the same interview he advocated de-monopolization of state enterprises, support for private enterprise, and opening of oil industry to foreign investment, because, he argued, neither Baku nor Moscow had any capital to modernize the aging oil sector.[65] In another interview, Mutalibov called on Moscow to raise the living standards of the people, because as he formulated, otherwise their confidence in the Soviet Union would be lost.[66]

Mutalibov made use of the same flexible interpretation of phenomena, when he described the recent omission of "Soviet and Socialist" from the official title of the republic. He said that the omission was a "reflection of the growth of national self-awareness."[67] Yet Mutalibov did not miss the opportunity to reiterate his allegiance to the Union. He stated: "[T]here are matters, such as dealings with foreign states, which republics should leave to the country [the USSR] as a whole."[68] On the issue of introducing more democracy into the people's lives Mutalibov spoke like a typical apparatchik. He stated that he was an ardent believer in democracy, but democracy actually meant respect for the laws. Criticizing the current lack of socio-political stability, Mutalibov added that many Azerbaijanis believed that democracy was doing whatever one desired, which he equated with anarchy.[69]

Another Moscow-loyalist, Elmira Kafarova, chairman of the Azerbaijan Supreme Soviet, also advocated the new union. She said that, despite grievances, as most Azeris, she preferred to remain within the to-be-established union. Kafarova said that Azerbaijan benefited from the 70-year partnership with Moscow, although, she admitted, Baku paid for the benefits by its oil. Like many of the ruling elite, she cautioned that despite the latter's enthusiasm for the new union, Moscow's failure to ensure Azerbaijan's territorial integrity would strengthen the separatist camp, and implied that the AzCP would not be able to stem people's zeal for independence.[70] This statement was very characteristic of how the NKAO problem had become a litmus test for the AzCP's, as well as the opposition's, commitment to Azerbaijan's well-being.

The Democratic Bloc deputies of the Supreme Soviet, for their part, also used the NKAO factor to justify why the republic should not take part in the union-wide referendum on the fate of the new union. On March 9, 1991 they argued that Azerbaijan's abstention from the referendum would show that the Azerbaijani people were dissatisfied with Moscow's lack of support on the NKAO issue.[71] A few days later, Heidar Aliev also opposed the referendum, arguing that the Soviet Communist Party had lost its legitimacy and that it should abdicate.[72] The AzCP deputies responded by stating that failing to join the new union could lead Moscow to back the Armenian cause. Several Democratic Bloc deputies threatened hunger strikes and forming an alternative national parliament, but could not sway the AzCP majority. The Supreme Soviet resolved to hold the referendum by a vote of 254 in favor, 43 against, with six abstentions.[73]

On March 17, 1991 a union-wide referendum on the preservation of the USSR as a union based on the participation of more autonomous republics took place. The Azerbaijani population seemed to have overwhelmingly voted for the new union, although the voting was typically Soviet: the outcome was known beforehand.[74] The APF argued that only 15 percent of the electorate had participated in the referendum, while the government-controlled "Central Election Commission" maintained that there was a Soviet-style large turnout. The ANM-ruled Armenia and five other republics boycotted the referendum.[75] Armenia declared that it would hold its own referendum on independence soon.[76]

"Operation Ring"

In the spring of 1991 the level of violence began to increase. Both sides raided villages and took hostages. Armenians made use of conventional and not-so-conventional weapons, including the Alazan rocket, a device that had not been designed for battle. It was "a two-pound explosive on a booster rocket shaft used for seeding clouds and making rain."[77] Alazans caused significant harm and could kill if they hit people. They were first used in combat in April 1991, when they were fired into Shusha, hitting several houses and wounding three people.[78] Soon Alazans were replaced by the RPGs, or rocket-propelled grenades, bought from Soviet troops or acquired by raiding arms depots. Later, the parties acquired BTRs, or Soviet-style armored personnel carriers, either rented or sold by corrupt garrison commanders in the region. "GRAD multiple missile launching units came next, followed by older and then newer model tanks and eventually attack helicopters and jet bombers."[79] The escalation in armaments would lead to an even higher escalation of casualty figures. A case in point is Polyanichko's survival of an attempt on his life when a rocket-propelled grenade was fired on his office in Stepanakert on May 10, 1991. Yet, in July 1993, not long after he left Azerbaijan he was killed by Armenian assassins in North Ossetia. The military commander serving under Polyanichko, General Safanov, escaped a similar assassination attempt in April 1991 in Rostov-on-Don.[80]

In late April, the proportions of warfare in Getashen (Chaykend) reached new proportions with the capture by Armenian paramilitaries of 13 Russian and one Azerbaijani Soviet Army servicemen. In order to free them, Soviet Army units and Azerbaijani OMON blockaded various villages in the Getashen area. [81] The Azerbaijani soldier was later executed. Azeris retaliated by besieging the nearby village of Martunashen, and eventually driving out the Armenian population.[82] Along the common border, fighting intensified in the center portion including Goris (Armenia) and Lachin (Azerbaijan), and in the north involving Idzhevan (Armenia) and Kazakh (Azerbaijan) border regions.[83]

In response to Baku's enthusiasm to join the new union Moscow agreed to the Azerbaijani operation aimed at pacifying the "illegal armed formations" who had grabbed control of the Shaumyan region including villages north of the NKAO. In Azerbaijan the operation was labeled "Passport Checking Operation", referring to the presence in the region of armed guerrillas who had infiltrated the region from Armenia. Yet it soon became known by its code name: "Operation Ring". The aim was to encircle the Shaumyan villages to check the *propiskas*, the official registration cards which displayed where one resided, and weed out dangerous outsiders.[84] In an interview later, Mutalibov suggested that plans for Operation Ring existed since 1990, but its implementation needed Moscow's support. He said that he convinced Moscow about the necessity of the operation by arguing Azerbaijani loyalty to the union depended on Moscow supporting Azerbaijan's territorial integrity.[85]

As a result, the entire 23rd Division of the Soviet 4th Army, based in Ganja, was made available for the operation in the Khanlar and Shaumyan

(Geranboy) regions. The 23rd Division, with its tanks and artillery, joined Azerbaijani OMON and Azerbaijani villagers to root out the *fedayin*. In the region there were only a few hundred *fedayin*, yet they enjoyed logistical support from the ANM Government in Armenia, including military helicopters, which helped their deployment where they were needed most.[86] In an interview in 2000, the then ANM Government's Minister of Interior, Ashot Manucharian, stated that he supplied the *fedayin* with illicitly bought weapons and provided transport to the region. He said that most of the arms were bought from Soviet bases in Georgia, presumably to hide the fact that they were going to be used in or around the NKAO. The weapons bought were mostly small arms, including rifles and grenade launchers, and were transported across the border by foot or by helicopters.[87]

The main battlefront in the Azerbaijani assault on Armenian militias was the wooded hills to the north of the Khanlar and Shaumyan regions. In the first stage of the operation, Getashen (Chaikend) and Martuneshen (Karabulakh) were raided by mostly Russian Soviet Interior Ministry troops. The second phase of the Operation Ring involved Azerbaijani forces taking over the main role in the operation. Erkech, Buzlukh, and Manashid villages were overrun; their Armenian inhabitants were deported first to Stepanakert and from there to Armenia proper. After their departure, some Azeri refugees who were deported from Armenia in 1988 and 1989 were settled in the region.[88] Those Armenian *fedayin* who were not captured or killed escaped through the mountain passes to Armenia. Nevertheless, after the demise of the USSR the region would be recaptured by the *fedayin*.[89] In the NKAO proper, 17 small villages in the Hadrut and Shusha regions were evacuated and around 500 of their inhabitants were deported to Armenia.[90]

In April 1991, Mutalibov continued to defend strong ties with Moscow and to denounce Armenian irredentism, while categorically refusing the establishment of a national army that could stand up to Armenian paramilitaries. In an interview with *Krasnaya Zvezda*, Mutalibov praised the 70-year-old Soviet experience, stating: "The breaking up of everything, which has until now been called the Union, is taking place to the advantage of a handful of newfound political mongers, but counter to the will of millions of people."[91] Arguing that it was necessary to keep the USSR intact, Mutalibov stated that he was in favor of "the conservation and consolidation of inter-republican economic and other mutual ties."

The assumptions on which Mutalibov based his expectations and his political career were no longer pertinent to the capabilities of the Soviet state, which was, it would turn out, on the brink of dismemberment. He assumed that Moscow would side with Azerbaijan for opting for the new union, while punishing Armenia for choosing independence. Mutalibov assumed that the possible retribution Armenia would have to cope with was the unequivocal re-establishment of Azerbaijani sovereignty over the NKAO. As it turned out, Mutalibov's calculations were too optimistic.

In the short term, however, Mutalibov did succeed in driving home to the NKAO Armenians that without Armenia's participation in the new union they could not expect Russia to support their autonomy, let alone their secession from Azerbaijan. Mutalibov's Moscow-supported strategy seemed to be working when on May 16 the NKAO Armenian leadership announced that it was interested in talks with Baku on the future of the oblast. This implied that the NKAO Armenians were canceling all the secession and unification with Armenia resolutions. The same day, they also wrote a letter to Gorbachev informing him that they wished the NKAO would join the new union.[92]

On June 19 the suspended Soviet of the NKAO adopted a resolution expressing the desire for dialogue instead of confrontation. The offer seemed to aim at a deal which would provide for the re establishment of the NKAO party organs in return for the latter revoking the secession resolution adopted earlier, and agreeing to the "demilitarization" of the oblast. It seemed the Moscow-supported strong-arm tactics of the Azerbaijani leadership was paying off.[93] A delegation of the NKAO party officials headed by Valery Grigorian went to Moscow and to Baku to hold talks "on the basis of the Constitution of the Soviet Union and the Republic of Azerbaijan and Union documents on Nagorno-Karabagh." The talks were to also determine the timing of the NKAO elections.[94] The Karabagh party officials' offer was practically capitulation in exchange for the return to the *status quo ante*, and thus not popular with the oblast's Armenian population.

On July 16, following up on its new stance adopted on May 16, 1991, the Armenian controlled NKAO administration, including the Bureau of the City Party Committee, City Soviet Executive Committee, the Oblast Soviet, the Oblast Soviet Executive Committee, and the Bureau of Oblast Party Committee rescinded resolutions adopted since 1988. Foremost among these resolutions was the NKAO's secession from Azerbaijan. Instead, they resolved that the NKAO Administration that was suspended on January 12, 1989 by the USSR Supreme Soviet should be restored, and elections to the oblast soviets at all levels should be held. In a separate letter to Gorbachev, the Armenian leadership of the NKAO stated that "all sides' decisions incompatible with the [USSR] Constitution" should be rescinded. The move by the NKAO Armenians indicated a veritable fear that Moscow was about to recognize Baku's decision to rescind the oblast's autonomy unless the NKAO Armenians displayed commitment to the new union.[95]

Other articles of the resolution included such demands as the demilitarization of the oblast's borders with Azerbaijan, restoration of the NKAO security forces, ending the Azerbaijani closure of the Goris–Stepanakert road, and repatriation of Armenians deported from the NKAO and Shaumyan. As suggested earlier, Armenia's Supreme Soviet, ironic as it may seem, once again supported the NKAO Armenians' resolution to join the new union as part of Azerbaijan. Yet the Armenian Supreme Soviet's vote was taken after Ter-Petrosyian's intensive lobbying, and passed by a margin of one vote, indicating the controversial nature of even tactical moves involving the NKAO.[96] Ter-Petrosyan accurately saw the dangers that would befall the NKAO Armenians in a new union without Armenia's participation, and had lobbied for the resolution. Interestingly, the administrative head of the NKAO Party Oblast Committee, Valeriy Grigoryan, who had begun to conduct negotiations with the Azerbaijani leadership in July 1991, was assassinated on August 10, 1991 in Stepanakert. Although the culprits were not apprehended, his murderers could have been Armenian extremists who desired secession at any cost.[97]

In Armenia also, Operation Ring had caused the republic's leadership to reconsider its policy on the NKAO. On July 20, 1991, during his one and only attendance at the talks on the New Union Treaty at Novo-Ogarevo, Ter-Petrosyan stated to Gorbachev his readiness to make concessions. The opposition ACP's chairman, Aram Sarkissian, took advantage of this and accused Ter-Petrosyan of trying to sell out to Moscow on the Shaumyan and Khanlar issues in return for a favorable settlement in the NKAO.[98] Gorbachev, who had approved the operation, was, however, apparently unaware of the deportations that followed. In an interview, Aram Sarkissian, then head of the opposition ACP, argued that when he talked about the operation to Gorbachev, the latter stated that he didn't know about the deportations.[99] Presumably those around him who desired more law and order, and opposed the creation of a looser new union, misled him. They would soon try to overthrow Gorbachev, contributing to the demise of the USSR.

Earlier, on April 19, 1991 official Azerbaijani media reported that President Mutalibov "directed" the military commander of Baku, Valeriy Buniatov, to lift the curfew, instituted after Black January, starting on April 20, 1991. Mutalibov's move implied that he wanted to show the home audience that he was capable of imposing his will on Moscow.[100] Yet Mutalibov's directive might actually have come after consultations with Moscow, which, for its part, would have desired an end to its heavy and unpopular involvement in Azerbaijani political life.

On May 28, 1991 Armenia celebrated the establishment of independent Armenia on May 28, 1918. Azerbaijan, likewise, commemorated the Azerbaijani statehood of May 28, 1918 on the same day, touting it as the "Azerbaijani Day of National Republic."[101] The fact that Ter-Petrosyan was swept to power for offering better leadership in the "national struggle", that is, unification with the NKAO, made the Armenian festivities look more genuine than the ones in Azerbaijan, where the AzCP, championing the virtues of a new union, was still in power.

The APF held its second congress in mid-July 1991 with the participation of 243 delegates. The congress, at which Elchibey was elected chairman once again, resolved to call for a boycott of the upcoming presidential elections because, as it argued, free elections were impossible under the emergency rule imposed by the Soviet military.[102] A few days after the congress, Etibar Mamedov, who for some time had sought to establish a rival organization, announced the formation of his *Milli Istiqlal Partiyasi* (National Independence Party.)[103] Mamedov, who had spent one year in jail at the Lefortivo prison in Russia for his participation in APF activities, had criticized the APF for having become heavily involved in deals and agreements with the AzCP, and for agreeing to operate within the narrow political confines drawn by Baku and Moscow.[104]

Visitors to Baku in the summer of 1991 were struck by the changes in the city's appearance. The portraits of Azerbaijan's first president, Mammad Emin Resulzada (1918–1920), were everywhere, as well as the red, green, and blue flag of the first Azerbaijan Republic with a crescent and star in the middle. The flag was even hung on the façade of the Supreme Soviet building. On the second floor of the Lenin Museum, formerly banned publications from the 1918–1920 era were put on display. Resulzada's famous phrase "Bir Kere Yükselen Bayrak Bir Daha İnmez" or "The Flag Raised Once Cannot Be Lowered" was placed beneath his portrait in the museum as well.[105]

The Anti-Gorbachev Coup and the Demise of the AzCP

On August 19, 1991 Soviet hardliners including Vice-President Gennady Yanayev, Prime Minister Valentin Pavlov, KGB Chairman Vladimir Kryuchkov, Interior Minister Boris Pugo, and others announced that their self-styled State Emergency Committee had taken over Gorbachev's powers as President, and claimed that they were acting to prevent the Soviet Union from disintegrating into chaos. The hardliners had for some time felt that Gorbachev's reform program and the New Union Treaty he had negotiated devolved too much of the central government's power to the republics. The coup collapsed in three days and Gorbachev returned to power, but the episode undermined the legitimacy of the CPSU and contributed to the collapse of the Soviet Union.[106]

During the first two days of the coup, Mutalibov was on an official visit to Iran, where he reportedly made pro-coup statements. On August 19, 1991 he stated that the coup and the related developments were the "natural consequences of the policies that had brought chaos during the past several years. ... We welcome the developments in the Soviet Union."[107] The Russian Interfax agency reported that Mutalibov stated on August 21 that the coup leadership would help solve the Karabagh problem.[108] The AzCP newspapers enthusiastically published the decrees of the State Emergency Committee. For his part, the Second Secretary of the AzCP, Polyanichko, also spoke on Azerbaijani radio, supporting the coup in more uncertain terms than Mutalibov.[109]

Yet when the coup unraveled on August 21, Mutalibov denied ever having supported the coup.[110] In response, the APF held demonstrations and denounced Mutalibov's support of the coup.[111] The August 23 issue of the APF paper *Azadlik* printed a message which showed that Mutalibov had welcomed the coup. This issue of *Azadlik* was confiscated by the police and could not reach the readers. It had called for the nationalization of the AzCP's property, the lifting of the state of emergency, and the cancellation of presidential elections scheduled for September 18, 1991.[112]

Heidar Aliev also accused Mutalibov for having supported the anti-Gorbachev coup. He demanded that the Azerbaijan Supreme Soviet eliminate the monopoly of the AzCP in Azeri politics and administration, arguing that the AzCP, as did the CPSU, supported the coup. He also called for an inquiry into the Black January events and the lifting of the state of emergency in Baku.[113] His demands were almost identical to those of the

APF, a good indication of the power and popularity of nationalism in the republic.

The coup's impact was so detrimental to the image of the CPSU that city officials ordered the removal of the Lenin monument from Azadlyg Square, which took place on August 26.[114] Since August 22, when Gorbachev returned to Moscow, rallies had been held in Baku denouncing Mutalibov's and the AzCP's support of the coup. The APF accused Mutalibov for being a cohort of the coup leaders.[115] Unabashed, Mutalibov was quick to embrace the forces of democracy after the demise of the coup. On August 22 he congratulated Russia's President Yeltsin, who had played a critical role in the failure of the coup. Later, on August 24, mimicking decisions made in Moscow with regard to the CPSU, he ordered the separation of the party and state administrations. Accordingly, the AzCP would sever its links to all state organs, including the police, the republican KGB, the Ministry of Internal Affairs, and the Ministry of Justice.[116]

The demise of the Soviet central administration after the August coup led to the juridical independence of all Soviet republics, including Azerbaijan. The Azerbaijani ruling elite, as did its counterparts in other Turkic republics, began to move into the power vacuum that emerged after the failed August coup.[117] Although the Mutalibov leadership had wholeheartedly subscribed to the notion that success in the NKAO dispute, as well as socio-economic welfare, depended on the preservation of the union, it nevertheless was compelled to embrace the idea of independence that it had long cast aside as counterproductive *vis-à-vis* the NKAO dispute.

Mutalibov went on to embrace and implement the demands of the opposition he once deemed unrealistic. On August 27 he invited all political forces to the conference table to join him in a government of national accord and to participate in the establishment of a national army.[118] The latter goal had been a major APF demand since late 1989 when Armenia set out to establish its own defense forces. Mutalibov thought that Armenia's decision to have its own army had set it on a collision course with Moscow, and had rejected the demand for a national army since late January 1991 when he became first secretary.

Mutalibov ordered most Azerbaijani enterprises and organizations subordinate to Union ministries to be brought under the jurisdiction of Azerbaijan's government ministries. For reasons of expediency, Mutalibov decreed that a few enterprises would, however, remain subsidiaries of Moscow-based parent organizations. Moreover, the AzCP's Lenin Museum was turned over to the Ministry of Culture and the AzCP's publishing house was transferred to the Press Committee of the Azerbaijan Republic.[119] The main square of Baku, Lenin Square, was renamed Azadlyg (independence) Square, and as suggested earlier, the Lenin monument in the square was sentenced to banishment to another, and less conspicuous, location.[120]

In autonomous Nakhichevan, the Aliev-controlled Supreme Soviet defied Baku by deciding to dissolve the Nakhichevani section of the AzCP on August 27. Its property was earmarked for nationalization and its offices were sealed. The same day, the Lenin monument in the central square was dismantled in the presence of Nakhichevan authorities.[121] Aliev stated that the AzCP in the rest of the country should also be shut down.[122] The coup actually strengthened the hand of Aliev, who had denounced the coup before its demise. The removal of the AzCP from Nakhichevan and Aliev's election to the post of Chairman of the Nakhichevan Supreme Soviet on September 3 augured what was yet to come: his rise to prominence once again.[123] His election as Chairman of the Nakhichevan Supreme Soviet meant that according to Article 112/2 of Azerbaijan's Constitution he was now deputy chairman of the republic's Supreme Soviet, a platform from which he could accelerate the demise of Mutalibov.

On August 24 Mikhail Gorbachev resigned from the office of the CPSU General Secretary, and next day Boris Yeltsin nationalized the property of the CPSU in Russia. On August, 1991, emulating other republican parties, the AzCP Central Committee held a plenum and decided to withdraw the AzCP from the CPSU. Other formalities followed. Mutalibov resigned from the CPSU Central Committee Politburo and the AzCP decided to withdraw Azerbaijani members from the CPSU Central Committee.[124]

Yet for the Democratic Bloc of the Supreme Soviet, which also included APF members, the AzCP's severance of ties with the CPSU was not enough. Like Aliev, the Bloc demanded the banning of the AzCP and an inquiry into the AzCP leadership's initial support of the anti-Gorbachev coup. During the Azerbaijani Supreme Soviet deliberations APF supporters gathered outside the assembly building to influence the outcome. Yet the AzCP majority in the Supreme Soviet rejected opposition demands.[125] Nevertheless, on August 29 Mutalibov resigned from his position as head of the AzCP. Anxious to keep up with developments in the NKAO, he stated that there were rumors that the Soviet Army was about to withdraw from along the Azerbaijan–Armenia border. In order to cope with the Armenian menace, he indicated that he would declare a state of emergency and set up paramilitary formations to cope with Armenia's armed forces.[126]

On August 30, 1991 the Azerbaijani Supreme Soviet decided to lift the state of emergency in Baku. In a symbolic move the Azerbaijani assembly also decided to restore the country's independence, which it characterized as being interrupted some seventy years previously. The adoption of a law to that effect, however, was to take place on October 18. The preamble of the law "On the Restoration of State Independence of the Azerbaijan Republic" stated that the Azerbaijan Democratic Republic was quashed as a result of the Red Army's invasion, and that all acts adopted and treaties passed by the republic since April 1920 were invalid.[127] Moreover, the assembly voted to establish a national guard and convert the Azerbaijani KGB to Azerbaijani Ministry of National Security, although the change was cosmetic.[128] Nevertheless, the independence resolution left the door open for renewed close ties with Moscow. It stated that Azerbaijan desired "to secure friendly relations in the future with all the republics that were part of the USSR."[129]

Two days after the Azerbaijani declaration of independence, on September 2, the Armenian-only NKAO Regional Council and the Shaumyan District Governing Council held a joint session and also declared independence. The new entity was named "Nagorno-Karabagh Armenian Republic".[130] This move reversed the NKAO Armenian leadership's mid-July cancellation of its secession resolution adopted earlier. The failed coup had created overnight a power vacuum in the oblast. For its part, Azerbaijan abolished in mid-September 1991 the so-called "Republican Organizing Committee", headed by the Second Secretary of the AzCP, Victor Polyanichko. The Committee was established in the wake of Black January, and took advantage of the presence of the Soviet Army to restore Azerbaijani control in the NKAO. The Azerbaijani independence, however, made the committee superfluous. Instead, the Azerbaijani Supreme Soviet let it be known that a multi-party "Coordination Committee" was going to be established.[131] Polyanichko and all the members of the Organizing Committee left the oblast, and the Soviet armed forces there were left without a civilian command and without a clear mission. Hence, in the following weeks the Armenian *fedayin* easily recaptured the Shaumyan region which they had abandoned during Operation Ring.[132]

Armenia, for its part, opted to hold a referendum for independence, which was held on September 21, 1991. Out of the 95 percent of voters who participated, 93 percent cast their votes in favor of independence. On September 23 the Supreme Soviet of Armenia unanimously declared independence.[133] Initially, however, Azerbaijan seemed poised to acquire more benefits than Armenia from independence. From the point of view of international law, independent statehood strengthened the Azerbaijani claim to the NKAO because the international community soon recognized all Soviet republics' borders as state borders.

Despite its own independence resolution, the Azerbaijani leadership seemed to be its old former self. Ironically, Mutalibov continued denouncing those who were pro-independence by labeling them "separatists".[134] The independence resolution had been passed unanimously and the opposition seemed to have lost a powerful propaganda instrument. Yet very soon Mutalibov joined the short-lived State Council, which was supposed to govern the former USSR in the absence of the Communist Party. Together with Central Asian leaders Mutalibov tried to salvage the now defunct union. Elchibey, meanwhile, characterized the independence resolution as "total nonsense", arguing that "so long as Azerbaijan … lacked such basic attributes of statehood as control over its own resources and territory", and relied on Moscow for the settlement of the NKAO dispute it could not claim to be really independent.[135]

In Azerbaijan, to prevent rival candidates from participating, presidential elections were held hastily on September 8, with Mutalibov running as the sole candidate. A one-time APF founder and the chairman of the Social Democratic Party, Zardusht Alizade, withdrew his candidacy one week before the elections. The Araz and Zardusht Alizade brothers had all along been considered to have been encouraged by the AzCP to set up their party in order to make the political system look more democratic.[136] The APF called for a boycott, and Heidar Aliev's stronghold of Nakhichevan did not allow polling to take place.

According to various estimates, there was around 50 percent turnout and official results showed that Mutalibov received 90 percent of the votes. The APF alleged widespread fraud and announced that it did not recognize the outcome of the elections.[137] It demanded once again the dissolution of the AzCP and the holding of general elections for a new democratically elected parliament.[138] The following day, September 14, holding its 33rd Extraordinary Congress, the AzCP did indeed dissolve itself.[139] This action was neither unexpected nor unique to Azerbaijan. Throughout the USSR, ruling communist parties were being dismantled or restructured under different names.

Despite Azerbaijan's declaration of independence on August 30, Mutalibov attended on September 16 the meeting of the so-called "State Council" in Moscow. Ter-Petrosyan, who had been more adamant with regard to independence, was also present.[140] Soon, however, Gorbachev's "State Council" would be outflanked by Yeltsin's Commonwealth of Independent States (CIS), which Russia established with Ukraine and Belarus on December 8. On December 21, 1991 all Central Asian states, Azerbaijan and Armenia joined the CIS at a summit in Almaty. Acknowledging defeat, Gorbachev resigned from the presidency of the Soviet Union, and the "State Council" ceased to exist.

Earlier, on September 12, when it seemed the Soviet Union was on the way out, fighting and mutual blockades had resumed between Azerbaijan and Armenia. The Azerbaijani railway blockade interrupted train services to Armenia from the Nakhichevan and Kazakh regions of Azerbaijan, which had not been interrupted since January 1990.[141] As before, the APF led the blockade efforts. Azerbaijanis felt the urge to act because on September 2, two days after the Azerbaijani declaration of independence, the NKAO Soviet had also declared independence.

On September 14 Azerbaijan stopped fuel shipments to Armenia by Azerbaijani trains, apparently in response to the shooting down of a helicopter in NKAO airspace carrying high government officials.[142] Armenian militants responded with a vengeance. In late September they cut off the railway between Azerbaijan and Nakhichevan at the southern Armenian railroad juncture in Megri.[143] Yet rail traffic resumed in October 1991, even if only for a short time.

In late September 1991, faced with an increase in interethnic fighting and his rapidly eroding popular support, Mutalibov decided to form an eight-member Defense Council, bringing together representatives from various political parties, including the Social Democratic Party, the National Independence Party, and the APF. Mutalibov was to chair the Council, and such prominent members from opposition parties as Rahim Gaziev, Etibar Mamedov, and Araz Alizade were to take part in the Council. Mamedov stated that he joined the Council because in cases of national security "there should not be talk of opposition."[144]

On September 26, 1991, the government announced that 50 percent of the Azerbaijani conscripts should serve within Azerbaijan.[145] This decision fell short of the APF's demand that no Azerbaijani draftee should serve outside the republic, and seemed oblivious to the fact that the Soviet Union was about to dissolve; it was nevertheless a radical departure from the government's earlier position. Unsatisfied with the government's half-hearted moves, on September 30, a pro-APF rally in the capital called for the establishment of a national army, the replacement of the Soviet-era government with a national unity government with the participation of all the major political parties in the country.[146] In the following days, the republic-wide fear of "Armenian expansionism" would grow, fed by the fact that Azerbaijan lagged far behind Armenia in the establishment of a national army.

Escalating hostilities in the NKAO seemed to have forced Mutalibov to theoretically embrace the idea of the national army, although its establishment would not take place during his tenure, which ended in March 1992. On October 12, he announced that "Azerbaijan [would] sign the [Economic Union Agreement with former Soviet republics] only when the Soviet armed forces suppl[ied] all the needs of the military forces that [were] being established in the republic."[147] Obviously this statement was just another indication that Mutalibov still desired to accomplish goals by blackmailing the center, or the former center, Moscow, as his predecessors had done before him. To succeed, he did not even shy away from making use of the fictional establishment of a "national army" which never materialized while he was in power. As later events would show, Mutalibov actually considered economic union with Russia as indispensable. Yet by attaching conditions to Azerbaijan's membership, he tried to reap benefits from what he actually sought, while at the same time hoping to appeal to the Azerbaijani public with his apparent commitment to national armed forces. To cope with the problem of arms that the to-be-established army would need, Mutalibov had another bright idea. His government objected to the withdrawal of the Soviet military forces from the republic, if they also took along their weaponry.[148] This objection was then interpreted as Mutalibov's attempt to acquire badly needed arms for Azerbaijan's future army, but in hindsight his move seemed like another attempt at blackmail to prevent the departure of former Soviet troops.

Nevertheless, despite the fact that a majority of the Supreme Soviet consisted of supporters of the government, Mutalibov faced an uphill battle to sell the economic union agreement to the assembly. Opposition deputies made up 26 of the 350 members of the assembly, but they were eventually able to block the adoption of the agreement by insisting that such an agreement was contrary to Azerbaijan's sovereignty. Hence, although by then ten republics had expressed willingness to join such a union, Azerbaijan opted out.[149]

The mediation attempt by the Russian and Kazakh Presidents, Yeltsin and Nazarbaev, also could not prevent the escalation of the crisis. During their visits to Azerbaijan, Armenia and the NKAO, in September 1991, they convinced the three parties to sign a preliminary joint communiqué, which provided for the restoration of the NKAO's pre-1989 legal status as well as its elected government organs, and the cessation of all hostilities. Ter-Petrosyan and Mutalibov, and NKAO spokesman, Samson Voskanyan, seemed to have agreed to the deal.[150] The APF's deputy chairman, Isa Gambar, stated that the APF opposed the agreement because it treated the Karabagh issue as an international problem, and the APF considered it only an internal matter of Azerbaijan.[151] Elchibey too dealt with the issue when he addressed a crowd at Azadlyg Square in the same week, arguing that the agreement failed to state whose laws would apply in the oblast: Azerbaijani laws, Armenian laws, or the already on the way out Soviet laws.[152]

The Yeltsin-Nazarbaev initiative led to bilateral talks between Azerbaijani and Armenian delegations, with Russian and Kazakhstani representatives acting as observers. The talks began to falter by the end of October 1991, after the Armenian militants' cross-border shelling of Azerbaijani villages in the northwestern Kazakh region, to which Azerbaijan responded by shutting down the gas pipeline. On November 19, 1991 Armenia announced that it would not continue its participation in the talks unless Azerbaijan resumed gas deliveries.[153] The Armenian militants' shooting down of an Azerbaijani helicopter in the Martuni district (part of Hojavend) of the NKAO on November 20, however, was a more deadly blow to the negotiation process. Twenty-three people, including Azerbaijani negotiators and Russian and Kazakh observers, were killed in the incident.[154] The dead included two high-ranking Azerbaijani officials, Vagif Jafarov, and Osman Mirzaev, as well as Russian and Kazakh observers associated with the Yeltsin-Nazarbaev Ten-Point Plan. There were bullet holes in the fuselage of the helicopter, strengthening the Armenian ground fire theory.[155]

In reaction to the downing of the helicopter, there were demonstrations in Ganja and Sheki, demanding the urgent establishment of a national army, dissolution of the Azerbaijani Supreme Soviet and the transfer of power to the eight-member National Defense Council. The Azerbaijani Supreme Soviet, for its part, voted on November 26 to eliminate the autonomous status of the NKAO. The vote was unanimous, uniting the government and opposition parties.[156] The vote was a radical step in revising Azerbaijan's NKAO thesis, in that the Azerbaijanis had all along insisted that the autonomy enjoyed by the oblast people rendered their demand for independence superfluous.

The following day, Mutalibov addressed the Supreme Soviet to make two promises: one popular and one controversial. The popular promise was that he undertook not to declare martial law in the country. The unpopular promise concerned a demand long advocated by the opposition: the recall of Azerbaijani troops and officers from the Soviet Army. He stated that he would not recall them. Instead he promised that the formation of the national army would be accelerated, and the equipment held by Soviet forces stationed in Azerbaijan would be inventoried, implying that he could ask for their handover if/when these troops were withdrawn. He also announced that the Soviet Army units on Azerbaijani soil should be under the command of the Azerbaijani Government.[157]

A corollary of Mutalibov's policy of banking on Moscow's support was his attempt to prevent Soviet troops based in Azerbaijan from leaving, even if their units were to pull out. Some ten days before the referendum on Azerbaijani independence, he met with commanders of the Soviet army and navy troops in Azerbaijan and asked them to remain in the country, promising that they would be welcome in independent Azerbaijan.[158] He pledged that Soviet troops opting to remain in the republic would not have to worry about housing and adequate salaries. They would be provided by Azerbaijan. He added that the republic would even assign subsidized plots for summer homes and would ensure the availability of decent kindergartens and schools for the troops' families. He also promised the return of arms taken away from Soviet Army depots by paramilitary units.[159]

7

The Road to Independence

On November 5, 1991 an Azerbaijani delegation, including Prime Minister Hasan Hasanov and Etibar Mamedov, arrived in Turkey and asked for the recognition of Azerbaijan's independence. Both men stated that they were part of the same delegation because for the sake of Azerbaijan's well-being they chose to ignore their differences. Mamedov also stated that the opposition parties withdrew their demand for Mutalibov's resignation, because at the moment, the survival of Azerbaijan was at stake. He added: "The most important problems facing Azerbaijan now are recognition of its independence, the lifting of the Russian pressure, and the Armenian [NKAO] question."[1] As expected, Turkey became the first country to recognize independent Azerbaijan on November 9, 1991.[2]

On November 26 Mutalibov took another step to appease the opposition. The Pro-Mutalibov Azerbaijani Supreme Soviet resolved to create the National Council (*Milli Majlis*). The new 50-member assembly would consist of 25 pro-government and all 25 opposition deputies of the Supreme Soviet, and would be virtually in constant session to cope with the ongoing crisis in the oblast.[3] The Supreme Soviet also remained in existence, which contributed to the multi-polarity of power in the country. From time to time the former passed important resolutions, including the annulment of the NKAO's autonomy on November 26, to which Karabagh Armenians responded by yet another declaration of independence on December 6.[4]

One of the first resolutions adopted by the National Council was to reject the November 27 resolution of the USSR State Council, which appealed to the Azerbaijani and Armenian Supreme Soviets to cancel all acts altering the NKAO's legal status and to restore the constitutional order there. The resolution was a clear reference to the Azerbaijani Supreme Soviet's abolition of the NKAO's autonomy on November 26. On December 9 the National Council announced that it considered Moscow's resolution only as a recommendation without any legal force.[5]

The NKAO Armenians reacted promptly. One day after the National Council's announcement, a referendum was held in the Armenian-controlled areas of the NKAO to once again declare independence from Azerbaijan. Armenian media organs reported that 99 percent of those who participated voted in favor of independence, though it was impossible to verify what percentage of NKAO Armenians took part in the vote.[6] As expected, on December 12 the NKAO People's Deputies Soviet announced its desire to join the CIS as an independent state, which it named the Nagorno-Karabagh Republic.[7]

The Azerbaijani reaction was one of rejection and denial. The National Council contested the validity of the referendum, suggesting that the so-called NKAO People's Deputies Soviet was an illegal entity, and thus it was not entitled to hold a referendum. The National Council resolution asked the Azerbaijani government to take all measures to prevent the implementation of all decisions of the NKAO People's Deputies Soviet.[8] Undeterred, the NKAO Armenian leadership held elections for a new parliament on December 28, 1991, and on January 6, 1992 the latter declared independence once again.[9]

Two weeks earlier, on December 18 Mutalibov had gone to Almaty to sign the CIS Treaty, although the National Council had unanimously voted to bar him from attending.[10] Mutalibov's advisor, Rasim Musabekov, stated that Mutalibov would sign the CIS Treaty because it was in Azerbaijan's interest to do so. He said: "Bearing in mind the rather high level of economic integration in the economic field, the proximity of political interests, and traditional cultural ties, all this determines the long-term future of cooperation … of the republics that used to form the USSR. [sic]"[11] After having signed the CIS Treaty on December 21, Mutalibov tried to appease the National Council. He stated rather feebly that during the process of ratification the National Council could still propose changes to the clauses of the CIS Treaty that they considered unacceptable.[12]

The APF member and deputy of the National Council, Tofik Kasumov, had earlier stated that the Slavic Union, comprising Russia, Ukraine and Belarus, was trying to recreate the Soviet Union under a different name because they wanted to dominate the republics.[13] This was how many in the Democratic Bloc, or the opposition, perceived the establishment of the

CIS. Etibar Mamedov too described the CIS as a new Soviet Union and called for its rejection by the National Council.[14] Supporters of Mutalibov, for their part, found it difficult to publicly stand up for the CIS Treaty, which many Azerbaijanis assumed was aimed at resuscitating the Soviet Union. Hence members of the National Council, including those who supported Mutalibov, chose not to vote on the CIS Treaty.

Believing that Armenia's remaining outside the CIS would strengthen Azerbaijan's hand in the NKAO dispute and that membership would be economically beneficial, Ter-Petrosyan had also attended the Almaty meeting and had signed the CIS Treaty. The Armenian Supreme Soviet, although more skeptical of the CIS than Ter-Petrosyan, ratified the treaty on December 30, 1991.[15] While in Almaty, Ter-Petrosyan stated that Armenia could forego the idea of unification with the NKAO if Azerbaijan were to grant a wide-ranging autonomy to the oblast.[16]

On January 19, 1992 the National Council adopted a law on the protection of state borders, authorizing Azerbaijan's border troops with border defense.[17] This seemingly awkward law became necessary, because by the first week of January all Soviet OMON troops had withdrawn from the NKAO. *Pravda* reported that the NKAO's Armenian paramilitaries were able to acquire a substantial portion of the arms of departing troops.[18] In the following months the NKAO-based 366th Regiment would disband, with many non-Armenian soldiers deserting and the mostly Armenian troops and officers joining the NKAO forces with their weapons.[19]

In late January NKAO Armenian militia and "volunteers" from Armenia went on the offensive once again. They attacked ethnic Azeri towns, focusing in particular on the strategically located Shusha and its villages. They also attacked the Azeri town of Aghdam, which is located outside the NKAO. The Azeris also tried to mount an offensive against the NKAO's Armenian towns, but their assault faced stiff resistance. The Azerbaijani side argued that Russian troops who remained behind when Soviet forces withdrew from the NKAO fought on the Armenian side.[20]

On February 2 Armenia's Defense Minister, Vazgen Sarkissian, stated that it was Armenia's objective to strengthen NKAO Armenians militarily, so that the NKAO became like an "impregnable fortress".[21] Deputy Foreign Minister and Ter-Petrosyan's foreign affairs adviser, Jirair (Gerard) Libaridian, admitted that Armenia gave to NKAO Armenians "whatever is necessary for their security and survival."[22] Armenia's Foreign Minister, Raffi Hovannisian, for his part, tried to project a neutral stance by arguing that Armenia desired the NKAO to be independent of both Azerbaijan and Armenia.[23]

The Fall of Khojaly and the Demise of Mutalibov

By early 1992 Armenian forces in the NKAO had begun to expand beyond Stepanakert. They captured nearby Azeri villages and expelled their inhabitants. Their next main target was the town of Khojaly five miles northeast of Stepanakert, with a population of 6,300.[24] Khojaly was located on the road that connected Stepanakert and Aghdam and was the base for the region's airport. According to reports from Helsinki Watch, Khojaly was used as a base for Azerbaijani forces shelling the city of Stepanakert and in turn was shelled by Armenian forces.[25]

In October 1991 Armenian militants had gone on the offensive cutting off the road between Khojaly and Aghdam, so that the only way to reach Khojaly was by air. By February 1992 the fall of Khojaly seemed imminent, and the Azeri government airlifted many inhabitants from the town. After the last helicopter to Khojaly on February 13, 3,000 inhabitants were left behind, defended by 160 lightly armed men under the command of Alif Hajiev. The final Armenian assault took place on the night of February 25, coinciding with the Sumgait massacres four years earlier. Armored vehicles of the former Soviet Army's 366th Regiment provided support to the attackers, giving credibility to the claim that Armenians not only employed former Soviet troops but also a significant portion of the Karabagh-based unit's armored vehicles.[26] Soon the attackers overwhelmed the defenders.[27]

By nightfall on February 26 Azeri defenses were overrun and the remaining Azeri forces and civilians were in retreat to the government-held areas. What ensued during the night was nothing short of ethnic cleansing or even genocide, which had far-reaching consequences. It turned out that many civilians were shot at close range after they surrendered to Armenian forces.[28] An Azerbaijani parliamentary investigation later put the death toll at 485. Even if this number included combatants and those who died of cold, the figure is still enormous.[29] Azeris also claimed that an additional 1,000 were wounded and 1,000 taken as prisoners of war.[30] Although the Armenian side initially rejected the charges, it later admitted that many civilian Azeris were killed while they were fleeing Khojaly. Armenians put the blame for the excesses on criminals and fanatics taking part in the operation, and some argued that refugees from Sumgait were also involved in the atrocities.[31] Autopsies performed on the recovered dead revealed severed penises, breasts and other body parts, attesting to the claim that widespread atrocities were committed.[32]

Initially, the Azeri government denied for two days that Khojaly had fallen. Later, it admitted the loss of Khojaly but tried to hide the proportions of the tragedy and declared that only two Azerbaijanis had lost their lives there.[33] The government's denial of the Khojaly massacre engendered a more confrontational style in Azerbaijani politics, eventually leading to Mutalibov's downfall. The opposition charged the government with treason or *satkinlig* (sell-out). The APF blamed the loss of Khojaly on Mutalibov's "deliberate delay" in creating a national army and attempted to avenge Khojaly's loss. Months later, after losing power, Mutalibov inadvertently conceded that his earlier rejection of the establishment of a national army contributed to the Khojaly massacre. He admitted that he was then against a national army because Moscow "… talk[ed] of the formation of unified armed forces of the CIS, of a common strategy, and of the fact that the security of each state would be protected."[34] Demonstrating a disturbing naïveté, Mutalibov suggested that he was taken by surprise that the Soviet Army's 366th Regiment fought alongside the Armenian forces in Khojaly against Azeri forces whose leadership had time and again professed loyalty to Moscow.[35] In apparent exasperation, APF heavyweight Rahim Gaziev deployed two GRAD multiple-rocket missile launchers in the mountaintop town of Shusha to fire at Stepanakert, which lay in the valley below. The GRAD launchers, though highly inaccurate, were terrifying weapons, which could fire up to 40 rockets on their targets. For Gaziev and others on the Azeri side, inaccuracy did not matter because these weapons were going to be used in retaliation to the Khojaly massacre, and in order to force the Armenians into submission. The fact that they were used indiscriminately against Stepanakert showed that the level of hatred felt toward "the other" was similar on both sides.[36] Soon Armenians also acquired GRADs and used them against Shusha until they captured the town in May 1992, though Shusha's higher altitude worked against the effectiveness of Armenian GRADs.[37]

Armenians, for their part, argued that the Azeri forces also committed a massacre in the northern NKAO village of Maragha (Leninavan), close to the Azerbaijani town of Terter. The Azeris had captured the town on April 10, 1992 and had withdrawn the next day. Armenians claimed that they found and buried the remains of 43 villagers. An additional fifty villagers were also reported to have been taken hostage, and Armenia claimed that 19 of them were never returned.[38] The fact that the "Christian Solidarity

Association", headed by the pro-Armenian Baroness Caroline Cox, undertook the exhumation of the mutilated bodies in Maragha undermines the credibility of the findings, though it wouldn't be unbelievable if such atrocities were also committed by unruly Azeri mobs as well.

On March 3 the National Council called for an emergency meeting of the Azerbaijani Supreme Soviet. The National Council itself tried to function as a parliament, but acted mostly as an "ineffectual irritant".[39] From the start it passed legislation that the opposition deemed essential, including the removal of former Soviet troops, establishment of a national army and the adoption of the Latin alphabet to replace the Cyrillic. Mutalibov would approve such legislation but postpone their implementation to an indefinite future. When impending critical issues were on the country's agenda, such as Azerbaijan joining the CIS, Mutalibov would ignore the Council's objections, claiming that it was his prerogative to decide on such issues.[40] It looked hence ironic that opposition members of the National Council decided to convene the Supreme Soviet where they were in the minority. While the opposition in the National Council hoped to challenge Mutalibov in the Supreme Soviet and dismiss him from presidency, the pro-government members planned to endorse his signing of the CIS Treaty.

The chairman of the Supreme Soviet, Elmira Kafarova, had resigned in September 1991 in the wake of protests over her remarks, accidentally carried live on Azerbaijani TV, in which she said that the opposition consisted of no one but "drunks and dope addicts", standard terminology used by Soviet authorities for dissidents.[41] The new chairman was the dean of Baku University's Medical Faculty, Dr Yagub "Dollar" Mamedov. Mamedov was a Mutalibov associate who had acquired the nickname due to his reputation for lowering university entrance requirements for a fee. Many assumed that he was a transition figure to mind parliamentary affairs until a hard core Mutalibov associate took over.

The APF-affiliated members of the Supreme Soviet brought the fall of Khojaly and the massacres committed there to the earliest session on March 5, 1992. Yet, despite demonstrations outside the parliament, former AzCP members seemed oblivious to the fates of those killed there and even tried to prevent its discussion. The conservatives also attempted to prevent the showing of the footage of those murdered lying strewn over a large field outside Khojaly as filmed by journalist Chingiz Mustafaev.[42] While the mayor of Khojaly, Elman Mahmedov, insisted on showing the footage, the conservatives refused on "procedural grounds". Soon, however, outside the protesters' noise became more difficult to ignore, and

Yagub Mamedov gave in. The film turned out to be gruesome and shocking: It showed mutilated bodies, bodies with fingers cut off and eyes gouged out by knives. Some bodies were even scalped.[43] The film had an immediate effect. All members, including the pro-Mutalibov ones were sobbing while the crowd outside chanted "*istifa*", demanding Mutalibov's resignation.

When the latter addressed the assembly, he seemed confused and insecure. He argued that the Russian policy was pro-Armenia because Azerbaijan had not ratified the CIS Treaty, and Azerbaijan would surely lose the NKAO if it did not sign the upcoming treaty on unified – that is, Russian – command of CIS troops. Mutalibov might have correctly diagnosed the reason for Russia's anti-Azerbaijani policy, yet his cold-hearted mention of the necessity of alliance with Russia, whose troops had just a few days ago participated in the massacre of Azeris, was rather tactless and insensitive.[44]

After Mutalibov, Rahim Gaziev, having just arrived from Shusha, took the floor. Gaziev scoffed at Mutalibov's idea of demobilization, urging instead that Azerbaijan should engage in universal mobilization. Gaziev, as well as Iskender Hamidov, another heavyweight of the APF, took the floor next and called for Mutalibov's resignation. Hamidov stated that Mutalibov was appointed First Secretary after Black January and had dutifully implemented Moscow's policies, and thus was "personally" responsible for the Khojaly disaster. Moreover, he accused Mutalibov for violating the Azerbaijani Constitution because despite the National Council's adoption of a law aiming at the establishment of a national army, Mutalibov chose not to implement it. Hence he suggested that Mutalibov should be impeached.

Etibar Mamedov, for his part, called Mutalibov a traitor for suggesting that Azerbaijan should attach its to-be-established army to the CIS forces whose leading power, Russia, had slaughtered Azerbaijani citizens in Khojaly. He then presented a draft resolution on behalf of the Democratic Bloc, demanding Mutalibov's resignation. Yagub Mamedov ignored the motion and called for a recess. The deliberations continued on and off till 2 p.m. next day.

Although some Democratic Bloc members, including "social democrat" Araz Alizade, supported Mutalibov and even called for the banning of political parties and the suspension of the parliament for six months, crowds outside the Supreme Soviet sounded more convincing: they asked for Mutalibov's resignation by 12 noon next day, then extended it till 2 p.m., threatening to storm the building if he did not comply. Belatedly, at 6 p.m. on March 6, 1992 Mutalibov gave in and resigned.[45] The constitution provided for Mamedov to act as interim president until presidential elections.[46]

After Mutalibov's departure, the APF's newly acquired influence helped the former's rival within the AzCP, the incumbent Prime Minister, Hasan Hasanov, to keep his seat. For some time, Hasanov had seemed interested in improving relations with the APF. After Mutalibov's resignation, he signed a protocol with Elchibey, which provided for the appointment of three APF members to ministerial positions. Moreover, Elchibey moved to the executive building, and although he did not have any official portfolio, he participated in most of the government meetings.[47]

At the time of Mutalibov's resignation, the new government faced numerous difficulties. As with many other republics, Azerbaijan was dependent on the supply channels and the markets of the Soviet Union. Their almost overnight disappearance in the immediate post-Soviet period brought the country to the brink of bankruptcy. There was also the problem of refugees, adding to socio-political and economic difficulties. The APF leadership lacked experience in running the country; hence it agreed to a coalition government with the AzCP elite.

Elchibey turned out to be ineffective and often naïve. He believed in lofty ideals including "… emancipation from Russia's all pervasive grip, drawing closer to Turkey and establishing firm ties with [Iranian Azeris] across the Araxes [Araz] frontier." Moreover, he sought to act upon these goals, only to find that they exacted a heavy price and could be mutually exclusive.[48] In refusing to join the CIS he argued that even Central Asian states would soon split from the CIS, saying that "in a few months the popular movement growing there will sweep away the present leadership stifling the people's aspirations to freedom."[49] Elchibey's lack of pragmatism was displayed even before his rise to power. At a time when Iran's neutrality was crucial to Azerbaijan's struggle in the NKAO, he prophesied independence for Iranian Azeris: "As an independent state rises in the north of Azerbaijan, it will make it easier for freedom to grow in the south."[50] In contrast, Heidar Aliev – even while in Nakhichevan – avoided any such talk, focusing on the opening of new mosques and visiting the tomb of Imam Reza in Meshed, Iran.[51]

On March 28 the Azerbaijani Supreme Soviet met to consider the establishment of the national army and the declaration of a state of emergency as suggested by Rahim Gaziev, now defense minister of the coalition government. Conservatives of the AzCP tried to postpone the establishment of the army till after the presidential elections, which led Abulfaz

Elchibey, who wasn't even a member of the assembly, to address those present. He denounced the lack of enthusiasm for the national army by saying: "Once we are sure we can defend ourselves – then, and only then, will we be able to speak about elections and other matters."[52]

Mutalibov formally established Azerbaijan's Defense Ministry in October 1991, but, unlike Armenians, there weren't many Azeri officers who had served in the Soviet Armed Forces. Azerbaijan's nascent Defense Ministry, for its part, had fewer than 100 staff. The appointment of four successive ministers to head the Defense Ministry within six months of its establishment complicated the situation more. The ministry had no weapons and no secure communications lines. Tajeddin Mekhtiev, who served for nine weeks in early 1992 as Defense Minister, stated in 2000 that all Azerbaijan's government phone lines went through the Russian Military Intelligence Network (GRU), which was thus able to learn of Azerbaijan's military decisions.[53] This meant that Russia could have supplied valuable military information to Armenia if/when the former desired to undermine Azerbaijan's war effort. The GRU might have supplied intelligence to Armenia, especially after the anti-Russian Elchibey became President in June 1992.

Azerbaijan's rather belated attempt to establish a national army faced several other difficulties. Earlier, in late September 1991, faced with an increase in inter-ethnic fighting and his lack of a legitimate claim to power, Mutalibov had formed an eight-member Defense Council, bringing together representatives from various political parties, including the Social Democratic Party, the National Independence Party, and the APF.[54] Yet Mutalibov dissolved the Defense Council on January 27, 1992 by a presidential decree. Etibar Mamedov, also a member of the Council, suggested that Mutalibov abolished the Council because he feared irregular forces under the control of various opposition figures could be used to topple him.[55]

After becoming Defense Minister in March 1992, Rahim Gaziev called on Azeri troops serving in the former Soviet Union's army to return home and serve in the to-be-established armed forces. This appeal was heeded by most. Yet a major portion of these conscripts were serving – as most Muslims from Turkic republics did – in construction battalions and had no military training. Those who had some military training were part of the existing OMON units, or gendarmes under the command of the Ministry of the Interior. Many OMON members had become supporters of

Iskender Hamidov's pan-Turkist Bozkurt Association, while others retained their pro-Moscow loyalties.

Nevertheless, paramilitaries, or private armies whose allegiance was due to regional loyalties, partisanship or wages paid by the warlords carried out most of the fighting in the NKAO. The Lachin, Fuzuli and Gubatli units looked like "extended families" whose loyalty depended on primordial ties, a factor that also influenced politics in the republic throughout the Soviet era. Alekram Hummatov's Lenkoran-based Talish brigade included Talish fighters from the southeast of the country. Etibar Mamedov also had by mid-1992 around 2,000 armed men, most of whom were students.

Another well-known paramilitary group was the so-called "Ganja Brigade" financed by Surat Huseinov, the young former director of the state wool combine in Ganja, whose illicitly acquired wealth helped to pay his troops well.[56] In front-line Aghdam, located in lower Karabagh near the eastern border of the NKAO, there existed six private armies controlled by outlaws and local mafia groups. Most of their men were ex-convicts and criminals. They not only did not coordinate their attacks on the NKAO Armenian forces, but they fought each other as well.[57]

Armenia too had gone through a process of army building, but started doing so much earlier than Azerbaijan. Two years prior to Azerbaijan's endeavor to form an army, Armenia began recruiting former Soviet officers, Russian and Armenian alike. Former Deputy Head of the Soviet General Staff Norad Ter-Grigoriants, an ethnic Armenian, was appointed Armenia's head of general staff. Some of the legionnaires were familiar with the region, including Lt. General Anatoly Zenevich, who had served in Armenia. Zenevich would go on working for the NKAO Armenians in 1992.[58]

Irregulars, or the *fedayin*, too did most of the fighting on the Armenian side. Especially after the demise of the Soviet Union, many Armenian volunteers, recruited by nationalist paramilitary groups, including the Dashnakt, flocked to the NKAO with little formal help from the Yerevan government. Yet those Armenians or the *fedayin* who had arrived earlier in the NKAO had served up to four years in the underground, which made them formidable adversaries. There were also many criminals and hooligans who went to the oblast in pursuit of riches and/or military adventure.[59] On the Azerbaijani side, similar dark characters also carved a niche for themselves on the war front. It was mostly, but not always, these groups on both sides who were responsible for the gruesome acts during the fighting.

At the end of 1991, when Soviet armed units ceased to be responsible for security in the NKAO, Azerbaijani villages there found themselves surrounded by dozens of Armenian villages, which made them vulnerable to ethnic cleansing. Yet Armenians in the NKAO were also exposed. Mostly-Armenian Stepanakert, the capital, was surrounded by Azerbaijani towns and villages which were situated on hills overlooking the capital. Fifteen miles to the east was Aghdam, a major Azerbaijani city and the center of Azerbaijani military activity. Five miles north of Stepanakert lay Khojaly, a large Azerbaijani village with an airport, which before its fall in February 1992, supplied Azeri military units throughout the oblast. Just above Stepanakert was Shusha, the Azerbaijani stronghold, which gave the Azeris at least temporary advantage *vis-à-vis* Armenians.

Armenians in the oblast took advantage of the demise of the Soviet Union by either illicitly buying arms from local Soviet commanders or acquiring them through raids on army depots.[60] One of the illicit ways used by Armenians and Azeris alike was the orchestration of explosions in the Russian army bases in Azerbaijan and Armenia, which enabled commanders not to account for missing weaponry. Robert Kocharian, the leader of the NKAO Armenians in those days said that his forces often paid the 366th Motorized Regiment of the Soviet 4th Army based in Stepanakert, in return for which the latter fired at Shusha.[61]

The major asset of the 366th Regiment was its ten tanks. In 1992 the NKAO Armenians hired these tanks on several occasions. In February 1992 the Moscow weekly *Argumenty i Fakty* printed a letter sent by a young conscript belonging to the 366th Regiment. He described the conditions the 366th Regiment had to cope with. He said that they didn't have anything to eat, didn't have any gas or water, and if they ventured out of their barracks they were either taken hostage by Armenians or were forced to serve for them.[62] Even Russian troops based in Armenia were recruited to serve in the NKAO conflict. In 1992 six Russian servicemen were captured by Azeri villagers near Kelbejar, and confessed that they were from a 7th Army base in Armenia and were allowed by their commander to serve in the NKAO as mercenaries.[63] While the 366th Regiment was working for the NKAO Armenians, the 23rd Division in Ganja began cooperating with Azerbaijani forces in late 1991.[64] Former Soviet troops' readiness to serve as mercenaries and sell weapons was witnessed by an American human rights activist, Scott Norton, who was mistaken for a businessman by Yury Nikolayevich, an officer, who attempted to sell him a tank for just US $3,000.[65]

The Fall of Shusha and the APF's Coup

By the spring of 1992 civilian and armed Azeris, after having been ousted from most of the NKAO, had sought refuge in Shusha and some of the surrounding villages. Yet Shusha itself was besieged. The only access to the town was through Lachin on the road linking Shusha to Armenia, hardly a reliable supply route for Azeri forces. Azerbaijan's second Defense Minister, Tajeddin Mekhtiev, had directed the war effort in January 1992, and after him Rahim Gaziev, APF's future defense minister, assumed responsibility for the defense of the town starting in February 1992. Despite the importance ascribed to the defense of Shusha, there was no unified command structure in the town. Four rival paramilitary groups, which often engaged in hostilities against each other, vied for power. There was no cooperation between them and no coordination of military activities.[66]

In March 1992 Gaziev was appointed defense minister and was replaced in Shusha by Lieutenant Colonel Elbrus Orujov, who, with a handful of government troops, tried to cope with the lack of coordination of the defense of the "fortress" town Shusha. The anticipated Armenian attack started at 2 a.m. on May 8, 1992, and by the evening many irregular fighters had left the town without fighting. Orujov could count on a few fighters, including the legendary Chechen commander, Shamil Basaev, who remained behind. Yet they were too few and could hold their own only if reinforcements arrived in a day or two. No reinforcements came, and the town fell by the evening of the 9th.[67]

The fall of Shusha spawned conspiracy theories. Many heard rumors that Gaziev had sold the town to the Russians to facilitate the return of Mutalibov to power.[68] Yet the Azeri commander Orujov, as well as the Armenian commander who took the town, Arkady Ter-Tatevosian, agreed that it was the poor defense and lack of coordination among the fighters which led to its speedy fall.[69] In an interview with ANS, a private Azerbaijani TV channel, Shamil Basaev stated that Shusha was simply abandoned. Otherwise, he said, the impregnable fortress could have held out with even 100 fighters for as long as a year.[70]

Shusha's loss was interestingly an embarrassment for the Armenian President Ter-Petrosyan as well. When the Armenian attack on Shusha started, he was holding talks with the acting President of Azerbaijan, Yagub Mamedov, in Tehran at an Iranian-mediated meeting. When the two signed a communiqué on the general principles of a peace agreement on May 9, 1992, Shusha had already fallen. The assault on Shusha was as much an attack on Ter-Petrosyan, who was against it, as it was on Azerbaijan. Ter-Petrosyan's foreign policy advisor, Ashot Manucharian, also admitted that the capture of Shusha was so timed as to embarrass Ter-Petrosyan who believed in a less-than-desirable settlement in the NKAO that would save face for the Baku leadership.[71]

The Armenian capture of Shusha on May 7, however, provided Mutalibov with the opportunity to organize his comeback. Acting President Yagub Mamedov accused Defense Minister Rahim Gaziev of being a traitor for failing to defend the city. He said that Gaziev hid the fall of Shusha from him as well as the public for three days, to which Gaziev replied that it wasn't him but "those traitors in Baku" who sold out Shusha, referring to the government's failure to send reinforcements and supplies.[72] On May 14 the Supreme Soviet was to hear the Khojaly Disaster Commission's report, when Mutalibov showed up unexpectedly, and the Soviet, sitting without quorum rescinded its earlier decision of March 6, which had accepted Mutalibov's resignation.[73] After his reinstatement, Mutalibov vowed to ban all political parties and impose martial law. It seemed certain that he would cancel the presidential elections scheduled for June 7, because after his return the post of the president was no longer vacant. He argued that it was time to join the CIS, and that he would travel to Tashkent the next day for the CIS meeting to sign the CIS Treaty.[74]

The same day, Elchibey addressed thousands gathered outside the APF headquarters facing the former "26 Commissars Park". While both the United States and Turkey announced that they didn't recognize Mutalibov's restoration as lawful, Elchibey gave Mutalibov till 2 p.m. next day to resign. Next day, after some trepidation and the ensuing reassurance from the Turkish Ambassador, Mehmet Ali Bayar, that Russia promised to Turkey not to oppose the APF's counter-coup, the APF decided to go on the offensive.[75] By the end of the 2 p.m. deadline, while Mutalibov supporters had surrounded the building of the presidency with Mutalibov inside, the APF fighters, including many of Iskender Hamidov's paramilitaries, surprised everyone by attacking and capturing first the parliament and the TV building and then advancing towards the presidency. The apparent ease of the APF troops in capturing initial targets led to chaos and an earlier than expected dispersal of the pro-Mutalibov forces, with fewer than a dozen casualties on both sides.[76] Mutalibov gave up the fight and fled to Moscow.[77] A new pro-APF government was formed next day.

The coup enabled the APF to replace speaker Yagub Mamedov, who had played a prominent role in the Mutalibov coup, with Isa Gambar, a heavyweight of the front. During the election of the speaker on May 18, some former AzCP members wanted to steal away the APF's victory at the last minute by suggesting Heidar Aliev as an alternative candidate. They tried to get in touch with Aliev in Nakhichevan, though he chose not to talk to them.[78] Aliev chose not to accept the offer either because he wasn't too fond of the Mutalibov-allies or he might have thought that the APF coup had increased the APF's power drastically, so that even though Heidar Aliev was still very popular, he could have lost the elections.

The new government included more APF members, though especially ministries dealing with the economy were handed to former AzCP affiliated politicians. Iskender Hamidov and Rahim Gaziev were reappointed as ministers of interior and defense respectively, while Tofik Kasumov became foreign minister and Sabit Baghirov head of the state oil company, SOCAR.[79] Some, including Etibar Mamedov, head of the National Independence Party, refused to support the new cabinet, arguing that they were against a coalition with the communists.[80]

The APF did, however, adopt a hard-line stance when it demanded the Supreme Soviet dissolve itself in favor of the 50-member National Council. The initial vote resulted 171 in favor and 48 against, with the former communists arguing that it was anti-democratic to abolish the Supreme Soviet in favor of an unelected body. The APF revolution brought about the adoption of tactics including brandishing of pistols in the Supreme Soviet chamber, as well as making threatening speeches. Arif Hajiev reflected the APF's mood when he told the deputies:

> There has been a revolution by the Popular Front. We are in control of the country – and there are thousands of people outside who are fed up with your games and who will not let you leave this building until you come to your senses. So, vote like we say.[81]

These tactics proved useful and the Supreme Soviet abrogated itself with 244 out of 255 members voting in favor.

The coup attempt by the pro-Mutalibov members gravely affected, however, the Azerbaijani defenses near the NKAO, because several APF military units were hurried back to Baku to suppress the coup. This left Lachin, the Azerbaijani stronghold on the short land corridor linking Armenia to the NKAO, exposed to an Armenian assault. Further contributing to the weakening of the front was the dismissal of Arif Pashaev as commander of the Lachin Regiment in February 1992. By the time the

Armenian attack began on May 16, no replacement had been sent. By May 18 the town was captured by Armenians, while the 3,000-strong Azeri unit fled, confused as to who was their commander. Lachin, theoretically another difficult to capture town, was seized by Armenians, who burnt the town and reopened the corridor to Armenia, which had been closed for more than two years.[82] Lachin had a majority Kurdish population, and Armenians initially tried to justify its capture as their attempt to free the Kurds from the yoke of Azerbaijan. After its capture, however, Lachin was ethnically cleansed and its population deported to Azerbaijan.[83]

The fall of Shusha, and later Lachin, deepened political divisions in Azerbaijan. In Baku, each faction accused the other of incompetence and betrayal. The most seemingly "uninvolved" was Heidar Aliev, who, located in distant Nakhichevan, continued to promote himself as the "third force" in Azerbaijani politics. He was close to accurately describing the situation when he decried that "there is no leadership in Baku at the moment", but contradicted himself, adding that it was necessary to postpone presidential elections and focus on the pressing matter of the war in and around the NKAO.[84]

The APF, for its part, blamed Aliev for military defeats in and around Karabagh because by keeping Nakhichevan out of the war he had supposedly enabled Armenians to transfer their troops from the border with Nakhichevan to Karabagh. Aliev admitted that he held meetings with Armenian officials on the Nakhichevan–Armenia border, but rejected Interior Minister Iskender Hamidov's claim that they strengthened the Armenian side in the conflict. Whatever his motives were, Aliev avoided Baku's control of Nakhichevan, which would have happened had he not refused the latter's demand that he introduce a state of emergency.[85]

On May 15, only two days prior to the fall Lachin, representatives from Azerbaijan, Armenia, Belarus, Kazakhstan, the Russian Federation, Ukraine, and Georgia had signed the Treaty on Conventional Armed Forces in Europe (CFE) and its associated documents as successors of the USSR. This agreement determined their share of the conventional weapons to be left behind by the withdrawing Soviet forces. Both Armenia and Azerbaijan were to receive equal numbers of battle tanks (220), armed combat vehicles (220), artillery pieces (285), 100 warplanes, and four armed attack helicopters.[86] Thus, with these new acquisitions, some of which were already acquired by the parties through illicit ways, the fighting power of Armenia and Azerbaijan escalated drastically.

Azerbaijan was more advantageous because while Armenia had only three divisions and no military airfields on its soil during the Soviet era, Azerbaijan was home to five divisions and five military airfields. Hence there was more potential for Azerbaijan to acquire more weaponry through deals with Russian commanders. With regard to ammunition, Azerbaijan seemed luckier as well. An Armenian estimate put the already stored ammunition in Armenia as capable of filling only 500 railroad cars, while the Azerbaijani storage facilities supposedly contained 10,000 cars of ammunition.[87] In November 1993 the Azerbaijani Foreign Ministry admitted that in May 1992 it took possession of 286 tanks and 842 armored vehicles, as well as 386 artillery pieces.[88]

On June 7, 1992 elections were held. The APF's candidate, Abulfaz Elchibey, and Nizami Suleymanov, supported by Heidar Aliev were the main contenders for the presidency. Aliev was unable to run because of a constitutional provision barring candidates over 65 years of age. Niyazi Suleymanov was an obscure academic, but unlike Elchibey who focused on independence, the rule of law, and democracy, Suleymanov promised prosperity and an end to economic problems. He also vowed to settle the NKAO problem within three months without any loss of life.[89] He also promised that after his election he would invite the *aksakal*, the old/wise man, to Baku "to lead us all". In Azerbaijan *aksakal* meant only one person: Heidar Aliev.[90]

Elchibey's staff did not pay much attention to Suleymanov, but when his "bread and butter" message caught on, they became worried. Other candidates included Tamerlan Karayev, deputy chairman of the parliament and an APF member. He justified his participation as "keeping the [election] process honest," and providing "constructive opposition".[91] Etibar Mamedov was also a candidate until the last week of the campaign. Both Karayev and Mamedov withdrew their candidacies before the elections. Apparently Mamedov's major goal was to use the broadcast time allotted to candidates on radio and television. After his withdrawal he threw his support to Elchibey.[92] Elchibey received 59.4 percent of more than 3.3 million votes cast. Suleimanov came second, with a surprising 33 percent of the vote. No other candidate received as much as 5 percent of the vote.[93]

The election campaign was dominated by partisan use of state broadcasts by the APF. Even after the ban on election campaigning on June 5, Elchibey held a press conference next day which was carried live on state television. The APF was using all the perks of being in power, as did the AzCP once. Elchibey promised constitutional, economic, and cultural reforms. He heralded structural changes to ensure national sovereignty, including the creation of a national army and a national currency backed by gold reserves.[94]

Five days after Elchibey winning the presidential elections, Azeri forces went on the offensive. The June 12 offensive led to the recapture of the Shaumyan region, north of the NKAO.[95] During the following three weeks the northern NKAO region of Agdere (Martakert) was captured as well and Azerbaijani rule re-established there by July 4. Armenian forces were caught off guard. After their more than easy capture of such fortress towns as Shusha and Lachin, many *fedayin* had returned to Armenia, and Armenians in the region were gripped by a false sense of security. Azeris attacked from the north while Armenians were expecting an assault from the east. This time Baku also utilized the services of Russian mercenaries. The Azerbaijani assault force included around 150 armored vehicles and tanks, most of them driven by Russians from the 23rd division of the 4th Army based in Ganja.[96]

In early July, facing imminent expulsion from the region, Armenia turned to Russia for help. According to several independent observers Russian aid came in the form of military attack helicopters flown by Russian pilots, and the Azeri assault was stopped in its tracks. Even Yerevan officials admitted that Russia's help was instrumental in containing the Azerbaijani offensive.[97] Nevertheless, the Armenian front was still frail and in disarray. Having recaptured almost half of the NKAO, Azerbaijan began to make use of mercenary Russian and Ukrainian pilots in air attacks on Stepanakert.[98]

The NKAO Armenians acted quickly to shore up their defenses and not wait for Armenia to take the initiative. A new State Defense Committee headed by Robert Kocharian was established, which introduced military rule and general mobilization of all males aged 18 to 45. While Kocharian chaired the committee, Serzh Sarkissian was put in charge of the logistics of the NKAO armed forces. Both men would come to power in Armenia later on.[99]

The failure of Azerbaijan to join the CIS and the fall from power of pro-Russian Mutalibov in May 1992 many argued, drew Russia and Armenia, which had joined the CIS, closer. Moreover, Armenia's signing of the CIS Collective Defense Treaty on May 15 ensured the continuation of Russian military assistance.[100] The election of Elchibey, who was adamantly opposed to the CIS, as President contributed to the Russo-Armenian rapprochement. Elchibey not only refused to join the CIS but he also rejected a bilateral military pact with Russia. Russia retaliated by increasing customs duties and by canceling the contracts of Russian enterprises with Azerbaijan. Moscow even tried to keep in check Azerbaijani petty traders who traditionally sold goods in Russia. Russia's retaliation came just after Elchibey visited Moscow with a large delegation to explain why Azerbaijan could not be part of the CIS, but still desired friendly relations.[101] Adding to Elchibey's problems was US Congress' adoption on October 24, 1992 of the Freedom Support Act, Section 907, banning all aid to Azerbaijan in response to Azerbaijan's blockade of Armenia.[102]

Besides, Elchibey declined Russian offers of a mediated settlement to the NKAO problem, which would have necessitated Russian peacekeepers.[103] Russia responded by refraining from demanding Armenia's withdrawal from Lachin after the latter captured this land corridor in May 1992. According to then Deputy Defense Minister, Leyla Yunusova, after Azerbaijani aircraft began attacking Stepanakert in late summer 1992, Russia built an anti-aircraft system there which made the town literally invulnerable.[104] In the wake of Armenia's seizure of additional land corridors in the spring of 1993, the Russian Defense Minister, Pavel Grachev, stated that Azerbaijan should accept the military and political realities and grant the NKAO its independence.[105]

Although the NKAO issue was a factor in the election of Elchibey, winning the war was only one of his priorities. Nation-building a-la-Turkey was one of Elchibey's major preoccupations during his shortened term in office. He openly advocated a clear break with Moscow, closer ties to Turkey and the West, and in the long run, reunification with Iranian Azerbaijan. Academics who belonged to the same intellectual stratum as Elchibey were brought into government or the National Assembly. They included historian and co-founder of the APF, Isa Gambar, historian Etibar Mamedov, poet Sabir Rustemkhanli, and others. They were endowed intellectually to remake the Azerbaijani man or woman through rewriting history and proposing desirable socio-cultural characteristics of a new de-Sovietized society. Instead, they not only had to govern a country but they also had to face a full-blown secessionist movement in the NKAO, backed by Armenia and – according to many – by Russia.

Yet Elchibey and his associates believed that they could fight the war in the NKAO, engage in nation-building efforts and work for the reunification with southern Azerbaijan simultaneously. Three days after the presidential elections, Elchibey was interviewed on issues he felt strongly about. He suggested that the APF was interested in the democratization of Iran, because while Iran was supporting the NKAO Armenians, it was culturally suppressing Iranian Azeris. He argued that his mission included the "creation and preservation of a truly independent Azerbaijan", adding that this would help the forces of democracy in Iranian Azerbaijan and in Central Asia.[106]

Within a few months after coming to power, Elchibey began to lose popular support, and by the time he was ousted by a military coup, he was no longer popular with most of the electorate. Although his government included quite a few brilliant intellectuals who had no ties to the ancien régime, some of them became corrupt, while others felt lost in the midst of a government apparatus staffed by disloyal Soviet era apparatchiks. On the managerial level, the APF's replacement of many qualified technocrats with politically correct but inept activists contributed to the socio-economic disruptions.[107] Popular discontent led to anti-government demonstrations which increasingly became difficult to contain.[108] The spread of petty crime, chaos and lawlessness, as well as the humiliating defeats on the Karabagh front, accelerated his demise.[109]

The decline in popular support for the regime was also seen in the radically diminished rates of recruitment for the war front. Whereas joining newly established military units and private militias was initially voluntary, recruitment numbers soared in early 1992. Yet battlefield defeats, together with the growing popular perception that the command staff was largely incompetent and corrupt contracted recruitment figures in a year. Faced with the dwindling of men under arms, the government introduced conscription, but many tried to elude it. Police raids of places where the youth congregated became common. Many tried to leave the country to avoid the draft.[110] All these took place while on the war front Azeri units suffered from low morale, higher desertion rates, and lack of discipline.

Elections for a new parliament might have added to the appeal of the new ruling elite, but for various reasons the adoption of a new election law was continuously postponed. A major reason the APF provided was that wartime conditions were unsuitable for such an endeavor: focusing on anything other than the NKAO would have undermined the Azeri war effort. Some, however, argued that more parochial motives were the reason: the parliament chairman Isa Gambar's Yeni Musavat party was rapidly losing popular support and Gambar thus tried to postpone the elections.[111]

Political and economic reforms under Elchibey were slow, partly because of the resistance of the bureaucracy, which was still dominated by former communists, and the sectarian rivalries within the bureaucracy. The government's "Azerification" policy, while keeping some, liquidated many capable Slavic bureaucrats and administrators inherited from the Soviet era. In their place, inexperienced, incapable, but politically and "ethnically" correct APF loyalists were installed.[112]

On the positive side, political parties flourished during this period. Among nationalist and to varying degrees pan-Turkist parties one could mention the APF, Isa Gambar's *Yeni Musavat* and Etibar Mamedov's *Milli Istiqlal*, which were real parties with headquarters and branches. Yeni Musavat claimed to be the main governing party, and Etibar Mamedov's *Milli Istiqlal* identified itself as the main opposition, though neither had taken part in elections. Former communists also established several political parties. They opposed close ties to Turkey, favored state-controlled economic liberalization and close ties to Russia and the CIS. These included Yeni Azerbaycan (Heidar Aliev), Mustaqil Azerbaijan (Nizami Suleymanov), Social Democracy (Zardusht Alizade), and Azerbaijan Demokratik Quvvalarin Hareketi (Ilyas Ismayilov). There were also parties representing ethnic minorities (Talish, Lezgin and others).[113]

Under Elchibey, the Government continued to control access to the media and was in charge of allocating office space to political parties, and paper to newspapers. As in the Soviet era, these kinds of control enabled the new ruling elite to extend or withhold favors at will. Yet, whereas Azerbaijani politics in the post-Soviet era continued to be shaped partly by compromises or political deals between bureaucratic cliques, local strongmen, or warlords increasingly acquired significance.

A good example of increasing lawlessness is the behavior of Iskender Hamidov, who had acquired fame by leading the pro-APF forces in the successful counter-coup against Mutalibov on May 14/15, 1992. He was appointed Interior Minister and was initially successful in restoring order in Baku by the use of strong-arm tactics. The fiery Interior Minister had his own pan-Turkist Bozkurt (Grey Wolf) party and militia, which was loosely affiliated with the Turkish pan-Turkists. Soon, however, he became unruly himself and acquired notoriety for beating up journalists and for issuing an empty threat against Yerevan that he possessed two tactical nuclear weapons and could use them against Yerevan.[114] This silly bravado and others finally led to his dismissal by Elchibey. The removal of Hamidov from power meant that Elchibey could no longer count on Hamidov's well-armed units which the latter had successfully used against Mutalibov in May 1992. Surat Huseinov's revolt started soon after Hamidov was fired.[115]

Until his dismissal from office in late February 1993, Defense Minister Rahim Gaziev too displayed signs that he thought the political situation in the republic developed into a free-for-all. Whereas Interior Minister Hamidov reserved himself the right to give battle orders to his OMON troops in and around the NKAO without consulting the Defense Ministry, Defense Minister Gaziev did the opposite. He did not shy away from using defense ministry troops in domestic politics. In one case, he ordered Etibar Mamedov's National Independence Party to hand over the party's headquarters to him. It took Elchibey's involvement until Gaziev backed down.

To the end, Gaziev insisted that all opposition political activity in the republic should cease so that the government could concentrate on the conduct of the war.[116] Unable to dictate his will on the government, Elchibey ended up settling for a muddle through policy to get through the political maze. Instead of ruling, he arbitrated disputes between ministers, not always successfully. The constant bickering between the two heavyweights, Gaziev and Hamidov, undermined any claim to the rule of law. Elchibey would fire Gaziev on February 8, 1993, and Hamidov soon thereafter, which ironically undermined his authority because men with guns who could prop him up disappeared from the scene.

Another government official, Panakh Huseinov, caused embarrassment and loss of popular support for the Elchibey administration. He was appointed to the position of state secretary in the office of the President. This position entailed Huseinov's programming of Elchibey's daily schedule, thus enabling him to receive kickbacks from those who wished to talk to the President. Soon he became one of the wealthiest in Baku. "He was soon known as the man who drove 'a white Mercedes during black times.'"[117]

In short, the Elchibey era was negatively influenced by Soviet era patterns of behavior, lack of democratic culture, as well as new forms of regional and bureaucratic rivalries and external manipulation attempts, including Russia's not so covert aid to the NKAO Armenians, or to the local Azerbaijani warlord Surat Huseinov, who ended up toppling Elchibey. The Elchibey government, like the preceding AzCP governments, tried to ban bad news. As an informed observer aptly put it:

> Increasingly, what we got instead [of real news] were images of the President meeting foreign dignitaries (mainly visiting Turks), pictures of the Minister of Culture opening yet another art exhibit (of mainly state-sanctioned artists), and endless invitations from either the protocol section of the information department of the Foreign Ministry

> to attend this briefing or that photo opportunity with a visiting US Congressman from Texas or a knot of MPs flown in by British Petroleum (BP).[118]

Nevertheless, unlike the Soviet era, the media was much freer. Almost all political parties and groups owned their own papers and used them to field charges against the new government's members, accusing Elchibey and others of being Russian, Turkish, and Armenian agents. Frequently, there were character assassination attempts. For instance, the pro-Aliev New Azerbaijan published a story which portrayed Elchibey as a coward for allegedly trying to cooperate with the KGB when he was jailed in the 1970s.[119]

One of the most controversial issues of the Elchibey era was the parliament's change of the name of the state language from "Azerbaijan language" to "Turk Dili" (Language of Turks) in mid-December 1992, which turned out to be a disaster for the government.[120] Most Azeris assumed that Turkish, and not Azeri, was now the state language, although this was not the case. The pro-Russian social democrat Araz Alizade exclaimed: "Today our language is changed to Turkish, tomorrow they will call us all Turks, and next we will be declared to be a province of Turkey!"[121] Azerbaijan's Helsinki Committee activists demonstrated in front of Elchibey's residence, and many opponents of the law argued that such an important decision should have been made by referendum, rather than by *Milli Majlis*.[122] There was widespread sentiment that the language law would further alienate minorities, including the non-Turkic Talish, Lezgin, and Kurds.

Actually, the early independence era was the least opportune period to try to implement an ethnic nationalism policy. Elchibey's adamant pursuit of Turkification appealed to some of his supporters, yet for many it was useless in dealing with economic hardships. Throughout almost all his presidency he was considered a patriot who lacked political skills. His opponents took advantage of his lack of acumen. In Ganja, the shady Soviet manager-turned-businessman-turned-self-styled colonel, Surat Huseinov, who later overthrew Elchibey, had surrounded himself with a large mercenary army and was acting on his own as a warlord in the region. Although an ethnic Azeri, Huseinov detested Elchibey's brand of nationalism, and the latter's anti-Russian stance. In the north, the secessionist Lezgin groups, including *Sadval*, were also planning to challenge the Azerbaijani authority to establish an independent Lezgin state to be carved out of Azerbaijan and Daghestan.[123] Most Kurds living in Azerbaijan were also worried about Elchibey's perceived Turkic emphasis.[124]

The Elchibey era also roughly coincided with the start of the OSCE's (then CSCE) mediation effort on the NKAO dispute. On February 26, 1992 the CSCE's foreign ministers created the Minsk Group on Nagorno-Karabagh, which consisted of Armenia, Azerbaijan, Belarus, Czechoslovakia, France, Germany, Italy, Russia, Sweden, Turkey, and the United States. Initially the Group planned to hold the Minsk Conference, but failed to do so because the parties could not agree on each other's preliminary conditions.[125] The Group agreed on a step by step ceasefire formula, though the ceasefire came belatedly in 1994 with Russia's unilateral mediation.

The fall of Kelbejar – situated outside the NKAO, between the latter and Armenia – to the Armenians in April 1993 was a decisive turning point in Elchibey's destiny. The raion or district of Kelbejar was situated to the north-west of the NKAO controlling the access road from Armenia to the NKAO. The region was surrounded by steep mountain ranges and was home to 45,000 Kurdish and Azeri villagers living in dozens of villages.[126] Although the Armenian side then argued that the capture of the region was for defensive purposes, the commander of the Armenian assault, Monte Melkonian, claimed later that its seizure was a strategic goal all along.[127]

Already, defeats of the Azeri forces in late March had forced them to retreat and begin evacuating civilians from the region. The final Armenian push started on March 27, 1993, and by March 31 they were able to overrun the disorganized and demoralized Azeri units as well as the remnants of the civilian Azeri population who were still in the area. During this final push many civilians became victims of advancing Armenian units, which the Armenian commander Monte Melkonian openly admitted.[128]

On April 2 Armenian forces attacked the last remaining stronghold of the region, the city of Kelbejar itself. The city was defended by a few dozen poorly armed and poorly maintained troops, some of whom even lacked boots.[129] The last Azeri evacuation helicopters had flown on April 1, so the thousands of Azeri and Kurdish civilians still remaining were forced to avoid capture by fleeing through the Murov pass to the east where they encountered heavy snow and freezing temperatures. Many civilians perished during the arduous trek.[130]

Husseinov's Revolt

The Kelbejar debacle strengthened Elchibey's opponents who hoped to capitalize on it in order to get rid of him and the APF government. After all, it was the battlefield defeats in 1991 and early 1992 that helped the APF and Elchibey to rise to power. The same "battlefield factor" should also do the trick, Elchibey's opponents probably thought, to engineer a regime change. Yet the government acted fast, declaring a state of emergency and postponing parliamentary elections expected to be held in the fall of 1993.[131] This eliminated the chance for his opponents, former communists, Etibar Mamedov and others, of democratically neutralizing Elchibey's or the APF's hold on power. Ironically, elections were delayed twice from spring 1993, and Rahim Gaziev, then Defense Minister and ally of Huseinov, had called for their postponement early in 1993.[132]

Among those who held a grudge against Elchibey was Surat Huseinov, who, together with Defense Minister Rahim Gaziev, was fired from his post as commander in Ganja in February 1993 for military failures and plotting against Elchibey. Both Rahim Gaziev and Surat Husainov were considered to have cultivated too close ties with the Russian forces based in the region. This was another reason for their dismissal. While managing the state wool combine in Yevlakh, Husseinov had made a fortune and with this money he had financed his private army. His well-paid troops fought better than other private armies, and this enabled him to earn the rank of colonel, although he had no military training. He was also given the title of "national hero", which was usually reserved for those killed in action.

Huseinov owed his reputation as a "good soldier" to his unit's success in the Azeri assaults against Shaumyan and Agdere (Martakert) in June 1992.[133] As discussed earlier, Azeri victory in these regions enabled the Azeris to keep substantial portions of these regions until March 1993 when the Armenians recaptured them as part of their assault on Kelbejar. It was widely reported that Huseinov owed his success to the participation of Russian troops operating out of Ganja where the 23rd division of the Soviet Fourth Army was based. His attack force included tanks and attack helicopters operated by Russian-speaking servicemen.[134]

However, after Russian units departed Azerbaijan, Azeri forces began to suffer heavy defeats. It was perhaps no coincidence that Huseinov decided to withdraw his troops from the battle zone in the Agdere (Martakert) region in mid-February 1993 and then returned to the barracks of the 23rd

Motor Rifle Division of the Fourth Army in Ganja. Once there, he avoided any involvement in the fighting in the NKAO, which, with the absence of his units, contributed to the humiliating defeat of Kelbejar in late March 1993.

Huseinov, however, linked Armenian victories on the battlefield to Elchibey's desire to give away land to the Armenians, so that – in his own words – "democratic forces in Armenia," that is, Ter-Petrosyan, remained in power. For Huseinov, Elchibey's major preoccupation was a negotiated deal with Armenia, which required that Baku did not humiliate Ter-Petrosyan, who was considered the peace party. The fact that it was the NKAO Armenians under Kocharian who decided matters on the ground in the NKAO seems to have gone unnoticed by Huseinov.[135]

Surat Huseinov had resisted Elchibey's demands that he integrated his forces into the national army's command structure. As long as he delivered victories large and small, the government tolerated his maverick behavior. When the Russian contingent in Ganja evacuated its base in May 1993, it turned over its weapons to Huseinov's forces. Some alleged that Russian military intelligence personnel and Special Forces units were left behind to aid Huseinov's revolt,[136] while others claimed that he was actually an operative of Russian military intelligence.[137]

Huseinov stated that Elchibey should be held accountable for the losses on the battlefield and the economic catastrophe. His claims were all the more delusional in that, although he accused Elchibey for battlefield losses, these losses did indeed take place after he had withdrawn his private army from the battlefield to the comfortable surroundings of the barracks of the Soviet 23rd Motor Rifle Division. Elchibey first tried to achieve a compromise with him, but failing that he attempted to suppress his revolt on June 4, 1993, which also failed.[138] After the unsuccessful attempt to suppress the mutiny, the military commanders told Elchibey that they would not fight Huseinov.

Huseinov's revolt took place on the eve of three important events: Elchibey was scheduled to arrive in London on June 30, to sign a grandiose oil contract with a Western consortium including seven multinational companies.[139] The consortium did not include Russia's oil companies, but included Turkey's state-owned TPAO and was perceived by the former as a hostile move.[140] At the time a CSCE-mediated ceasefire seemed within reach; and Azerbaijan was preparing to leave the Ruble zone and shift to the sole use of Manat, the national currency.[141] Huseinov's putsch stopped progress on all three fronts, and was thus perceived as pro-Russian.

The CSCE effort involved American, Turkish and Russian peacemaking aimed at bringing together Armenia and Azerbaijan for talks in Moscow. At the start of the last week in May, as a goodwill gesture, Azerbaijan announced a unilateral five-day ceasefire. After meeting President Boris Yeltsin, Levon Ter-Petrosyan of Armenia agreed to the plan, although he awaited the NKAO leadership's acquiescence before formally endorsing it. The major stumbling block seemed to be Robert Kocharian, who rejected it, saying "[t]his initiative does not guarantee the safety of Karabagh's civilians."[142]

The agreement called for a 60-day ceasefire, the end of all blockades on Armenia and peace talks. There was no consensus yet whether international peacekeepers would be sent into disputed territory. If the parties had agreed to the plan, Armenia would have to withdraw from Kelbejar by June 4, and peace talks would have started on June 6 in Geneva under the auspices of the CSCE.[143] Even after the demise of the plan, Ter-Petrosyan's foreign policy adviser, Jirair (Gerard) Libaridian, showed enthusiasm for it by suggesting in late July 1993 that for talks to start NKAO Armenians should withdraw from Kelbejar and Aghdam.[144]

As suggested earlier, the NKAO leadership disliked Ter-Petrosyan's moderation and would have tried to undermine the plan by another Shusha-like fait accompli. Russian hardliners, including Defense Minister Pavel Grachev, who did not hide their enthusiasm for a strong role in the near abroad might have been inclined to disrupt the peace effort in which President Yeltsin was also publicly involved. During the early 1990s, major conflicts of opinion as well as interest within the Russian elite, was a rule rather than an exception. The two schools which competed to determine Russia's new role in world politics included Eurasianists and Atlanticists. The first, among others, aspired to have Russia continue to play a predominant role in its neighborhood, that is, the former Soviet republics. The Atlanticists, who left their imprint on Russian politics in the early 1990s, aimed at a clean break with the Soviet or autocratic past in order to fully embrace Western democratic traditions.[145] Gradually, by 1993 Eurasianists acquired the upper hand in this competition. Russia's alleged involvement in the coup to overthrow Elchibey might have been closely related to Russia's overall reorientation.

The coup attempt of Surat Huseinov began to unfold when the CSCE had just managed to convince both Armenia and Azerbaijan to a ceasefire and hold peace talks. Was he acting as proxy of the Russian military by revolting against Elchibey, and thus throwing a monkey wrench into the negotiations deal, we may never know. Yet his revolt practically eliminated the peace deal by forcing the Azerbaijani leadership to face the prospect of a fratricidal war. As we shall see later, the coup demoralized many Azeri troops, enabling the NKAO forces to advance with impunity on the battlefield. Their seemingly inevitable all-out defeat of the Azeri forces undercut Ter-Petrosyan's attempts to reach a compromise settlement.[146]

On June 9, while his forces advanced towards Baku, Huseinov called not only for the resignation of undesirable cabinet members but also, for the first time, of Elchibey. As demanded earlier by Huseinov, Prime Minister Panakh Huseinov had resigned on June 8, and Elchibey had asked for the resignation of Isa Gambar, chairman of the Parliament and since November 1992 head of the Musavat party. Gambar did so on June 13. Nevertheless, Huseinov kept advancing towards Baku upping the ante by also demanding Elchibey's head.[147] As a last recourse, Elchibey, with significant prodding from Turkey, invited Aliev on June 15 to take over as the new chairman of the Supreme Soviet.[148] The expectation was that with Aliev in the second most important post in Azerbaijan, Huseinov would stop his advance. Yet Huseinov did not stop, and his forces entered the city on June 23.[149] Aliev's appointment had wide public support. Even those who earlier blamed him for his Soviet past rushed to embrace him as the "savior". One of those was Etibar Mamedov, head of the opposition National Independence Party.[150]

Elchibey had flown out of the capital on June 18 for his native Nakhichevan. On June 21, 37 of the 50 members of the *Milli Majlis* voted to declare their support for Huseinov, and called Elchibey back to Baku to assume responsibility for his role in the crisis.[151] On June 24 *Milli Majlis* voted to strip Elchibey of presidency for failing to return to Baku, and Aliev took over as Acting President. The same day, he appointed Huseinov as Prime Minister, and the *Milli Majlis* approved the appointment. Huseinov was given direct responsibility for the military, security and police forces.[152] As many then assumed these three huge responsibilities would serve as nooses that would help Huseinov hang himself with in the years to come.

For his part, as soon as he arrived in Baku, Aliev started to rebuild his image and authority. The state television aired daily programs saluting his achievements, and he often spoke on TV endlessly to explain his positions on various issues.[153] On August 28, 1993 a referendum was held to confirm Elchibey's ouster.[154] Former chairman of the Supreme Soviet, Isa Gambar, was stripped of his immunity. He was later arrested and spent a month in jail. The deputy chairman of the Supreme Soviet, Tamerlan Karayev, was appointed Ambassador to China, a virtual political exile. Some other APF deputies were removed from the Supreme Soviet after the pro-Aliev deputies lifted their immunity. Some of them were also arrested and tried for various crimes, including sell-out in the NKAO war, abuse of power, graft, bribery and corruption.[155] On October 3, 1993 presidential elections were held, which Aliev won by a Soviet style 98.8 percent.[156]

One of the first actions of Aliev was to have the Cabinet of Ministers cancel on June 23 Elchibey's oil agreement.[157] Later, he renegotiated it, and on September 20, 1994 he signed a new treaty, the so-called "Contract of the Century", allocating a 10 percent share to the Russian Lukeoil. Aliev's anticipation was that Russia's involvement in the consortium would put an end to its objection to any Caspian state's unilateral exploitation of off-shore hydrocarbon resources, which would allow Azerbaijan to exploit its oil and gas deposits. Moscow's participation in the consortium was also expected to convince it that Baku respected Russian national interests in the region, thus reducing the latter's perceived pro-Armenian inclinations.

Aliev argued that without Russian help, and without joining the CIS, Azerbaijan could not solve the Karabagh problem.[158] On September 20, 1993 *Milli Majlis* voted by 31 to 13 to make Azerbaijan a member of the CIS.[159] Yet Aliev also tried to appease Turkey, a one-time supporter of Elchibey, by visiting Ankara in February 1994, and continuing to implement various bilateral agreements signed by Elchibey. He also curried favor with the West. In March 1994 Azerbaijan joined NATO's Partnership for Peace program, and signed on September 20, 1994 the Contract of the Century with the Azerbaijan International Oil Consortium. The latter move was aimed at not only enlisting the support of Russia but also of such countries as the United States, France and Britain, whose oil companies participated in the consortium. Iran welcomed Aliev's presidency, and he was hailed by the Iranian media as a politician Iran could deal with.[160]

Aliev ruled by temporarily siding with the powerful until such time when he would be able to challenge them. He appointed Surat Huseinov as Prime Minister, Minister of Interior, and Minister of Defense because Husainov had arrived in Baku with a huge military force, and with Russia's not so subtle support. Aliev appointed Hasan Hasanov, who was a rival of Mutalibov, as foreign minister. Layla Shovkat Hajieva, known to be pro-Russia, was appointed State Secretary.

In conformity with his promise to bring back law and order to the country, Aliev moved against Alekram Hummatov, an ethnic Talish and a one-time Deputy Defense Minister of the APF. When Surat Huseinov's coup started, Hummatov had sided with him and had declared the Talish-

Mughan Republic in Lenkoran on August 7, 1993. On August 23 government troops attacked his headquarters, forcing him to flee.[161] He was later arrested. Despite a successful escape from the Ministry of National Security facility in September 1994, he was captured in August 1995, tried and sentenced to death. Later his sentence was changed to life in prison, and in 2005 he was pardoned by a presidential decree.[162]

Although Aliev initially shared power with Surat Huseinov, the latter soon turned against him as well. On October 4, 1994 his forces once again mutinied in Ganja, and units loyal to him attempted to overthrow Aliev next day in Baku. On September 29, a few days prior to the coup attempt, Aliev loyalists, Afiyaddin Jalilov, vice-chairman of the parliament, and Shamsi Ragimov, head of Aliev's security apparatus, were assassinated, presumably to reduce the President's ability to clamp down on the rebellion. Aliev's suppression of the mutiny led Huseinov to flee to Russia from where he was extradited back to Azerbaijan in March 1997 to serve a life sentence.[163]

It is interesting to note that just as during his rebellion against Elchibey, the oil factor seems to have played an important role in Huseinov's putsch. It came less than two weeks after the signing of the Contract of the Century, and before its ratification by the parliament on December 2, 1994. Huseinov had not shied away from expression of dissatisfaction with the oil deal, which he considered an infringement on Russian interests.[164] Similarly, the oil factor might have played an important role in Russia's extradition of Huseinov to Azerbaijan, because it coincided with the former's signing a contract providing for Russian Lukeoil to explore for hydrocarbon resources in Azerbaijan's Yalama oil field.[165]

Heidar Aliev escaped two more coup attempts in the following months. The first took place from March 15 to 17, 1995, during which Deputy Interior Minister Rovshan Javadov's Interior Ministry troops (OPON) rebelled against Aliev. The mutiny was rumored to have been supported by rogue elements of Turkey's Interior Ministry and Intelligence Service, although their involvement was neither fully investigated nor openly acknowledged by Baku or Ankara. Aliev successfully suppressed this revolt as well, and liquidated many disloyal personnel from police units. Elchibey's Interior Minister, Iskender Hamidov, who was a member of the parliament and chairman of the National-Democratic Party of Azerbaijan, was also accused of involvement. He was arrested on March 17, but was not tried for his involvement in the coup. Hamidov was accused of embezzlement and convicted and sentenced to 14 years. Yet he was released in December

2003 after President Ilham Aliev granted an amnesty for political prisoners.[166]

Summer 1993: The Rout of the Azerbaijani Army

During and in the immediate aftermath of the political crisis of the summer of 1993 Azerbaijan lost significant patches of territory in and around the NKAO. Already militarily inferior, Azeri units began to suffer more from low morale, higher desertion rates, and lack of discipline. During the four crucial months from June 1993, Azerbaijan lost control of five regions in and out of the NKAO. In late June, Azeri forces lost control of Agdere (Martakert), their last remaining stronghold in the oblast. In July, Aghdam, a major district just a few kilometers to the east of the NKAO border was attacked. Azeri units made little effort to defend the district as well as the city by the same name, and joined civilians in their flight.[167] By mid-July the city was practically in the hands of Armenian forces. A *New York Times* reporter described the scene as:

> Heavy shelling of Aghdam, just east of the Nagorno-Karabagh border, began on Sunday. Today, witnesses said, the only open road out of the town was clogged with trucks, cars and donkey carts. Even a few construction cranes piled high with possessions lumbered out of the threatened town. Smoke rose from villages to the south, west and north that had reportedly been seized by Armenians over the last two days.[168]

The fate of Aghdam also befell other regions outside the NKAO. By late August 1993 the southern cities of Fuzuli, Jebrail and Zangelan, and the various villages around them were almost literally handed over by Azeri units after some token but ineffective resistance. As a result, some 200,000 residents of these regions fled hastily to reach safer territories in the east. The Armenian capture of the city of Goradiz near the Iranian border in early September 1993, however, cut off the only highway used by the refugees.[169] For a while the only escape option was to cross into Iran by swimming across the Araz River, which could have led to a human catastrophe. Yet Armenian forces held back and allowed the refugees to use the highway to Baku. The defeat on the southern front led the Azeri refugee population to rise to above one million.[170]

Hostilities resumed in earnest in November 1993 after Ter-Petrosyan and Aliev met for ceasefire talks in Moscow in late September 1993. The parties agreed in principle on goodwill gestures, providing that in return for an end to Azerbaijani blockades Armenians would withdraw from some territories they occupied.[171] Nevertheless, by late November 1993 hostilities were again in full swing. It's not clear who started them, but Armenian forces attacked and captured the Khudaferin bridge south of Fuzuli which served as a border crossing into Iran. After a five-hour fight, Azeri border guards escaped to Iran, and the only remaining foothold in the region was lost.[172]

In late December 1993 Azeri forces under the command of "national hero" Prime Minister Surat Huseinov, who also held the Defense and Interior Ministry portfolios, went on the offensive. Azeri units attacked Armenian positions around Fuzuli, lying to the southeast of the NKAO. They were repulsed, suffering heavy losses.[173] In early January 1994 Azeri forces went on the offensive once again on three fronts: in the east, north and the northeast of the NKAO, though most of the fighting took place near the northeastern NKAO city of Agdere (Martakert).

By mid-January, fighting spread to larger areas. Azeri forces went on the offensive near Aghdam, Fuzuli and Martakert (Agdere).[174] They were able to capture some territory, but by spring Armenian units recovered them.[175] The offensives and counter-offensives lasted through early May, with Azeris suffering heavy casualties.[176] Most of those were young new recruits with rudimentary training whose deployment the Azeri command decided as a last resort.[177] Their human-wave assaults resulted in a military fiasco. The 1,000-strong Afghan Mujahedin, borrowed from the Afghan warlord, Gulbiddin Hekmetyar, also failed to make a difference in the overall war-fighting ability of the Azeri forces.[178]

The fizzling out of the Azerbaijani offensive by May 1994 left Baku with no option other than to seek a truce. Having successfully defended all the territorial gains it had made earlier, the Armenian side was also favorably disposed to stop fighting. Representatives of all three warring parties met in Moscow and signed the ceasefire agreement on May 16. Defense Ministers Serzh Sarkissian of Armenia, Mamedrafi Mamedov of Azerbaijan, and Samvel Babayan of the NKAO agreed to stop hostilities and to seek deployment of peacekeepers from Russia and other CIS countries in the conflict zone.[179]

Despite his initial willingness to invite peacekeepers, Aliev soon reneged on his promise, believing that Russian peacekeepers would serve to preserve the status quo while reducing his maneuver room diplomatically. The Azeri public was also very much opposed to Russia's peace-keeping mission, believing that Russia was pro-Armenia. Nevertheless, the ceasefire was extended in July 1994, and has remained in place ever since despite occasional exchanges of fire between opposing parties in the no-man's-land.

OSCE's Peace Plans

Russia also had to give up its unilateral mediation efforts by late 1994, although till then it had arranged meetings in Moscow between Armenian, Azerbaijani and Karabagh Armenian representatives.[180] As suggested earlier, the Conference on Security and Cooperation in Europe's (CSCE) 11-country Minsk Group had also tried to mediate between the parties since its inception in August 1992 without achieving much.[181] Nevertheless, Azerbaijan insisted that the more neutral CSCE should continue its mediation, which the latter accepted in December 1994 when its name was changed to Organization for Security and Cooperation in Europe (OSCE). The organization also instituted co-chairmanship for the Minsk Group, and Russia and Sweden became the first co-chairs.[182]

In early 1997, when France replaced Finland, which in April 1995 had succeeded Sweden as co-chair, Baku insisted on the United States becoming the third mediator to balance Russia and France, which it perceived were pro-Armenian. During June and July 1997 the co-chairs suggested a staged withdrawal of Armenians from occupied Azeri territory situated outside the NKAO in return for unspecified Azeri concessions. Ter-Petrosyan's enthusiasm for this less than desirable plan brought his downfall in February 1998 when Prime Minister Robert Kocharian and top ministers Vazgen Sarkissian and Serzh Sarkissian considered it unacceptable.[183]

After the demise of the OSCE's 1997 proposal, Aliev and Kocharian held 15 direct talks from 1999 to April 2001, at the end of which the United States organized a conference in Key West, Florida, bringing together Aliev and Kocharian, as well as the three co-chairs. Despite high expectations, not much progress was made.[184] After a few more talks between the parties, Aliev died on December 12, 2003, leaving the stage to his son Ilham Aliev, who was already elected president in October.

The 2000s witnessed the continuation of the OSCE mediation, while the respective parties met in summits at presidential and foreign ministerial levels. In November 2007 the OSCE's three co-chairs presented to the parties the Madrid Proposals, which were not made public. Yet soon the major characteristics became known. They included the withdrawal of Armenian troops from most occupied Azeri territory outside the NKAO, while Armenian presence in Lachin and Kelbejar would remain until the final settlement. After the Armenian withdrawals, Azeri refugees would return to their homes, while an international peace-keeping force would ensure that the region remained demilitarized. During this period the region would enjoy an interim status that would be acceptable to both sides. The final stage would be the holding of a referendum in the NKAO to determine its final status.[185]

The Madrid Proposals failed to meet both parties' expectations. The Armenian side desired that Azerbaijan agreed beforehand to the holding of a referendum in the NKAO for the status of the breakaway region in five years after Armenian troops evacuated occupied Azerbaijani territories outside the NKAO. Without Azerbaijani agreement to the holding of a referendum, Yerevan believed, Armenia's withdrawal would mean a grandiose gesture without a quid pro quo that would eliminate Armenia's bargaining cards.

Azerbaijani leadership, despite its enthusiasm for the initial stage of the plan, avoided agreeing to the referendum in the NKAO, which would inevitably result in a majority vote for the NKAO's joining Armenia. This is why Aliev demanded that the first and second stages of the plan should be separate stages, while promising that Baku would grant to the NKAO the utmost autonomy, which the Azeris would characterize as virtual independence, though not real independence.

The lack of progress in the negotiations is essentially related to both parties' "buying time strategy", as suggested by Sabine Freizer of the International Crisis Group. She argued that the Armenian government believed that "the de-facto reality" of the NKAO as a state and the principle of self-determination, as in the case of Kosovo, would sooner than later lead the international community to recognize its independence. The Azeri government, for its part, was convinced that the principles of sovereignty and territorial integrity would ensure that the NKAO remained part of Azerbaijan.[186]

An astute observer, Vefa Gulizade, who served as foreign policy adviser to both Elchibey and Heidar Aliev, succinctly described the negotiation process in November 2007 by suggesting that all progress reports of the OSCE co-chairs are a "collective bluff" and that the parties were "as far from peace now as [they] were at the beginning of the process in 1994."[187] Similarly, Ilgar Mammadov, an independent political analyst, argued:

> The negotiation process and [any] peace agreement have to answer the main question: Who will enjoy sovereignty over Nagorno-Karabagh territory after a settlement? It is clear that any decision that goes beyond the territorial integrity of Azerbaijan is unacceptable for Baku. … I cannot understand what fuels so much optimism for the OSCE Minsk Group's co-chairs.[188]

Conclusion

This book suggested that there are strong links between the growth of Azerbaijani nationalism and such factors as: 1) the post-Stalin revival of the study of once-taboo historical and literary subjects; 2) the national elite's tolerance of subtle nationalist expression in the form of the rediscovery of the past; 3) the relative relaxation of controls over political expression during Gorbachev's latter years; and 4) the escalation of tensions between Azerbaijan and Armenia over the Karabagh dispute and the full-blown war that ensued. The existence of these links was explained by reference to sociopolitical events, international developments, articles and reports in Azerbaijani journals and newspapers pointing to the retrieval of the past, policy decisions, statements and arguments of the various parties involved in Azerbaijani politics between 1988 and 1994. Moreover, links between events and the views and arguments of the Azerbaijani historians and cultural literati also show that the assumptions of this book, which were outlined at the beginning, seem to be valid. The historical and literary articles evolved from being regime-supportive and apolitical to anti-regime and radically nationalist within a short period between 1985 and 1991.[1]

There is ample evidence that the first three of the above mentioned factors, namely the post-Stalin resilience, tolerance shown toward subtle nationalist expression, and Gorbachev's relaxation of controls were responsible for the emergence of a more liberal atmosphere in the Azerbaijani historical and literary publications by the mid-1980s. As a result, issues including Moscow's responsibility for environmental degradation, its emphasis on cotton monoculture, the second-class status of Azerbaijani Turkish and overemphasis on Russification, the depletion of Azerbaijan's oil for all-Union needs, and unfavorable terms of trade for Azerbaijani products had all begun to be freely discussed. Yet the Azerbaijan-Armenian dispute over Nagorno-Karabagh and Moscow's inability or unwillingness to arbitrate drastically changed the political discourse. Starting in 1988, Moscow's policies regarding nationalities, the lack of Azeri sovereignty and Moscow's perceived tilt toward Yerevan began to be widely debated. The way political developments took their own course was, however, significantly related to how the AzCP responded to the individual phases of the NKAO conflict, and increasingly to its reactions to opposition initiatives. I extensively discussed that the AzCP's policy of reliance on Moscow undermined the war effort, substantially diminished the ruling elite's credibility, and, in the final analysis, was responsible for the loss of the NKAO.

Not only during Abulfaz Elchibey's presidency (June 1992–June 1993) but also under President Heidar Aliev, the themes of independence and sovereignty were constantly placed to the forefront. Given that at the time of independence Azerbaijan was engaged in a virtual interstate war with Armenia and had eventually lost 20 percent of its territory, it should not be surprising that a nationalist discourse had dominated the political landscape. Although democracy was a major demand of the APF and other pro-independence groups in the late 1980s and early 1990s, it was in general not understood as a Western-style multi-party political system. Democracy was perceived rather as the will of the people to get rid of Russian dominance, defeat the enemy, and restore Azerbaijani rule over the NKAO.

By manipulating ethnic or national symbols, Heidar Aliev – and his successor Ilham Aliev – projected himself as a nationalist leader in pursuit of national goals. Even though street demonstrations, which were commonplace during 1988 and 1993, ceased under Aliev, Azerbaijan continued to be a country where nationalist discourse is more widespread than in any other Turkic state. This state of affairs is primarily due to the simmering Karabagh dispute and the continuing occupation of Azeri territory by Armenian forces. The dispute is not only an international conflict but also it involves the lives of more than one million refugees from the occupied territories. Hence, it would not be much of a prophesy to say that the persistence of the Armeno-Azeri conflict will ensure that any incumbent Azeri president will try not to look soft on the national, read Karabagh, issue. Yet, this does not mean that the rather mundane bread and butter issues have not influenced the political agenda in the republic. Economic issues or the mismanagement of the economy by successive Elchibey and

Aliev administrations have very much preoccupied the ordinary Azeri since independence.

The once all-powerful APF and its offshoots no longer enjoy the popularity they once enjoyed, partly because of their failure during 1992 and 1993 to recover Armenian-occupied territories. Azeri people are also more preoccupied these days with economic hardships, so that they are less interested in nationalist rhetoric.[2] This is not to say, however, that Heidar Aliev, who used nationalist discourse sparingly, did not engage in nation building. Although Aliev, unlike the APF, avoided anti-Russian or anti-Iranian rhetoric, he distanced Azerbaijan from Russia by refusing the return of Russian troops either as peacekeepers in Karabagh or as border guards.

Like his predecessor, Heidar Aliev also faced coup attempts in the initial years of his presidency. In October 1994, March 1995 and August 1995, Surat Huseinov, disgruntled OMON and several generals and defense ministry officials undertook coup attempts, which were suppressed with difficulty.[3] He turned the incidents to his advantage by liquidating "unreliable" officials and reorganizing OMON in such a way as to prevent further coup attempts. The earlier coup attempts were not simply consequences of frustrated OMON units' attempts to revise the country's foreign or domestic policies. Some of these units were recruited in the early 1990s to fight in the NKAO, that is, they didn't have links to the establishment. But soon the decay set in. They also became institutions to pursue parochial goals or self-aggrandizement. As will be discussed below, security forces are well placed to do favors for those who would like to enjoy immunity from prosecution while engaging in various illegal activities.

As in other Transcaucasian states, "clans" or "mafias" are patronage networks. Such networks form around individuals who come to enjoy favorable treatment by higher echelons of the economic or political apparatus. Exchanges of favors and privileges provide for the acquisition of political influence and upward mobility in the economic entrepreneurship area. In Azerbaijan, the major network centers on the Aliev "clan", which remains in place even after the death of Heidar Aliev. One time rival networks, including one led by the former speaker of the parliament, Resul Guliev, and the former foreign minister, Hasan Hasanov, were already eliminated before the elder Aliev handed over the reins of government to his son.

The Nakhichevan factor is often important in that many high government officials originate from there, and regionalism requires that one look after his/her close and distant relatives and those originating from the same region. A second major network is called *Yerazi* or Yerazi Clan, consisting of Azeris who had moved to Azerbaijan from Armenia during Soviet rule when both republics increasingly became more homogeneous. Heidar Aliev belonged to both of these clans at the same time because although he was born in Nakhichevan, his family originated from Zangezur, which became part of Armenia in December 1920. Like the Nakhichevanis, the Yerazi also control a patronage network which promotes nepotism. Nevertheless, since independence, people not belonging to any of the clans have also become part of the ruling elite due to their loyalty to the president and reputation for getting the job done. Moreover, those in important governmental positions, that is, powerful officials, might and do create their own networks based on self-interest.

Beside nepotism, bribing of high-level officials and buying of civil service posts seem a common practice.[4] "Profitable" posts enable the office holder to receive substantial sums from entrepreneurs in return for turning a blind eye to irregularities. Often businesses are subject to frequent inspections, which function as harassments and continue until the requisite bribes are paid. It is hence little surprise that Azerbaijan has consistently ranked very low in the Corruptions Perceptions Index of the Transparency International. According to the 2007 Index, Azerbaijan ranked 31st out of 180 countries in terms of perceived corruption.

Ministers who control security forces and economic affairs are in positions to provide favors, often in return for kickbacks and secret partnerships with the recipients of these favors. Control over borders (border guards), or urban law enforcement provide ample opportunities to receive bribes for looking the other way. Government mafias could even engage in their own operations by hiring common criminals as undertakers. Positions that allocate import-export licenses and levy taxes or distribute foreign loans are well placed to reap "benefits". Favored entrepreneurs could even acquire monopoly status for their enterprises in return for the adequate fee. A clan member financier would hear the news of a radical change in exchange rates a few hours before others, and this would make all the difference.

It is undeniable that the legacy of Soviet-era control of the economy by the ruling elite had a major impact on the post-independence situation. The post-1991 governments, including that of Elchibey, appointed network-members to important positions in administration or economic enterprises. The latter acquired unhindered access to the resources of major state companies and they were the first to be considered as the new owners of the to-be-privatized state-owned enterprises. In short, Soviet-era habits did play a major role in the post-Soviet practices of usurping.

Yet the post-Soviet conditions also do play a role. While Soviet-era lack of the rule of the law and an effective institutional framework is to blame for the omnipresence of networks, other factors should also be taken into account. Most of the time there are too many laws (Soviet-era laws as well as post-Soviet) to go around. Over-regulation and under-regulation exist side by side. Many times, citizens as well as foreign businessmen have no idea as to which government agency or government official is responsible for a given issue. It is often not clear whether local or central government is authorized to make decisions. Hence people turn to networks to guide them through the legal and administrative maze. To disgruntled citizens the judiciary is of little help, partly because of the Soviet legacy of its subservience to the executive.

Given the indisputable predominance of the president in making all major decisions, one could hardly talk of a Western-style democracy. Surely there is a constitution, a parliament, and, theoretically, separation of powers. Elections for the office of presidency and parliament take place, though their fairness is highly suspect. The president constitutionally has extensive powers, yet Heidar Aliev and his son Ilham Aliev have exercised powers unfettered even by the very presidential constitution, which is already in place. Both Alievs also desired to have a cult of personality status, which their subordinates worked hard to promote.

In almost all elections since independence, observers pointed to major nationwide fraud, including election commission members and government officials interfering illegally in the counting and tabulation of votes.[5] Due to the ruling Yeni Azerbaycan Party's (YAP) domination of the parliament, the former determines various election commission members and the existing election code. The crucial two-thirds majority in central and local election commissions consists of members of YAP and other pro-government parties. This enables YAP to nominate all election commission chairpersons and to have a two-thirds majority in every commission to make the decisions.[6]

The YAP functions more or less the same as the AzCP and membership is a prerequisite for state employment and favorable treatment of businessmen by the government. State officials are often spotted campaigning for the YAP. State resources are used to support YAP candidates, and state employees are pressured to vote for the latter and to avoid attending opposition demonstrations.[7] The problem is so acute that President Ilham

Aliev issued an executive order to officials asking them to refrain from interfering in the election campaign.[8] He later complained that authorities continued to support some candidates.[9] Although in recent elections opposition candidates are provided with free airtime, most prime time news and year-round coverage disproportionately favor pro-government candidates and the incumbent president. As a result, few opposition parties are represented in parliament.

Policy-making is mostly a presidential prerogative, and presidents rely on advisors and several ministers who are considered well informed, shrewd, wise, and most importantly loyal. The government functions as an agency essentially to implement the president's directives, and the parliament, mostly comprising pro-Aliev members, has remained a rubber stamp chamber. The president's monopoly of power inevitably leads to charges of authoritarianism, graft, and callousness. Although initially the elder Aliev shared power with Surat Huseinov, Resul Guliev and Hasan Hasanov, he took advantage of various crises to get rid of them one by one without paying much attention to constitutional provisions. Since the mid-1990s, the elder and younger Alievs ensured that close relatives dominated the YAP. Heidar Aliev's brothers, Jalal and Agil Aliev, his nephew Jamil Aliev and his son-in-law, Vasif Talibov have held high-profile YAP posts. Jalal Aliev is also a parliamentarian and holds a controlling share of Azercell, the country's major mobile phone operator.[10] Other relatives and in-laws, including Ilham Aliev's sister, Sevil Alieva, are also involved in business activities and/or are heavily represented in prominent YAP positions and government and high-level state bureaucracy.[11]

Newspapers critical of the government have little impact on public opinion, not only because they face various restrictions, financial pressures, and intimidation but also because they have a very small readership. There are national TV channels and radio stations, many of which are privately owned. Yet some of them are owned or controlled by the president's relatives and members of the ruling elite. Consequently, they could not be considered private or independent. Other private TV channels and radio stations are owned by businessmen who in general own non-media companies and factories, and are, for that reason, vulnerable to government pressure Therefore, they also try to avoid adopting "too critical" positions *vis-à-vis* the ruling elite.[12]

Azerbaijan's Soviet past contributes to the population's acquiescence in, if not demand for, strong leadership. Elchibey's inability to re establish law and order and the chaotic years of early independence, including the immediate post-Soviet period's socio-economic hardships and the war in and around the NKAO, further strengthened the popular respect for omnipotent but wise rulers. At the time of the ouster of Elchibey, Aliev opponents feared that he would steer the country back to a pro-Russia line, but he proved that he was his own man. He showed that he had considerable acumen by courting Russia by dropping the anti-Russian rhetoric of his predecessor and involving the latter's Lukoil in the Azerbaijan International Oil Consortium's projects, while refusing the deployment of Russian peacekeepers in and around the NKAO. He also improved relations with Iran by moving away from Elchibey's anti-Iranian stance, dropping the latter's irredentism *vis-à-vis* Iranian Azerbaijan.

Nevertheless, life in Azerbaijan is tough for ordinary citizens who live below the poverty line even though they are in employment. Life is even tougher for many who don't have jobs or those who are retired with pensions, which are in general very inadequate. The free market reforms since independence seem to have treated much better those "New Azeris" who frequent posh restaurants, drive expensive cars and live in palace-like villas. As suggested above, they are the products of graft, which has enabled them to amass huge fortunes. The discrepancy in living standards between the haves and have-nots is obvious for even the most uninitiated visitor to the country.

Average monthly salaries range from $20 to $100, which are not sufficient for even bare subsistence. Economic hardships are all the more surprising in a country whose exports surpassed $32 billion while imports were only $7.5 billion in 2008. Although per capita GDP reached $6,637 (from $2,250 in 2000) and exports increased by 34.5 percent in 2006 and 25.1 percent in 2007, many ordinary Azeris try to eke out a living.[13] Obviously, earnings from oil and gas exports do not trickle down to ordinary citizens either because they are siphoned off by networks or because they are used for projects that could raise living standards in the long run. The latter explanation seems hard to believe given the obvious lack of investment in industry and agriculture. Public education and health care have also deteriorated and long forgotten epidemics have resurfaced since the Soviet era.

There are a multitude of stories depicting how money in state coffers could be misappropriated. In one case, former foreign minister Hasan Hasanov spent $10 million to build a hotel and a casino in Baku although the money was supposed to be spent on Azeri legations abroad. After an investigation directed by Prime Minister Arthur Rasizade in 1998, he was sacked as minister but kept his parliamentary seat. Another example involves Resul Guliev, former speaker of the parliament, who had served as director of the Baku oil refinery and later as vice-president of the State Oil Company of Azerbaijan Republic (SOCAR). By the time he left the country for New York in 1997 he had allegedly appropriated $76 million.[14]

Ilham Aliev's succeeding his father as president looked very much like the introduction of hereditary rule. The March 2009 referendum, which provided for indefinite extension of a president's tenure beyond the two-term limit, further served to accentuate this impression. Yet, despite Azerbaijani political system's malaise, the ruling elite are not as authoritarian or oppressive as those in Central Asia. Despite various obstacles, opposition parties are able to openly criticize the government and hold public demonstrations. The fact that elections are less than fair accounts for only part of the ability of the ruling party and the incumbent president to cling on to power. Political opposition is splintered into numerous parties that bicker with each other and thus prevent the emergence of one or two formidable alternatives to the YAP.[15] An additional factor is popular indifference to politics, which is due to the average Azeri's preoccupation with bread and butter issues and frustration with the general lawlessness and economic misery experienced during the 1988–1993 period when political participation and mobilization had reached unprecedented heights.

Public apathy and resignation to helplessness might, however, prove to be a passing phase. The enormous gap between the affluent and the deprived has so far failed to cause civil unrest. The continuation of corruption and the popular perception that the regime is not accountable to the people might lead to instability and turmoil, especially if living standards of the ordinary Azeri do not improve. While the Azeri ruling elite and their Western allies believe that the man on the street values strong leadership, the latter notion could prove of only ephemeral value if not accompanied by action to reduce material inequalities. The fate that befell the Shah of Iran is as instructive for Azerbaijan as for any other Third World state that relies on petro-dollars to prop up an increasingly out of touch and autocratic leadership that is perceived to grant favors to a small minority at the expense of destitute masses.

Notes

Introduction

1 Ernest Gellner, *Thought and Change* (Chicago: University of Chicago Press, 1964), p. 164.

2 Alexander J. Motyl, *Sovietology, Rationality, Nationality: Coming to Grips with Nationalism in the USSR* (New York: Columbia University Press, 1990), p. 55.

3 See Eugene Kamenka, "Nationalism: Ambiguous Legacies and Contingent Futures", *Political Studies*, Vol. 41 (1993), Special Issue, pp. 78–92.

4 See Mark Hagopian's description of nationalism as an ideal in *Ideals and Ideologies of Modern Politics* (New York: Longman, 1985), pp. 2 and 70.

5 For various views, see Ian Bremmer, Ras Taras, eds., *Nations and Politics in the Soviet Successor States* (New York: Cambridge University Press, 1993); Ronald Grigor Suny, *The Revenge of the Past: Nationalism, Revolution, and the Collapse of the Soviet Union* (Stanford, CA: Stanford University Press, 1993); Motyl, *Sovietology, Rationality, Nationality.*

6 I borrowed this categorization from Suny, *Ibid.*, pp. 102–122.

7 Audrey L. Altstadt, "Decolonization in Azerbaijan", in Donald Schwartz, Razmik Panossian, eds., *Nationalism in History* (Toronto: University of Toronto Press, 1994).

8 See Alexander J. Motyl, ed., *Thinking Theoretically About Soviet Nationalities: History and Comparison in the Study of the USSR* (New York: Columbia University Press, 1992).

9 See John A. Armstrong, "The Autonomy of Ethnic Identity: Historic Cleavages and Nationality Relations in the USSR", in Alexander J. Motyl, ed., *Thinking Theoretically About Soviet Nationalities* (New York: Columbia University Press, 1990), pp. 59–71.

10 Michael Hechter, *Internal Colonialism* (Berkeley, CA: University of California Press, 1975), p. 49. See also John P. Willerton, "Azerbaidzhan and the Aliev Network", *Patronage and Politics in the USSR* (New York: Cambridge University Press, 1992), pp. 191–279.

11 Ernest Gellner, *Nations and Nationalism* (Ithaca, NY: Cornell University Press, 1983); Eric Hobsbawm, *Nations and Nationalism since 1780: Programme, Myth, Reality* (Cambridge: Cambridge University Press, 1990).

12 Miroslav Hroch, *Social Preconditions of National Revival in Europe* (Cambridge: Cambridge University Press, 1985), pp. 22–23.

13 Peter Palmer Ekeh, "Colonialism and the Two Publics in Africa", *Comparative Studies in Society and History*, Vol. 17 (1975), p. 108.

14 See Christopher Clapham, *Third World Politics* (Madison: The University of Wisconsin Press, 1985).

15 International Crisis Group, *Azerbaijan: Turning over a New Leaf* (Baku/Brussels: Europe Report 156, 2004), p. 10.

16 Audrey L. Altstadt, *The Azerbaijani Turks: Power and Identity under Russian Rule* (Stanford, CA: Hoover Institution Press), 1992, p. 2.

17 See Zia Buniatov, *O Khronoligicheskom nesootvetsvii glav 'Istorii Agvan' Moiseya Kagankatvatsi* (Baku, 1965).

18 See Roman Girshman, *Iran from the Earliest Times to the Islamic Conquest* (London: Penguin Books, 1954), p. 339; Shireen T. Hunter, *The Transcaucasus in Transition* (Washington: CSIS, 1994), pp. 6–12.

19 Altstadt, *The Azerbaijani Turks*, p. 7; See also Keith Hitchens, "The Caucasian Albanians and the Arab Caliphate in the Seventh and Eight Centuries", in Bedi Kartlisa, *Revue de Kartvélologie* (Paris) Vol. 42 (1984), pp. 238–240.

20 Tadeusz Swietochowski, *Russian Azerbaijan, 1905–1920: The Shaping of National Identity in a Muslim Community* (New York: Cambridge University Press, 1985), p. 2.

21 Swietochowski, *Russian Azerbaijan*, p. 3.

22 See Thomas de Waal, *Black Garden: Armenia and Azerbaijan through Peace and War* (New York: New York University Press, 2003), p. 96.

23 *Ibid.*, p. 9; Swietochowski, *Russian Azerbaijan*, p. 7.

24 Stephan H. Astourian, "In Search of Their Forefathers: National Identity and the Historiography and Politics of Armenian and Azerbaijani Ethnogenesis", in Donald Schwartz, Razmik Panossinian, eds., *Nationalism and History* (Toronto: Toronto University Press, 1994), p. 53.

25 Dmitriy Furman, "Return to the Third World: The Sorry Tale of Azerbaijani Democracy", *Svobodnaya Mysl*, No. 11 (July 1993), in *FBIS-USR* (*Foreign Broadcast Information Service, USSR*), December 14, 1993, p. 39.

26 *Kommunist*, Baku, in Azeri, September 28, p. 4, in *FBIS/SOV*, October 31, 1989, p. 77.

27 International Crisis Group, *Azerbaijan's 2005 Elections: Lost Opportunity* (Baku/Brussels: Europe Briefing, No. 156, 2005), p. 1.

28 International Crisis Group, *Azerbaijan's 2005 Elections*, p. 13.

29 Robert Ebel and Rajan Menon, eds., *Energy and Conflict in Central Asia and the Caucasus* (Lanham, MD: Rowman and Littlefield, 2000), p. 13, in International Crisis Group, *Azerbaijan's 2005 Elections*, p. 8.

1
Pre-Soviet Era and Sovietization

1 *Azerbayjan Tarikhi*, (Baku: Academy of Sciences, 1958–1963), Vol. 1, p. 109; Altstadt, *The Azerbaijani Turks*, p. 2.
2 Ronald G. Suny, *The Revenge of the Past* (Stanford, CA: Stanford University Press, 1993), p. 38.
3 See De Waal, *Black Garden*, p. 152.
4 Altstadt, *The Azerbaijani Turks*, p. 2.
5 Swietochowski, *Russian Azerbaijan Turks*, p. 1.
6 Buniatov, *O Khronoligicheskom.*
7 Buniatov, *O Khronoligicheskom*, and Buniatov, *Mxitar Gosh, Albanskaya Khronika.* De Waal suggests that Buniatov's aforementioned two monographs were actually translations of two articles written by C. F. J. Dowsett, see De Waal, *Black Garden*, pp. 152–153.
8 Vladimir Minorsky, "Caucasia IV: Sahl ibn Sunbat of Shakki and Arren: The Caucasian Vassals of Mazruban in 344–955", in Vladimir Minorsky, *The Turks, Iran and the Caucasus in the Middle Ages* (London: Variorum Reprints, 1978); Altstadt, *The Azerbaijani Turks*, p. 5.
9 Altstadt, *The Azerbaijani Turks*, p. 5.
10 Cyril Tourmanoff, "Introduction to Christian Caucasian History: The Formative Centuries", *Traditio*, Vol. 15 (1959).
11 Chantal Lemercier Quelquejay, "Islam and Identity in Azerbaijan", *Central Asian* Survey, Vol. 3, No. 2 (1984), p. 32.
12 Ronald G. Suny, *The Revenge of the Past*, p. 39.
13 Muriel Atkin, *Russia and Iran, 1780–1828* (Minneapolis: University of Minnesota Press, 1980), pp. 11–13.
14 Peter B. Golden, "The Turkic Peoples and Caucasia", in Ronald G. Suny, *Transcaucasia: Nationalism and Social Change* (Ann Arbor: University of Michigan Slavik Publications, 1983), pp. 46–49; Swietochowski, *Russian Azerbaijan*, p. 2; F. Sümer, "Azerbaycan'in Türkleşmesi Tarihine Umumi Bir Bakiş", *Belleten* (Turk Tarih Kurumu), Vol. 21 (1957), pp. 429–447.
15 Swietochowski, *Russian Azerbaijan*, p. 2.
16 Swietochowski, *Russian Azerbaijan*, p. 3.
17 De Waal, *Black Garden*, p. 96.
18 Imam Shamil was the leader of Muridism, a religious-social order which was an offshoot of the Sufi Naqshbandi order. See Swietochowski, *Russian Azerbaijan*, p. 11.
19 Altstadt, *The Azerbaijani Turks*, pp. 7–8.
20 Atkin, *Russia and Iran, 1780–1828*, p. 6.
21 Swietochowski, *Russian Azerbaijan*, p. 3.
22 Altstadt, *The Azerbaijani Turks*, pp. 8–9.
23 Altstadt, *The Azerbaijani Turks*, p. 9; Swietochowski, *Russian Azerbaijan*, p. 7.

24 George A. Bournatian, *Eastern Armenia in the Last Decades of Persian Rule, 1807–1828: A Political and Socioeconomic Study of the Khanate of Yerevan on the Eve of the Russian Conquest* (Malibu, California: 1982), pp. 74–77.

25 L. H. Rhinelander, "Viceroy Vorontsov's Administration of the Caucasus", in Ronald G. Suny, *Transcaucasia: Nationalism and Social Change* (Ann Arbor: University of Michigan Slavik Publications, 1983).

26 Brenda Shaffer, *Borders and Brethren: Iran and the Challenge of Azerbaijani Identity* (Cambridge: MIT Press, 2002), p. 24.

27 Atkin, *Russia and Iran, 1780–1828*, p. 150; Shaffer, *Borders and Brethren*, p. 24.

28 Testimony of David Nissman, "The Nagorno-Karabagh Crisis: Prospects for Resolution", *Hearing Before the Commission on Security and Cooperation in Europe*, 102nd Congress, 1st Session, 23 October 1991, Washington: G.P.O., 1992, p. 125.

29 *Ibid.*, p. 126.

30 Naselenie imperii po perepisi 28-go ianvaria 1897 goda po uezdam (St Petersburg: S.P. Iakovlev, 1897); *Bakinskaia guberniia: Vol. 63: Elizavetpolskaia* (St Petersburg, 1905), in Altstadt, *The Azerbaijani Turks*, p. 28.

31 Altstadt, *The Azerbaijani Turks*, pp. 29–30.

32 Russia was concerned because Imam Shamil had successfully used the Sufi orders in his long resistance to Russian rule in the late eighteenth century.

33 Audrey L. Altstadt, "Baku City Duma: Arena for Elite Conflict", *Central Asian Survey*, Vol. 5, Nos. 3–4 (1986).

34 Ronald G. Suny, *The Baku Commune, 1917–1918: Class and Nationality in the Russian Revolution* (Princeton: Princeton University Press, 1972), p. 14.

35 Audrey L. Altstadt, "Azerbaijan's Struggle toward Democracy", in Karen Dawisha, Bruce Parrott, eds., *Conflict, Cleavage, and Change in Central Asia and the Caucasus* (Cambridge: Cambridge University Press, 1997), p. 113.

36 There was an interval of state monopoly from 1834 to 1850. See Altstadt, *The Azerbaijani Turks*, p. 20.

37 Robert W. Tolf, *The Russian Rockefellers: The Saga of the Nobel Family and the Russian Oil Industry* (Stanford: Hoover Institution Press, 1976).

38 See Chs. 1–3 in: Atkin, *Russia and Iran, 1780–1828.*

39 Altstadt, *The Azerbaijani Turks*, p. 31.

40 Edmund M. Hertzig, "Armenians", in Graham Smith, ed., *The Nationalities Question in the Soviet Union* (New York, London: Longman, 1990), p. 152.

41 Gerard J. Libaridian, "Revolution and Liberation in the 1892 and 1907 Programs of the Dashnaksutiun", in Suny, ed., *Transcaucasia*, pp. 196–197.

42 Altstadt, "The Baku City Duma".

43 Quelquejay, "Islam and Identity", p. 33.

44 Quelquejay, "Islam and Identity", p. 33.

45 Audrey L. Altstadt, "Azerbaijani Turks' Response to Russian Conquest", *Studies in Comparative Communism*, Vol. 19, Nos. 3–4 (Fall–Winter 1986), pp. 267–286.

46 Edward Lazzerini, *Ismail Bey Gasprinski and Muslim Modernism in Russia* (University of Washington: PhD Thesis, 1973).

47 *Fuyuzat*, Baku, No. 20 (1907), in Swietochowski, *Russian Azerbaijan*, p. 60.

48 Samet Ağaoğlu, *Babamdan Hatıralar* (Ankara, 1940).

49 Stephan H. Astourian, "In Search of Their Forefathers", p. 53.
50 Quelquejay, "Islam and Identity", p. 33.
51 Quelquejay, "Islam and Identity", pp. 33–34.
52 Astourian, "In Search of Their Forefathers", p. 53.
53 Adeeb Khaled, *The Politics of Muslim Cultural Reform: Jadidism in Central Asia* (Berkeley, CA: University of California Press, 1999); Edward A. Allworth, *Central Asia: One Hundred Thirty Years of Russian Dominance: A Historical Overview* (Durham, NC: Duke University Press 1994).
54 Audrey L. Altstadt, "O Patria Mia: National Conflict in Mountainous Karabagh", in Raymond Duncan, Paul Holman Jr., eds. *Ethnic Nationalism & Regional Conflict: The Former Soviet Union and Yugoslavia* (Boulder, CO: Westview, 1994), p. 106.
55 Sultan M. Äfändiev, "Himmät'in Yaranması", *Azerbayjan Elmi Savhasi*, Nos. 1 and 2 (1932), pp. 83–89.
56 N. M. Mikayilov, "Milli Mäsälädä Marksizm-Leninizm Ideyaları Ughrunda Azärbayjan Bolshevik Mätbuatının Mübarizäsi, 1905–1911 illär", *A. N. Az. S. S. R., Izvestiia*, Ser. Ob. N., No. 1 (1963), pp. 21–61, in Tadeusz Swietochowski, "The Himmät Party: Socialism and the National Question in Russian Azerbaijan, 1904–1920", *Cahiers du Monde Russe et Soviétique*, Vol. 19, Nos. 1–2 (1978), pp. 119–142.
57 Tadeusz Swietochowski, "The Himmät Party: Socialism and the National Question in Russian Azerbaijan, 1904–1920", *Cahiers du Monde Russe et Soviétique*, Vol. 19, Nos. 1–2 (1978), p. 124.
58 Mammad Emin Resulzada, *Azerbaijan Cumhuriyeti* (Istanbul, 1341), p. 22, in Swietochowski, *Russian Azerbaijan*, p. 73.
59 Swietochowski, "The Himmät Party", p. 123.
60 Edward Abrahamian, *Iran between Two Revolutions* (Princeton: Princeton University Press, 1964), pp. 103–104.
61 Altstadt, *The Azerbaijani Turks*, p. 73.
62 Ziya Gökalp, *The Principles of Turkism* (Leiden, 1968), p. 17.
63 *Fuyuzat*, No. 23 (1907), in Swietochowski, *Russian Azerbaijan*, p. 59.
64 Suny, *The Revenge of the Past*, p. 42.
65 Swietochowski, *Russian Azerbaijan*, p. 39.
66 Altstadt, *The Azerbaijani Turks*, p. 64.
67 Christopher J. Walker, *Armenia: The Survival of A Nation* (New York: St Martin's Press, 1980), pp. 73–81.
68 Altstadt, *The Azerbaijani Turks*, p. 40.
69 For the Armenian version of events, see various chapters in Richard Hovannissian's edited book: *The Armenian Genocide in Perspective* (New Brunswick, NJ: Transaction Books, 1986).
70 Quelquejay, "Islam and Identity", p. 54.
71 S. Zenkovsky, *Pan-Turkism and Islam in Russia* (Cambridge: Cambridge University Press, 1960), pp. 45–51.
72 E. G. Browne, *The Persian Revolution, 1905–1909* (London: Cambridge University Press: 1912), p. 250, in Swietochowski, *Russian Azerbaijan*, p. 69.
73 Jody Emami-Yeganeh, "Iran vs. Azerbaijan: Divorce, Separation or Reconciliation", *Central Asian Survey*, 1984, p. 7.

74 The new name of the Musavat became Turk Adem-i Merkeziyyet: Musavat Firqasi. See Swietochowski, *Russian Azerbaijan*, p. 88.

75 Swietochowski, "The Himmät Party", p. 124.

76 Swietochowski, *Russian Azerbaijan*, pp. 107–108.

77 Swietochowski, "The Himmät Party", p. 125.

78 Firuz Kazemzadeh, *The Struggle for Transcaucasia, 1917–1921* (New York: Philosophical Library, 1951), p. 70; Ronald G. Suny, *The Baku Commune: Class and Nationality in the Russian Revolution* (Princeton: Princeton University Press, 1972), p. 224.

79 Gerard J. Libaridian, *Armenia at the Crossroads: Democracy and Nationhood in the post-Soviet Era* (Watertown, MA: Blue Crane Books, 1991), p. 21.

80 Georgia declared independence on May 26 and Armenia followed suit on May 28, 1918. See Richard Pipes, *The Formation of the Soviet Union: Communism and the Soviet Union, 1917–1923* (Cambridge: Harvard University Press, 1964), pp. 193–195.

81 Swietochowski, *Russian Azerbaijan*, p. 130. Karabagh literally means black garden or black orchard. The name is probably related to the fertility of the region, which is famous for its grapes and mulberries.

82 Swietochowski, *Russian Azerbaijan*, p. 130.

83 Pipes, *The Formation of the Soviet Union*, p. 205; M. Mirza Bala, *Milli Azerbaycan Hareketi: Milli Azerbaycan Musavat Halk Fırkası'nın Tarihi* (Berlin: Parti Divani, 1938), p. 148.

84 Kazemzadeh, *The Struggle for Transcaucasia, 1917–1921*, pp. 143–144; A. H. Aslanian, "Britain and the Transcaucasian Nationalities during the Russian Civil War", in Ronald G. Suny, ed., *Transcaucasia: Nationalism and Social Change*; Quelquajay, "Islam and Identity", p. 36.

85 Swietochowski, *Russian Azerbaijan*, p. 139.

86 Richard H. Ullman, *Britain and Russian Civil War* (Princeton: Princeton University Press, 1968), pp. 68, 77–78; Altstadt, *The Azerbaijani Turks*, pp. 105–106.

87 De Waal, *Black Garden*, p. 128.

88 Swietochowski, "The Himmät Party", p. 128.

89 Swietochowski, *Russian Azerbaijan*, p. 148; Altstadt, *The Azerbaijani Turks*, p. 95.

90 De Waal, *Black Garden*, p. 128; See also Artin H. Arslanian, "Britain and the Transcaucasian Nationalities during the Russian Civil War", in Ronald G. Suny, ed., *Transcaucasia, Nationalism, and Social Change* (Ann Arbor: University of Michigan Press, 1983).

91 Kazim Karabekir, *Istiklal Harbimiz* (Istanbul: Turkiye Yayınları, 1960), pp. 466–467; Swietochowski, *Russian Azerbaijan*, p. 163.

92 Swietochowski, *Russian Azerbaijan*, p. 171.

93 *Fukara Sedasi*, August 27, 1919, in Swietochowski, *Russian Azerbaijan*, p. 172.

94 For July 1919 resolution of the Politbureau of the RCP(b) recognizing Azerbaijani independence see *Azerbaycan communist partiiasinin tarikhi* (History of the Azerbaijan Communist Party) (Baku, 1958), Vol. I, p. 335, in Swietochowski, "The Himmät Party", p. 130.

95 Swietochowski, *Russian Azerbaijan*, pp. 181–182; Altstadt, *The Azerbaijani Turks*, p. 98.

96 Altstadt, *The Azerbaijani Turks*, p. 114.

97 Pipes, *The Formation of the Soviet Union*, Ch. 5.
98 Among the first presidents of the Sovnarkom (Council of Ministers) were Dr Nariman Narimanov, M. D. Huseyinov and S. M. Efendiev. Other commissars were Dadash Buniatzada, A. G. Karayev, and G. G. Sultanov.
99 Altstadt, *The Azerbaijani Turks*, p. 110.
100 Stephen Blank, "Bolshevik Organizational Development in Early Soviet Transcaucasia: Autonomy vs Centralization, 1918–1924", in Suny, ed., *Transcaucasia*, p. 334.
101 Altstadt, "O Patria Mia", p. 116.
102 Pipes, *The Formation of the Soviet Union*, p. 269.
103 Blank, "Bolshevik Organizational", p. 334; Audrey L. Altstadt, "Nagorno-Karabagh: Apple of Discord in the Azerbaijani SSR", *Central Asian Survey*, Vol. 7, No. 4 (1988), pp. 63–78.
104 De Waal, *Black Garden*, p. 80.
105 Altstadt, "O Patria Mia", p. 109.
106 Libaridian, Gerard J., ed., *The Karabagh File* (Cambridge, MA: Zoryan Institute, 1988), p. 34.
107 *K istorii obrazovaniia nagorno-Karabaghskoi avtonomnoi oblast: Azerbaidzhanskoi SSR: Dokumenty i materialy* (Baku: Azerneshr, 1989), cited in Altstadt, "O Patria Mia", p. 109.
108 Altstadt, "O Patria Mia", p. 109.
109 Shireen T. Hunter, *The Transcaucasus in Transition*, p. 98.
110 See Richard C. Hovannissian, "Armenia and the Caucasus in the Genesis of the Soviet-Turkish Entente", *International Journal of Middle East Studies*, Vol. 4, No. 2 (1973), pp. 129–147.
111 See Kars and Moscow Treaties in *Caucasian Boundaries: Documents and Maps 1802–1946*, in *Archive Editions* (www.archiveeditions.co.uk).
112 A. S. Mil'man, *Azerbaidzhanskaya SSR – Suverennoe gosudartsvo v sostave SSSR* (Baku, 1971), p. 249; Altstadt, "Nagorno-Karabagh: Apple of Discord", p. 66.
113 Altstadt, "Nagorno-Karabagh: Apple of Discord", p. 66.
114 See Sadulla Shahverdyoglu Aslani, *Obrazovanie Iranskoi partii 'Edzhtimaiiun-e Amiiun (Mudzhakhid)'*, cited in Altstadt, " O Patria Mia", pp. 117–118.
115 De Waal, *Black Garden,* p. 130.
116 De Waal, *Black Garden*, p. 130.
117 *K istorii obrazovanii Nagorno-Karabaghskoi avtonomnoi oblasti Azerbaidzhanskoi SSR: Dokumenty I materialy* (Baku: Azerneshr, 1989), pp. 90–92; Altstadt, "O Patria Mia", p. 103.
118 Altstadt, "Nagorno-Karabagh: Apple of Discord", pp. 66–67.
119 Between 1923–1937 the NKAO was called the Autonomous Region of Nagorno Karabagh. In 1937 the name was changed to Nagorno-Karabagh Autonomous Oblast (NKAO).
120 The village of Khankendi was made regional capital and renamed Stepanakert after the Baku Bolshevik commissar Stepan Shaumian.
121 George A. Bournatian, "The Ethnic Composition and the Socio-Economic Condition of Eastern Armenia in then First Half of the Nineteenth Century", in Suny, ed., *Transcaucasia*, p. 79.

122 De Waal, *Black Garden*, p. 140.
123 Altstadt, "O Patria Mia", p. 110.

2
Azerbaijan during the Soviet Era

1 Altstadt, *The Azerbaijani Turks*, pp. 123–124.
2 Altstadt, *The Azerbaijani Turks*, pp. 128–129.
3 Turkey's adoption of the Latin alphabet in the late 1920s might also have influenced Moscow's decision.
4 Altstadt, *The Azerbaijani Turks*, p. 132.
5 Altstadt, *The Azerbaijani Turks*, p. 146.
6 Zbigniew Brezezinski, *The Permanent Purge: Politics in Soviet Totalitarianism* (Cambridge, MA: Harvard University Press, 1956), p. 190.
7 A. Vahap Yurtsever, "Azerbaycan İstiklal Savaşında Sahneler", *Azerbaycan* (Ankara), May–June 1956; Altstadt, *The Azerbaijani Turks*, p. 164.
8 Tadeusz Swietochowski, *Russia and Azerbaijan: A Borderline in Transition* (New York: Columbia University Press, 1995), p. 164.
9 Touraj Atabaki, *Azerbaijan: Ethnicity and Autonomy in Twentieth-Century Iran* (London: British Academic Press, 1993).
10 Swietochowski, *Russia and Azerbaijan*, p. 165.
11 M. Chesmazer, "Muhammad Biriya", *Novruz*, Vol. 5, No. 22 (1991), in Swietochowski, *Russia and Azerbaijan*, p. 165.
12 Swietochowski, *Russia and Azerbaijan*, p. 174.
13 A. Vahap Yurtsever, "Bagirof'un İdamı", *Azerbaycan* (Ankara), May–June 1956, pp. 8–12; A. Azertekin, "Bir İdamdan alınacak Ders", *Azerbaycan* May–June 1956, pp. 19–20.
14 Swietochowski, *Russia and Azerbaijan*, p. 175.
15 Sattar Khan and Khiabani actively took part in the Iranian constitutional struggle in the early twentieth century, but were apparently considered lacking proletarian credentials. See Swietochowski, *Russia and Azerbaijan*, p. 176.
16 See Mammäd Jafar, *Azärbaijanda Romantizm* (Baku: Izd-vo ANAzSSR, 1966); Swietochowski, *Russia and Azerbaijan*, p. 169.
17 Swietochowski, *Russia and Azerbaijan*, p. 176.
18 Swietochowski, *Russia and Azerbaijan*, p. 169.
19 Prior to the reform, students were required to learn both Russian and the language of the republic where they resided. See Swietochowski, *Russia and Azerbaijan*, p. 176.
20 Swietochowski, *Russia and Azerbaijan*, p. 176.
21 Yaroslav Bilinsky, "The Soviet Education Laws of 1958–59 and Soviet Nationalities Policy", *Soviet Studies*, Vol. 14, No. 2 (October 1962), pp. 138–157.
22 Steven E. Hegaard, "Nationalism in Azerbaidzhan in the Era of Brezhnev", in George W. Simmonds, ed., *Nationalism in the USSR and Eastern Europe in the Era of Brezhnev and Kosygin* (Detroit, MI: University of Detroit Press, 1977), p. 193.

23 Martin McAuley, "The Soviet Muslim Population: Trends in Living Standards, 1960–1975", in Yaakov Ro'i, ed., *The USSR and the Muslim World* (London: George Allen & Unwin, 1984), p. 99.

24 Since Akhundov had to implement an unpopular language law that cost his predecessor's seat, he probably felt that he should compensate for this by tolerating national assertiveness by some of his subordinates. See Altstadt, *The Azerbaijani Turks*, p. 169.

25 Azade-Ayse Rorlich, "Not by History Alone: The Retrieval of the Past among the Tatars and the Azeris", *Central Asian Survey*, Vol. 3, No. 2 (1984), p. 91.

26 See Azerbaijan, Baku, No. 11 (1966), pp. 198–201; Altstadt, *The Azerbaijani Turks*, p. 174.

27 Suny, "Transcaucasia", p. 230.

28 See also Suny, "Transcaucasia", p. 231.

29 Swietochowski, *Russia and Azerbaijan*, p. 183.

30 Elizabeth Fuller, "The Transcaucasian Republics During the Brezhnev Era", *Radio Liberty*, January 7, 1983, pp. 2–3.

31 1967 and 1968 figures from: Narodnoe khoziaistvo SSSR v 1967 g. (Moscow: Statistica, 1968), pp. 211–212; v 1968 g. (1969), pp. 149, 558. 1973 figures cited from: Narodnoe khoziaistvo SSSR v 1973 g. (Moscow: Statistika, 1974), pp. 181–194, 574, in Suny, "Transcaucasia", p. 232.

32 Shireen T. Hunter, *The Transcaucasus in Transition*, p. 65.

33 Suny, *The Revenge of the* Past, pp. 118–119; Hunter, *The Transcaucasus in Transition*, p. 65.

34 Suny, "Transcaucasia", p. 231.

35 Rorlich, "Not By History Alone", p. 88.

36 Thomas Goltz, *Azerbaijan Diary: A Rogue Reporter's Adventures in an Oil-Rich, War-Torn, post-Soviet Republic* (Armonk, New York, 1998), p. 71.

37 See his daughter Turan Javid's recollections in Turan Javid, "The Night Father was Arrested", *Azerbaijan International*, Vol. 4, No. 1 (Spring 1996), p. 24.

38 See Bäkir Näbiyäv's article in *Azerbaijan*, No. 7 (1986) in Altstadt, *The Azerbaijani Turks*, p. 190.

39 Cited in David B. Nissman, *The Soviet Union and Iranian Azerbaijan: The Use of Nationalism for Political Penetration* (Boulder, Westview, 1987), p. 71.

40 *The Times*, London, November 29, 1982, in Swietochowski, *Russia and Azerbaijan*, p. 192.

41 Swietochowski, *Russia and Azerbaijan*, p. 192.

42 Z. M. Buniatov, *Gosudarstvo Atabekov Azerbaidzhana: 1136–1225 gody* (Baku, 1978); Sh. Farzaliev, *Aksan at-Tavarikh Khasan beka Rumlu kak istochnik po istorii Azerbaidzhana* (Baku, 1981); A. S. Farandzhev, *Zarozhdenie i razvitie ekonomicheskoi mysli v Azerbaidzhane v epokhu feodalizma* (Baku, 1981).

43 Rorlich, "Not By History Alone", p. 96.

44 See A. M. Akhmedov, *Filosofiia Azerbaidzhanskogo prosveshcheniia* (Baku: Azerneshr, 1983), pp. 183–267, in Rorlich, "Not By History Alone", pp. 94–95.

45 Mammad Dadashzada, "Dada Gorgud destanlarinda Azerbaijan etnografiyasina dair bazi malumatlar", *Azerbaijanin etnografik mechmuasi* (Azerbaijan Journal of Ethnography), No. 3 (Baku: Elm, 1977), pp. 182–194.

46 Dadashzada, "Dada Gorgud".
47 Hasan B. Paksoy, *Central Asia Reader* (Armonk, NY: M. E. Sharpe, 1994).
48 Paksoy, *Central Asia Reader*, p. 64.
49 I. Guseinov, *Sudnyi Den'* (Baku, 1981).
50 A. Jafarzada, *Baku-1501* (Baku, 1981), p. 252, in Rorlich, "Not By History Alone", p. 96.
51 Swietochowski, *Russia and Azerbaijan*, p. 181.
52 Richard B. Dobson, "Georgia and the Georgians", in Zev Katz, Rosemary Rogers, and Frederic Harned, eds., *Handbook of Major Soviet Nationalities* (New York: The Free Press, 1975), p. 177; Suny, "Transcaucasia", p. 235.
53 The discrimination factor also played a role in the ethnic Azeris leaving Armenia. See USSR, People's Deputies from Azerbaijan, *On Forcible Deportation of Azerbaijanis from Azerbaijan*, [n.d.], p. 2.
54 De Waal, *Black Garden*, p. 133.
55 De Waal, *Black Garden*, p. 140.
56 De Waal, *Black Garden*, p. 140.
57 Altstadt, "O Patria Mia", p. 113.
58 Altstadt, *The Azerbaijani Turks*, pp. 183–184; Suny, "Transcaucasia", pp. 236–237.
59 Suny, "Transcaucasia", pp. 234–235.
60 Suny, "Transcaucasia", pp. 236–237.
61 Dobson, "Georgia and the Georgians", p. 177.
62 Suny, *The Revenge of the Past*, p. 126.
63 See *Azerbaijan*, No. 18 (September 1948).
64 Suleyman Aliyarov, "Bizim Sorgu: Tarikhimiz, Abidalarimiz, Darsliklarimiz", *Azerbaijan*, No. 7, 1988, p. 175.
65 Igrar Aliev, "Raspolagaet li nauką dokazatel'stvami v pol'zu iranoiazychnosti Midian i Atropatentsev? Mozhno li schitat' Midian odnimi iz predkov azerbaidzhanskogo naroda?" Part 2, in *Khäberlär/Izvestiia*, No. 4 (1990), pp. 80–88, in Astourian, "In Search of Their Forefathers", p. 55.
66 Astourian, "In Search of Their Forefathers", p. 55.
67 J. B. Guliev, *Istoriia Azerbaijana* (Baku: Elm Publications, 1979), pp. 26–30.
68 See "Albaniya", and "Daghliq Garabagh Mukhtar Vilayati", *Azerbayjan Sovet Ensiklopediyasi*, pp. 215, 308; Astourian, "In Search of Their Forefathers", p. 58.
69 *Azerbayjan Sovet Ensiklopediyasi*, p. 217; Astourian, "In Search of Their Forefathers", p. 59.
70 Guliev, *Istoriia Azerbaijana*, p. 64, in Astourian, "In Search of Their Forefathers", p. 60.
71 Nissman, *The Soviet Union*, p. 10.
72 Bakhtyar Vahabzade and Suleyman Aliyarov's letter in: "Redaksiyamizin Pochtudan", *Azerbaijan*, No. 2 (February 1988), pp. 188–189.
73 M. K. Sharifli, *IX Asrin Ikinji-XI Asrlarda Azerbaijan Feodal Dövlatlari* (Baku: Elm, 1978), p. 37.
74 See Suleyman Aliyarov's letter in: "Redaksiyamizin Pochtudan", *Azerbaijan*, No. 9 (1988), p. 182.
75 His monographs mentioned earlier were: *Mxitar Gosh* (Baku, 1960), and *O Khronoligisheskom* (Baku, 1965).

76 De Waal, *Black Garden*, p. 153.
77 De Waal, *Black Garden*, p. 153.
78 De Waal, *Black Garden*, p. 153.
79 Robert H. Hewsen, "Ethno-History and the Armenian Influence upon the Caucasian Albanians", in Thomas J. Samuelian, ed., *Classical Armenian Culture: Influences and Creativity* (Atlanta, Georgia: Scholars Press, 1982).
80 Vasil Velichko, *Kavkaz: Russkoye Deb i Mezhduplemmenye voprosy* [The Caucasus: Russia's Work and Inter-Tribal Questions], in De Waal, *Black Garden*, p. 143.
81 De Waal, *Black Garden*, p. 143.
82 Igrar Aliev, Kamil Mamedzade, *Albanskiye Pamyatniki Karabakha* [The Albanian Monuments of Karabakh] (Baku: Azerbaijab Devlet Nshriyaty, 1997), p. 19, in De Waal, *Black Garden*, p. 153.
83 At the time of his murder in February 1997 Buniatov was a member of the Azerbaijani Parliament. See http://www.hri.org/news/balkans/rferl/2001/01-02-22.rferl.html and De Waal, *Black Garden*, p. 153.
84 Suny, *The Revenge of the Past*, p. 125.
85 Martha B. Olcott, "Gorbachev's Nationalities Policy and Central Asia", in Rajan Menon, Daniel N. Nelson, eds., *Limits to Soviet Power* (Lexington, MA: Lexington Books, 1989), pp. 69–70.
86 Suny, *The Revenge of the Past*, p. 128.
87 Suny, *The Revenge of the Past*, p. 128.
88 Steven L. Burg, "Nationality Elites and Political Change in the Soviet Union", in Lubomyr Hajda and Mark Beissinger, eds., *The Nationalities Factor in Soviet Politics and Society* (Boulder, CO: Westview Press, 1990), p. 27.
89 See "Kommunizm gurujulughu täjrübäsi vä ädäbi-bädii näshlar", *Azerbaijan Kommunisti*, No. 6 (1986), in Altstadt, *The Azerbaijani Turks*, p. 193.
90 See R. Allahverdiev, "Bashlija Istiqamat Uzra", *Azerbaijan Kommunisti*, No. 9 (1986).
91 *Azerbaijan*, No. 2 (1987), in Altstadt, *The Azerbaijani Turks*, p. 194; *Azerbaijan Kommunisti*, No. 4 (1987).
92 Mirza Michaeli, William Reese, "Unofficial Publications in Azerbaijan", *RFE/RL Report on the USSR*, September 15, 1989, pp. 20–21.
93 Suny, *The Revenge of the Past*, p. 130.
94 De Waal, *Black Garden*, p. 142.
95 De Waal, *Black Garden*, p. 142.
96 De Waal's interview with Kaputikian on September 26, 2000 in De Waal, *Black Garden*, pp. 136–137. She died in August 2006.
97 Suny, *The Revenge of the Past*, p. 144.
98 *Azerbaijan*, No. 10 (1989).
99 Raoul Motika, "Glastnost in der Sowjetrepublik Aserbaidschan am Beispiel der Zeitschrift Azärbaijan", *Orient*, Vol. 32, No. 4 (December 1991), p. 576.
100 *Azerbaijan*, No. 1 (1986), pp. 3–7.
101 *Azerbaijan*, No. 10 (1987) in Motika, "Glastnost in der Sowjetrepublik Aserbaidschan…", p. 582.

102 For Jabir Bovruz's comments, see *Ädäbiyyat vä Injäsänat*, July 31, 1987, in Abbasali Djavadi, "Glastnost and Soviet Azerbaijani Literature", *Central Asian Survey*, Vol. 9, No. 1 (1990), pp. 97–103, p. 98.

103 Motika, "Glastnost in der Sowjetrepublik Aserbaidschan...", p. 579.

104 *Azerbaijan*, No. 1 (1989).

105 Aitmatov: Nos. 7 and 8 (1985); Rasputin: No. 8 (1987); Ahmatova: No. 6 (1989).

106 *Azerbaijan*, No. 10 (1987); No. 3 (1988); No. 6 (1990).

107 Motika, "Glastnost in der Sowjetrepublik Aserbaidschan...", p. 581.

108 *Encyclopedia of Soviet Azerbaijan*, Vol. 10 (1988), in Djavadi, "Glastnost and Soviet Azerbaijani Literature", p. 100.

109 See M. Ismayilov, "Tariximiz va Tadqiqatimiz", in *Ädäbiyyat vä Injäsänat*, July 15, 1988, in Djavadi, p. 101.

110 Djavadi, "Glastnost and Soviet Azerbaijani Literature", p. 100.

111 The article was originally published in the Russian journal *Neva*. See *Azärbaijan*, No. 7 (1989), pp. 130–164, in Motika, "Glastnost in der Sowjetrepublik Aserbaidschan...", p. 583.

112 Swietochowski, *Russia and Azerbaijan*, p. 197.

113 *Ädäbiyyat vä Injäsänat*, March 6, 1988, in Djavadi, p. 100.

114 Described by some as the mysticism or esotericism of Islam. See Yasin Ceylan, "Al Ghazali between Philosophy and Sufism", *American Journal of Islamic Social Sciences*, Vol. 12, No. 4, Winter 1995, p. 587.

115 See "Sarraf va La'li", in *Janubi Azärbaijan Ädäbiyyati Antologiyasi* (Baku: [ ], 1983) Vol. II, in Djavadi, "Glastnost and Soviet Azerbaijani Literature", p. 102.

116 *Azerbaijan*, No. 12 (1988), pp. 155–162.

117 *Azerbaijan*, No. 10 (1989), p. 130.

118 Abulfaz Aliyev, "Tarikhin Darin Gatlarina Doghru", *Azerbaijan*, No. 10 (1989), p. 130.

119 *Azerbaijan*, No. 6 (1988), p. 153; No. 9 (1989), pp. 163–171.

120 See Mammad Emin Resulzada, "Gafgasiya Turkleri", *Azerbaijan*, No. 12 (December 1990), p. 143.

121 Suleyman Aliyarov's letter in "Redaksiyamizin Pochtudan", *Azerbaijan*, No. 9 (1988), p. 182.

122 Mirza Bala, "Azerbaijan Tarikhinda Turk Albaniya", *Azerbaijan*, No. 10 (1989), pp. 120–127.

123 See Nissman, *The Soviet Union*, pp. 69, 71; *Azerbaijan*, No. 6 (1989), p. 184.

124 See A. Abbasov's article in: *Azerbaijan*, No. 2 (1989), pp. 124–141.

125 *Azerbaijan*, No. 6 (1985), pp. 92–97, 108–110.

3
Armenia Claims Mountainous Karbagh
Start of Hostilities

1 De Waal, *Black Garden,* p. 137.

2 Ronald G. Suny, "Nationalism and Democracy in Gorbachev's Soviet Union: The Case of Karabagh", *Michigan Quarterly Review,* Vol. 28, No. 3 (Summer 1989), pp. 484–485.

3 De Waal, *Black Garden*, pp. 137–138.

4 *Interview with Ohanjenian*, in De Waal, *Black Garden*, p. 138.

5 De Waal, *Black Garden*, pp. 238–239.

6 For these figures see P. H. Clandenning, "Armenian Unrest in the Caucasus", *Soviet Observer*, March 1–16, 1988, pp. 1, 3, in Altstadt, "O Patria Mia", p. 115.

7 De Waal, *Black Garden*, p. 137.

8 Swietochowski, *Russia and Azerbaijan*, p. 182.

9 De Waal, *Black Garden*, p. 137.

10 *L'Humanité*, November 18, 1987, p. 17, in Altstadt, *The Azerbaijani Turks*, p. 195.

11 De Waal, *Black Garden*, p. 22.

12 De Waal, *Black Garden*, p. 29.

13 Their open letter is examined in the previous chapter. *Azerbaijan,* No. 2 (February 1988). For an English translation see *Journal of the Institute of Muslim Minority Affairs* (London), Vol. 9, No. 2 (July 1988).

14 Altstadt, *The Azerbaijani Turks*, p. 196.

15 De Waal, *Black Garden*, p. 189.

16 Bulbul's real name was Murtuza Mashadi Rza oglu Mammadov.

17 Johann Schiltberger, *The Bondage and Travels of Johann Schiltberger, a Native of Bavaria, in Europe, Asia and Africa, 1396–1427* (London: 1878); and Baron von Haxthausen, *Transcaucasia: Sketches of the Nations and Races between the Black Sea and the Caspian* (London: 1854), p. 438, in De Waal, *Black Garden*, p. 149.

18 De Waal, *Black Garden*, p. 149.

19 De Waal, *Black Garden*, p. 16.

20 Libaridian, *Armenia at the Crossroads*, p. 31.

21 De Waal, *Black Garden*, p. 18.

22 De Waal, *Black Garden*, p. 17.

23 *Haratch*, Yerevan, November 19, 1987, cited in Levon Chorbajian, Patrick Danabedian, and Claude Mutafian, *The Caucasian Knot: The History and Geopolitics of Nagorno-Karabakh* (London and Atlantic Highlands, NJ: Zed Books, 1994), p. 148.

24 Georgy K. Shakhnazarov, *Tsena Svobody* [The Price of Freedom], p. 206 in De Waal, *Black Garden*, p. 16.

25 De Waal, *Black Garden*, p. 17.

26 Goltz, *Azerbaijan Diary*, p. 68.

27 *FBIS/SOV*, February 23, 1988, p. 52.

28 De Waal, *Black Garden*, p. 304, footnote 4.

29 *Komsomolskaia Pravda*, Moscow, 23 July 1988, p. 4, in *FBIS/SOV*, July 25, 1988, p. 46.

30 Seven of them were academics and four of them became leaders in post-1991 Armania. See De Waal, *Black Garden*, p. 56.
31 De Waal, *Black Garden*, p. 56.
32 *Hayk*, Nos. 4–5, 1990 in Gerard J. Libaridian, *Armenia at the Crossroads*, p. 44.
33 Interview with Ter-Petroysan, May 24, 2000, in De Waal, *Black Garden*, p. 57.
34 Libaridian, *Armenia at the Crossroads*, pp. 30–31.
35 Libaridian, *Armenia at the Crossroads*, p. 31.
36 Libaridian, *Armenia at the Crossroads*, p. 93; Charles van der Leeuw, *Azerbaijan: A Quest for Identity* (Richmond, UK: Curzon, 1999), p. 164.
37 Leeuw, *Azerbaijan: A Quest for Identity* p. 160.
38 *Moscow's TV Service*, in Russian, February 24, 1988, in *FBIS/SOV*, February 24, 1988, p. 37.
39 *Tass*, February 23, 1988, in De Waal, *Black Garden*, p. 13.
40 See http://www.departments.bucknell.edu/russian/const/1977toc.html.
41 De Waal, *Black Garden*, pp. 27–28. Kaputikian died in August 2006.
42 *Baku Domestic Service*, in Azeri, February 23, 1988, in *FBIS/SOV*, February 26, 1988, p. 39.
43 *AFP*, Paris, in English, February 27, 1988, in *FBIS/SOV*, February 29, 1988; *Bakinskiy Rabochiy*, in Russian, March 30, 1988, p. 55.
44 Leeuw, *Azerbaijan: A Quest for Identity*, p. 156.
45 *DPA* in German, February 26, 1988, in *FBIS/SOV*, February 26, 1988, p. 42.
46 *Pravda*, February 25, 1988, in *FBIS/SOV*, February 25, 1988, p. 38.
47 *Bakinskiy Rabochiy*, Baku, in Russian, March 2, 1988, p. 3 in *FBIS/SOV*, March 16, 1988; Also see *Baku Domestic Service,* in Azeri, March 1, 1988, in *FBIS/SOV*, March 2, 1988, p. 42.
48 De Waal, *Black Garden*, p. 28.
49 De Waal, *Black Garden*, p. 62. Soviet reports argued then that by February 1989, 141,000 Azeris had left Armenia, and 158,800 Armenians had left Azerbaijan. See *TASS*, Moscow, in Russian, February 7, 1989, in *FBIS/SOV*, February 7, 1989, p. 56.
50 De Waal, *Black Garden*, p. 63.
51 Arif Yunusov, "Pogromy v Armenii v 1988–1989 Godakh", [Pogroms in Armenia in 1988–1989], *Express-Khronika*, 9:186 (February 26, 1991), in De Waal, *Black Garden*, pp. 62–63.
52 De Waal, *Black Garden*, pp. 62–63.
53 Politburo Session of February 29, 1988, Transcript, in the *Russian Archives Project: State Archive Service of Russia* (Hoover Institution). Hereafter: Russian Archives Project, Reel 1003 (89/42/18), in De Waal, *Black Garden*, p. 26.
54 *Russian Archives Project*, Fond 89, Reel 1.003, 89/42/18, in De Waal, *Black Garden*, p. 58.
55 *Libération*, Paris, March 11, 1988, p. 25, in *FBIS/SOV*, March 16, 1988, p. 40.
56 *Tass*, Moscow, in English, March 4, 1988, in *FBIS/SOV*, March 7, 1988, p. 44.
57 De Waal, *Black Garden*, p. 34.
58 De Waal, *Black Garden*, p. 39.
59 *AFP*, Paris, March 1, 1988, in *FBIS/SOV*, March 1, 1988, p. 43.
60 *Bakinskiy Rabochiy*, Baku, March 17, 1988, in *FBIS/SOV*, March 30, 1988, p. 55.

61 *Bakinskiy Rabochiy*, Baku, March 30, 1988, in *FBIS/SOV*, March 30, 1988, p. 54.
62 *AFP*, in English, October 17, 1988, in *FBIS/SOV*, October 17, 1988, p. 35.
63 De Waal, *Black Garden*, p. 41.
64 *Kommunist Sumgaita*, May 13, 1988, in Samvel Shahmuratian, ed., *The Sumgait Tragedy: Pogroms against Armenians in Soviet Azerbaijan*, Vol. I (New Rochelle, NY: Aristide D Caratzas, 1990), p. 7, in De Waal, *Black Garden*, p. 43.
65 Leeuw, *Azerbaijan: A Quest for Identity*, p. 156.
66 Leeuw, *Azerbaijan: A Quest for Identity*, p. 156.
67 *Sovetskaya Kultura*, Moscow, in Russian, March 26, 1988, p. 2, in *FBIS/SOV*, April 5, 1988, p. 45.
68 *Elm* [Weekly of the Azerbaijan's Academy of Sciences], May 13, 1989, in De Waal, *Black Garden*, p. 42.
69 *Politburo Session*, February 29, 1988, in *Russian Archive Project* (http://www.yale.edu/rusarch/archive.html), in De Waal, *Black Garden*, pp. 38–39.
70 *Libération*, Paris, in French, March 12–13, 1988, p. 16, in *FBIS/SOV*, March 18, 1988, p. 46.
71 Interview with Gukasian, October 7, 2000, in De Waal, *Black Garden*, p. 44.
72 *AFP*, Paris, in English, March 18, 1988, in *FBIS/SOV*, March 18, 1988, p. 44.
73 *AFP*, in English, March 30, 1988, in *FBIS/SOV*, March 30, 1988, p. 52.
74 *AFP*, Paris, in English, April 1, 1988, in *FBIS/SOV*, April 1, 1988, p. 37.
75 *Moscow News*, in English, No. 12 (March 20, 1988), p. 10, in *FBIS/SOV*, March 23, 1988, p. 64.
76 *Moscow News*, in English, No. 12 (March 20, 1988), p. 10, in *FBIS/SOV*, March 23, 1988, p. 64.
77 *Le Monde*, March 16, 1988, p. 4.
78 De Waal, *Black Garden*, p. 139.
79 See *Bakinskiy Rabochiy*, March 11, 1988, and *Azärbaijan Khalg täsärrufaty*, No. 7 (1988), pp. 8–16, in Altstadt, "O Patria Mia", p. 116.
80 *Antinji Chaghirish Azerbaijan SSR Ali Sovetinin Ijlaslari, 9ju sessiya (21–22 dekabr 1965–ji il); Stenografik hesabat* (Baku, 1966), pp. 107–111; *Bakinskiy Rabochiy*, November 12, 1988, in Altstadt, "O Patria Mia", p. 116.
81 Altstadt bases her argument on the 1979 data: *Chislennost'I sostav naseleniia SSSR; Po dannym vsesoiuznoi perepisi naseleniia 1979 goda* (Moscow, 1984), in Altstadt, "O Patria Mia", p. 116.
82 De Waal, *Black Garden*, p. 139.
83 Kocharian interviewed on *Ostankino* Russian TV with Andrei Karaulov on the *Moment Istiny* [Moment of Truth] program. January 10, 1994. The transcript is in V. B. Harutrinian, *Sobytiya v Nagorno Karabakhe. Khronika* [Events in Nagorno Karabagh: A Chronicle], Parts I–VI (Yerevan: Izdatel'stvo AN ASSR, 1990–1997), in De Waal, *Black Garden*, p. 139.
84 *AFP*, Paris, in English, March 18, 1988, in *FBIS/SOV*, March 18, 1988, p. 44.
85 *Pravda*, Moscow, March 24, 1988, p. 5, in *FBIS/SOV*, March 24, 1988, p. 39.
86 *Pravda*, Moscow, March 25, 1988, second ed., in *FBIS/SOV*, March 25, 1988, p. 32.
87 See various news reports from Azerbaijan and Armenia cited in *FBIS/SOV*, March 24–29, 1988.

88 *Trud*, Moscow, in Russian, March 25, 1988, p. 3, in *FBIS/SOV*, March 30, 1988, p. 49.

89 *Kommunist*, Yerevan, in Russian, October 9, 1988, p. 1, in *FBIS/SOV*, October 21, 1988, pp. 69–70.

90 *Kommunist*, Yerevan, in Russian, March 26, 1988, in *FBIS/SOV*, April 20, 1988, p. 65.

91 Both Airikyan and Grigoryants were prominent organizers of 'unification' demonstrations. See *Kommunist*, Yerevan, in Russian, April 7, 1988, p. 3, in *FBIS/SOV*, April 26, 1988, pp. 49–51.

92 *Budapest Domestic Service*, May 18, 1988, in *FBIS/SOV*, May 19, 1988, p. 38.

93 "Samizdat", *Central Asian Newsletter*, London, Vol. 7, No. 3 (August 1988), pp. 4–5.

94 "Samizdat from Baku", *Central Asia and the Caucasus Chronicle*, Vol. 8, No. 2 (May 1989), pp. 3–4.

95 *AFP*, Paris, in English, May 31, 1988, in *FBIS/SOV*, May 31, 1988, p. 42; *AFP*, Paris, in English, May 31, 1988, in *FBIS/SOV*, June 1, 1988, p. 38.

96 *AFP*, Paris, May 31, 1988, in *FBIS/SOV*, June 1, 1988, p. 38.

97 *Pravda*, Moscow, in Russian, May 29, 1988, 2nd ed., p. 6.

98 *AFP*, Paris, in English, May 21, 1988.

99 *Bakinskiy Robochiy*, in Russian, May 18, 1988, p. 1.

100 *TASS International Service*, in Russian, May 21, 1988, in *FBIS/SOV*, May 23, 1988, p. 57.

101 De Waal, *Black Garden*, p. 61.

102 *Pravda*, Moscow, in Russian, June 10, 1988, 1st ed., p. 4.

4
Inter-Communal Fighting and Ethnic Cleansing

1 *Yerevan Domestic Service*, in Armenian, June 9, 1988, in *FBIS/SOV*, June 13, 1988, p. 55.

2 *Baku Domestic Service*, in Armenian, June 14, 1988, p. 23, in *FBIS/SOV*, June 14, 1988, p. 23.

3 *AFP*, in English, June 14, 1988, in *FBIS/SOV*, June 14, 1988, p. 24.

4 *AFP*, Paris, June 15, 1988, in *FBIS/SOV*, June 15, 1988, pp. 40–41.

5 *Yerevan Domestic Service*, in Russian, June 16, 1988, in *FBIS/SOV*, June 16, 1988, p. 33.

6 *Yerevan Domestic Service*, in Armenian, June 6, 1988, in *FBIS/SOV*, June 8, 1988, pp. 51–52.

7 *Baku Domestic Service*, in Azeri, July 10, 1988, in *FBIS/SOV*, July 11, 1988, p. 68.

8 *Pravda*, Moscow, in Russian, June 30, 1988, 2nd ed., p. 7, in *FBIS/SOV*, June 30, 1988, pp. 25–28.

9 *Moscow Domestic Service*, in Russian, June 29, 1988, in *FBIS/SOV*, June 30, 1988, pp. 33–34.

10 *Izvestiya*, Moscow, in Russian, July 5, 1988, p. 28, morning edition, p. 6, in *FBIS/SOV*, July 5, 1988, p. 28.
11 *Tass*, Moscow, in English, July 13, 1994, in *FBIS/SOV*, July 13, 1988, p. 55.
12 Altstadt, *The Azerbaijani Turks*, p. 198.
13 De Waal, *Black Garden*, p. 67.
14 De Waal, *Black Garden*, p. 68.
15 De Waal, *Black Garden*, p. 68.
16 *Pravda*, Moscow, in Russian, July 20, 1988, pp. 1–4, in *FBIS/SOV*, July 20, 1988, p. 43.
17 *TASS*, Moscow, in English, July 19, 1988, in *FBIS/SOV*, July 19, 1988, p. 59.
18 *TASS*, Moscow, in English, July 19, 1988, in *FBIS/SOV*, July 19, 1988, p. 61.
19 *TASS*, Moscow, September 19, 1988, in *FBIS/SOV*, September 19, 1988, p. 62.
20 *Moscow Domestic Service*, in Russian, October 17, 1988, in *FBIS/SOV*, October 18, 1988, p. 52.
21 *Pravda*, in Russian, September 22, 1988, 2nd ed., p. 6.
22 *AFP*, September 14, 1988, in *FBIS/SOV*, September 14, 1988, p. 55; *Daily Telegraph*, London, September 20, 1988, p. 11, in *FBIS/SOV*, September 21, 1988, p. 80.
23 *Central Asia Newsletter*, Vol. 7, Nos. 5–6 (December 1988–January 1989), p. 7.
24 *Central Asia Newsletter*, p. 7.
25 Audrey L. Altstadt, "Decolonization in Azerbaijan", Donald Schwartz, Razmik Panossian, eds., *Nationalism and History* (Toronto: University of Toronto Press, 1994), pp. 101–102.
26 *AFP*, Paris, November 24, 1988, in English in *FBIS/SOV*, November 25, 1988, p. 36.
27 *BBC World Service*, London, in English, November 24, 1988, in *FBIS/SOV*, November 25, 1988, p. 38.
28 *BBC World Service*, London, in English, November 24, 1988, in *FBIS/SOV*, November 25, 1988, p. 38.
29 *Armenpress International Service*, Yerevan, in Armenian, November 9, 1988, in *FBIS/SOV*, November 17, 1988, p. 51.
30 *Armenpress International Service*, Yerevan, in Armenian, October 18, 1988, in *FBIS/SOV*, November 1, 1988, pp. 65–66.
31 *Armenpress International Service*, Yerevan, in Armenian, October 18, 1988, in *FBIS/SOV*, November 1, 1988, pp. 65–66.
32 *AFP*, Paris, in English, November 23, 1988, in *FBIS/SOV*, November 23, 1988, pp. 38–39; *Baku Domestic Service*, in Azeri, November 30, 1988, in *FBIS*/SOV, December 1, 1988, p. 63.
33 Swietochowski, *Russia and Azerbaijan*, p. 196.
34 *Baku Domestic Service*, in Azeri, November 22, 1988, in *FBIS/SOV*, November 23, 1988, pp. 39–40.
35 Altstadt, *The Azerbaijani Turks*, p. 200.
36 *Baku Domestic Service*, in Azeri, December 29, 1988, in *FBIS/SOV*, December 30, 1988, p. 37.
37 *TASS*, Moscow, in English, December 5, 1988, in *FBIS/SOV*, December 6, 1988, p. 39.

38 *Izvestiya*, Moscow, in Russian, November 28, 1988, p. 4, in *FBIS/SOV*, November 29, 1988, p. 62.
39 *TASS*, Moscow, in English, December 5, 1988, in *FBIS/SOV*, December 6, 1988, p. 39.
40 *Kommunist*, Yerevan, in Russian, November 29, 1988, p. 4, in *FBIS/SOV*, December 9, 1988, p. 53.
41 Altstadt, *The Azerbaijani Turks*, p. 203.
42 *Sotsialistichekaya Industria*, Moscow, in Russian, December 7, 1988, p. 1, in *FBIS/SOV*, December 8, 1988, p. 64.
43 Suny, *The Revenge of the Past*, p. 135.
44 *Komsomolskaya Pravda*, Moscow, in Russian, March 26, 1988, p. 4, in *FBIS/SOV*, March 29, 1988, p. 41.
45 Suny, *The Revenge of the Past*, p. 135.
46 Tofiq Gasymov, "The War against the Azeri Popular Front", *Uncaptive Minds*, Vol. 3, No. 5 (1990), p. 12, in Swietochowski, *Russia and Azerbaijan*, p. 199.
47 The APF was only one of the organizations that sprung up during 1988. There were others, including *Gaygy* (Concern), which focused on the plight of the refugees and distributed aid to them. *Gaygy*'s chairman was Imam D. Mustafaev, former First Secretary of the AzCP.
48 De Waal, *Black Garden*, p. 82.
49 *Central Asia and Caucasus Chronicle*, Vol. 8, No. 4 (August 1989), pp. 7–9.
50 De Waal, *Black Garden*, p. 82.
51 *Central Asia and Caucasus Chronicle*, Vol. 8, No. 4 (August 1989), p. 7.
52 *Central Asia and Caucasus Chronicle*, Vol. 8, No. 4 (August 1989), p. 8.
53 *Central Asia and Caucasus Chronicle*, Vol. 8, No. 4 (August 1989), p. 8.
54 *Central Asia and Caucasus Chronicle*, Vol. 8, No. 4 (August 1989), p. 8.
55 *Central Asia and Caucasus Chronicle*, Vol. 8, No. 4 (August 1989), p. 8.
56 *Central Asia and Caucasus Chronicle*, Vol. 8, No. 4 (August 1989), p. 9.
57 *Central Asia and Caucasus Chronicle*, Vol. 8, No. 4 (August 1989), p. 9.
58 *Central Asia and Caucasus Chronicle*, Vol. 8, No. 4 (August 1989), p. 10.
59 *Central Asia and Caucasus Chronicle*, Vol. 8, No. 4 (August 1989), p. 9.
60 De Waal, *Black Garden*, p. 83.
61 Swietochowski, *Russia and Azerbaijan*, p. 202.
62 Swietochowski, *Russia and Azerbaijan*, p. 202.
63 Motyl, *Sovietology, Rationality, Nationality*, p. 187.
64 Alexander J. Motyl, *Will the Non-Russians Rebel? State, Ethnicity, and Stability in the USSR* (Ithaca, NY: Cornell University Press, 1987); Alexander J. Motyl, "Reassessing the Soviet Crisis: Big Problems, Muddling Through, Business as Usual", *Political Science Quarterly*, Vol. 104, No. 2 (Summer 1989), pp. 269–280.
65 Motyl, *Sovietology, Rationality, Nationality*, p. 187.
66 Motyl, *Sovietology, Rationality, Nationality*, p. 187.
67 Ted Robert Gurr, *Why Men Rebel* (Princeton: Princeton University Press, 1970).
68 Robert V. Barylski, "The Caucasus, Central Asia, and the Near-Abroad Syndrome", *Central Asia Monitor*, Nos. 5 & 6 (1993), p. 32.
69 *Moscow Domestic Service*, in Russian, January 20, 1989, in *FBIS/SOV*, January 23, 1989, p. 64.

70 *Izvestiya*, Moscow, in Russian, January 21, 1989, morning ed., p. 1, in *FBIS/SOV*, January 23, 1989, p. 62.
71 *Izvestiya*, Moscow, in Russian, January 21, 1989, morning ed., p. 1, in *FBIS/SOV*, January 23, 1989, p. 62.
72 *Pravda*, Moscow, in Russian, January 18, 1989, 2nd ed., p. 2, in *FBIS/SOV*, January 23, 1989, p. 73.
73 *Bakinskiy Rabochiy*, Baku, in Russian, January 15, 1989, pp. 1–2, in *FBIS/SOV*, February 1, 1989, pp. 61–67.
74 *Kommunist*, Yerevan, in Russian, January 18, 1989, in *FBIS/SOV*, February 6, 1989, p. 68.
75 *Daily Telegraph*, London, January 9, 1989, p. 12.
76 *Sotsialisticheskaya Industriya*, Moscow, in Russian, April 30, 1989, in *FBIS/SOV*, May 11, 1989, pp. 54, 56.
77 The Congress was recreated as part of Gorbachev's reforms, via a 1988 amendment to the 1977 Constitution. Only one Congress was elected, in March 1989. It remained in existence until the end of the Soviet Union in 1991.
78 De Waal, *Black Garden*, p. 70.
79 *International Service in Armenian*, Yerevan, March 12, 1989, in *FBIS/SOV*, March 14, 1989, p. 54.
80 *Armenpress International Service*, Yerevan, in Armenian, March 7, 1989, in *FBIS/SOV*, March 14, 1989, p. 54.
81 The cooperative was Gorbachev's brainchild to promote free enterprise. *Armenpress International Service*, Yerevan, in Armenian, April 21, 1989, in *FBIS/SOV*, May 4, 1989, p. 69.
82 *Armenpress International Service*, Yerevan, May 16, 1989, in *FBIS/SOV*, May 17, 1989, p. 80.
83 The Congress was held for the first time in June 1989. For Khanzadyan's speech see *Khorhrdayin Hayastan*, Yerevan, in Armenian, June 16, 1989, p. 2, in *FBIS/SOV*, August 3, 1989, p. 78.
84 *Komsomolskaya Pravda*, Moscow, in Russian, August 23, 1989, p. 1, in *FBIS/SOV*, August 24, 1989, p. 51.
85 *Armenpress International Service*, in Armenian, Yerevan, August 23, 1989, in *FBIS/SOV*, August 28, 1989, p. 63.
86 *Domestic Service*, Moscow, in Russian, August 5, 1989, in *FBIS/SOV*, August 7, 1989, p. 79.
87 *Pravda*, Moscow, in Russian, September 14, 1989, 2nd ed., p. 3, in *FBIS/SOV*, September 14, 1989, p. 36.
88 *Pravda*, Moscow, in Russian, September 14, 1989, 2nd ed., p. 3, in *FBIS/SOV*, February 14, 1989, p. 36.
89 *Kommunist*, Yerevan, in Russian, October 31, 1989, p. 3, in *FBIS/SOV*, December 29, 1989, p. 68.
90 Van der Leeuw, *Azerbaijan: A Quest for Identity*, p. 160.
91 *Central Asia and Caucasus Chronicle*, Vol. 8, No. 6 (December 1989/January 1990), pp. 11–13; *Pravda*, Moscow, 2nd ed., September 10, 1989, p. 2, in *FBIS/SOV*, September 11, 1989, p. 33.

92 *Baku Domestic Service*, in Azeri, August 19, 1989, in *FBIS/SOV*, August 21, 1989, p. 82.

93 *Central Asia and Caucasus Chronicle*, Vol. 8, No. 6 (December 1989/January 1990), p. 8.

94 *Bakinskiy Rabochiy*, September 21, 1989, pp. 3–4, in *Central Asia and Caucasus Chronicle*, Vol. 8, No. 6 (December 1989/January 1990), pp. 8–9.

95 *AFP*, Paris, in English, September 10, 1989, in *FBIS/SOV*, September 11, 1989, p. 36.

96 *AFP*, Paris, in English, September 10, 1989, in *FBIS/SOV*, September 11, 1989, p. 36.

97 *Central Asia and Caucasus Chronicle*, Vol. 8, No. 6 (December 1989/January 1990), pp. 11–13.

98 *Domestic Service*, Baku, in Azeri, September 18, 1989, in *FBIS/SOV*, September 19, 1989, pp. 48–49.

99 Swietochowski, *Russia and Azerbaijan*, p. 201.

100 For the full text of the law, see *Kommunist* (Baku), 17:9 (1989). See also: *Central Asia and Caucasus Chronicle*, Vol. 8, No. 6 (December 1989/January 1990), pp. 11–13.; and Swietochowski, *Russia and Azerbaijan*, p. 201.

101 *Kommunist*, Baku, in Azeri, September 28,1989, p. 4, in *FBIS/SOV*, October 31, 1989, p. 77.

102 *Central Asia and Caucasus Chronicle*, Vol. 8, No. 6 (December 1989/January 1990), pp. 11–13.

103 Suny, *The Revenge of the Past*, pp. 136–137.

104 *Bakinskiy Rabochiy*, October 5, 1989, in *Central Asia and Caucasus Chronicle*, Vol. 8, No. 5 (October 1989/January 1989), p. 1.

105 *Television Service in Russian*, Moscow, October 5, 1989, in *FBIS/SOV*, October 6, 1989, p. 42.

106 Altstadt, *The Azerbaijani Turks*, pp. 205–206.

107 William Keller, "Nationalists in Azerbaijan Win Big Concessions from Party Chief", *The New York Times*, October 12, 1989, in Altstadt, *The Azerbaijani Turks*, pp. 205–206.

108 *Yerevan International Service*, in Armenian, September 8, 1989, in *FBIS/SOV*, September 11, 1989, p. 37.

109 De Waal, *Black Garden*, pp. 68–69.

110 *Moscow Domestic Service*, in Russian, September 28, 1989, in *FBIS/SOV*, September 28, 1989, p. 60.

111 *Pravda*, Moscow, in Russian, October 12, 1989, 2nd ed., p. 2, in *FBIS/SOV*, October 12, 1989, p. 45.

112 *Domestic Service*, Moscow, in Russian, October 11, 1989, in *FBIS/SOV*, October 11, 1989, p. 57.

113 *Moscow Domestic Service*, in Russian, September 29, 1989 in *FBIS/SOV*, October 2, 1989, pp. 57–58.

114 *Pravda*, Moscow, in Russian, October 12, 1989, 2nd ed., p. 2, in *FBIS/SOV*, October 12, 1989, p. 45.

115 *Moscow News*, Moscow, in English, No. 40 (October 1, 1989), p. 40, in *FBIS/SOV*, October 5, 1989, p. 55.

116 *Domestic Service*, Moscow, in Russian, October 11, 1989, in *FBIS/SOV*, October 11, 1989, p. 57.

117 *International Service in Armenian*, Yerevan, November 4, 1989; *Tass*, Moscow, in English, November 4, 1989, in *FBIS/SOV*, November 7, 1989, pp. 46–48.

118 *AFP*, Paris, in English, November 6, 1989, in *FBIS/SOV*, November 7, 1989, p. 49; *Komsomolets*, Yerevan, in Russian, November 4, 1989, p. 2, in *FBIS/SOV*, December 5, 1989, p. 53.

5
Black January and After

1 *Domestic Service*, Baku, November 29, 1989; and *AFP*, Paris, in English, November 29, 1989, in *FBIS/SOV*, November 29, 1989, p. 89.

2 *Domestic Service*, Baku, in Azeri, December 5, 1989, in *FBIS/SOV*, December 6, 1989, pp. 72–73.

3 *Domestic Service*, Baku, in Azeri, December 5, 1989, in *FBIS/SOV*, December 6, 1989, pp. 72–73.

4 *AFP*, Paris, in English, December 1, 1989; *Yerevan Domestic Service*, in Armenian, December 2, 1989; *Moscow Domestic Service*, in Russian, December 2, 1989, in *FBIS/SOV*, December 4, 1989, pp. 112–114.

5 The Congress of USSR People's Deputies was Gorbachev's brainchild, formed in the latter half of 1989. Through it, Gorbachev intended to have more popular political participation from outside the Communist Party.

6 Izvestiya, Moscow, in Russian, December 1, 1989, morning ed., p. 2, in *FBIS/SOV*, December 1, 1989, p. 49.

7 *Domestic Service*, Baku, in Azeri, December 5, 1989, in *FBIS/SOV*, December 6, 1989, p. 73. For the 1977 Soviet Constitution, see http://www.departments.bucknell.edu/russian/const/1977toc.html.

8 *Domestic Service*, Baku, in Azeri, December 5, 1989, in *FBIS/SOV*, December 6, 1989, p. 73.

9 De Waal, *Black Garden*, p. 71.

10 *Teheran Radio*, October 24, 1989, in *SWB*, SU/0605 (November 4, 1989), p. B/6.

11 *BBC Summaries of World Boradcasts* (*SWB*), SU/0605 (November 4, 1989), p. B/5.

12 *SWB*, SU/0615 (November 16, 1989).

13 *Domestic Service*, Baku, in Azeri, December 30, 1989, in *FBIS/SOV*, January 2, 1990, p. 49.

14 *Kommunist*, Baku, in Azeri, June 4, 1989.

15 *Kommunist*, Yerevan, October 31, 1989, p. 3, in *FBIS/SOV*, December 29, 1989, p. 71.

16 De Waal, *Black Garden*, p. 88.

17 De Waal, *Black Garden*, p. 88.

17 *Izvestiia*, Moscow, January 9, 1990, pp. 1, 6, in Shaffer, *Borders and Brethren*, pp. 136–137.

18 *Moscow Domestic Service*, in Russian, January 3, 1990, in *FBIS/SOV*, January 4, 1990, pp. 63–64.

19 *Moscow Television Service*, in Russian, January 2, 1990, in *FBIS/SOV*, January 3, 1990, p. 32.

20 *Azadlik*, January 14, 1990; *Moscow Domestic Service*, in Russian, January 3, 1990, in *FBIS/SOV*, January 4, 1990, pp. 63–64.

21 *Reuters*, Moscow, December 30, 1989, and Y. Samad Oghlu, *Washington Post*, January 3, 1990, in Shaffer, *Borders and Brethren*, p. 137; "Ob istoricheskom edinstve severnoi i iuzhnoi chastei Azerbaidzhana", *Azerbaijan*, Vol. 1, No. 11 (1990), in Swietochowski, *Russia and Azerbaijan*, p. 203.

22 *Azadlik*, January 14, 1990.

23 *IRNA*, in English, January 21, 1990, in Shaffer, *Borders and Brethren*, p. 140.

24 *IRNA*, in English, January 21, 1990, in Shaffer, *Borders and Brethren*, p. 140.

25 *AFP*, Paris, in English, January 2, 1990, in *FBIS/SOV*, January 2, 1990, p. 47.

26 *Bakinskiy Rabochiy*, Baku, in Russian, June 2, 1990, p. 2, in *FBIS/SOV*, July 10, 1990, p. 65.

27 De Waal, *Black Garden*, p. 88.

28 De Waal, *Black Garden*, p. 88.

29 Outside of the NKAO, such cities as Aghdam, Askeran, and such regions as Martakert and Shaumyan had mixed Azeri and Armenian populations.

30 *Izvestiya*, Moscow, in Russian, January 17, 1990, morning ed., p. 6, in *FBIS/SOV*, January 17, 1990, p. 70.

31 *AFP*, Paris, January 10, 1990, in *FBIS/SOV*, January 11, 1990, p. 93.

32 *International Service*, Yerevan, January 11, 1990, in *FBIS/SOV*, January 12, 1990, p. 79.

33 *Domestic Service*, Moscow, in Russian, January 9, 1990, in *FBIS/SOV*, January 10, 1990, p. 71.

34 *Domestic Service*, Moscow, in Russian, January 14, 1990, in *FBIS/SOV*, January 16, 1990, p. 59.

35 *Krasnaya Zvezda*, Moscow, in Russian, January 14, 1990, 1st ed., p. 1, in *FBIS/SOV*, January 16, 1990, p. 59.

36 *AFP*, Paris, December 30, 1989, in *FBIS/SOV*, January 2, 1990, p. 46.

37 *Pravda*, Moscow, in Russian, February 16, 1990, p. 8, in *FBIS/SOV*, February 20, 1990, pp. 83–87.

38 A. Gorokhov and V. Okulov, "A 'Front' Against Whom? Echo of the Baku Crisis", in *Pravda*, in Russian, February 16, 1990, 2nd ed., p. 8, in *FBIS/SOV*, February 20, 1990, p. 85.

39 *Pravda*, in Russian, January 11, 1990, 2nd ed., p. 1, in *FBIS/SOV*, January 11, 1990, p. 95.

40 *Domestic Service*, Yerevan, in Armenian, January 11, 1990, in *FBIS/SOV*, January 12, 1990, p. 79.

41 *Izvestiya*, Moscow, January 15, 1990, morning ed., p. 2, in *FBIS/SOV*, January 16, 1990, p. 65.

42 De Waal, *Black Garden*, p. 205.

43 Leonidas T. Chrysanthopolous, *Caucasus Chronicles: Nation-Building and Diplomacy in Armenia* (Princeton: Gomidas Institute Books, 2002); De Waal, *Black Garden*, p. 206.
44 *Domestic Service*, Baku, in Azeri, January 11, 1990; *AFP*, Paris, in English, January 11, 1990, in *FBIS/SOV*, January 12, 1990, pp. 80–81; *Tass*, Moscow, January 12, 1990, in *FBIS/SOV*, January 16, 1990, p. 57.
45 *Komsomolskaya Pravda*, Moscow, in Russian, January 20, 1990, p. 4, in *FBIS/SOV*, January 25, 1990, pp. 44–45.
46 *Domestic Service*, Baku, in Azeri, January 11, 1990; *AFP*, Paris, in English, January 11, 1990, in *FBIS/SOV*, January 12, 1990, pp. 80–81; *Tass*, Moscow, January 12, 1990, in *FBIS/SOV*, January 16, 1990, p. 57.
47 *Komsomolskaya Pravda*, Moscow, in Russian, January 20, 1990, p. 4, in *FBIS/SOV*, January 25, 1990, pp. 44–45.
48 De Waal, *Black Garden*, p. 90.
49 Some estimate the death toll to be close to 90 although in the absence of an official investigation it is difficult to forecast exact numbers. Black January events soon descended on Baku, and an official investigation did not occur. For the higher figure see De Waal, *Black Garden*, p. 90.
50 *Izvestiya*, in Russian, January 15, 1990, morning ed., p. 2, in *FBIS/SOV*, January 16, 1990, p. 65. See also *AACAR Bulletin* (Massachusetts), Vol. 2, No. 2 (Fall 1990); *Azadlik*, Baku, January 18, 1990, and Altstadt, *The Azerbaijani Turks*, p. 213.
51 *Trud*, Moscow, in Russian, January 19, 1990, p. 4.
52 De Waal, *Black Garden*, p. 90.
53 See *Tass*, in English, January 18, 1990, in *FBIS/SOV*, January 19, 1990, p. 60.
54 *Azadlik*, January 14, 1990.
55 De Waal, *Black Garden*, p. 91.
56 De Waal, *Black Garden*, p. 92.
57 *Pravda*, in Russian, January 16, 1990, 2nd ed., p. 1, in *FBIS/SOV*, January 16, 1990, pp. 77–78.
58 *Komsomolskaya Pravda*, Moscow, in Russian, January 19, 1990, p. 1.
59 *Izvestiya*, in Russian, January 19, 1990, morning ed., p. 6.
60 *Tass*, International Service, in Russian, January 18, 1990, in *FBIS/SOV*, January 19, 1990, p. 53.
61 *Tass*, International Service in Russian, January 18, 1990, in *FBIS/SOV*, January 19, 1990, p. 59.
62 *Yerevan Domestic Service*, in Armenian, January 19, 1990, in *FBIS/SOV*, January 22, 1990, p. 106.
63 De Waal, *Black Garden*, p. 92.
64 De Waal, *Black Garden*, p. 92.
65 *AFP*, Paris, January 19, 1990, in *FBIS/SOV*, January 22, 1990, p. 108.
66 In January 1993, Azerbaijan Public Prosecutor, Ikhtiyar Shirinov suggested that the then KGB chief in Baku, Vagif Huseinov, gave the order to blow up the power units. See Aydyn Mekhtiyev, "Baku Blames the USSR Leadership Three Years after the Bloodshed", *Nezavisimaya Gazeta*, January 21, 1993, p. 1, in *FBIS-URS*, January 29, 1993, p. 60; For the sabotage operation see *Moskovskie novosti*, August 12, 1990, reprinted in *Bakinskiy Rabochiy*, August 17, 1990, p. 3.

67 *Vilnius Domestic Service*, in Lithuanian, January 22, 1990, in *FBIS/SOV*, January 23, 1990, p. 43; *TASS*, Moscow, in English, January 20, 1990, in *FBIS/SOV*, January 22, 1990, p. 56; *AFP*, Paris, in English, January 20, 1990, in *FBIS/SOV*, January 22, 1990, p. 190.

68 *AFP*, Paris, in English, January 20, 1990, in *FBIS/SOV*, January 22, 1990, p. 190.

69 *Moscow Domestic Service*, in Russian, January 20, 1990, *FBIS/SOV*, January 22, 1990, p. 56, 114.

70 *Tass*, Moscow, in English, January 20, 1990, in *FBIS/SOV*, January 22, 1990, pp. 55–57.

71 See *Krasnaya Zvezda*, January 21, 1990, p. 1, in *FBIS/SOV*, January 22, 1990, pp. 63–64.

72 *TASS*, Moscow, in English, January 20, 1990, in *FBIS/SOV*, January 22, 1990, pp. 55–57.

73 Altstadt, *The Azerbaijani Turks*, p. 218; *AFP*, Paris, in English, January 22, 1990, in *FBIS/SOV*, January 22, 1990, pp. 107–108.

74 *AFP*, Paris, in English, January 20, 1990, in *FBIS/SOV*, January 22, 1990, p. 109.

75 *Baku Domestic Service*, in Azeri, January 20, 1990, in *FBIS/SOV*, January 22, 1990, p. 99.

76 *Tass*, Moscow, in English, January 20, 1990, in *FBIS/SOV*, January 22, 1990, p. 55. For Vezirov's nervous breakdown see De Waal, *Black Garden*, p. 93.

77 *Tass*, Moscow, in English, January 20, 1990, in *FBIS/SOV*, January 22, 1990, p. 56.

78 *Baku Domestic Service*, in Azeri, January 25, 1990, in *FBIS/SOV*, January 25, 1990, p. 36.

79 De Waal, *Black Garden*, pp. 95, 307.

80 *Baku Domestic Service in Azeri*, January 21, 1990, in *FBIS/SOV*, January 22, 1990, p. 101.

81 Goltz, *Azerbaijan Diary*, p. 128.

82 *Baku Domestic Service*, in Azeri, January 21, 1990, in *FBIS/SOV*, January 22, 1990, p. 102.

83 *KUNA*, Kuwait, in English, January 21, 1990, in *FBIS/SOV*, January 22, 1990, p. 114.

84 *IRNA*, Tehran, January 20, 1990, in *FBIS/SOV*, January 22, 1990, p. 112.

85 *Radio Liberty Daily* Report, February 20, 1990, in Altstadt, *The Azerbaijani Turks*, p. 218.

86 *Izvestiya*, Moscow, in Russian, January 27, 1990, morning ed., pp. 1–2, in *FBIS/SOV*, January 29, 1990, p. 36.

87 *Pravda*, in Russian, January 25, 1990, 2nd ed., p. 3, in *FBIS/SOV*, January 25, 1990, pp. 48–49.

88 *Moscow Domestic Service*, in Russian, February 1, 1990, in *FBIS/SOV*, February 2, 1990, p. 50.

89 *Tass*, Moscow, January 31, 1990, in *FBIS/SOV*, January 31, 1990, p. 97.

90 *IRNA*, Tehran, in English, January 20, 1990, in *FBIS/SOV*, January 22, 1990, p. 113; Moscow *Television Service*, January 28, 1990, in *FBIS/SOV*, January 29, 1990, p. 32.

91 *Moscow Television Service*, in Russian, January 25, 1990, in *FBIS/SOV*, January 26, 1990, p. 28.
92 *AFP*, Paris, in English, January 27, 1990, in *FBIS/SOV*, January 29, 1990, pp. 26–27.
93 *Baku Domestic Service*, in Azeri, January 28, 1990, in *FBIS/SOV*, January 29, 1990, p. 35.
94 *Izvestiya*, in Russian, January 22, 1990, morning ed., p. 1.
95 Interview with Scott Horton, a human rights activist who visited the NKAO in the summer of 1991. January 2, 2001, in De Waal, *Black Garden*, p. 109.
96 De Waal, *Black Garden*, p. 110.
97 De Waal, *Black Garden*, p. 110.
98 De Waal, *Black Garden*, p. 110.
99 *Yerevan Domestic Service*, in Armenian, January 20, 1990, in *FBIS/SOV*, January 22, 1990, p. 103.
100 *Armenpress International Service*, in Armenian, Yerevan, February 27, 1990, in *FBIS/SOV*, March 2, 1990, p. 96.
101 *Baku Domestic Service*, in Azeri, February 4, 1990, in *FBIS/SOV*, February 7, 1990, p. 89.
102 *Baku Domestic Service*, in Azeri, February 4, 1990, in *FBIS/SOV*, February 7, 1990, p. 89.
103 Interview with Byrkin, June 1, 2000, in De Waal, *Black Garden*, pp. 110–111.
104 *Pravda*, Moscow, in Russian, February 7, 1990, 2nd ed., p. 3.
105 *Pravda*, Moscow, in Russian, February 7, 1990, 2nd ed., p. 3.
106 *Izvestiya*, Moscow, in Russian, January 22, 1990, morning ed., p. 1.
107 *Krasnaya Zvezda*, in Russian, January 21, 1990, 1st ed., p. 1.
108 *Yerevan Domestic Service*, in Armenian, January 20, 1990, in *FBIS/SOV*, January 22, 1990, p. 103.
109 *Yerevan Domestic Service*, January 20, 1990, in *FBIS/SOV*, January 22, 1990, p. 107.
110 I disagree with Alexander J. Motyl, who argued that before Black January the APF was not nationalist as such, but thereafter it acquired the characteristics of a fleeting national liberation organization. Prior to Black January, too, the APF articulated nationalist demands as the APF Program attests. See Alexander J. Motyl, *Sovietology, Rationality, Nationality*, p. 176.
111 *La Republica*, Rome, in Italian, January 24, 1990, p. 13.
112 *AFP*, Paris, in English, January 25, 1990, in *FBIS/SOV*, January 29, 1990, p. 25.
113 *Baku Domestic Service*, in Azeri, January 26, 1990, in *FBIS/SOV*, January 29, 1990, p. 25.
114 *Krasnaya Zvezda*, in Russian, January 21, 1990, 1st ed., p. 4.
115 *Pravda*, in Russian, February 4, 1990, 1st ed., p. 5; *AFP*, Paris, in English, February 3, 1990, in *FBIS/SOV*, February 5, 1990, pp. 60–62.
116 *Baku Domestic Service*, in Azeri, February 13, 1990, in *FBIS/SOV*, February 15, 1990, p. 74.
117 *Baku Domestic Service*, February 10, 1990, in *FBIS/SOV*, November 14, 1990, p. 96.
118 *Baku Domestic Service*, in Azeri, March 13, 1990, in *FBIS/SOV*, April 6, 1990, p. 109.

119 *Bakinskiy Rabochiy*, in Russian, April 13, 1990, p. 1.
120 *Bakinskiy Rabochiy*, in Russian, April 13, 1990, p. 1.
121 *Bakinskiy Rabochiy*, in Russian, April 13, 1990, p. 1.
122 *Bakinskiy Rabochiy*, in Russian, April 13, 1990, p. 1.
123 *Bakinskiy Rabochiy*, in Russian, May 19, 1990, p. 1.
124 The same day, Elmira Kafarova, the serving chairman of the AzSSR Supreme Soviet Presidium, was elected chairman of the Republic's Supreme Soviet. See *Baku Domestic Service*, in Azeri, May 18, 1990, in *FBIS/SOV*, May 21, 1990, p. 116.
125 *Pravda*, Moscow, in Russian, May 17, 1990, second ed., p. 2.
126 *Pravda*, Moscow, in Russian, May 17, 1990, second ed., p. 2.
127 *Tercuman*, Istanbul, May 14, 1990, p. 6.

6
Baku Courts Moscow while the ANM Comes to Power in Yerevan

1 *Yerevan Domestic Service*, in Armenian, March 27, 1990, in *FBIS/SOV*, March 28, 1990, p. 116.
2 *Krasnaya Zvezda*, Moscow, April 10, 1990, 1st ed., p. 1.
3 *Yerevan Domestic Service*, in Armenian, April 1, 1990, in *FBIS/SOV*, April 2, 1990, p. 111.
4 *Yerevan International Service*, in Armenian, February 21, 1990, in *FBIS/SOV*, February 23, 1990, p. 76.
5 *Yerevan International Service*, in Armenian, February 17, 1990, in *FBIS/SOV*, February 20, 1990, p. 90.
6 *Baku Domestic Service*, in Azeri, March 25, 1990, in *FBIS/SOV*, March 27, 1990, p. 119.
7 *Baku Domestic Service*, in Azeri, March 31, 1990, in *FBIS/SOV*, April 2, 1990, p. 112.
8 *AFP*, Paris, in English, April 13, 1990, in *FBIS/SOV*, April 16, 1990, p. 128.
9 *Krasnaya Zvezda*, in Russian, May 6, 1990, 1st ed., p. 4.
10 *Krasnaya Zvezda*, in Russian, May 6, 1990, 1st ed., p. 4.
11 *Yerevan International Service*, May 27, 1990, in *FBIS/SOV*, May 31, 1990, p. 100; *Moscow Domestic Service*, in Russian, May 23, 1990, in *FBIS/SOV*, May 25, 1990, p. 119.
12 *AFP*, Paris, in English, August 4, 1990, in *FBIS/SOV*, August 6, 1990, p. 82.
13 *Armenpress International Service*, Yerevan, August 3, 1990, in *FBIS/SOV*, August 6, 1990, p. 86.
14 *Moscow Television Service*, in Russian, July 31, 1990, in *FBIS/SOV*, July 31, 1990, p. 99.
15 *Tass, Moscow*, in English, August 18, 1990, in *FBIS/SOV*, August 20, 1990, pp. 98–99.
16 De Waal, *Black Garden*, p.111.
17 *TASS*, Moscow, August 9, 1990, in *FBIS/SOV*, August, 1990, p. 79.

18 *Tass International Service*, in Russian, Moscow, May 28, 1990, in *FBIS/SOV*, May 29, 1990, p. 143.
19 *Krasnaya Zvezda*, in Russian, Moscow, May 27, 1990, 1st ed., p. 3.
20 *Tass*, in English, Moscow, June 8, 1990, in *FBIS/SOV*, June 8, 1990, p. 68.
21 *Tercuman*, Istanbul, in Turkish, June 7, 1990, p. 6.
22 *Tass, in English*, Moscow, June 28, 1990, in *FBIS/SOV*, June 28, 1990, p. 119.
23 *Baku Domestic Service*, in Azeri, June 20, 1990, in *FBIS/SOV*, June 25, 1990, p. 117.
24 *Moscow Domestic Service*, in Russian, June 11, 1990, in *FBIS/SOV*, June 12, 1990, p. 115.
25 *Moscow Domestic Service*, in Russian, June 15, 1990, in *FBIS/SOV*, June 18, 1990, p. 116.
26 For a speech of Mutalibov, in which he demanded greater economic and political sovereignty, equitable prices for Azerbaijani products, and a guarantee from Moscow of Azerbaijan's territorial integrity, see *Adabiyyat va Injasanat*, May 22, 1990, pp. 1–2.
27 *Baku Domestic Service*, in Azeri, June 21, 1990, in *FBIS/SOV*, p. 121.
28 *Tass*, in English, Moscow, November 22, 1990, in *FBIS/SOV*, November 29, 1990, p. 95.
29 *Azerbaijan*, Baku, May 4, 1990; *Azadlik*, Baku, November 22, 1990, in Audrey L. Altstadt, "Baku, 1991: One Year after Black January", in *AACAR Bulletin*, Vol. 4, No. 1 (Spring 1991), p. 10.
30 *Pravda*, in Russian, Moscow, July 7, 1990, 2nd ed., p. 4.
31 *Milliyet*, in Turkish, Istanbul, July 16, 1990, p. 14.
32 *Milliyet*, in Turkish, Istanbul, July 16, 1990, p. 14.
33 *TASS*, Moscow, in English, August 23, 1990, in *FBIS/SOV*, August 23, 1990, p. 98.
34 *TASS*, Moscow, in English, August 23, 1990, in *FBIS/SOV*, August 23, 1990, p. 98.
35 Libaridian, *Armenia at the Crossroad*, p.110.
36 *Yerevan Domestic Service*, in Armenian, August 29, 1990, in *FBIS/SOV*, August 29, 1990, p. 83.
37 *Yerevan Domestic Service*, in Armenian, August 29, 1990, in *FBIS/SOV*, August 29, 1990, p. 83.
38 The APF, *Yeni Musavat* (New Musavat), Karabagh Relief Committee, and various refugee associations. fielded candidates. *Moscow World Service*, in Russian, November 14, 1990, in *FBIS/SOV*, November 16, 1990, p. 89; *TASS International Service*, in Russian, February 4, 1991, in *FBIS/SOV*, February 6, 1991, p. 99.
39 *Azadlik*, September 8, 1990, in Altstadt, *The Azerbaijani Turks*, p. 224; Altstadt, "Baku, 1991: One Year after Black January", p. 8.
40 For the program see *Azadlik*, September 8, 1990, in Altstadt, *The Azerbaijani Turks*, p. 224; Altstadt, "Baku, 1991: One Year after Black January", p. 8.
41 *Milliyet*, Istanbul, September 15, 1990, p. 7.
42 *Baku Domestic Service*, in Azeri, December 21, 1990, in *FBIS/SOV*, December 24, 1990, p. 99.
43 Swietochowski, *Russia and Azerbaijan*, p. 210.

44 S. Abdullayeva, G. Tagiyeva, "The Parliament of Our Hopes?", *Bakinskiy Rabochiy*, October 12, 1990, in *FBIS-USR*, December 14, 1993, p. 42. See also Swietochowski, *Russia and Azerbaijan*, p. 210.
45 Swietochowski, *Russia and Azerbaijan*, p. 212.
46 Goltz, *Azerbaijan Diary*, p. 53.
47 Goltz, *Azerbaijan Diary*, p. 53.
48 Goltz, *Azerbaijan Diary*, p. 52.
49 *Central Television Second Program Network*, Moscow, in Russian, February 17, 1991, in *FBIS/SOV*, February 19, 1991, p. 74.
50 *Central Television Second Program Network*, Moscow, in Russian, February 17, 1991, in *FBIS/SOV*, February 19, 1991, p. 74.
51 "Interview with Panakhov", November 8, 2000, in De Waal, *Black Garden*, p. 85.
52 Elm, Baku, 8:25, in Swietochowski, *Russia and Azerbaijan*, p. 214.
53 *Tass, International Service*, in Russian, Moscow, February 5, 1991, in *FBIS/SOV*, February 6, 1991, p. 99.
54 *Central Television First Program Network*, Moscow, in Russian, February 7, 1991, in *FBIS/SOV*, February 8, 1991, pp. 68–69.
55 *Russian Archives Project*, Fond 89, Reel 1.989 89/4/17, in De Waal, *Black Garden*, pp. 113–114.
56 De Waal, *Black Garden*, p. 114.
57 Melkonian was killed in June 1993. De Waal, *Black Garden*, p. 207.
58 *Rabochaya Tribuna*, Moscow, in Russian, February 20, 1991, p. 2, in *FBIS/SOV*, February 25, 1991, p. 92; *Domestic Service*, in Armenian, Yerevan, February 18, 1991, in *FBIS/SOV*, February 21, 1991, p. 89.
59 *Bakinskiy Rabochiy*, Baku, in Russian, November 27, 1990, p. 1.
60 *Tercuman*, Istanbul, in Turkish, December 7, 1990, p. 8.
61 *Baku Domestic Service*, in Azeri, January 14, 1991, and *Yerevan Domestic Service*, in Armenian, January 15, 1991, in *FBIS/SOV*, January 16, 1991, pp. 101–102; *Armenpress International Service*, in Armenian, Yerevan, February 12, 1991, in *FBIS/SOV*, February 14, 1991, p. 76.
62 *Domestic Service*, Yerevan, February 25, 1991, in *FBIS/SOV*, February 27, 1991, pp. 91–92.
63 *Domestic Service*, Baku, in Azeri, February 21, 1991, in *FBIS/SOV*, February 25, 1991, p. 94.
64 *Izvestiya*, Moscow, in Russian, March 6, 1991, Union edition, p. 3.
65 *Izvestiya*, Moscow, in Russian, March 6, 1991, Union edition, p. 3.
66 *Moscow Central Television Second Program Network*, in Russian, April 7, 1991, in *FBIS/SOV*, April 19, 1991, pp. 71–74.
67 *Izvestiya*, Moscow, in Russian, March 6, 1991, Union edition, p. 3.
68 *Moscow Central Television Second Program Network*, in Russian, April 7, 1991, in *FBIS/SOV*, April 19, 1991, pp. 71–74.
69 *Moscow Central Television Second Program Network*, in Russian, April 7, 1991, in *FBIS/SOV*, April 19, 1991, pp. 71–74.
70 *Krasnaya Zvezda*, Moscow, in Russian, 1st ed., January 23, 1991, p. 2.
71 *Moscow Domestic Service*, in Russian, March 9, 1991, in *FBIS/SOV*, March 11, 1991, pp. 83–84.

72 *Rabochaya Tribuna*, Moscow, March 12, 1991, p. 1.

73 *Moscow Domestic Service*, in Russian, March 9, 1991, in *FBIS/SOV*, March 11, 1991, pp. 83–84.

74 According to official figures 93.3 percent of Azeris voted in favor of the new union.

75 *Izvestiya*, Moscow, March 28, 1991, Union edition, p. 1. Armenia was scheduled to hold its own referendum on September 21, 1991 on independence from the USSR.

76 De Waal, *Black Garden*, p. 114.

77 Goltz, *Azerbaijan Diary*, p. 75.

78 De Waal, *Black Garden*, p. 115.

79 Goltz, *Azerbaijan Diary*, p. 75.

80 De Waal, *Black Garden*, p. 116.

81 *Armenpress International Service*, in Armenian, Yerevan, May 1, 1991; *Radio Rossii Network*, in Russian, May 2, 1991, in *FBIS/SOV*, May 3, 1991, p. 54; *TASS*, Moscow, in English, May 6, 1991, in *FBIS/SOV*, May 7, 1991, p. 55.

82 *Armenpress International Service*, in Armenian, Yerevan, May 1, 1991; *Radio Rossii Network*, in Russian, May 2, 1991, in *FBIS/SOV*, May 3, 1991, p. 54; *TASS*, Moscow, in English, May 6, 1991, in *FBIS/SOV*, May 7, 1991, p. 55.

83 *Armenpress International Service*, in Armenian, Yerevan, May 1, 1991; *Radio Rossii Network*, in Russian, May 2, 1991, in *FBIS/SOV*, May 3, 1991, p. 54.

84 De Waal, *Black Garden*, p. 114.

85 De Waal, *Black Garden*, p. 115.

86 De Waal, *Black Garden*, p. 115.

87 De Waal, *Black Garden*, p. 115.

88 *Argumenty i Fakty*, February 7, 1992, in De Waal, *Black Garden*, pp. 308–309. See also David Murphy, "Operation 'Ring': The Black Berets in Azerbaijan", *Soviet Military Studies*, Vol. 5, No. 1 (March 1992), pp. 487–498.

89 De Waal, *Black Garden*, p. 121.

90 De Waal, *Black Garden*, p. 118.

91 *Krasnaya Zvezda*, Moscow, April 25, 1991, pp. 1–2.

92 *Armenpress International Service*, in Armenian, Yerevan, July 17, 1991, in *FBIS/SOV*, July 19, 1991, pp. 85–87.

93 De Waal, *Black Garden*, p. 118.

94 Erik Melander, "The Nagorno-Karabakh Conflict Revisited: Was the War Inevitable", *Journal of Cold War Studies*, Vol. 3, No. 2 (Spring 2001), p. 70, in De Waal, *Black Garden*, p. 120.

95 *Armenpress International Service*, in Armenian, Yerevan, July 17, 1991, in *FBIS/SOV*, July 19, 1991, pp. 85–87.

96 *Armenpress International Service*, in Armenian, Yerevan, July 17, 1991, in *FBIS/SOV*, July 19, 1991, pp. 85–87.

97 *Radio Yerevan Network*, in Armenian, Yerevan, August 10, 1991, in *FBIS/SOV*, August 12, 1991, p. 67; See also Melander, "The Nagorno-Karabakh Conflict Revisited", p. 71, in De Waal, *Black Garden*, p. 120.

98 Interview with Sarkissian, May 4, 2000, in De Waal, *Black Garden*, p. 122.

99 De Waal, *Black Garden*, p. 123.

100 *Baku Domestic Service*, in Azeri, April 19, 1991, in *FBIS/SOV*, April 22, 1991, p. 91.

101 *All Union Radio First Program, Radio-1 Network*, in Russian, Moscow, May 28, 1991; and *Radio Yerevan Network*, in Armenian, Yerevan, May 28, 1991, in *FBIS/SOV*, May 30, 1991, p. 70.

102 *Komsomolskaya Pravda*, Moscow, in Russian, July 19, 1991, p. 1.

103 *Komsomolskaya Pravda*, Moscow, in Russian, July 25, 1991, p. 2.

104 Altstadt, "Decolonization in Azerbaijan", pp. 105–106.

105 Goltz, *Azerbaijan Diary*, p. 61.

106 Among others see Hill, "Managing Ethnic Conflict", *Journal of Communist Studies and Transition Politics*, Vol. 9, No. 1 (March 1993), pp. 57–74.

107 *FBIS, NES-90-27*, in Swietochowski, *Russia and Azerbaijan*, p. 214.

108 *Interfax*, Moscow, in English, August 22, 1991, in *FBIS/SOV*, August 23, 1991, p. 104.

109 *Radio Baku Network*, in Azeri, Baku, July 23, 1991, in *FBIS/SOV*, August 27, 1991, p. 126; *Armenpress International Service*, in Armenian, Yerevan, August 26, 1991, in *FBIS/SOV*, August 28, 1991, p. 111.

110 *FBIS, NES-90-015*, in Swietochowski, *Russia and Azerbaijan*, p. 214.

111 *Komsomolskaya Pravda*, in Russian, Moscow, August 24, 1991, p. 1; *Milliyet*, in Turkish, Istanbul, August 24, 1991, p. 14.

112 *Interfax*, in English, Moscow, August 24, 1991, in *FBIS/SOV*, August 26, 1991, p. 106.

113 *Radio Rossii Network*, in Russian, Moscow, August 27, 1991, in *FBIS/SOV*, August 27, 1991, p. 125.

114 *Radio Rossii Network*, in Russian, Moscow, August 27, 1991, in *FBIS/SOV*, August 27, 1991, p. 125.

115 *Interfax*, Moscow, in English, August 22, 1991, in *FBIS/SOV*, August 23, 1991, p. 104.

116 *Radio Rossii Network*, in Russian, Moscow, August 24, 1991, in *FBIS/SOV*, August 26, 1991, p. 104.

117 See Barnett Rubin, "Contradictory Trends in the International Relations of Central Asia", *Central Asia Monitor*, No. 6 (1993), p. 11.

118 *All-Union Radio First Program, Radio-1 Network*, in Russian, Moscow, August 27, 1991, in *FBIS/SOV*, August 28, 1991, p. 113.

119 *Interfax*, in English, Moscow, August 27, 1991, in *FBIS/SOV*, August 28, 1991, p. 113.

120 *TASS*, in English, Moscow, August 26, 1991, in *FBIS/SOV*, August 28, 1991, p. 114.

121 *Interfax*, Moscow, in English, August 27, 1991, in *FBIS/SOV*, August 28, 1991, p. 113.

122 *Russian Television Network*, Moscow, September 5, 1991, in *FBIS/SOV*, September 6, 1991, p. 98.

123 *Radio Rossii Network*, Moscow, October 22, 1991, in *FBIS/SOV*, October 25, 1991, p. 56.

124 *Radio Baku Network*, in Azeri, Baku, August 29, 1991, in *FBIS/SOV*, September 4, 1991; *TASS*, Moscow, August 29, 1991, in *FBIS/SOV*, August 30, 1991, p. 122.

125 *Central Television First Program Network*, in Russian, Moscow, August 29, 1991, in *FBIS/SOV*, August 30, 1991, pp. 122–123.
126 *Russian Television Network*, Moscow, in Russian, August 29, 1991, in *FBIS/SOV*, August 30, 1991, pp. 122–123.
127 *Interfax*, in English, Moscow, October 18, 1991, in FBIS/SOV, October 21, 1991, p. 92.
128 *Radio Baku Network*, in Azeri, Baku, August 30, 1991, in *FBIS/SOV*, September 3, 1991, p. 109.
129 Swietochowski, *Russia and Azerbaijan*, p. 216.
130 *Radio Yerevan Network*, in Armenian, Yerevan, September 2, 1991, in *FBIS/SOV*, September 3, 1991, p. 110.
131 *Interfax*, in English, Moscow, September 16, 1991, in *FBIS/SOV*, September 17, 1991, p. 64.
132 De Waal, *Black Garden*, p. 160; Polyanichko was assassinated on August 1, 1993 near Vladikaskaz, capital of North Ossetia. Some suggested that NKAO Armenians could be his assassins. See Eric Pace, "Victor Polyanichko: Russia Aide", *The New York Times*, August 9, 1993
133 *Radio Yerevan Network*, in Armenian, September 21, 1991, in *FBIS/SOV*, September 23, 1991, p. 74.
134 Swietochowski, *Russia and Azerbaijan*, p. 217.
135 Goltz, *Azerbaijan Diary*, p. 61.
136 Goltz, *Azerbaijan Diary*, p. 53.
137 *AFP*, Paris, September 8, 1991, in *FBIS/SOV*, September 10, 1991, p. 97.
138 *Interfax*, Moscow, in English, September 13, 1991, in *FBIS/SOV*, September 16, 1991, p. 98.
139 *TASS*, in English, Moscow, September 14, 1991, in *FBIS/SOV*, September 16, 1991, p. 99.
140 *TASS International Service*, in Russian, September 16, 1991, in *FBIS/SOV*, September 17, 1991, p. 64.
141 *Russian Television Network*, Moscow, September 13, 1991, in *FBIS/SOV*, September 16, 1991, p. 99.
142 Swietochowski, *Russia and Azerbaijan*, p. 219.
143 *Azerbaijan Radio Network*, in Azeri, Baku, September 27, 1991, in *FBIS/SOV*, October 1, 1991, p. 71.
144 *Izvestiya*, Moscow, in Russian, Union Edition, October 1, 1991, p. 1.
145 *Radio Rossii Network*, in Russian, Moscow, September 26, 1991, p. 79.
146 *Interfax*, in English, Moscow, September 30, 1991, in *FBIS/SOV*, October 1, 1991, p. 71.
147 *Radio Baku Network*, in Azeri, Baku, October 12, 1991, in *FBIS/SOV*, October 16, 1991, p. 83.
148 *Central Television First Program Network*, Moscow, in Russian, October 19, 1991, in *FBIS/SOV*, October 21, 1991, p. 92.
149 *Baku Radio*, in Azeri, Baku, November 15, 1991, in *FBIS/SOV*, November 18, 1991, p. 70.
150 *Interfax*, Moscow, September 24, 1991, in *FBIS/SOV*, September 25, 1991, p. 72.

151 *Interfax*, in English, Moscow, October 8, 1991, in *FBIS/SOV*, October 9, 1991, p. 71.
152 Goltz, *Azerbaijan Diary*, p. 49.
153 *TASS*, in English, Moscow, November 21, 1991, in *FBIS/SOV*, November 22, 1991, p. 79.
154 *TASS*, in English, Moscow, November 21, 1991, in *FBIS/SOV*, November 22, 1991, p. 79; *Tass International Service*, in Russian, Moscow, November 23, 1991, in *FBIS/SOV*, November 25, 1991, p. 91.
155 Goltz, *Azerbaijan Diary*, p. 112.
156 *Baku Radio*, in Azeri, Baku, November 26 and 27, 1991, in *FBIS/SOV*, November 27, 1991, pp. 63–64.
157 *Baku Radio*, in Azeri, Baku, November 26 and 27, 1991, in *FBIS/SOV*, November 27, 1991, pp. 63–64.
158 *Interfax*, in English, Moscow, December 30, 1991, in *FBIS/SOV*, December 31, 1991, p. 64.
159 *Postfactum*, in English, Moscow, December 18, 1991, in *FBIS/SOV*, December 19, 1991, p. 47. See also *Milliyet*, Istanbul, January 15, 1992, p. 10.

7
The Road to Independence

1 *Tercuman*, in Turkish, Istanbul, November 7, 1991, p. 83.
2 See http://www.fas.org/man/crs/92-109.htm.
3 *Baku Radio*, in Azeri, Baku, November 26 and 27, 1991, in *FBIS/SOV*, November 27, 1991, p. 64.
4 *Baku Radio*, in Azeri, Baku, November 26 and 27, 1991, in *FBIS/SOV*, November 27, 1991, pp. 63–64; Helsinki Watch, *Bloodshed in the Caucasus: Escalation of the Armed Conflict in the Nagorno-Karabagh*, September 1992, p. 6.
5 *Interfax*, in English, Moscow, December 9, 1991, in *FBIS/SOV*, December 10, 1991, p. 66.
6 *Radio Yerevan Network*, in Armenian, Yerevan, December 11, 1991, in *FBIS/SOV*, December 12, 1991, p. 55.
7 *Radio Yerevan Network*, in Armenian, Yerevan, December 12, 1991, in *FBIS/SOV*, December 13, 1991, p. 79.
8 *Baku Radio Network*, in Azeri, Baku, December 10, 1991, in *FBIS/SOV*, December 11, 1991, p. 76.
9 *TASS International Service*, in Russian, Moscow, January 5, 1992, in *FBIS/SOV*, January 7, 1991, p. 76.
10 "Ongoing Political Power Struggle in Azerbaijan", *RFE/RL Report*, May 1, 1992.
11 *All-Union Radio First Program, Radio-1 Network*, in Russian, Moscow, December 19, 1991, in *FBIS/SOV*, December 20, 1991, p. 73.
12 *Baku Radio Network*, in Azeri, Baku, December 23, 1991, in *FBIS/SOV*, December 27, 1991, p. 63.
13 *Hurriyet*, in Turkish, Istanbul, December 12, 1991, p. 11.

14 *Armenpress International Service*, in Armenian, Yerevan, December 27, 1991, in *FBIS/SOV*, January 8, 1992, p. 75.

15 *Interfax*, in English, Moscow, December 30, 1991, in *FBIS/SOV*, December 31, 1991, p. 64.

16 *AND*, in German, Berlin, December 26, 1991, in *FBIS/SOV*, December 27, 1991, p. 61.

17 *Mayak Radio*, in Russian, Moscow, January 19, 1992, in *FBIS/SOV*, January 21, 1992, p. 91.

18 *Pravda*, in Russian, Moscow, January 9, 1992, pp. 1–2.

19 A. Kasatov, "Sama ne svoya. Rossiiskaya armiya za rubezhom", *Stolitsa*, No. 48 (1992), pp. 1–4, in Alexei Zverev, "Nagorno-Karabakh and the Azeri-Armenian Conflict, 1988–94", Bruno Coppitiers, ed., *Contested Borders in the Caucasus* (Brussels, VUB University Press, 1996), p. 32.

20 *AFP*, Paris, in English, February 1, 1992 and *Mayak Radio Network*, in Russian, Moscow, January 28, 1992, in *FBIS/SOV*, February 4, 1992, pp. 76–77.

21 *Radio Rossii Network*, in Russian, Moscow, February 2, 1992, in *FBIS/SOV*, February 3, 1992, p. 72.

22 Raymond Bonner, "War in the Caucasus Shows Ethnic Hate's Front Line", *The New York Times*, August 2, 1993.

23 *TASS International Service*, in Russian, January 30, 1992, in *FBIS/SOV*, January 30, 1992, p. 72.

24 Arif Yunusov, "Tragediya Khodjaly" [The Tragedy of Khojaly], *Zerkalo*, No. 25 (June 13–18, 1992), in De Waal, *Black Garden*, p. 312.

25 Rachel Denber, and Robert Kogod Goldman, *Bloodshed in the Caucasus: Escalation of the Armed Conflict in Nagorno Karabakh* (New York, NY: 1992).

26 "Nagorno-Karabagh Victims Buried in Azerbaijani Town", *Washington Post*, February 28, 1992; "Massacre by Armenians Being Reported", *The New York Times*, March 3, 1992.

27 De Waal, *Black Garden*, p. 170.

28 Human Rights Watch World Report 1993 – The Former Soviet Union (http://www.hrw.org/reports/1993/WR93/Hsw-07.htm).

29 Figures vary. Human Rights Watch had reported more than 300 dead, while the Azerbaijani paper *Ordu* reported in issues 9, 16, and 20 (1992) the death toll at 636. See De Waal, *Black Garden*, p. 313.

30 Denber, and Robert Kogod Goldman, *Bloodshed in the Caucasus.*

31 Paul Quinn-Judge, "Armenians, Azerbaijanis Tell of Terror; Being an Alleged Massacre, A Long Trail of Revenge", *Boston Globe*, March 15, 1992, in De Waal, *Black Garden*, p. 313.

32 Goltz, *Azerbaijan Diary*, p. 130.

33 Goltz, *Azerbaijan Diary*, p. 130.

34 V. Simonov, "'Ex,' the Prefix of Disgrace: Who is Hounding Ayaz Mutalibov and for What Reason", *Komsomolskaya Pravda*, Moscow, December 23, 1992, p. 2, in *FBIS-USR*, January 4, 1993, p. 66.

35 Simonov, "'Ex,' the Prefix of Disgrace: Who is Hounding Ayaz Mutalibov and for What Reason", *Komsomolskaya Pravda*, Moscow, December 23, 1992, p. 2, in *FBIS-USR*, January 4, 1993, p. 66.

36 De Waal, *Black Garden*, p. 174.
37 De Waal, *Black Garden*, p. 175.
38 Human Rights Watch, *Bloodshed in the Caucasus: Escalation of the Armed Conflict in Nagorno-Karabakh*, September 1992, p. 29; De Waal, *Black Garden*, p. 176.
39 Goltz, *Azerbaijan Diary*, p. 132.
40 Goltz, *Azerbaijan Diary*, p. 133.
41 Goltz, *Azerbaijan Diary*, p. 133.
42 Brian Killen, "Atrocity Reports Horrify Azerbaijan", *The Washington Times*, March 3, 1992.
43 Goltz, *Azerbaijan Diary*, p. 134.
44 Goltz, *Azerbaijan Diary*, p. 136.
45 "Heavy Fighting Goes On for Town In Disputed Region of Caucasus", *The New York Times*, March 9, 1992; Goltz, *Azerbaijan Diary*, pp. 136–139.
46 Elizabeth Fuller, "Azerbaijan after the Presidential Elections", *RFE/RL Research Report*, June 26, 1992, pp. 1–3.
47 Goltz, *Azerbaijan Diary*, p. 215.
48 Swietochowski, *Russia and Azerbaijan*, p. 221.
49 *Svoboda*, No. 21, June 19, 1992, in *FBIS-USR*, December 14, 1993, p. 43.
50 *Azadlik*, Baku, July 19, 1991, p. 9, in Swietochowski, *Russia and Azerbaijan*, p. 221.
51 *Iran Times*, June 15, 1993, in Swietochowski, *Russia and Azerbaijan*, p. 221.
52 Goltz, *Azerbaijan Diary*, p. 147.
53 Interview with Tajeddin Mekhtiev, March 31, 2000, in De Waal, *Black Garden*, p. 163.
54 *Izvestiya*, Moscow, in Russian, Union Edition, October 1, 1991, p. 1.
55 Interview with Etibar Mamedov, November 22, 2000, in De Waal, *Black Garden*, p. 165.
56 Goltz, *Azerbaijan Diary*, p. 150.
57 De Waal, *Black Garden*, p. 165.
58 De Waal, *Black Garden*, pp. 162–163.
59 De Waal, *Black Garden*, pp. 162–163.
60 Interview with Robert Kocharian, May 25, 2000, in De Waal, *Black Garden*, p. 166.
61 Interview with Robert Kocharian, May 25, 2000, in De Waal, *Black Garden*, p. 166.
62 De Waal, *Black Garden*, p. 167. For more details see Paul Quinn-Judge, "In Armenian Unit, Russian Is Spoken", *Boston Globe*, March 16, 1992.
63 Goltz, *Azerbaijan Diary*, p. 248.
64 The 366th Regiment was part of the 23rd division, and both belonged to the Azerbaijan-based 4th Army.
65 De Waal, *Black Garden*, pp. 166–167.
66 For rival paramilitary groups see Alexei Zverev, "Nagorno-Karabakh and the Azeri-Armenian Conflict, 1988–94", Bruno Coppitiers, ed., *Contested Borders in the Caucasus* (Brussels, VUB University Press, 1996), pp. 35–37.
67 De Waal, *Black Garden*, pp. 177–178; Raymond Bonner, "War in Caucasus Shows Ethnic Hate's Front Line", *The New York Times*, August 2, 1993.
68 Although Gaziev had been anti-Russia, by the spring of 1992 he came to believe that Russian help was necessary to keep the NKAO.
69 Interview with Orujev and Ter-Tatevosian, in De Waal, *Black Garden*, p. 209.

70 *ANS TV* Interview with Basaev, July 17, 2000, as reported by *BBC Monitoring*, in De Waal, *Black Garden*, p. 181. Basaev died on July 10, 2006 in Ingushetia.

71 De Waal, *Black Garden*, pp. 178–179, 314.

72 Goltz, *Azerbaijan Diary*, p.185.

73 There was no quorum because fewer than 240, the minimum for a quorum, were in attendance. See Goltz, *Azerbaijan Diary*, p.186.

74 Goltz, *Azerbaijan Diary*, p.188.

75 Goltz, *Azerbaijan Diary*, p.198.

76 Goltz, *Azerbaijan Diary*, p.199.

77 Hunter, *The Transcaucasus in Transition*, pp. 73–74; Moffitt, *op. cit.*, p. 29; "Briefing on Azerbaijan: Presidential Election", *Hearing before the Commission on Security and Cooperation in Europe*, 102nd Congress, Second Session, June 22, 1992 (Washington, DC: G.P.O., 1992), p. 3.

78 Goltz, *Azerbaijan Diary*, p. 200.

79 Goltz, *Azerbaijan Diary*, p. 199.

80 Goltz, *Azerbaijan Diary*, p.199.

81 Goltz, *Azerbaijan Diary*, p.205.

82 De Waal, *Black Garden*, pp. 182–183.

83 *Gamk*, Paris, in Armenian, November 21–22, 1992, in *FBIS-USR*, January 6, 1993, pp. 49–50. See also: Mehrdad Izadi, "You Too, Armenia?" *Kurdish Life*, Spring 1994, in Goltz, *Azerbaijan Diary*, p. 347.

84 David Ljunggren, "Azerbaijanis Say Armenians Attack Town Near Karabakh", *Reuters*, Baku, May 12, 1992; Elif Kaban, "Azeri Strongman Says War Makes Elections Futile", *Reuters*, Ankara, May 11, 1991, in De Waal, *Black Garden*, pp. 181–182.

85 Vladimir Yemelyanenko, "Former KGB Chief Turned into Allah's Messenger", *Moscow News*, in English, Apr. 30, 1993, p. 4, in *FBIS-USR*, June 18, 1993, p. 86.

86 http://www.dod.mil/acq/acic/treaties/cfe/agreements/tashkent.htm

87 David Petrosian, "What are the Reasons for Armenians' Success in the Military Phase of the Karabakh Conflict (1991–mid-1994)", *Noyan Tapan Highlights*, Nos. 19, 20, 21 (May 18 and 25, June 1, 1994), in De Waal, *Black Garden*, p. 198.

88 Dmitry Danilov, "Russia's Search for an International Mandate in Transcaucasia", in Bruno Coppieters, ed., *Contested Borders in the Caucasus* (Brussels: VUB Press, 1996), footnote 161.

89 Goltz, *Azerbaijan Diary*, p. 217.

90 Goltz, *Azerbaijan Diary*, p. 226.

91 Goltz, *Azerbaijan Diary*, p. 216.

92 Goltz, *Azerbaijan Diary*, p. 216.

93 http://countrystudies.us/azerbaijan/30.htm

94 http://countrystudies.us/azerbaijan/30.htm

95 Carey Goldberg, "Azerbaijan Troops Launch Karabakh Offensive", *The Los Angeles Times*, June 14, 1992.

96 Alexei Zverev, "Nagorno-Karabakh and the Azeri-Armenian Conflict, 1988–94", in Coppitiers, ed., *Contested Borders*; Thomas Goltz, "Letter from Eurasia: The Hidden Hand", *Foreign Policy*, No. 92 (Fall 1993), p. 112.

97 Interview with a senior Armenian official, in De Waal, *Black Garden*, p. 112.

98 John-Tor Dahlburg, "Azerbaijan Accused of Bombing Civilians", *Chicago Sun-Times*, August 24, 1992.
99 De Waal, *Black Garden*, p. 197.
100 Barylski, *op. cit.*, p. 34.
101 Carol Migdalovitz, "Armenia-Azerbaijan Conflict", *Issue Brief for Congress* (Library of Congress, Congressional Research Service, 2002).
102 Migdalovitz, "Armenia-Azerbaijan Conflict", p. 17.
103 Hunter, *The Transcaucasus in Transition*, p. 89.
104 De Waal, *Black Garden*, p. 209.
105 See Alexander Sychev's article in *Izvestiya*, May 14, 1993.
106 Goltz, *Azerbaijan Diary*, p. 228; Zverev, "Nagorno-Karabakh and the Azeri-Armenian Conflict", p. 31.
107 "Economic Crisis' in Republic Viewed", *Izvestiya*, September 15, 1993, p. 5, in *FBIS-USR*, November 4, 1993, pp. 5–9.
108 Zverev, "Nagorno-Karabakh and the Azeri-Armenian Conflict", p.31.
109 Swietochowski, "The Sprit of Baku, Summer 1993", *Central Asia Monitor*, No. 4 (1993), p. 19.
110 "Military Draft, Unemployment Spur Emigration", *Novaya Yezhednevnaya*, Moscow, November 10, 1993, p. 5, in *FBIS-USR*, December 4, 1993, pp. 5–6.
111 Goltz, *Azerbaijan Diary*, p. 286.
112 Goltz, *Azerbaijan Diary*, p. 284.
113 Hunter, *The Transcaucasus in Transition*, pp. 79–81.
114 Altstadt, "Azerbaijan's Struggle Toward Democracy", p. 136.
115 Altstadt, "Azerbaijan's Struggle Toward Democracy", p. 136.
116 Aydyn Mekhtiyev, "Azerbaijan: Internal Political Conflicts Grow Sharper: The Popular Front is Accused of Trying to Settle Accounts with the Opposition", *Nezavisimaya Gazeta*, December 23, 1992, pp. 1, 3, in *FBIS-USR*, January 6, 1993, p. 52.
117 Goltz, *Azerbaijan Diary*, pp. 280–281.
118 Goltz, *Azerbaijan Diary*, p. 290.
119 Goltz, *Azerbaijan Diary*, p. 286.
120 For the text of the law, see "On the State Language in the Azerbaijan Republic", *Khalg Gezeti*, Baku, in Azeri, February 2, 1993, p. 2, in *FBIS-USR*, June 9, 1993, pp. 87–89.
121 Goltz, *Azerbaijan Diary*, p. 257.
122 Aydyn Mekhtiyev, "Procurator General Warns the Opposition: A Decision on Renaming the Language May Deepen the Political Crisis", *Nezavisimaya Gazeta*, December 29, 1992, p. 3, in *FBIS-USR*, January 13, 1993, p. 104.
123 See Barylski, *op. cit.*, p. 23.
124 For the "Kurdish Liberation Movement", see *Gamk*, Paris, in Armenian, November 21–22, 1992, in *FBIS-USR*, January 6, 1993, pp. 49–50.
125 "Hearing before the Commission on Security and Cooperation in Europe", 103rd Congress, 1st Session, *Ethnic Violence in Transcaucasia*, March 8, 1993 (Washington, DC: G.P.O., 1993), pp. 9–10.
126 Human Rights Watch/Helsinki Watch, *Azerbaijan: Seven Years of Conflict in Nagorno-Karabakh* (New York: Human Rights Watch, 1995), p. 9.

127 Markar Melkonian, *My Brother's Road: An American's Faithful Journey to Armenia* (New York: I.B.Tauris, 2005), pp. 244–245.

128 Melkonian, *My Brother's Road*, pp. 245–246; "Armenia Takes Town in Western Azerbaijan", *The New York Times*, April 4, 1993.

129 "Armenia Accused of Major Attack", *The New York Times*, April 5, 1993; See also Melkonian, *My Brother's Road*, p. 247.

130 "Attacks in the Caucasus Bring New Tide of Refugees", *The New York Times*, April 13, 1993, p. A5.

131 "Armenia Accused of Major Attack", *The New York Times*, April 5, 1993.

132 Arif Huseinov, "Azerbaijan: Moratorium on Democracy", *Rossiyskaya Gazeta*, January 9, 1993, p. 7, in *FBIS-USR*, January 27, 1993, p. 121.

133 "Azerbaijan Forces Report Advances", *Boston Globe*, August 9, 1992.

134 "Suret Guseynov's Rise to Power Detailed", *Rossiyskiye Vesti*, July 8, 1993, p. 2, in *FBIS-USR*, July 23, 1993, p. 5.

135 "Suret Guseynov Explains Recent Actions", *Literaturnaya Gazeta* (Moscow), in Russian, No. 26 (June 30, 1993), p. 2, in *FBIS-USR*, July 23, 1993, p. 4.

136 The Russian Ambassador, however, dismissed the claims, saying that any Russians involved were only mercenaries. See Altstadt, "Decolonization in Azerbaijan", p. 114.

137 Goltz, *Azerbaijan Diary*, p. 243.

138 "Suret Guseynov Career Detailed", *Komsomolskaya Pravda*, Moscow, June 11, 1993, p. 1, in *FBIS-USR*, June 30, 1993, p. 3.

139 Rustam Narzikulov, "Geidar Aliev's First Economic Act", *Segodnya*, Moscow, July 9, 1993, p. 5, in *FBIS-USR*, July 30, 1993, p. 5.

140 Suha Bolukbasi, "The Controversy over the Caspian Mineral Resources: Conflicting Perceptions, Clashing Interests", *Europe-Asia Studies*, Vol. 50, No. 3 (1998), p. 398.

141 "Armenia and Azerbaijan Agree on a Peace Plan", *The New York Times*, May 27, 1993.

142 "Armenia and Azerbaijan Agree on a Peace Plan", *The New York Times*, May 27, 1993.

143 "Armenia and Azerbaijan Agree on a Peace Plan", *The New York Times*, May 27, 1993.

144 Bonner, "War in the Caucasus Shows Ethnic Hate's Front Line", *The New York Times*, August 2, 1993.

145 See Graham E. Fuller, "Russia and Central Asia: Federation or Fault Line", in Michael Mandelbaum, *Central Asia and the World* (New York: Council of Foreign Relations, 1994), pp. 120–122.

146 For a similar argument, see Dmitriy Furman, "The Sorry Tale of Azerbaijani Democracy", *Svobodnaya Mysl*, No. 11, July 1993, in *FBIS-USR*, December 14, 1993, p. 44.

147 "Azerbaijan Chief Offers to Resign", *The New York Times*, June 8, 1993; "Azerbaijani Quits: Ex-Communist Steps in", *The New York Times*, June 14, 1993.

148 "Ex-KGB Aide Grabs Helm in Baku", *The New York Times*, June 19, 1993.

149 "Rebels Close In on Capital of Azerbaijan", *Los Angeles Times*, June 21, 1993, p. 8; Sonni Efron, "Rebel Claims Azerbaijani Presidency Caucasus: Suret Guseynov

Says 'the People' Support His Bid for Power. His forces are Now Camped outside the Capital", *Los Angeles Times,* June 22, 1993, p. 4.

150 Andrey Polonskiy, "He Who Laughs Last, Laughs Louder", *Obshchaya Gazeta*, Moscow, July 9–16, 1993, p. A5, in *FBIS-USR*, July 30, 1993, p. 3.

151 "Azerbaijan Rebel Claims Power and Support", *The New York Times*, June 22, 1993.

152 "Aliyev Fires 3 Azerbaijani Officials", *Los Angeles Times*, June 27, 1993, p. 4; "Azerbaijan Strips Leader of Power", *Los Angeles Times*, June 25, 1993, p. 12.

153 Serge Schmemann, "Veteran Communist Crowns a Comeback in Azerbaijan", *The New York Times*, July 1, 1993.

154 John-Thor Dahlburg , "Azerbaijani Vote Likely to Ratify Ouster Caucasus: The Ballot Asks, 'Do you Trust President Abulfaz Elchibey?' He was Deposed in Rebellion. His Supporters are Boycotting the Election", *Los Angeles Times*, August 30, 1993, p. 4.

155 Human Rights Center of Azerbaijan, "Political Arrests and Trials in Azerbaijan", (Baku, 1995).

156 Only two obscure candidates challenged Aliev. See Hugh Pope, "Aliyev Declared Azerbaijan Winner Caucasus: He takes 98.8% of Vote in Election Marred by Irregularities. But Shattered Nation's Support for ex-KGB Figure Seems Genuine and Broad", *Los Angeles Times*, October 8, 1993, p. 19.

157 Rustam Narzikulov, "Geidar Aliev's First Economic Act", *Segodnya*, Moscow, July 9, 1993, p. 5, in *FBIS-USR*, July 30, 1993, p. 5; Schmemann, "Veteran Communist Crowns a Comeback in Azerbaijan", *The New York Times*, July 1, 1993.

158 *Izvestiya*, June 17, 1993.

159 "Azerbaijan Moves to Rejoin Ex-Soviets' Commonwealth", *The New York Times*, September 21, 1993.

160 Tadeusz Swietochowski, "The Sprit of Baku, Summer 1993", *Central Asia Monitor*, No. 4 (1993), p. 19.

161 "Pro-Iranian is Ousted", *The New York Times*, August 24, 1993.

162 "129 Prisoners Pardoned by the President", *Baku Sun*, March 19, 2004.

163 Ekaterina Fartova. *Beloruskaya Delovaya Gazeta*, February 19, 1999; Human Rights Center, *Political Arrests and Trials in Azerbaijan, June 1993–November 1995* (Baku, 1995). In 2004 Huseinov was pardoned by President Ilham Aliev and released from jail.

164 Neil MacFarlane, Larry Minear, *Humanitarian Action and Politics: the Case of Nagorno-Karabakh*, Occasional Paper No. 25 (Thomas J. Watson Jr. Institute for International Studies, Brown University: 1997).

165 "The Caucasus and the Caspian: 1996–1997" (Harvard University: John F. Kennedy School of Government Seminar Series, 1997). See http://www.ciaonet.org/conf/jfk01/index.html#22

166 International Crisis Group, *Azerbaijan: Defense Sector Management and Reform*, (Brussels: Policy Briefing, October 29, 2008), p. 4; "129 Prisoners Pardoned by the President", *Baku Sun*, March 19, 2004.

167 Alexis Rowell, "Azerbaijani Stronghold in Karabakh Falls Caucasus: Armenian Forces Take Advantage of Political Turmoil to Capture Last Bastion: Defenders and 20,000 Residents Flee, *Los Angeles Times*, June 28, 1993, p. 10; Bonner, "War

in Caucasus Shows Ethnic Hate's Front Line", *The New York Times*, August 2, 1993.

168 "2 Caucasus Regions Sinking Deeper Into Civil War", *The New York Times*, July 6, 1993; "Azerbaijani Forces Flee In Battle With Armenians Over Key Town", *The Boston Globe*, July 25, 1993. For how the city looked like after eight years, see Michael Wines, "Trying to Tell a Truce From a War", *The New York Times,* May 27, 2001.

169 "Azerbaijan Claims Armenians Seized a Key Town", *The New York Times*, September 5, 1993.

170 "Azerbaijan, Armenia Forces Break Truce", *The Boston Globe*, August 8, 1993; "Armenians Near Iran In Azerbaijan Attack", *The Boston Globe*, August 19, 1993; "Armenians Take A Key Town, Azeris Say", *The Boston Globe*, August 20, 1993; "War in Azerbaijan Spurs Exodus", *The New York Times*, August 28, 1993.

171 "Armenia, Azerbaijan Leaders Seek Truce", *The Boston Globe*, September 26, 1993, p. 7.

172 "Azerbaijan Post Taken by Armenians", *The Boston Globe*, November 26, 1993, p. 26.

173 "High Azerbaijan Toll is Reported", *The Boston Globe*, December 24, 1993, p. 64.

174 "Armenia Reports Renewed Clashes", *The Boston Globe*, January 4, 1994, p. 54; "Azerbaijan Says Losses are Heavy", *The Boston Globe*, January 9, 1994, p. 15.

175 "Azerbaijan Claims Territorial Gains", *The Boston Globe*, January 25, 1994, p. 55.

176 "High Tolls Cited in Karabakh War",*The Boston Globe*, April 23, 1994, p. 67.

177 Steve LeVine, "Azerbaijan Throws Raw Recruits into Battle", *The Washington Post*, April 21, 1994, p. A20.

178 Tim Weiner, "Blowback from the Afghan Battlefield", *The New York Times*, March 13, 1994; Steve LeVine, "Afghan Fighters Aiding Azerbaijan in Civil War", *The Washington Post*, November 3, 1993, p. A14.

179 "New Truce Set Around Disputed Azerbaijan Area", *The Boston Globe*, May 17, 1994, p. 92.

180 For Radio Free Europe/Radio Liberty's account of negotiations see "Nagorno-Karabakh: Timeline of the Long-Road to Peace", *Radio Free Europe/Radio Liberty*, February 10, 2006, in www.rferl.org/content/Article/1065626.html.

181 David Binder, "New Hostilities Threaten Azerbaijan Peace Talks", *The New York Times*, April 2, 1993.

182 "Nagorno-Karabakh: Timeline of the Long-Road to Peace".

183 "Nagorno-Karabakh: Timeline of the Long-Road to Peace".

184 "Nagorno-Karabakh: Timeline of the Long-Road to Peace".

185 "Analysis: Presidents Give Green Light for Continuation of Karabakh Talks", *Radio Free Europe/Radio Liberty*, June 12, 2008, in www.rferl.org/content/Article/1144604; See also Jean-Christophe Peuch, "Nagorno-Karabakh: Mediators Strive to Keep Peace-Talk Participants on the Same Page", *Eurasianet*, in www.eurasianet.org/departments/insight/articles/eav120707.shtml.

186 www.rferl.org/content/Article/1078613.html.

187 Rovshan Ismayilov, "Karabakh Talks Grind to a Holt, Again", in www. eurasianet.org/insight/articles/eav061107a.shtml.

188 Ismayilov, "Karabakh Talks Grind to a Holt, Again".

Conclusion

1 Some of the articles include: Azamat Rustamov, "Dada Gorkut'la Bagly Yer Adlary", *Elm va Hayat*, 1987, No. 9; Kamal Veliyev, "Bir Daha Dada Gorgud Shairlari Hakkynda", *Azerbaijan,* 1981, No.11; Mahmut Ismayilov, "Tariximiz va Tadqiqatimyz", *Adabiyyat va Injasanat*, 15 July 1988; R.Allahverdiyev, "Bashlyja Istimaqat Uzra", *Azerbaijan Kommunisti*, No.9 (1986); Akif Huseynov, "Nashrimiz va Kechmishimiz", *Azerbaijan*, No.10 (1982); Zemfira Verdiyeva, "Mavzumuz: Tarikhimiz, Abidalarimiz, Darsliklarimiz", *Azerbaijan*, No.6 (1988); Memmed Dadashzade, "Dada Gorgud Dastanlarynda Azerbaijan Ethnografiyasýna Dair Bazi Malumatlar", *Azerbaijanyn Ethnografik Mechmuasi*, No.3 (1977). Books that also show the evolution include: T. I. Hajiev, K. N. Veliyev, *Azerbaijan Dili Tarikhi: Ocherklar va Materiallar* (Baku: Maarif, 1983); Sabir Rustemkhanli, *Omur Kitaby* (Baku: Genjlik, 1988); *Azerbaijan Filologiya Masalalari*, Vol. 2 (Baku: Institute of Philology, Azerbaijan Academy of Sciences, 1984); V. Allahverdiyev, S. Mehdiyev, *Azerbaijan Demokratik Respublikasy: Azerbaijan Hokumaty, 1918–1920* (Baku: Genjlik, 1990); *Mirali Seidov*, Azerbaijan Khalgynyn Soikokunu Dushunarkan (Baku: Yazychy, 1990); Ali Saladdin, Azerbaijan She'ri va Folklor, 19–20 Asrlar (Baku: Elm, 1982).

2 One should also refer to Isa Gambar's Musavat party which has been more pan-Turkist than the APF, or Etibar Mamedov's Milli Istiqlal party as well as a plethora of similar parties which have shared the same fate as the APF in terms of loss of popularity.

3 Human Rights Center of Azerbaijan, "Political Arrests and Trials in Azerbaijan", November 14, 1995.

4 International Crisis Group, *Azerbaijan: Turning over a New Leaf*, p 9.

5 International Crisis Group, *Azerbaijan's 2005 Elections*, p. 3.

6 International Crisis Group, *Azerbaijan's 2005 Elections*, p. 15.

7 Human Rights Watch, "Azerbaijan Parliamentary Elections, 2005: Lessons Not Learned", October 31, 2005, p. 11.

8 Executive Order of the President, "On Improvement of Election Practice in the Republic of Azerbaijan", May 11, 2005.

9 Executive Order of the President, "On Urgent Measures in Connection with Preparation and Conducting of the Elections to the Milli Majlis of the Republic of Azerbaijan", October 25, 2005; See also OSCE/ODHIR Election Observation Mission, Republic of Azerbaijan, "Parliamentary Elections 2005", Interim Report No. 3, October 8–21, 2005, p.3.

10 *Turkish Daily News,* June 19, 1999; *Azernews,* January 8, 2004, in International Crisis Group, *Azerbaijan: Turning over a New Leaf*, p. 12.

11 See "Azeri Paper Publishes List of President's High-Ranking Relatives", *BBC Monitoring*, Central Asia (http://www.monitor.bbc.co.uk/).

12 See The Media Rights Institute, "Media During Elections and Status of Media Related Laws", November 3, 2003, in International Crisis Group, *Azerbaijan: Turning over a New Leaf*, p. 12.

13 See Asian Development Bank, *Key Indicators for Asia and the Pacific*, 2008, p. 151 (hhtp://www.adb.org/Documents/Books/Key_Indicators/2008/pdf/Regional-Tables.pdf).

14 Alec Rasizade, "Azerbaijan Descending into the Third World after a Decade of Independence", *Comparative Studies of South Asia, Africa, and the Middle East*, Vol. 22, Nos. 1 & 2 (2002), p.131.

15 See Rasizade, "Azerbaijan Descending into the Third World", p. 132.

Bibliography

Newspaper Articles, Radio and TV Broadcasts, Foreign Broadcast Information Service (FBIS) and BBC Summaries of World Broadcasts (BBC-SWB) Reports, and Official Statements

Abdullayeva S. and Tagiyeva G. "The Parliament of Our Hopes?" *Bakinskiy Rabochiy*, 12 October 1990, in *FBIS-USR*, 14 December, 1993, p. 42.

AFP 27 February 1988, in *FBIS/SOV*, 29 February 1988.

AFP 1 March 1988, in *FBIS/SOV*, 1 March 1988, p. 43.

AFP 18 March 1988, in *FBIS/SOV*, 18 March 1988, p. 44.

AFP 30 March 1988, in *FBIS/SOV*, 30 March 1988, p. 52.

AFP 1 April 1988, in *FBIS/SOV*, 1 April 1988, p. 37.

AFP 19 May 1988, in *FBIS/SOV*, 19 May 1988, p. 36.

AFP 31 May 1988, in *FBIS/SOV*, 31 May 1988, p. 42.

AFP 31 May 1988, in *FBIS/SOV*, 1 June 1988, p. 38.

AFP 14 June 1988, in *FBIS/SOV*, 14 June 1988, p. 24.

AFP 15 June 1988, in *FBIS/SOV*, 15 June 1988, pp. 40–41.

AFP 17 October 1988, in *FBIS/SOV*, 17 October 1988, p. 35.

AFP 14 September 1988, in *FBIS/SOV*, 14 September 1988, p. 55.

AFP 23 November 1988, in *FBIS/SOV*, 23 November 1988, pp. 38–39.

AFP 24 November 1988, in *FBIS/SOV*, 25 November 1988, p. 36.

AFP 13 August 1989, in *FBIS/SOV*, 14 August 1989, p. 64.

AFP 2 September 1989, in *FBIS/SOV*, 5 September 1989, p. 61.

AFP 10 September 1989, in *FBIS/SOV*, 11 September 1989, p. 36.

AFP 4 October 1989, in *FBIS/SOV*, 5 October 1989, p. 51.

AFP 6 November 1989, in *FBIS/SOV*, 7 November 1989, p. 49.

AFP 29 November 1989, in *FBIS/SOV*, 29 November 1989, p. 89.

AFP 30 December 1989, in *FBIS/SOV*, 2 January 1990, p. 46.

AFP 2 January 1990, in *FBIS/SOV*, 2 January 1990, p. 47.

AFP 10 January 1990, in *FBIS/SOV*, 11 January 1990, p. 93.
AFP 11 January 1990, in *FBIS/SOV*, 12 January 1990, pp. 80–81.
AFP 19 January 1990, in *FBIS/SOV*, 22 January 1990, p. 108.
AFP 20 January 1990, in *FBIS/SOV*, 22 January 1990, p. 190.
AFP 22 January 1990, in *FBIS/SOV*, 22 January 1990, pp. 107–108.
AFP 25 January 1990, in *FBIS/SOV*, 29 January 1990, p. 25.
AFP 27 January 1990, in *FBIS/SOV*, 29 January 1990, pp. 26–27.
AFP 3 February 1990, in *FBIS/SOV*, 5 February 1990, pp. 60–62.
AFP 13 April 1990, in *FBIS/SOV*, 16 April 1990, p. 128.
AFP 4 August 1990, in *FBIS/SOV*, 6 August 1990, p. 82.
AFP 8 September 1991, in *FBIS/SOV*, 10 September 1991, p. 97.
AFP 26 December 1991, in *FBIS/SOV*, 27 December 1991, p. 61.
AFP 1 February 1992 in *FBIS/SOV*, 4 February 1992, pp. 76–77.
Akhundova, Elmira. "A Second Karabakh on the Banks of the Samur," *Literaturnaya Gazeta*, 23 December 1992 in *FBIS-USR*, 4 January 1993, pp. 63–66.
"Aliyev Fires 3 Azerbaijani Officials," *Los Angeles Times* 27 June 1993, p. 4.
Argumenty i Fakty 7 February 1992.
"Armenia Accused of Major Attack," *The New York Times* 5 April 1993.
"Armenia and Azerbaijan Agree on a Peace Plan," *The New York Times* 27 May 1993.
"Armenia, Azerbaijan Leaders Seek Truce," *Boston Globe* 26 September 1993, p. 7.
"Armenia Reports Renewed Clashes," *Boston Globe* 4 January 1994, p. 54;
"Armenia Takes Town In Western Azerbaijan," *The New York Times* 4 April 1993.
"Armenians Near Iran In Azerbaijan Attack," *Boston Globe* 19 August 1993.
"Armenians Take A Key Town, Azeri's Say," *Boston Globe* 20 August 1993.
Armenpress International Service 16 August 1988, in *FBIS/SOV*, 23 August 1988, p. 42.
Armenpress International Service 18 October 1988, in *FBIS/SOV*, 1 November 1988, pp. 65–66.
Armenpress International Service 9 November 1988, in *FBIS/SOV*, 17 November 1988, p. 51.
Armenpress International Service 7 March 1989, in *FBIS/SOV*, 14 March 1989, p. 54.
Armenpress International Service 21 April 1989, in *FBIS/SOV*, 4 May 1989, p. 69.
Armenpress International Service 16 May 1989, in *FBIS/SOV*, 17 May 1989, p. 80.
Armenpress International Service 15 August 1989, in *FBIS/SOV*, 17 August 1989, p. 49.
Armenpress International Service 27 February 1990, in *FBIS/SOV*, 2 March 1990, p. 96.
Armenpress International Service 3 August 1990, in *FBIS/SOV*, 6 August 1990, p. 86.
Armenpress International Service 12 February 1991, in *FBIS/SOV*, 14 February 1991, p. 76.
Armenpress International Service 17 July 1991, in *FBIS/SOV*, 19 July 1991, pp. 85–87.
Armenpress International Service 26 August 1991, in *FBIS/SOV*, 28 August 1991, p. 111.
Armenpress International Service 27 December 1991, in *FBIS/SOV*, 8 January 1992 p. 75.

"Attacks in the Caucasus Bring New Tide of Refugees," *The New York Times* 13 April 1993, p. A5.

Azadlik 14 January 1990.

Azadlik 18 January 1990.

Azadlik 8 September 1990.

Azadlik 22 November 1990.

Azerbaijan Radio Network 27 September 1991, in *FBIS/SOV*, 1 October 1991, p. 71.

"Azerbaijan Accused of Bombing Civilians," *Chicago Sun-Times* 24 August 1992.

"Azerbaijan, Armenia Forces Break Truce," *Boston Globe* 8 August 1993.

"Azerbaijan Chief Offers to Resign," *The New York Times* 8 June 1993.

"Azerbaijan Claims Armenians Seized a Key Town," *The New York Times* 5 September 1993.

"Azerbaijan Claims Territorial Gains," *Boston Globe* 25 January 1994, p. 55.

"Azerbaijan Forces Report Advances," *Boston Globe* 9 August 1992.

"Azerbaijan Moves to Rejoin Ex-Soviets' Commonwealth," *The New York Times* 21 September 1993.

"Azerbaijan Post Taken by Armenians," *Boston Globe* 26 November 1993, p. 26.

"Azerbaijan Rebel Claims Power and Support," *The New York Times* 22 June 1993.

"Azerbaijan Says Losses are Heavy," *Boston Globe* 9 January 1994, p. 15.

"Azerbaijan Strips Leader of Power," *Los Angeles Times* 25 June 1993, p.12.

"Azerbaijani Forces Flee In Battle With Armenians Over Key Town," *Boston Globe* 25 July 1993.

"Azerbaijani Quits: Ex-Communist Steps," *The New York Times* 14 June 1993.

Bakinskiy Rabochiy 2 March 1988, p. 3, in *FBIS/SOV*, March 16, 1988.

Bakinskiy Rabochiy 17 March 1988, in *FBIS/SOV*, 30 March 1988, p.55.

Bakinskiy Rabochiy 30 March 1988, in *FBIS/SOV*, 30 March 1988, p.54.

Bakinskiy Rabochiy 15 January 1989, pp. 1–2, in *FBIS/SOV*, 1 February 1989, pp. 61–67.

Bakinskiy Rabochiy 2 June 1990, p. 2, in *FBIS/SOV*, 10 July 1990, p. 65.

Baku Domestic Service 23 February 1988, in *FBIS/SOV*, 26 February 1988, p. 39.

Baku Domestic Service 1 March 1988, in *FBIS/SOV*, 2 March 1988, p. 42.

Baku Domestic Service 19 May 1988, in *FBIS/SOV*, 19 May 1988, p. 37.

Baku Domestic Service 19 May 1988, in *FBIS/SOV*, 20 May 1988, p. 25.

Baku Domestic Service 14 June 1988, p. 23, in *FBIS/SOV*, 14 June 1988, p. 23.

Baku Domestic Service 10 July 1988, in *FBIS/SOV*, 11 July 11 1988, p. 68.

Baku Domestic Service 22 November 1988, in *FBIS/SOV*, 23 November 1988, pp. 39–40.

Baku Domestic Service 30 November 1988, in *FBIS/SOV*, 1 December 1988, p. 63.

Baku Domestic Service 29 December 1988, in *FBIS/SOV*, 30 December 1988, p. 37.

Baku Domestic Service 19 August 1989, in *FBIS/SOV*, 21 August 1989, p. 82.

Baku Domestic Service 18 September 1989, in *FBIS/SOV*, 19 September 1989, pp. 48–49.

Baku Domestic Service 5 December 1989, in *FBIS/SOV*, 6 December 1989, pp. 72–73.
Baku Domestic Service 30 December 1989, in *FBIS/SOV*, 2 January 1990, p. 49.
Baku Domestic Service 20 January 1990, in *FBIS/SOV*, 22 January 1990, p. 99.
Baku Domestic Service 21 January 1990, in *FBIS/SOV*, 22 January 1990, pp. 101–102.
Baku Domestic Service 25 January 1990, in *FBIS/SOV*, 25 January 1990, p. 36.
Baku Domestic Service 26 January 1990, in *FBIS/SOV*, 29 January 1990, p. 25.
Baku Domestic Service 28 January 1990, in *FBIS/SOV*, 29 January 1990, p. 35.
Baku Domestic Service 4 February 1990, in *FBIS/SOV*, 7 February 1990, p. 89.
Baku Domestic Service 10 February 1990, in *FBIS/SOV*, 14 November 1990, p. 96.
Baku Domestic Service 13 February 1990, in *FBIS/SOV*, 15 February 1990, p. 74.
Baku Domestic Service, 13 March 1990, in *FBIS/SOV*, 6 April 1990, p. 109.
Baku Domestic Service 25 March 1990, in *FBIS/SOV*, 27 March 1990, p. 119.
Baku Domestic Service 31 March 1990, in *FBIS/SOV*, 2 April 1990, p. 112.
Baku Domestic Service 18 May 1990, in *FBIS/SOV*, 21 May 1990, p. 116.
Baku Domestic Service 20 June 1990, in *FBIS/SOV*, 25 June 1990, p. 117.
Baku Domestic Service 21 June 1990, in *FBIS/SOV*, p. 121.
Baku Domestic Service 21 December 1990, in *FBIS/SOV*, 24 December 1990, p. 99.
Baku Domestic Service 14 January 1991, in *FBIS/SOV*, 16 January 1991, pp. 101–102.
Baku Domestic Service 21 February 1991, *in FBIS/SOV*, 25 February 1991, p. 94.
Baku Domestic Service 19 April 1991, in *FBIS/SOV*, 22 April 1991, p. 91.
Baku Domestic Service 27 April 1991, in *FBIS/SOV*, 29 April 1991, p. 57.
Baku Radio Network 26 and 27 November 1991, in *FBIS/SOV*, 27 November 1991, pp. 63–64.
Baku Radio Network 10 December 1991, in *FBIS/SOV*, 11 December 1991, p. 76.
Baku Radio Network 21 December 1991, in FBIS/SOV, 27 December 1991, p. 63.
Baku Radio Network 23 December 1991, in *FBIS/SOV*, 27 December 1991, p. 63.
Baku Radio Network 11 January 1992, in *FBIS/SOV*, 16 January 1992, p. 77.
BBC World Service 24 November 1988, in *FBIS/SOV*, 25 November 1988, p. 38.
Budapest Domestic Service 18 May 1988, in *FBIS/SOV*, 19 May 1988, p. 38.
Central Television First Program 29 August 1991, in *FBIS/SOV*, 30 August 1991, pp. 122–123.
Central Television First Program 19 October 1991, in *FBIS/SOV*, 21 October 1991, p. 92.
Central Television First Program 6 November 1991, in *FBIS/SOV*, 7 November 1991, p. 82.
Central Television Second Program 7 February 1991, in *FBIS/SOV*, 8 February 1991, pp. 68–9.
Central Television Second Program 17 February 1991, in *FBIS/SOV*, 19 February 1991, p. 4.
Central Television Second Program 7 April 1991, in *FBIS/SOV*, 19 April 1991, pp. 71–74.
DPA 26 February 1988, in *FBIS/SOV*, 26 February 1988, p. 42.
DPA in German 24 September 1989, in *FBIS/SOV*, 25 September 1989, p. 114.

"Ex-KGB Aide Grabs Helm in Baku," *The New York Times* 19 June 1993.

Fuller, Elizabeth. "Azerbaijan after the Presidential Elections," *RFE/RL Research Report*, 26 June 1992, pp. 1–3.

Furman, Dmitriy. "Return to the Third World: The Sorry Tale of Azerbaijani Democracy," *Svobodnaya Mysl.* 11 July 1993, in *FBIS-USR*, 14 December 1993, p. 39.

Gamk 21–22 November 1992, in *FBIS-USR*, 6 January 1993, pp. 49–50.

Goldberg, Carey. "Azerbaijan Troops Launch Karabakh Offensive," *The Los Angeles Times* 14 June 1992.

Gorokhov A. and V. Okulov. "A 'Front' Against Whom? Echo of the Baku Crisis," *Pravda* 16 February 1990, p. 8, in *FBIS/SOV*, 20 February 1990, p. 85.

"Heavy Fighting Goes On for Town In Disputed Region of Caucasus," *The New York Times* 9 March 1992.

"High Azerbaijan Toll is Reported," *Boston Globe* 24 December 1993, p. 64.

Human Rights Center of Azerbaijan. "Political Arrests and Trials in Azerbaijan, June 1993–November 1995" (1995).

Human Rights Watch/Helsinki Watch. "Seven Years of Conflict in Nagorno-Karabakh" (1995).

Huseinov, Arif. "Azerbaijan: Moratorium on Democracy," *Rossiyskaya Gazeta*, 9 January 1993, p. 7, in *FBIS-USR*, 27 Jan. 1993, p. 121.

Huseinov, Arif. "Suret Guseynov Explains Recent Actions," *Literaturnaya Gazeta*, 30 June 1993, p. 2, in *FBIS-USR*, 23 July 1993, p. 4.

Interfax 5 August 1991, in *FBIS/SOV*, 6 August 1991, p. 70.

Interfax 22 August 1991, in *FBIS/SOV*, 23 August 1991, p. 104.

Interfax 24 August 1991, in *FBIS/SOV*, 26 August 1991, p. 106.

Interfax 27 August 1991, in *FBIS/SOV*, 28 August 1991, p. 113.

Interfax 13 September 1991, in *FBIS/SOV*, 16 September 1991, p. 98.

Interfax 24 September 1991, in *FBIS/SOV*, 25 September 1991, p. 72.

Interfax 30 September 1991, in *FBIS/SOV*, 1 October 1991, p. 71.

Interfax 8 October 1991, in *FBIS/SOV*, 9 October 1991, p. 71

Interfax 18 October 1991, in *FBIS/SOV*, 21 October 1991, p. 92.

Interfax 10 November 1991, in *FBIS/SOV*, 13 November 1991, p. 80.

Interfax 9 December 1991, in *FBIS/SOV*, 10 December 1991, p. 66.

Interfax 30 December 1991, in *FBIS/SOV*, 31 December 1991, p. 64.

International Crisis Group. *Azerbaijan: Turning over a New Leaf*, Europe Report, 156 (2004).

International Crisis Group. *Azerbaijan's 2005 Elections: Lost Opportunity*, Europe Briefing, 156 (2005).

International Crisis Group. *Azerbaijan: Defense Sector Management and Reform*, 29 October 2008.

International Service in Armenian 12 March 1989, in *FBIS/SOV*, 14 March 1989, p. 54.

International Service in Armenian 1 August 1989, in *FBIS/SOV*, 8 August 1989, p. 55.

International Service in Armenian 11 January 1990, in *FBIS/SOV*, 12 January 1990, p. 79.

IRNA 20 January 1990, *in FBIS/SOV*, 22 January 1990, pp. 112–113.

Izvestiya 5 July 1988, pp. 6, 28 in *FBIS/SOV*, 5 July 1988, p. 28.

Izvestiya 28 November 1988, p. 4, in *FBIS/SOV*, 29 November 1988, p. 62.

Izvestiya 21 January 1989, in *FBIS/SOV*, 23 January 1989, p. 62.

Izvestiya 9 September 1989, p. 2, in *FBIS/SOV*, 8 September 1989, p. 34.

Izvestiya 1 December 1989, p. 2, in *FBIS/SOV*, 1 December 1989, p. 49.

Izvestiya 15 January 1990, p. 2, in *FBIS/SOV*, 16 January 1990, p. 65.

Izvestiya 17 January 1990, p. 6, in *FBIS/SOV*, 17 January 1990, p. 70.

Izvestiya 27 January 1990, pp. 1–2, in *FBIS/SOV*, 29 January 1990, p. 36.

Izvestiya 15 September 1993, p. 5, in *FBIS-USR*, 4 Nov. 1993, pp. 5–9.

Kaban, Elif. "Azeri Strongman Says War Makes Elections Futile," *Reuters* 11 May 1991.

Keller, William. "Nationalists in Azerbaijan Win Big Concessions from Party Chief," *The New York Times* 12 October 1989.

Khorhrdayin Hayastan 16 June 1989, p. 2, in *FBIS/SOV*, 3 August 1989, p. 78.

Killen, Brian. "Atrocity Reports Horrify Azerbaijan," *The Washington Times* 3 March 1992.

Kommunist 26 March 1988, in *FBIS/SOV*, 20 April 1988, p. 65.

Kommunist 7 April 1988, p. 3, in *FBIS/SOV*, 26 April 1988, pp. 49–51.

Kommunist 9 October 1988, p. 1, in *FBIS/SOV*, 21 October 1988, pp. 69–70.

Kommunist 29 November 1988, p. 4, in *FBIS/SOV*, 9 December 1988, p. 53.

Kommunist 18 January 1989, in *FBIS/SOV*, 6 February 1989, p. 68.

Kommunist 28 September 1989, p. 4, in *FBIS/SOV*, 31 October 1989, p. 77.

Kommunist 31 October 1989, p. 3, in *FBIS/SOV*, 29 December 1989, p. 68.

Komsomolets 4 November 1989, p. 2, in *FBIS/SOV*, 5 December 1989, p. 53.

Komsomolets 18 January 1990, p. 2, in *FBIS/SOV*, February 16, 1990, pp. 64–67.

Komsomolskaya Pravda 26 March 1988, p. 4, in *FBIS/SOV*, 29 March 1988, p. 41.

Komsomolskaya Pravda 23 July 1988, p. 4, in *FBIS/SOV*, 25 July 1988, p. 46.

Komsomolskaya Pravda 22 August 1989, in *FBIS/SOV*, 28 August 1989, pp. 63–64.

Komsomolskaya Pravda 23 August 1989, p. 1, in *FBIS/SOV*, 24 August 1989, p. 51.

Komsomolskaya Pravda 20 January 1990, p. 4, in *FBIS/SOV*, 25 January 1990, pp. 44–45.

Komsomolskaya Pravda 11 June 1993, p. 1, in *FBIS-USR*, 30 June 1993, p. 3.

Krasnaya Zvezda 4 December 1988, p. 4, in *FBIS/SOV*, 5 December 1988, p. 101.

Krasnaya Zvezda 14 January 1990, p. 1, in *FBIS/SOV*, 16 January 1990, p. 59.

Krasnaya Zvezda 21 January 1990, pp. 1, 3, in *FBIS/SOV*, 22 January 1990, pp. 63–64.

Krasnaya Zvezda 14 January 1992, p. 3, in *FBIS/SOV*, 16 January 1992, p. 77.

La Republica 24 January 1990, p. 13.

Le Monde 16 March 1988, p. 4.

L'espresso 31 July 1989, in *FBIS/SOV*, 4 August 1989, pp. 69–71.

LeVine, Steve. "Afghan Fighters Aiding Azerbaijan in Civil War," *The Washington Post* 3 November 1993, p. A14.

LeVine, Steve. "Azerbaijan Throws Raw Recruits into Battle," *The Washington Post* 21 April 1994, p. A20.

Libération 11 March 1988, p. 25, in *FBIS/SOV*, 16 March 1988, p. 40.

Libération 12–13 March 1988, p. 16, in *FBIS/SOV*, 18 March 1988, p. 46.

Ljunggren, David. "Azerbaijanis Say Armenians Attack Town Near Karabakh," *Reuters* 12 May 1992.

"Massacre by Armenians Being Reported," *The New York Times* 3 March 1992.

Mayak Radio 19 January 1992 in *FBIS/SOV*, 21 January 1992, p. 91.

Mayak Radio 28 January 1992, in *FBIS/SOV*, 4 February 1992, pp. 76–77.

Mekhtiyev, Aydyn. "Azerbaijan: Internal Political Conflicts Grow Sharper: The Popular Front is Accused of Trying to Settle Accounts with the Opposition," *Nezavisimaya Gazeta* 23 December 1992, pp. 1, 3, in *FBIS-USR*, 6 January 1993, p. 52.

Mekhtiyev, Aydyn. "Baku Blames the USSR Leadership Three Years after the Bloodshed," *Nezavisimaya Gazeta* 21 Jan. 1993, p. 1, in *FBIS-URS*, 29 Jannuary 1993, p. 60.

Mekhtiyev, Aydyn. "Procurator General Warns the Opposition: A Decision on Renaming the Language May Deepen the Political Crisis," *Nezavisimaya Gazeta* 29 December 1992, p. 3, in *FBIS-USR*, 13 January 1993, p. 104.

Michaeli, Mirza and William Reese. "Unofficial Publications in Azerbaijan," *RFE/RL Report on the USSR* 15 September 1989, pp. 20–21.

"Military Draft, Unemployment Spur Emigration," *Novaya Yezhednevnaya* 10 November 1993, p. 5, in *FBIS-USR*, 4 December 1993, pp. 5–6.

Milliyet 16 July 1990, p. 14.

Milliyet 15 September 1990, p. 7.

Milliyet 24 August 1991, p. 14.

Milliyet 15 January 1992, p. 10.

Moscow Domestic Service 29 June 1988, in *FBIS/SOV*, 30 June 1988, pp. 33–34.

Moscow Domestic Service 17 October 1988, in *FBIS/SOV*, 18 October 1988, p. 52.

Moscow Domestic Service 20 January 1989, in *FBIS/SOV*, 23 January 1989, p. 64.

Moscow Domestic Service 5 August 1989, in *FBIS/SOV*, 7 August 1989, p. 79.

Moscow Domestic Service 28 September 1989, in *FBIS/SOV*, 28 September 1989, p. 60.

Moscow Domestic Service 29 September 1989 in *FBIS/SOV*, 2 October 1989, pp. 57–58.

Moscow Domestic Service 11 October 1989, in *FBIS/SOV*, 11 October 1989, p. 57.

Moscow Domestic Service 2 December 1989, in *FBIS/SOV*, 4 December 1989, pp. 112–114.

Moscow Domestic Service 3 January 1990, in *FBIS/SOV*, 4 January 1990, pp. 63–64.

Moscow Domestic Service 9 January 1990, in *FBIS/SOV*, 10 January 1990, p. 71.

Moscow Domestic Service 14 January 1990, in *FBIS/SOV*, 16 January 1990, p. 59.

Moscow Domestic Service 20 January 1990, in *FBIS/SOV*, 22 January 1990, pp. 56, 114.

Moscow Domestic Service 1 February 1990, in *FBIS/SOV*, 2 February 1990, p. 50.

Moscow Domestic Service 23 May 1990, in *FBIS/SOV*, 25 May 1990, p. 119.

Moscow Domestic Service 11 June 1990, in *FBIS/SOV*, 12 June 1990, p. 115.

Moscow Domestic Service 15 June 1990, in *FBIS/SOV*, 18 June 1990, p. 116.

Moscow Domestic Service 9 March 1991, in *FBIS/SOV*, 11 March 1991, pp. 83–84.

Moscow News 20 March 1988, p. 10, in *FBIS/SOV*, 23 March 1988, p. 64.

Moscow News 26 June 1988, p. 11, in *FBIS/SOV*, 6 July 1988, p. 53.

Moscow News 1 October 1989, p. 40, in *FBIS/SOV*, 5 October 1989, p. 55.

Moscow TV Service 25 January 1990, in *FBIS/SOV*, 26 January 1990, p. 28.

Moscow TV Service 24 February 1988, in *FBIS/SOV*, 24 February 1988, p. 37.

Moscow TV Service 2 January 1990, in *FBIS/SOV*, 3 January 1990, p. 32.

Moscow TV Service 28 January 1990, in *FBIS/SOV*, 29 January 1990, p.32.

Moscow TV Service 31 July 1990, in *FBIS/SOV*, 31 July 1990, p. 99.

Moscow World Service 7 June 1990, in *FBIS/SOV*, 8 June 1990, p. 67.

Moscow World Service 14 November 1990, in *FBIS/SOV*, 16 November 1990, p. 89.

"Nagorno-Karabagh Victims Buried in Azerbaijani Town," *Washington Post* 28 February 1992.

Narzikulov, Rustam. "Geidar Aliev's First Economic Act," *Segodnya* 9 July 1993, p. 5, in *FBIS-USR*, 30 July 1993, p. 5.

"New Truce Set Around Disputed Azerbaijan Area," *Boston Globe* 17 May 1994, p. 92.

Nezavisimaya Gazeta 1 February 1992, p. 3, in *FBIS/SOV*, 4 February 1992, p. 76.

"Ongoing Political Power Struggle in Azerbaijan," *RFE/RL Report* 1 May 1992.

"On the State Language in the Azerbaijan Republic," *Khalg Gezeti* 2 February 1993, p. 2, in *FBIS-USR*, 9 June 1993, pp. 87–89.

Postfactum 18 December 1991, in *FBIS/SOV*, 19 December 1991, p. 47.

Pravda 25 February 1988, in *FBIS/SOV*, 25 February 1988, p. 38.

Pravda 24 March 1988, in *FBIS/SOV*, 24 March 1988, p. 39.

Pravda 25 March 1988, in *FBIS/SOV*, 25 March 1988, p. 32.

Pravda 30 June 1988, p. 7, in *FBIS/SOV*, 30 June 1988, pp. 25–28.

Pravda 20 July 1988, pp. 1–4, in *FBIS/SOV*, 20 July 1988, p. 43.

Pravda 3 December 1988, pp. 1, 3, in *FBIS/SOV*, 5 December 1988, p. 86.

Pravda 18 January 1989, p. 2, in *FBIS/SOV*, 23 January 1989, p. 73.

Pravda 23 August 1989, p. 2, in *FBIS/SOV*, 23 August 1989, p. 37.

Pravda 10 September 1989, p. 2, in *FBIS/SOV*, 11 September 1989, p. 33.

Pravda 15 September 1989, p. 8, in *FBIS/SOV*, 18 September 1989, p. 45.

Pravda 12 October 1989, p. 2, in *FBIS/SOV*, 12 October 1989, p. 45.

Pravda 11 January 1990, p. 1, in *FBIS/SOV*, 11 January 1990, p. 95.

Pravda 16 January 1990, p. 1, in *FBIS/SOV*, 16 January 1990, pp. 77–78.

Pravda 25 January 1990, p. 3, in *FBIS/SOV*, 25 January 1990, pp. 48–49.

Pravda 16 February 1990, p. 8, in *FBIS/SOV*, 20 February 1990, pp. 83–87.

"Pro-Iranian is Ousted," *The New York Times* 24 August 1993.

Quinn-Judge, Paul. "Armenians, Azerbaijanis Tell of Terror; Behind an Alleged Massacre, A Long Trail of Revenge," *Boston Globe* 15 March 1992.

Quinn-Judge, Paul. "In Armenian Unit, Russian Is Spoken," *Boston Globe* 16 March 1992.

Rabochaya Tribuna 20 February 1991, p. 2, in *FBIS/SOV*, 25 February 1991, p. 92.

Radio-1 Network 27 August 1991, in *FBIS/SOV*, 28 August 1991, p. 113.

Radio-1 Network 19 December 1991, in *FBIS/SOV*, 20 December 1991, p. 73.

Radio Baku Network 23 July 1991, in *FBIS/SOV*, 27 August 1991, p. 126.

Radio Baku Network 29 August 1991, in *FBIS/SOV*, 4 September 1991.

Radio Baku Network 30 August 1991, in *FBIS/SOV*, 3 September 1991, p. 109.

Radio Baku Network 12 October 1991, in *FBIS/SOV*, 16 October 1991, p. 83.

Radio Rossii Network 2 May 1991, in *FBIS/SOV*, 3 May 1991, p. 54.

Radio Rossii Network 24 August 1991, in *FBIS/SOV*, 26 August 1991, p. 104.

Radio Rossii Network 27 August 1991, in *FBIS/SOV*, 27 August 1991, p. 125.

Radio Rossii Network 22 October 1991, in *FBIS/SOV*, 25 October 1991, p. 56.

Radio Rossii Network 2 February 1992, in *FBIS/SOV*, 3 February 1992, p. 72.

Radio Yerevan Network 28 May 1991, in *FBIS/SOV*, 30 May 1991, p. 70.

Radio Yerevan Network 10 August 1991, in *FBIS/SOV*, 12 August 1991, p. 67.

Radio Yerevan Network 2 September 1991, in *FBIS/SOV*, 3 September 1991, p. 110.

Radio Yerevan Network 21 September 1991, in *FBIS/SOV*, 23 September 1991, p. 74.

Radio Yerevan Network 12 December 1991, in *FBIS/SOV*, 13 December 1991, p. 79.

Raymond Bonner. "War in the Caucasus Shows Ethnic Hate's Front Line," *The New York Times* 2 August 1993.

"Rebels Close In on Capital of Azerbaijan," *Los Angeles Times* 21 June 1993, p. 8, *Reuters* 30 December 1989.

Russian Television Network 29 August 1991, in *FBIS/SOV*, 30 August 1991, pp. 122–123.

Russian Television Network 5 September 1991, in *FBIS/SOV*, 6 Sept. 1991, p. 98.

Russian Television Network 13 September 1991, in *FBIS/SOV*, 16 September 1991, p. 99.

Schmemann, Serge. "Veteran Communist Crowns a Comeback in Azerbaijan," *The New York Times* 1 July 1993.

Simonov, V. "'Ex,' the Prefix of Disgrace: Who is Hounding Ayaz Mutalibov and for What Reason," *Komsomolskaya Pravda* 23 December 1992, p. 2, in *FBIS-USR*, 4 January 1993, p. 66.

Sotsialisticheskaya Industriya 7 December 1988, p. 1, in *FBIS/SOV*, 8 December 1988, p. 64.

Sotsialisticheskaya Industriya 30 April 1989, in *FBIS/SOV*, 11 May 1989, pp. 54, 56.

Sovetskaya Kultura 26 March 1988, p. 2, in *FBIS/SOV*, 5 April 1988, p. 45.

"Suret Guseynov's Rise to Power Detailed," *Rossiyskiye Vesti* 8 July 1993, p. 2, in *FBIS-USR*, 23 July 1993, p. 5.

SWB, SU/0605, 4 November 1989, p. B/5.

SWB, SU/0605, 16 November 1989.

Svoboda 19 June 1992, in *FBIS-USR*, 14 December 1993, p. 43.

TASS 23 February 1988, in *FBIS/SOV*, 24 February 1988, p. 36.

TASS 4 March 1988, in *FBIS/SOV*, 7 March 1988, p. 44.

TASS 13 July1994, in *FBIS/SOV*, 13 July 1988, p. 55.

TASS 19 July 1988, in *FBIS/SOV*, 19 July 1988, pp. 59, 61, 63.

TASS 14 September 1991, in *FBIS/SOV*, 16 September 1991, p. 99.

TASS 19 September 1988, in *FBIS/SOV*, 19 September 1988, p. 62.

TASS 5 December 1988, in *FBIS/SOV*, 6 December 1988, p. 39.

TASS 7 February 1989, in *FBIS/SOV*, 7 February 1989, p. 56.

TASS 1 August 1989, in *FBIS/SOV*, 2 August 1989, p. 72.

TASS 4 November 1989, in *FBIS/SOV*, 7 November 1989, pp. 46–48.

TASS 12 January 1990, in *FBIS/SOV*, 16 January 1990, p. 57.

TASS 18 January 1990, in *FBIS/SOV*, 19 January 1990, p. 60.

TASS 20 January 1990, in *FBIS/SOV*, 22 January 1990, pp. 55–57.

TASS 31 January 1990, in *FBIS/SOV*, 31 January 1990, p. 97.

TASS 8 June 1990, in *FBIS/SOV*, 8 June 1990, p. 68.

TASS 28 June 1990, in *FBIS/SOV*, 28 June 1990, p. 119.

TASS 9 August 1990, in *FBIS/SOV*, August 1990, p. 79.

TASS 18 August 1990, in *FBIS/SOV*, 20 August 1990, pp. 98–99.

TASS 23 August 1990, in *FBIS/SOV*, 23 August 1990, p. 98.

TASS 22 November 1990, in *FBIS/SOV*, 29 November 1990, p. 95.

TASS 6 May 1991, in *FBIS/SOV*, 7 May 1991, p. 55.

TASS 25 July 1991, in *FBIS/SOV*, 26 July 1991, p. 7

TASS 26 August 1991, in *FBIS/SOV*, 28 August 1991, p. 114.

TASS 29 August 1991, in *FBIS/SOV*, 30 August 1991, p. 122.

TASS 21 November 1991, in *FBIS/SOV*, 22 November 1991, p. 79

TASS International Service 21 May 1988, in *FBIS/SOV*, 23 May 1988, p. 57.

TASS International Service 18 January 1990, in *FBIS/SOV*, 19 January 1990, pp. 53, 59.

TASS International Service 4 February 1991, in *FBIS/SOV*, 6 February 1991, p. 99.

TASS International Service 28 May 1990, in *FBIS/SOV*, 29 May 1990, p. 143.

TASS International Service 5 February 1991, in *FBIS/SOV*, 6 February 1991, p. 99.

TASS International Service 16 September 1991, in *FBIS/SOV*, 17 September 1991, p. 64.

TASS International Service 23 November 1991, in *FBIS/SOV*, 25 November 1991, p. 91.

TASS International Service 5 January 1992, in *FBIS/SOV*, 7 January 1991, p. 76.

TASS International Service 30 January 1992, in *FBIS/SOV*, 30 January 1992, p. 72.

Teheran Radio 24 October 1989, in *SWB*, SU/0605, 4 November 1989, p. B/6.

Tercuman 14 May 1990, p. 6.

Tercuman 7 June 1990, p. 6.

Tercuman 7 December 1990, p. 8.

Tercuman 7 November 1991, p. 3.

Testimony of David Nissman. "The Nagorno-Karabagh Crisis: Prospects for Resolution," *Hearing before the Commission on Security and Cooperation in Europe*, 102nd Congress, 1st Session, 23 October 1991, Washington: G.P.O., 1992.

Trud 25 March 1988, p. 3, in *FBIS/SOV*, 30 March 1988, p. 49.

"Two Caucasus Regions Sinking Deeper Into Civil War," *The New York Times* 6 July 1993.

Vilnius Domestic Service 22 January 1990, in *FBIS/SOV*, 23 January 1990, p. 43.

"War in Azerbaijan Spurs Exodus," *The New York Times* 28 August 1993.

Weiner, Tim. "Blowback from the Afghan Battlefield," *The New York Times* 13 March 1994.

Wines, Michael. "Trying to Tell a Truce From a War," *The New York Times* 27 May 2001.

Yemelyanenko, Vladimir. "Former KGB Chief Turned into Allah's Messenger," *Moscow*

News 30 April 1993, p. 4, in *FBIS-USR*, 18 June 1993, p. 86.

Yerevan Domestic Service 9 June 1988, in *FBIS/SOV*, 13 June 1988, p. 55.

Yerevan Domestic Service 6 June 1988, in *FBIS/SOV*, 8 June 1988, pp. 51–52.

Yerevan Domestic Service 16 June 1988, in *FBIS/SOV*, 16 June 1988, p. 33.

Yerevan Domestic Service 18 August 1989, in *FBIS/SOV*, 30 August 1989, p. 31.

Yerevan Domestic Service 29 August 1990, in *FBIS/SOV*, 29 August 1990, p. 83.

Yerevan Domestic Service 12 September 1989, in *FBIS/SOV*, 13 September 1989, p. 65.

Yerevan Domestic Service 19 September 1989, in *FBIS/SOV*, 20 September 1989, p. 57.

Yerevan Domestic Service 11 January 1990, in *FBIS/SOV*, 12 January 1990, p. 79.

Yerevan Domestic Service 19 January 1990, in *FBIS/SOV*, 22 January 1990, p. 106.

Yerevan Domestic Service 20 January 1990, in *FBIS/SOV*, 22 January 1990, pp. 103, 107.

Yerevan Domestic Service 27 March 1990, in *FBIS/SOV*, 28 March 1990, p. 116.

Yerevan Domestic Service 1 April 1990, in *FBIS/SOV*, 2 April 1990, p. 111.

Yerevan Domestic Service 15 January 1991, in *FBIS/SOV*, 16 January 1991, pp. 101–102.

Yerevan Domestic Service 18 February 1991, in *FBIS/SOV*, 21 February 1991, p. 89.

Yerevan Domestic Service 25 February 1991, in *FBIS/SOV*, 27 February 1991, pp. 91–92.

Yerevan International Service 26 February 1988, in *FBIS/SOV*, 29 February 1988, p. 65.

Yerevan International Service 12 July 1988, in *FBIS/SOV*, 13 July 1988, p. 57.

Yerevan International Service 8 September 1989, in *FBIS/SOV*, 11 September 1989, p. 37.

Yerevan International Service 24 September 1989, in *FBIS/SOV*, 27 September 1989, p. 69.

Yerevan International Service 17 February 1990, in *FBIS/SOV*, 20 February 1990, p. 90.

Yerevan International Service 21 February 1990, in *FBIS/SOV*, 23 February 1990, p. 76.

Yerevan International Service 27 May 1990, in *FBIS/SOV*, 31 May 1990, p. 100.

Yerevan International Service 28 June 1990, in *FBIS/SOV*, 3 July 1990, p. 100.

Yerevan International Service 12 March 1991, in *FBIS/SOV*, 14 March 1991, pp. 81–82.

Yerevan International Service 12 April 1991, in *FBIS/SOV*, 26 April 1991, p. 57.

Books, Articles and Book Chapters

Abrahamian, Edward. *Iran between Two Revolutions*. Princeton: Princeton University Press, 1964.

Äfändiev, Sultan M. "Himmät'in Yaranması." *Azerbayjan Elmi Savhasi,* Nos. 1 & 2, 1932.

Ağaoğlu, Samet. *Babamdan Hatıralar.* Ankara, 1940.

Akçuraoğlu, Yusuf. "Türkçülük." *Türk Yılı*, 1928.

Akhmedov, A. M. *Filosofiia Azerbaidzhanskogo prosveshcheniia.* Baku: Azerneshr, 1983.

Akhundov, A.F. *Eserleri.* 3 Vols. Baku: Izd-vo A.N. Az. SSR, 1958–1962.

Aliev, Igrar. Kamil Mamedzade, *Albanskiye Pamyatniki Karabakha* [The Albanian Monuments of Karabakh]. Baku: Azerbaijab Devlet Nshriyaty, 1997.

Aliyarov, Suleyman. "Bizim Sorgu: Tarikhimiz, Abidalarimiz, Darsliklarimiz." *Azerbaijan* 7 (1988): 175.

Aliyev, Abulfez. "Tarikhin Darin Gatlarina Doghru." *Azerbaijan* 10, 1989.

Allahverdiev, R. "Bashlija Istiqamat Uzra." *Azerbaijan Kommunisti*, No. 9, 1986.

Allworth, Edward A. *Central Asia: One Hundred Thirty Years of Russian Dominance: A Historical Overview.* Durham, NC: Duke University Press, 1994.

Altstadt, Audrey L. "Azerbaijani Turks' Response to Russian Conquest." *Studies in Comparative Communism* 19 (Fall–Winter 1986): 267–286.

Altstadt, Audrey L. "Baku City Duma: Arena for Elite Conflict." *Central Asian Survey* 5 (1986): 49–66.

Altstadt, Audrey L. "Nagorno-Karabagh: Apple of Discord in the Azerbaijani SSR." *Central Asian Survey* 7, (1988): 63–78.

Altstadt, Audrey L. "Baku, 1991: One Year after Black January." *AACAR Bulletin* 4 (Spring 1991): 10.

Altstadt, Audrey L. *The Azerbaijani Turks: Power and Identity under Russian Rule.* Stanford, CA: Hoover Institution Press, 1992.

Altstadt, Audrey L. "Decolonization in Azerbaijan," in Donald Schwartz, Razmik Panossian, eds. *Nationalism in History.* Toronto: University of Toronto Press, 1994.

Altstadt, Audrey L. "O Patria Mia: National Conflict in Mountainous Karabagh," in Raymond Duncan, Paul Holman, Jr., eds. *Ethnic Nationalism & Regional Conflict: The Former Soviet Union and Yugoslavia.* Boulder, CO: Westview, 1994.

Altstadt, Audrey L. "Azerbaijan's Struggle toward Democracy," in Karen Dawisha, Bruce Parrott, eds. *Conflict, Cleavage, and Change in Central Asia and the Caucasus.* Cambridge: Cambridge University Press, 1997.

Antologiia literatury Iuzhnogo Azerbaidzhana VI. Baku, 1981.

Armstrong, John A. "The Autonomy of Ethnic Identity: Historic Cleavages and Nationality Relations in the USSR," in Alexander J. Motyl, ed. *Thinking Theoretically About Soviet Nationalities.* New York: Columbia University Press, 1990.

Aslanian, A. H. "Britain and the Transcaucasian Nationalities during the Russian Civil War," in Ronald G. Suny, ed. *Transcaucasia: Nationalism and Social Change.* Ann Arbor: Michigan Slavik Series, 1983.

Astourian, Stephan H. "In Search of Their Forefathers: National Identity and the Historiography and Politics of Armenian and Azerbaijani Ethnogenesis," in Donald Schwartz, Razmik Panossian, eds. *Nationalism and History: The Politics of Nation Building in Post-Soviet Armenia, Azerbaijan and Georgia.* Toronto: Toronto University Press, 1994.

Atabaki, Touraj. *Azerbaijan: Ethnicity and Autonomy in Twentieth-Century Iran.* London: British Academic Press, 1993.

Atkin, Muriel. *Russia and Iran, 1780–1828.* Minneapolis: University of Minnesota Press, 1980.

Azarsina, Habib. "An Independent Azerbaijan: Does It Pose a Question for Iran." *Azerbaijan International* 1, 1993.

Azerbaijan Filologiya Meseleleri, Vol. II. Baku: Institute of Philology, Azerbaijan Academy of Sciences, 1984.

Azerbayjan Tarikhi, 3 Vols. Baku: Academy of Sciences, 1958–1963, Vol. 1.

Bahry, Donna. "Perestroika and the Debate over Territorial Economic Decentralization." *Harriman Institute Forum* 2 (May 1989): 1–8.

Bala, Mirza. "Azerbaijan Tarikhinda Turk Albaniya." *Azerbaijan* 10 (1989): 120–127.

Balayan, Zori. *Between Hell and Heaven: The Struggle for Karabakh.* Yerevan: Amaras, 1997.

Barylski, Robert V. "The Caucasus, Central Asia, and the Near-Abroad Syndrome." *Central Asia Monitor* 5 & 6 (1993): 22.

Bennigsen, Alexander and Chantal Lemercier-Quelquejay. *Islam in the Soviet Union.* New York: Praeger, 1967.

Bennigsen, Alexander and Enders Wimbush. *Muslims of the Soviet Empire: A Guide.* Bloomington, Indiana University Press, 1986.

Bilinsky, Yaroslav. "The Soviet Education Laws of 1958–59 and Soviet Nationalities Policy." *Soviet Studies* 14 (October 1962): 138–157.

Blank, Stephen. "Bolshevik Organizational Development in Early Soviet Transcaucasia: Autonomy vs Centralization, 1918–1924," in Ronald G. Suny, ed.

Transcaucasia: Nationalism and Social Change. Ann Arbor: Michigan Slavik Series, 1983.

Bolukbasi, Suha. "The Controversy over the Caspian Mineral Resources: Conflicting Perceptions, Clashing Interests." *Europe-Asia Studies* 50 (1998).

Bournatian, George A. *Eastern Armenia in the Last Decades of Persian Rule, 1807–1828: A Political and Socioeconomic Study of the Khanate of Yerevan on the Eve of the Russian Conquest.* Malibu, California: 1982.

Bournatian, George A. "The Ethnic Composition and Socio-Economic Condition of Eastern Armenia in the First Half of the Nineteenth Century," in Ronald G. Suny, ed. *Transcaucasia: Nationalism and Social Change.* Ann Arbor, MI: University of Michigan Press, 1983.

Bournatian, George A. "The Ethnic Composition and Socio-Economic Condition of Eastern Armenia in the First Half of the Nineteenth Century," in Donald Schwartz, Razmik Panossian, eds. *Nationalism and History: The Politics of Nation Building in Post-Soviet Armenia, Azerbaijan and Georgia.* Toronto: Toronto University Press, 1994.

Bremmer, Ian and Ras Taras, ed. *Nations and Politics in the Soviet Successor States.* New York: Cambridge University Press, 1993.

Brezezinski, Zbigniew. *The Permanent Purge: Politics in Soviet Totalitarianism.* Cambridge, MA: Harvard University Press, 1956.

Browne, E. G. *The Persian Revolution, 1905–1909.* London: Cambridge University Press, 1912.

Buniatov, Z. M. *Gosudarstvo Atabekov Azerbaidzhana: 1136–1225 gody*: Baku, 1978.

Buniatov, Z. M. *O Khronoligicheskom nesootvetsvii glav 'Istorii Agvan' Moiseya Kagankatvatsi.* Baku, 1965.

Burg, Steven L. "Nationality Elites and Political Change in the Soviet Union," in Lubomyr Hajda and Mark Beisinger, eds. *The Nationalities Factor in Soviet Politics and Society,* Boulder, CO: Westview Press, 1990.

Caucasian Boundaries: Documents and Maps 1802–1946, in Archive Editions (http://www.archiveeditions.co.uk/).

Central Asia Newsletter Vol. 7 (5–6) (December 1988–January 1989).

Central Asia and Caucasus Chronicle Vol. 8 (3) (July 1989).

Central Asia and Caucasus Chronicle Vol. 8 (4) (August 1989).

Central Asia and Caucasus Chronicle Vol. 8 (5) (October 1989).

Central Asia and Caucasus Chronicle Vol. 8 (6) (December 1989–January 1990).

Ceylan, Yasin. "Al Ghazali between Philosophy and Sufism." *American Journal of Islamic Social Sciences* 12 (Winter 1995).

Chesmazer, M. "Muhammad Biriya." *Novruz* 5 (1991).

Chorbajian, Levon and Patrick Danabedian, and Claude Mutafian. *The Caucasian Knot: The History and Geopolitics of Nagorno-Karabakh.* London and Atlantic Highlands, NJ: Zed Books, 1994.

Chrysanthopolous, Leonidas T. *Caucasus Chronicles: Nation-Building and Diplomacy in Armenia.* Princeton: Gomidas Institute Books, 2002.

Clapham, Christopher. *Third World Politics.* Madison: The University of Wisconsin Press, 1985.

Dadashzada, Mammad. "Dada Gorgud destanlarinda Azerbaijan etnografiyasina dair bazi malumatlar." *Azerbaijanin etnografik mechmuasi* (Azerbaijan Journal of Ethnography) 3 (1977): 182–194.

Danilov, Dmitry. "Russia's Search for an International Mandate in Transcaucasia," in Bruno Coppieters, ed. *Contested Borders in the Caucasus.* Brussels: VUB Press, 1996.

De Waal, Thomas. *Black Garden: Armenia and Azerbaijan Through Peace and War.* New York: New York University Press, 2003.

Denber, Rachel and Robert Kogod Goldman. *Bloodshed in the Caucasus: Escalation of the Armed Conflict in Nagorno Karabakh.* New York, NY: 1992.

Djavadi, Abbasali. "Glasnost and Soviet Azerbaijani Literature." *Central Asian Survey* 9 (1990): 97–103.

Dobson, Richard B. "Georgia and the Georgians," in Zev Katz, Rosemary Rogers and Frederic Harned, eds. *Handbook of Major Soviet Nationalities.* New York: The Free Press, 1975.

Duncan Raymon and Paul Holman, Jr. *Ethnic Nationalism & Regional Conflict: The Former Soviet Union and Yugoslavia.* Boulder, CO: Westview, 1994.

Ebel, Robert and Rajan Menon. *Energy and Conflict in Central Asia and the Caucasus.* Lanham, MD: Rowman and Littlefield, 2000.

Ekeh, Peter Palmer. "Colonialism and the Two Publics in Africa." *Comparative Studies in Society and History* 17 (1975): 91–112.

Emami-Yeganeh, Jody. "Iran vs. Azerbaijan (1945–46): Divorce, Separation or Reconciliation." *Central Asian Survey* 3 (1984): 1–27.

Farandzhev, A. S. *Zarozhdenie i razvitie ekonomicheskoi mysli v Azerbaidzhane v epokhu feodalizma.* Baku, 1981.

Farzaliev, Sh. *Aksan at-Tavarikh Khasan beka Rumlu kak istochnik po istorii Azerbaidzhana.* Baku, 1981.

Gasymov, Tofiq. "The War against the Azeri Popular Front." *Uncaptive Minds* 3, 1990.

Gellner, Ernest. *Thought and Change.* Chicago: University of Chicago Press, 1964.

Gellner, Ernest. *Nations and Nationalism.* Ithaca, NY: Corrnell University Press, 1983.

Girshman, Roman. *Iran from the Earliest Times to the Islamic Conquest.* London: Penguin Books, 1954.

Golden, Peter B. "The Turkic Peoples and Caucasia", in Ronald G. Suny, *Transcaucasia: Nationalism and Social Change.* Ann Arbor: University of Michigan Slavik Publications, 1983.

Goltz, Thomas. "Letter from Eurasia: The Hidden Hand." *Foreign Policy* 92 (Fall 1993).

Goltz, Thomas. *Azerbaijan Diary: A Rogue Reporter's Adventures in an Oil-Rich, War-Torn, post-Soviet Republic.* Armonk, New York, 1998.

Gorgud: Dada. "Passionate Tales of the Middle Ages." *Azerbaijan International* 4(1996): 24.

Gökalp, Ziya. *The Principles of Turkism.* Leiden, 1968.

Guliev, J. B. *Istoriia Azerbaijana*, Baku: Elm Publications, 1979.

Gurr, Ted Robert. *Why Men Rebel.* Princeton: Princeton University Press, 1970.

Guseinov, I. *Sudnyi Den'.* Baku, 1981.

Hagopian, Mark. *Ideals and Ideologies of Modern Politics.* New York: Longman, 1985.

Halilov, Penah. "Kitabi Dada Gorgud'un joghrafiyasi," *Elm va Hayat* 8 (1988).

Harris, George S. *The Origins of Communism in Turkey.* Stanford: CA, 1967.

Hechter, Michael. *Internal Colonialism.* Berkeley, CA: University of California Press, 1975.

Hegaard, Steven E. "Nationalism in Azerbaidzhan in the Era of Brezhnev," in George W. Simmonds, ed. *Nationalism in the USSR and Eastern Europe in the Era of Brezhnev and Kosygin.* Detroit, MI: University of Detroit Press, 1977.

Helsinki Watch. *Bloodshed in the Caucasus: Escalation of the Armed Conflict in the Nagorno-Karabagh.* 1992.

Hertzig, Edmund M. "Armenians," in Graham Smith, ed. *The Nationalities Question in the Soviet Union.* New York, London: Longman, 1990.

Hewsen, Robert H. "Ethno-History and the Armenian Influence upon the Caucasian Albanians," in Thomas J. Samuelian, ed. *Classical Armenian Culture: Influences and Creativity.* Atlanta, Georgia: Scholars Press, 1982.

Hill, Ronald J. "Managing Ethnic Conflict." *Journal of Communist Studies and Transition Politics* 9 (March 1993): 57–74.

Hitchens, Keith. "The Caucasian Albanians and the Arab Caliphate in the Seventh and Eight Centuries", in Bedi Kartlisa, *Revue de Kartvélologie.* Vol. 42, Paris, 1984, pp. 238–240.

Hobsbawm, Eric. *Nations and Nationalism since 1780: Programme, Myth, Reality.* Cambridge: Cambridge University Press, 1990.

Hovannissian, Richard. "Armenia and the Caucasus in the Genesis of the Soviet-Turkish Entente." *International Journal of Middle East Studies* 4 (1973): 129–147.

Hovannissian, Richard. *The Republic of Armenia: The First Year, 1918–1919.* Berkeley, CA: University of California Press, 1974.

Hovannissian, Richard. *The Armenian Genocide in Perspective.* New Brunswick, NJ: Transaction Books, 1986.

Hroch, Miroslav. *Social Preconditions of National Revival in Europe.* Cambridge: Cambridge University Press, 1985.

Huddle, Frank. "Azerbaidzhan and the Azerbaidzhanis," in Zev Katz, Rosemarie Rogers, Frederic Harned, eds. *Handbook of Major Soviet Nationalities.* New York: Free Press, 1975.

Hunter, Shireen T. *The Transcaucasus in Transition.* Washington: CSIS, 1994.

Huseynov, Akif. "Nashrimiz ve Kechmishimiz." *Azerbaijan* 10 (1982).

Ibragimov, Sh. *Natsional'no-osvoboditel'noe dvizhenie v iuzhnykh vilaietakh Irana v period pervoi miravoi voiny*. Baku, 1981.

Ismayilzada, I. "Obalardan Galan Seslar." [Voices from the Diaspora] *Azerbaijan* 2 (1990).

Jafar, Mammäd. *Azärbaijanda Romantizm*, Baku: Izd-vo ANAzSSR, 1966.

Javid, Turan. "The Night Father was Arrested." *Azerbaijan International* 4 (Spring 1996): 24.

Kamenka, Eugene. "Nationalism: Ambigious Legacies and Contingent Futures." *Political Studies* 41(1993): 78–92.

Karabekir, Kazim. *Istiklal Harbimiz*. Istanbul: Turkiye Yayınları, 1960.

Kasatov, A. "Sama ne svoya. Rossiiskaya armiya za rubezhom." *Stolitsa* 48 (1992): 1–4.

Kazemzadeh, Firuz. *The Struggle for Transcaucasia, 1917–1921*. New York: Philosophical Library, 1951.

Khaled, Adeeb. *The Politics of Muslim Cultural Reform: Jadidism in Central Asia*. Berkeley, CA: University of California Press, 1999.

Lazzerini, Edward. *Ismail Bey Gasprinski and Muslim Modernism in Russia*. University of Washington: PhD Thesis, 1973.

Libaridian, Gerard J. "Revolution and Liberation in the 1892 and 1907 Programs of the Dashnaksutiun," in Ronald G. Suny, ed. *Transcaucasia: Nationalism and Social Change*. Ann Arbor: Michigan Slavik Series, 1983.

Libaridian, Gerard J., ed. *The Karabagh File*. Cambridge, MA: Zoryan Institute, 1988.

Libaridian, Gerard J. *Armenia at the Crossroads: Democracy and Nationhood in the post-Soviet Era*. Watertown, MA: Blue Crane Books, 1991.

Mandelbaum, Michael. *Central Asia and the World*. New York: Council of Foreign Relations, 1994.

McAuley, Martin. "The Soviet Muslim Population: Trends in Living Standards, 1960–1975," in Yaakov Ro'i, ed. *The USSR and the Muslim World*. London: George Allen & Unwin, 1984.

Melander, Erik. "The Nagorno-Karabakh Conflict Revisited: Was the War Inevitable." *Journal of Cold War Studies* 3 (Spring 2001).

Melkonian, Markar. *My Brother's Road: An American's Faithful Journey to Armenia*. New York: I.B.Tauris, 2005.

Migdalovitz, Carol. "Armenia-Azerbaijan Conflict." *Issue Brief for Congress*. Library of Congress, Congressional Research Service, 2002.

Minorsky, Vladimir. *The Turks, Iran and the Caucasus in the Middle Ages*. London: Variorum Reprints, 1978.

Mirza Bala, M. *Milli Azerbaycan Hareketi: Milli Azerbaycan Musavat Halk Fırkası'nın Tarihi*. Berlin: Parti Divani, 1938.

Mollazade, Jeyhun. "The Karabakh Problem: The Legal Aspect of the Conflict." *Azerbaijan International* 1(1993).

Motika, Raoul. "Glastnost in der Sowjetrepublik Aserbaidschan am Beispiel der Zeitschrift Azärbaijan." *Orient* 32 (December 1991).

Motyl, Alexander J. *Will the Non-Russians Rebel? State, Ethnicity, and Stability in the USSR.* Ithaca, NY: Cornell University Press, 1987.

Motyl, Alexander J. "Reassessing the Soviet Crisis: Big Problems, Muddling Through, Business as Usual." *Political Science Quarterly* 104 (Summer 1989), pp. 269–280.

Motyl, Alexander J. *Sovietology, Rationality, Nationality: Coming to Grips with Nationalism in the USSR.* New York: Columbia University Press, 1990.

Motyl, Alexander J. *Thinking Theoretically About Soviet Nationalities: History and Comparison in the Study of the USSR.* New York: Columbia University Press, 1992.

Murphy, David. "Operation 'Ring': The Black Berets in Azerbaijan." *Soviet Military Studies* 5 (March 1992): 487–498.

Nabiev, Bekir. "Epik Janr ve muasir hayat." *Azerbaijan* 7 (1982).

Nissman, David. *The Soviet Union and Iranian Azerbaijan: The Use of Nationalism for Political Penetration.* Boulder: Westview, 1987.

Olcott Martha B. "Gorbachev's Nationalities Policy and Central Asia," in Rajan Menon, Daniel N. Nelson, eds. *Limits to Soviet Power.* Lexington, MA: Lexington Books, 1989.

Paksoy, Hasan B. *Central Asia Reader.* Armonk, NY: M. E. Sharpe, 1994.

Pipes, Richard. *The Formation of the Soviet Union: Communism and the Soviet Union, 1917–1923.* Cambridge: Harvard University Press, 1964.

Quelquejay, Chantal Lemercier. "Islam and Identity in Azerbaijan." *Central Asian Survey* 3 (1984).

Reiss, Tom. *The Orientalist: The Many Lives of Lev Nussimbaum.* New York: Chatto and Windus, 2005.

Resulzada, Mammad Emin. *Azerbaycan Cumhuriyeti.* Istanbul, 1923.

Resulzada, Mammad Emin. "Gafgasiya Turkleri." *Azerbaijan* 12 (December 1990).

Rhinelander, L. H. "Viceroy Vorontsov's Administration of the Caucasus", in Ronald G. Suny, *Transcaucasia: Nationalism and Social Change.* Anne Arbor: University of Michigan Slavik Publications, 1983.

Rorlich, Azade-Ayse. "Not by History Alone: The Retrieval of the Past among the Tatars and the Azeris." *Central Asian Survey* 3, (1984): 87–98.

Rubin, Barnett. "Contradictory Trends in the International Relations of Central Asia." *Central Asia Monitor* 6 (1993): 11.

Rustamov, Azamat. "Dada Gorkut'la bagli yer adlari." *Älm vä Häyat* 10 (1987).

Rustamov, Azamat. "Dada Gorgut gahramanlarinin kökünü düshünürken." *Älm vä Häyat* 10 (1987).

"Samizdat." *Central Asian Newsletter.* Vol. 7 (3), London, 1988, pp. 4–5.

"Samizdat from Baku." *Central Asia and the Caucasus Chronicle*. Vol. 8 (2), 1980, pp. 3–4.

"Sarraf va La'li." *Janubi Azärbaijan Ädäbiyyati Antologiyasi* . Vol. II, Baku, 1983.

Shaffer, Brenda. *Borders and Brethren: Iran and the Challenge of Azerbaijani Identity*. Cambridge: MIT Press, 2002.

Shahmuratian, Samvel, ed. *The Sumgait Tragedy: Pogroms against Armenians in Soviet Azerbaijan* (Vol. l). New Rochelle, NY: Aristide D Caratzas, 1990.

Sharifli, M. K. *IX Asrin Ikinji-XI Asrlarda Azerbaijan Feodal Dövlatlari*. Baku: Elm, 1978.

Sultan, Garip. "Demographic and Cultural Trends among Turkic Peoples of the Soviet Union," in Erich Goldhagen, ed. *Ethnic Minorities in the Soviet Union*. New York: Frederick A. Praeger, 1968.

Sultanli, A. *Azerbayjan Dramaturgiasinin Inkishafi Tarikhinden*. Baku, 1964.

Sümer, F. "Azerbaycan'in Türkleşmesi Tarihine Umumi Bir Bakiş." *Belleten* (Turk Tarih Kurumu) 21 (1957), pp. 429–447.

Suny, Ronald Grigor. *The Baku Commune, 1917–1918: Class and Nationality in the Russian Revolution*. Princeton: Princeton University Press, 1972.

Suny, Ronald Grigor. *Transcaucasia: Nationalism and Social Change*. Ann Arbor: University of Michigan Slavik Publications, 1983.

Suny, Ronald Grigor. "Nationalism and Democracy in Gorbachev's Soviet Union: The Case of Karabagh." *Michigan Quarterly Review* 28 (Summer 1989).

Suny, Ronald Grigor. "Transcaucasia: Cultural Cohesion and Ethnic Revival in a Multinational Society," in Lubomyr Hajda and Mark Beissinger, eds. *The Nationalities Factor in Soviet Politics and Society*. Boulder, CO: Westview, 1990.

Suny, Ronald Grigor. *The Revenge of the Past: Nationalism, Revolution, and the Collapse of the Soviet Union*. Stanford, CA: Stanford University Press, 1993.

Swietochowski, Tadeusz. "The Himmät Party: Socialism and the National Question in Russian Azerbaijan, 1904–1920." *Cahiers du Monde Russe et Soviétique* 19 (1978): 119–142.

Swietochowski, Tadeusz. *Russian Azerbaijan, 1905–1920: The Shaping of National Identity in a Muslim Community*. New York: Cambridge University Press, 1985.

Swietochowski, Tadeusz. "The Spirit of Baku, Summer 1993." *Central Asia Monitor* 4 (1993).

Swietochowski, Tadeusz. *Russia and Azerbaijan: A Borderline in Transition*. New York: Columbia University Press, 1995.

Tolf, Robert W. *The Russian Rockefellers: The Saga of the Nobel Family and the Russian Oil Industry*. Stanford: Hoover Institution Press, 1976.

Tourmanoff, Cyril. "Introduction to Christian Caucasian History: The Formative Centuries." *Traditio* 15 (1959).

Ullman, Richard H. *Britain and Russian Civil War*. Princeton: Princeton University Press, 1968.

Vahabzade, Bakhtiyar and Suleyman Aliyarov. "Redaksiyamizin Pochtudan." *Azerbaijan* 2 (February 1988): 188–189.

Van der Leeuw, Charles. *Azerbaijan: A Quest for Identity*. Richmond, UK: Curzon, 1999.

Veliyev, Kamal. "Bir Daha Dada Gorgud Shairlari Hakkynda." *Azerbaijan* 11 (1981).

Walker, Christopher J. *Armenia: The Survival of A Nation*. New York: St Martin's Press, 1980.

Willerton, John P. *Patronage and Politics in the USSR*. New York: Cambridge University Press, 1992.

Wimbush, S. Enders. "Why Geidar Aliev." *Central Asian Survey* 1 (1983): 1–7.

Wimbush, S. Enders. "The Soviet Muslim Borderlands," in Robert Conquest, ed. *The Last Empire: Nationality and the Soviet Culture*. Stanford: Hoover Institution Press, 1986.

Yunusov, Arif. "Tragediya Khodjaly." *Zerkalo* 25 (June 13–18, 1992).

Zenkovsky, S. *Pan-Turkism and Islam in Russia*. Cambridge: Cambridge University Press, 1960.

Zverev, Alexei. "Nagorno-Karabakh and the Azeri-Armenian Conflict, 1988–94," Bruno Coppitiers, ed. *Contested Borders in the Caucasus*. Brussels: VUB University Press, 1996.

Index